AF843548

Institutions of Global Governance

LEUVEN GLOBAL GOVERNANCE

Series Editor: Jan Wouters, *KU Leuven, Belgium*

The Leuven Global Governance series comprises high-quality monographs and edited volumes dedicated to innovative research on global governance. The series covers a wide range of themes, from the EU and global multilateral governance to trade, sustainable development, peace and security, human rights, democracy and rule of law, private standards, and global commons. In full recognition of the complex issues involved, the series favours studies approaching global governance from a multidisciplinary, multi-level and multi-actor perspective.

For a full list of Edward Elgar published titles, including the titles in this series, visit our website at www.e-elgar.com.

Institutions of Global Governance

Shifting Dynamics in a Turbulent World

Edited by

Jacint Jordana

Professor of Political Science, Universitat Pompeu Fabra and Institut Barcelona d'Estudis Internacionals, Barcelona, Spain

Axel Marx

Deputy Director, Leuven Centre for Global Governance Studies, KU Leuven, Belgium

Marie Vandendriessche

Senior Researcher and Research Coordinator, EsadeGeo – Center for Global Economy and Geopolitics, Esade, Spain

Jan Wouters

Full Professor, Jean Monnet Chair and Director, Institute for International Law and Leuven Centre for Global Governance Studies, KU Leuven, Belgium

LEUVEN GLOBAL GOVERNANCE

Edward Elgar
PUBLISHING

Cheltenham, UK • Northampton, MA, USA

© The Editors and Contributors Severally 2025

Every effort has been made to trace all the copyright holders but if any have been inadvertently overlooked please notify the publisher.

All rights reserved. No part of this publication may be reproduced, stored in a retrieval system or transmitted in any form or by any means, electronic, mechanical or photocopying, recording, or otherwise without the prior permission of the publisher.

Published by

Edward Elgar Publishing Limited
The Lypiatts
15 Lansdown Road
Cheltenham
Glos GL50 2JA
UK

Edward Elgar Publishing, Inc.
William Pratt House
9 Dewey Court
Northampton
Massachusetts 01060
USA

Authorised representative in the EU for GPSR queries only: Easy Access System Europe – Mustamäe tee 50, 10621 Tallinn, Estonia, gpsr.requests@easproject.com

A catalogue record for this book is available from the British Library

Library of Congress Control Number: 2025944037

This book is available electronically in the **Elgar**online
Political Science and Public Policy subject collection
https://doi.org/10.4337/9781035302581

MIX
Paper | Supporting responsible forestry
FSC® C013056

ISBN 978 1 0353 0257 4 (cased)
ISBN 978 1 0353 0258 1 (eBook)
ISBN 978 1 0353 7702 2 (ePub)

Printed and bound in Great Britain by
TJ Books, Padstow, Cornwall

Contents

PART IV CONCLUSION

List of contributors

Lili Yulyadi Arnakim is Associate Professor at the Department of International Relations and editor of *Journal of ASEAN Studies* (JAS). His latest works have been published in JAS, *Intellectual Discourse, AEI Insights: An International Journal of Asia-Europe Relations, Transylvanian Review, Revista De Cercetare Si Interventie Sociala, SEJARAH: Journal of the Department of History, Contemporary Chinese Political Economy and Strategic Relations: An International Journal (CCPS)*, and *Journal of Southeast Asian Studies*. He completed the PhD program at the Department of International and Strategic Studies, University of Malaya.

Andrea C. Bianculli is an Associate Professor at Institut Barcelona d'Estudis Interncionals (IBEI). Her research explores the interplay between governance, regulation, and development from a comparative, regional, and multi-level perspective, with a focus on Latin America and Europe. She has published extensively in prominent journals in these fields, including *Global Social Policy*, the *Journal of Ethnic and Migration Studies*, the *Journal of International Relations and Development*, *Politics and Governance*, and *Regulation and Governance*, among others. Additionally, she has significant experience leading research projects funded by national, international and European Union agencies.

Ilana Blumsack is a former research assistant at the Hebrew University of Jerusalem in Israel. She received her BA in Economics and Political Science from Hebrew University in 2020, and her MS in Applied Economics from Johns Hopkins University in 2024.

Miriam Bradley is a Senior Lecturer in Humanitarian Studies at the University of Manchester. Her research focuses on international responses to conflict, violence and displacement. As well as several journal articles and chapters in edited volumes, she is the author of two books: *Protecting Civilians in War: The ICRC, UNHCR, and their Limitations in Internal Armed Conflicts* (OUP 2016) and *The Politics and Everyday Practice of International Humanitarianism* (OUP 2023).

Tomer Broude is Professor and Dean of the Faculty of Law at the Hebrew University of Jerusalem, and Bessie and Michael Greenblatt, Q.C., Chair in Public and International Law at the Faculty of Law and Department of International Relations. He specializes in public international law and international economic law, particularly international trade and investment, human rights, dispute settlement, development and cultural diversity. He has published several books as well as numerous articles on these topics.

David Coen is Pro Vice Provost Global Engagement and Professor of Public Policy at University College London (UCL). Previously he was Director of School of Public Policy and founding Director of the Global Governance Institute. Prior to joining UCL he held appointments at the London Business School and Max Planck Institute in Cologne, and he wrote his PhD at the European University Institute, Florence. He has held visiting appointments as a Schuman Distinguished Fellowship at the Institute of Advance Studies at the European University Institute and the Fulbright Distinguished Fellowship at the Kennedy School of Government at Harvard University. His research explores business and government relations, EU public policy, global governance, and public and private actors in climate change.

Charline Depoorter is a postdoctoral researcher in the Sustainability Research Group at the University of Basel and a Research Fellow at the Leuven Centre for Global Governance Studies at KU Leuven (PhD, 2024). She conducts research on global sustainability governance, with a particular focus on the design and implementation of public and private trade-based sustainability governance instruments in tropical agri-food sectors. She has published in several leading journals, including *Regulation and Governance*, *Sustainable Development*, and *Applied Economic Perspectives and Policy.*

Catalina Espinosa Notrica holds a degree in International Studies from the University Torcuato Di Tella and a Master's in Political Science from the University of Copenhagen. She has worked as a lecturer and researcher specializing in international political economy and gender. Her work focuses on gender equality policies, feminist international political economy, and welfare state regimes with a focus on Latin America.

Dalit Flaiszhaker's research focuses on financial regulation and monetary policy. She received her PhD from Tel-Aviv University in 2022. Dalit worked at the Bank of Israel, and participated in a doctoral program at the International Monetary Fund. Dalit holds an LL.M (summa cum laude) and an LL.B (magna cum laude) from Tel-Aviv University.

Yoram Z. Haftel is Professor and the Giancarlo Elia Valori Chair in the Study of Peace and Regional Cooperation in the Department of International Relations at the Hebrew University of Jerusalem. His research agenda touches on the sources, design, and effects of international organizations (IOs) and international investment agreements (IIA). His recent work examines such topics as the evolution of the IIA regime, the effect of global crises on IOs, the relationships between IO overlap and authority and regime complexity.

Kyle S. Herman has over 15 years of experience in climate and environmental policymaking, representing a myriad of constituents, including NGOs, multinational corporations, and institutions such as the UNFCCC. He has explored multilateral environmental policies and the inducement of innovation, and more recently industrial decarbonization and firm-level climate transitions. He deploys econometric and language processing methods in this research and is particularly interested in how stringent domestic climate policies exhibit influence across other regions and countries.

Adam Holesch is a Research Fellow at the Institut Barcelona d'Estudis Internacionals. In his research, Adam analyses European politics by going up and down the ladder of multi-level governance, focusing on democratic backsliding, regionalism and global governance. He has published, among others, in the journals *West European Politics*; *Journal of Common Market Studies*; *Journal of European Integration*; *East European Politics*; *Territory, Politics and Governance*; *Political Research Exchange*; *Acta Politica*; and *Global Governance*.

Kari Irwin Otteburn is a postdoctoral researcher at the Leuven Centre for Global Governance Studies of KU Leuven. She researches global economic governance and business and human rights, with a focus on regulatory initiatives to address trade, investment, and corporate impacts on human rights and the environment. She holds a PhD from KU Leuven (2024) and has published in leading journals, such as *The International Journal of Human Rights*, *The Journal of World Investment and Trade*, and *Asia Europe Journal*.

Jacint Jordana is Professor of Political Science and Administration at Universitat Pompeu Fabra (Barcelona) and ICREA Academia researcher. From 2005 to 2024 he directed the Institut Barcelona d'Estudis Internacionals. Currently, he is the president. He was the academic coordinator of the European project GLOBE (Horizon 2020), a research project oriented to the study of emerging trends and future scenarios in global governance and the role of the European Union. His main research area focuses on the comparative analysis of public policies, with special emphasis on regulatory policy and its specialist institutions. His most recent publications include articles on the globalization of regulatory institutions, public decision-making and trans-governmental policy networks.

Robert Kissack is an Associate Professor and Head of Studies at the Institut Barcelona d'Estudis Internacionals and a Senior Visiting Fellow to the Department of International Relations, London School of Economics. He researches European Union foreign policy, focusing on international organizations and the changing dynamics of the multilateral order.

Julia Kreienkamp is a Research Fellow at the UCL Global Governance Institute. Her work with the Institute has focused on the changing landscape for global policymaking, with a particular focus on climate change and other environmental sustainability challenges, as well as the implications of complexity thinking for governing catastrophic global risks.

David Levi-Faur is the Wolfson Family Chair in Public Administration. He is Professor at the Department of Political Science and the Federmann School of Public Policy at the Hebrew University of Jerusalem. He is a leading and foundational scholar in the field of regulation and governance and has pioneered theoretical breakthroughs, specifically through his research on diffusion, regulatory governance, and regulatory capitalism. He is a founding editor of *Regulation and Governance*, a top journal that serves as the leading platform for the study of regulation and governance in the social sciences.

Axel Marx is Deputy Director of the Leuven Centre for Global Governance Studies (KU Leuven). He has managed over 80 funded research projects for several national and international organizations, including the European Parliament, the European Commission, International Labour Organization, UNIDO, UNFSS, UNCTAD, OECD, European governments, science funding agencies and several private actors. His research interests include voluntary sustainability standards, sustainable trade, human/labour rights, global governance and EU trade policy.

Pablo Nemiña holds a PhD in Social Sciences and a BA in Sociology from the University of Buenos Aires. He is a full researcher at the National Council of Scientific and Technical Research (CONICET), based at the National University of San Martín, and an Associate Researcher in the Department of International Relations at FLACSO, Argentina. His research focuses on the evolution of the practices, ideas, and roles of the IMF and Multilateral Development Banks, the politics of relations between international financial institutions and developing countries, and the political economy of climate change financing.

Tirta Nugraha Mursitama is a full professor in International Business at the Department of International Relations at Bina Nusantara University (BINUS), Indonesia, and editor in chief of the *Journal of ASEAN Studies*. His research focuses on the interaction between business, international relations and diplomatic issues in Asia from an international political economic perspective. He has been conducting research on economic regionalism, digital economy, sustainability, high-tech industries in emerging economies and internationalization of firms.

Sukmawani Bela Pertiwi is Assistant Professor at the Department of International Relations and Coordinator for European Studies at the Centre for Business and Diplomatic Studies, BINUS University. She teaches Indonesia's foreign policy, diplomacy, ASEAN and EU regionalism, international organization and global governance. She researches regionalism and political security of Southeast Asia and Europe as well as global governance on key issues for both regions.

Charles Roger is a Ramón y Cajal Associate Professor at the Institut Barcelona d'Estudis Internacionals. He is the author of *The Origins of Informality: Why the Legal Foundations of Global Governance are Shifting, and Why It Matters* (OUP 2020) and a coauthor of *Transnational Climate Change Governance* (CUP 2014).

Lewin Schmitt's research focuses on global governance and the politics of artificial intelligence. He obtained his PhD from Pompeu Fabra University in 2024, he worked for the European Commission's internal think tank, covering foreign affairs and technology policy. Lewin holds a BSc in European Economic Studies from the University of Bamberg and an MSc in Latin American Studies from the University of Oxford. Currently, he works on digital transformation projects in the public sector.

Alexandros Tokhi is a postdoctoral researcher at Goethe University Frankfurt and holds a PhD in Political Science from Freie Universität Berlin. His research focuses on international organizations, democracy and authoritarianism in world politics, and challenges to international human rights and security. His work has appeared in *Global Policy*, the *Journal of European Integration*, and *International Studies Quarterly*.

Juan Carlos Triviño-Salazar is an Assistant Professor in Public Policy at the Department of Political and Social Sciences at the Universitat Pompeu Fabra Barcelona. His field of expertise is primarily focused on governance processes from multi-level and regulatory perspectives in multiple policy sectors but with a special focus on immigration and integration. He has published in top-ranking journals, such as *Public Administration*, *Governance*, *Journal of European Integration*, *the Lancet*, and *Journal of Ethnic and Migration Studies*, among others. Since September 2022, he has been the principal investigator of the Spanish project MUNMIGRA on local policy responses to the presence of precarious migrants in Spanish cities.

İrem Tuncer Ebetürk is a postdoctoral researcher at the WZB Berlin and holds a PhD in Sociology from Emory University. Her research explores global sociology, anti-gender movements, children's rights, global health, and the intersections of authoritarianism and technology. She has recently published in *International Affairs*, the *British Journal of International Relations*, and *Democratization*, with award-winning work on anti-feminist backlash in the United Nations.

Diana Tussie heads the Department of International Relations at FLACSO/Argentina where she teaches in the areas of international political economy, economic diplomacy and global economic governance. Dr Tussie holds a PhD in International Relations from the London School of Economics. She has published extensively in English and Spanish. She has been co-editor of *Global Governance* in the period 2014–2018. From 2006 to 2009 she served on the Committee for Development Policy of the United Nations. She has been a visiting scholar at the University of Chile, Universidad de la República de Uruguay, Manchester, Oxford, Córdoba and the German Institute of Global and Area Studies. In 2017 she was awarded the Distinguished Scholar, Global South Caucus Award from the International Studies Association.

Marie Vandendriessche is a Senior Researcher and Research Coordinator at the EsadeGeo Center for Global Economy and Geopolitics and a teaching fellow at Esade Business & Law School. Her work focuses on global governance and geopolitics, with a special interest in the interface between energy and climate change. Marie is also a PhD candidate in Politics, Policies and International Relations at the Universitat Autònoma de Barcelona, where she investigates global governance complexity and institutional choice.

Jan Wouters is Full Professor of International Law and International Organizations, Jean Monnet Chair ad personam, Director of the Institute for International Law and Leuven Centre for Global Governance Studies (Jean Monnet Centre of Excellence and University Centre of Excellence), Administrator at America Europe Fund, KU Leuven, a Visiting Professor at the College of Europe, Université Panthéon-Assas and Columbia University, a Member of the Belgian Royal Academy, and practises law as Of Counsel at Omega Law. He has published widely on international and EU law, international organizations, global governance and corporate and financial law. He recently coordinated a large Horizon 2020 Project, RECONNECT, and frequently advises and trains international organizations and governments.

Michael Zürn is Director at the WZB Berlin Social Science Center and Professor of International Relations at the Freie Universität Berlin. His work focuses on global governance, international institutions and their legitimacy, and contestations of liberal-democratic orders. From 2019 to 2023, he was co-spokesperson of the Cluster of Excellence "Contestations of the Liberal Script" (SCRIPTS) that was funded by the German Research Foundation (DFG) and served as Founding Dean of the Hertie School of Governance (Berlin) from 2004 to 2010. He is a member of the Berlin-Brandenburg Academy of Sciences and Humanities (BBAW) and the Academia Europaea. He received several prizes, among them the prestigious Berlin Science Award in 2021 and the Thomas Mann House Fellowship.

Preface

The current book is a spin-off of the international project "Global Governance and the European Union: Future Trends and Scenarios" (GLOBE) funded by the European Commission's Horizon 2020 programme (Grant Agreement 822654). GLOBE addressed the strategic priorities identified in the EU Global Strategy of 2016 – such as trade, development, security and climate change – as well as migration and global finance, in order to identify the major roadblocks to effective and coherent global governance by varied stakeholders in a multipolar world. The project also focused on a variety of specific problems, to address the challenges that the transformations of global politics are placing to international insitutions during the 2020s decade. The project was framed under the challenge "Europe in a changing world – Inclusive, innovative and reflective societies", in the "Governance for the Future" section of the EU's Horizon 2020 programme. The project was coordinated by Institut Barcelona d'Estudis Internacionals (IBEI) and brought together an academic consortium of partners from eight countries, composed of European and international academics and policymakers, including EsadeBusiness and Law School, Leuven Centre for Global Governance Studies (KU Leuven), University College London (UCL), Wissenschaftszentrum Berlin fur Socialforschung (WZB), Hebrew University of Jerusalem (HUJI), Facultad Latinoamericana de Ciencias Sociales (FLACSO Argentina), Universitas Bina Nusantara (BINUS), Barcelona Institute for Global Health (IS Global) and Peking University (PKU). The participating institutions acknowledge the important financial contribution by the European Commission thatmade this project possible. This book was realised in part with support from the Research Foundation – Flanders (FWO) funding for the scientific research network on 'Global Governance Through Informal Intergovernmental Institutions' (W000223N_WOG) and the ICREA foundation in Barcelona.

The editors thank all participating researchers in the GLOBE consortium, several of which contributed to this book, for their valuable contribution to the success of the project. GLOBE researchers including Adam Holesch, Angel Saz, David Coen, David Levi-Faur, Charles Roger, Michael Zürn, Alexandros Tokhi, Kari Otteburn, Lewin Schmitt, Carlota Moreno Villar, Andrea Bianculli, Fulya Apaydin, Miriam Bradley, Juan Carlos Triviño,

Robert Kissack, Emily Jones, Diego Badell Sánchez, Bart Kerremans, Nuria Agell, Ana Sanchez, Athanasios Kouliopoulos, Jennifer Thanh Van Nguyen, Irem Ebetürk, Tom Pegram, Julia Kreienkamp, Kyle Herman, Yoram Haftel, Tomer Broude, Tirta Nugraha Mursitama, Charanpal Singh Bal, Sukmawani Bela Pertiwi, Lili Yulyadi, Paramitaningrum, Diana Tussie, Melisa Deciancio, Pablo Nemiña, Juliana Peixoto Batista, Charline Depoorter, Vineet Hegde, Guillaume Van der Loo, Josep M. Antó and Cathryn Tonne.

The project also benefitted from valuable feedback and insights from the advisory board members of the project including Sharon Friel, Antoni Estevadeordal, Miles Kahler, Uttara Sahasrabuddhe, Anna Triandafyllidou and Pascal Lamy.

The finalization of the book would not have been possible without the research assistance of Carlos Sanchez, Lluc Fortuny and Iris Aurelia Raunu, and the supportive effors of the EE publishing team.

The editors
Jacint Jordana
Marie Vandendriessche
Axel Marx
Jan Wouters

1. Contemporary global governance: institutions, complexes and approaches

Axel Marx, Jacint Jordana, Marie Vandendriessche and Jan Wouters

1. GLOBAL GOVERNANCE: PAST, PRESENT AND FUTURE

With the fall of the Berlin Wall in 1989, a new era of international cooperation dawned. Large international conferences, such as the 1992 United Nations (UN) Conference on Environment and Development (also called the 'Earth Summit') in Rio, resulted in international agreements and commitments. Amid a fresh landscape where global confrontation had subsided, important formal intergovernmental organisations such as the World Trade Organization (WTO) (Van den Bossche & Zdouc, 2021) and the International Criminal Court (Alter, 2014) were established. Some of these organisations, such as the WTO, exemplified a novel form of international cooperation with far-reaching powers to overrule domestic policy-making, for example, through strong dispute settlement mechanisms. In parallel, other institutions were reformed, gaining more autonomy in their day-to-day operations. In Europe, the launch of the single market and the Euro as a common currency were hallmarks of the further integration of the European Union (EU), which some came to see as a model for other regional organisations (Lenz, 2021).

Outside the realm of large-scale multilateralism, it also became increasingly common for government officials to collaborate in smaller 'clubs' and informal settings, either to discuss specific policies or to engage in top-level diplomacy – as was the case of the G7/8 and the G20. This trend led to a boom in the establishment of transnational regulatory networks (Jordana, 2017; Jordana, Hoelsch, & Trivino-Salazar, 2022), which contributed to the establishment of a new regulatory order worldwide (Slaughter, 2000; Slaughter & Zaring, 2006). Informal intergovernmental organisations and law-making (Pauwelyn,

Wessel, & Wouters, 2012; Pauwelyn, Wessel, & Wouters, 2014; Roger, 2020), as well as global administrative law (Kingsbury, Krisch, & Stewart, 2005) were on the rise.

The 1990s thus saw a golden age of international cooperation spread across the globe. This opened the door to what is now commonly known as 'global governance', which includes multilevel international and supranational collaboration in varying geographical and thematic configurations. The concept of global governance emerged from the recognition that in an increasingly interconnected world, traditional forms of cooperation between nation-states might not be sufficient to address global challenges, such as environmental degradation and human rights violations (Marx & Westerwinter, 2022). Global governance therefore also includes hybrid and non-state actors, which are valued for their specific capabilities in policy-making and solutions to global challenges (Abbott & Faude, 2021a). New global governance initiatives involving private actors took off in the shape of multi-stakeholder initiatives (Marx et al., 2024), public–private partnerships (Westerwinter, 2021, 2022; Pattberg et al., 2012) and private initiatives (Fuchs, 2004; Mikler, 2018), among others. A 'law of global governance' was on the rise (Benvenisti, 2014; Wouters, 2024).

However, more than three decades later, optimism regarding the benefits of international cooperation and global governance has faded. Since the 2010s, but particularly in the 2020s, geopolitical tensions have surged, hindering the further development of global governance and its capacity to deliver global public goods, and even upending achievements of the past. Several international organisations are currently engulfed in crises. One of the most effective global multilateral organisations, the WTO, is paralysed in one of its most important functions (dispute settlement on trade disputes) and is struggling to find consensus on many outstanding challenges. Powerful informal bodies such as the G20, which took on an important role in tackling the 2008 financial crisis, are hamstrung by internal power struggles. In some cases, commitments to international cooperation are dwindling, with states withdrawing from international organisations, reneging on their commitments, or vacillating in their implementation of international initiatives like the Sustainable Development Goals (SDGs). Doubts are growing regarding the effectiveness of private governance initiatives, further impeding their capacity to complement or replace the flagging public side of global governance (Abbott & Snidal, 2009; Marx et al., 2024).

We are moving to a world where international cooperation is increasingly difficult. After decades of economic globalisation, some commentators observe a possible shift towards 'slowbalization' (Aiyar & Ilyina, 2023). The 2008 financial crisis, followed by the Covid-19 pandemic a decade later, may have been turning points in this evolution. Both emergencies have distorted fundamental assumptions and dynamics of global governance. They revealed some of the fault lines in addressing challenges globally, which often stem from the influence of major powers with diverging interests and visions of global cooperation. Some observers assert that deeply rooted domestic factors are generating opposition towards global cooperation and integration. This trend, which is driven by significant shifts in political preferences and reinforced by a diminishing influence of Western countries, seems to be structural in nature, according to current literature on geopolitics and geo-economics (Trubowitz & Burgoon, 2023). The anti-globalisation sentiment, partly fed by a number of civil society actors in response to trade liberalisation, affects the strategies and behaviour of national leaders in global affairs. As a result, we are witnessing a backlash against global governance: international organisations are confronting a myriad of internal and external challenges, from wavering member states to a lack of reform dynamics. This is the current context in which global governance is evolving and undergoing (re)configuration.

How all of this will play out for global governance in the end is still unknown. Yet, we are clearly at a crossroads. Debates about possible directions for global governance are proliferating, both in the academic and policy-making arenas. Miles Kahler (2018), for example, identifies three possible scenarios. A first scenario, fragmentation, entails the exit of major powers from global governance and a reconfiguration around regional centres of power ('new regionalism'), including the emergence or strengthening of regional multilateral organisations. A second scenario, stagnation, sees major powers persisting as parties to existing global governance institutions, but as acting blockers who create conditions for sustained gridlock, including by obstructing any options for reform. A third scenario considers prospects for transformation through the rise of new, more complex, global governance arrangements where subnational and non-state actors play bigger roles. Similarly, Saz-Carranza et al. (2023) combine a set of premises and uncertainties about the future to generate four scenarios for the world in 2035 and for global governance in those worlds. The first scenario is a drifting, bipolar world with two distinct spheres of influence (a US and a China-based one) and high levels of confrontation. Global governance is waning in this world, becoming fragmented, with international organisations increasingly falling into either the US or the Chinese sphere of influence, minilateral and highly informal. In the second scenario, the world is shifting: instability and distrust reign while alliances between states continuously fluctuate. The shadow of distrust makes formal international organisations largely ineffective here as well; what is left of global governance takes place through informal, minilateral and ad hoc frameworks. A third scenario shows a world where globalisation resumes amid high economic growth; interstate relations are non-confrontational and non-state actors play a large role. Multilateralism experiences a modest revival, and traditional international organisations undergo superficial reforms. In parallel, global governance arrangements containing private members rise in number and importance. Finally, a fourth scenario shows a less state-centric world: intergovernmental relations are fluid, but regions take on a larger role, as do non-state actors, including civil society. Multilateralism improves, participatory governance booms and formal international organisations undergo hybridisation processes and extensive reforms.

2. AIMS OF THE BOOK AND CONTRIBUTIONS

This book aims to improve our understanding of the complexities of contemporary global governance. By uncovering and analysing significant trends, including some of the ones outlined above, it also aspires to inform debates on possible future scenarios for global governance. The perspective the book adopts is a particular one. We analyse the 'cartography' of global governance – cutting across sectors and geographies – to identify key developments and discuss the main challenges for the institutions involved. The book's ultimate objective is to provide analysts with new insights on how research on global governance is evolving and to identify key trends in this research field.[1]

The contributions to this edited book have as their first common purpose to highlight the complexity of global governance and provide frameworks to analyse it. The chapters discuss the current state of global governance research, show how to map global governance, provide insights into issues that arise in global governance settings, and analyse the possibilities and limitations of addressing some of these issues. It is not our objective, though, to provide a full map of contemporary global governance. We are not particularly convinced that this can be a fruitful objective: the scope of global governance has become too broad for a complete mapping, going beyond conventional drawings based on geopolitical insights. The relative absence of hierarchical patterns within most areas of global governance spawns multiple alternatives for decision-making and increases complexity. Moreover, collapsing the map

---

[1] Throughout this book, different terms are used for similar types of global governance institutions. Some authors prefer to refer to international organisations as defined by the International Law Commission, which implies that international organisations are intergovernmental. Other authors prefer to explicitly add 'intergovernmental' and refer to international intergovernmental organisations to distinguish them from international private organisations. Still others prefer to refer to a distinction between formal and informal international intergovernmental organisations or formal and informal international organisations. Given that the authors in this book stem from different academic streams, we chose to respect their choice of terminology. We ensured that the terminology within each chapter is clearly introduced and used consistently.

of global governance into a scale based only on the larger, state-based international organisations (IOs) is no longer an option, as a mapping exercise of this type would omit important entities, such as private and hybrid actors, and therefore provide an incomplete and unreliable image. This being said, individual chapters do contribute careful, structured mappings of the global governance architectures working on particular issues, thereby revealing both issue-specific and overarching trends.

The second common purpose of this book is to provide insights on cross-cutting challenges, issues, and trends that lie at the centre of global governance controversies. Challenges in contemporary global governance can be analysed at the level of individual institutions, specific types of institutions, or the regime complex. The problems examined in the book are those that generate the brunt of tension and gridlock at the international level and consequently hinder the provision of global public goods, coordination of transnational regulatory frameworks, and positive collaboration among public and private actors. This book does not offer individual case studies of IOs, given the wealth of existing studies. Instead, the book examines the challenges – such as resource constraints, organisational autonomy issues, and authority and legitimacy concerns – that IOs face more generally and questions which role they can continue to play in global governance. Looking beyond traditional IOs, the book also focuses on trends and shifts that have been reshaping global governance over the past decade. These include increasing complexity, norm contestation and questions of effectiveness, the impact of emerging institutions and emerging powers, the increasing role of the private sector in regulation, novel forms of global governance, such as global compacts, and goal-based approaches to global governance.

In the remainder of this introduction, we present in detail the chapters that are part of this book, highlighting their contributions to global governance research. We begin with a series of chapters offering transversal perspectives. This part starts by taking stock of trends in academic research on global governance, before focusing on changes and challenges to the role of international organisations in global governance. Subsequently, we move to the level of global governance complexes (configurations of global governance institutions addressing a particular issue), highlighting the high degree of fragmentation and complexity in many different issue areas. Here we focus on how to think about global governance architectures and systems and how they have been conceptualised in global governance literature. We also examine what drives their evolution, with a specific focus on the role of domestic actors. From this point on, the book delves deeper into the practice of global governance to uncover how these configurations of institutions operate while exploring the potential and limitations to addressing complexity through coordination and orchestration. We furthermore assess what can be expected from relatively new initiatives in global governance, such as those based on goals and global compacts. We end with a conclusion highlighting important findings and suggesting avenues for future research.

2.1 Understanding Current Developments in Global Governance Research

There is no single clear point of origin for the concept of global governance, which started to emerge in policy documents before spilling over to academic literature. Global governance as a field of study emerged in the 1990s as a subfield of international relations and international political economy and later, in a second phase, expanded to fields such as international law, economics, and public policy (Coen & Pegram, 2018). In the inaugural issue of the journal *Global Governance*, the late James Rosenau conceived global governance to 'include systems of rule at all levels of human activity – from the family to IOs – in which the pursuit of goals through the exercise of control has transnational repercussion' (1995, p. 13). Years later, definitions of global governance expanded, with a strong focus on the range of actors involved (Abbott & Snidal, 2009; Abbott, Green, & Keohane, 2016) as well as the transnational public policy problems and common goods – such as security, climate protection, and economic prosperity – it aims to govern (Stone, 2019; Stone & Moloney, 2019; Zürn, 2018).

An important element across all definitions is the recognition that multiple actors of a different nature and at various levels play an important role in governance processes. Akin to the shift from government to governance identified at the national level in the 1980s (Lobel, 2004, 2012; Rhodes, 2012), global governance constitutes a shift from constellations where states and traditional intergovernmental organisations are the central actors towards configurations where several global governance institutions complement, but also sometimes substitute and antagonise, these actors (Abbott & Faude, 2021b; Barnett, Pevehouse, & Raustiala, 2021; Roger, 2020; Saz-Carranza et al., 2023). As a result, global governance has expanded and become increasingly complex in recent decades: it is now characterised by many public, private, formal, and informal organisations and processes at different levels of governance (local, national, regional, cross-regional, global), constituting global governance architectures and clusters. A significant body of academic literature on global governance and the actors involved has developed in tandem with this evolution.

This progression in academic research on global governance is analysed and described in depth in the chapter by Charles Roger, Adam Holesch, Jacint Jordana, and Lewin Schmitt on 'The evolution of global governance research'. They observe that at the start of the 1990s, global governance was hardly discussed by either scholars or policy-makers. Of late, it has grown into a research discipline in its own right. Hundreds of academic articles are published each year, and global governance is discussed at the highest levels of government and across civil society. In their chapter, Roger et al. examine the evolution of the idea of global governance and highlight some of the main advances made in research on the subject. They use a novel dataset of academic articles to identify major trends and distinguish three important periods of research. In a first, formative stage, significant attention went into clarifying the initially vague concept of global governance and highlighting how it challenged more traditional approaches and perspectives in international relations. In a second stage, the concept was further developed through mainly qualitative case studies, demonstrating the complexity of contemporary transnational rule-making and the many actors involved. At this stage, most research focused on specific global governance actors and institutions, yet attention also turned to cross-cutting discussions in world affairs of issues of legitimacy, accountability, and effectiveness. In a third stage, research expanded in two directions. On the one hand, researchers increasingly relied on datasets and quantitative methods to analyse major trends in global governance. On the other hand, attention turned to complex inter-institutional relations in global governance. Roger et al. conclude by outlining theoretical, methodological, and institutional priorities for future research, to which we return in the conclusion of this book.

2.2 Challenges to the Centrality of International Organisations in Global Governance

Since the post-World War II era, formal intergovernmental organisations have played a key role in global governance. They are characterised by the fact that they are established by an international treaty or instrument, have states as members, and have – amidst other organs – a permanent secretariat that has some degree of autonomy to pursue policies. Next to states, formal IOs were for a considerable time the main rule-makers in global governance. Over the last decade and a half, IOs have been confronted with several challenges that affect their autonomy and authority. Autonomy refers to the degree to which IOs can develop and pursue policy goals. Some IOs have a relatively high degree of autonomy, while others are very much constrained by their member states and their constituent treaties and instruments (Barnett & Finnemore, 2004; Bauer & Ege, 2016). If an IO's autonomy is constrained, this may affect its capacity to deliver global public goods (Lall, 2023) as well as how much authority it holds (Zürn, Binder, & Ecker-Ehrhardt, 2012). Research on the authority and autonomy of IOs has been expanding and has mainly looked at the variation in levels of autonomy and how this might influence effectiveness. In this book, we contribute to these debates from two different perspectives.

The chapter by Alexandros Tokhi, İrem Tuncer Ebetürk, and Michael Zürn on 'Global governance and intergovernmental organizations: features and developments of authority beyond the nation state' explores developments in the authority of IOs and their link to autonomy. Based on a new dataset, the authors seek to understand how IOs exercise authority within and across key issue areas in global governance. This inquiry leads them to compare and qualify the relative authoritativeness of specific issue areas and organisations over others, while identifying general patterns in the exercise of authority across IOs and specific sectors. The first trend they identify is that IOs are, on average, only moderately authoritative, and that there is considerable variation in levels of authority between them. Second, the authority of IOs has increased significantly over time, though recent contributions show that this growth may have levelled off after 2015. Tokhi et al. note that the distribution and growth of IOs' authority appears to have halted and has remained frozen since 2013 (end date of their data). Over the last decade, the growth in the number of IOs has slowed down (Pevehouse et al., 2020). Moreover, the competencies of existing IOs – with the possible exception of the EU – have not been deepened in significant ways, limiting their ability to autonomously develop and implement policies. This suggests that the formal-legal authority with which states have endowed IOs has not changed much since its peak in the early 2000s and is currently even being challenged.

This final point is explored further in the chapter by Kari Irwin Otteburn and Axel Marx, 'Designed for different times? Institutional challenges of international organisations and the rise of informality'. Their chapter starts from the premise that in the last two decades, IOs have had to operate in a changing geopolitical and global governance context, which presents several challenges. This chapter takes a cross-issue or sector approach and aims to identify general challenges IOs face, through an in-depth analysis of reports mapping global governance complexes in six issue areas (trade, security, climate change, migration, development, and finance). The chapter identifies three primary institutional limitations. First, IOs face difficulties balancing the needs of a diverse set of stakeholders and members due to inappropriate decision-making rules or the inflexibility of governance structures. Second, IOs' mandates often do not grant them sufficient policy autonomy or scope of action to meet their goals. Third, IOs frequently lack the necessary resources, including funding, staff, and access to information. A shift in funding from general budgetary contributions to earmarked voluntary contributions further exacerbates this point. These limitations create challenges for IOs and their capacity to govern autonomously. By limiting the ability of IOs to address global challenges, such constraints directly affect their autonomy and authority. This, in turn, undermines IOs' credibility and legitimacy as global governance actors. In the next step, the chapter assesses to what degree the rise of informal IOs, as identified by Roger (2020) and Vabulas and Snidal (2013), presents a solution to the institutional challenges outlined above. Otteburn and Marx suggest that the structural institutional limitations of IOs are unlikely to be fully resolved through increased informality in certain issue areas.

2.3 Global Governance Complexes: Approaches and Evolution

The book subsequently moves to the next level of global governance, the meso level, which takes a collection of public and private actors involved in an issue area as its unit of analysis. These collections have been referred to as 'regime complexes' or 'global governance architectures', among other terms. The number of global governance actors active in specific issue areas has increased significantly over the last two decades. A series of contextual trends facilitated this surge in the density and diversity of global governance actors, including falling transaction costs, a strengthening of private actors as political agents (Mikler, 2018), and the rise of private governance initiatives (Marx et al., 2024). As a result, most global issues today are not governed by a single, monolithic institution, but instead by a set of varied institutions which overlap, complement, substitute, and antagonise each other to varying degrees. This development has been captured and analysed under different concepts in the global governance literature.

The chapter by Marie Vandendriessche, Jacint Jordana, and Alex Marx, 'Beyond the formal intergovernmental organization: studying the complexity of global governance', focuses on this literature and maps the various approaches that have been taken. It shows that different authors focus on a similar phenomenon, but through a range of concepts that are operationalised with a focus on distinct dimensions. The chapter sheds light on extant scholarship relating to complexes of global governance institutions, focusing on the lenses that are used, the main dimensions under study, and significant debates in the field. It starts with an examination of five of the frameworks (regime complexes, global governance complexes, hybrid institutional complexes, global governance architectures, and supercluster complexes) that have been used, including an analysis of their defining features and key debates. This overview also provides insights into the main dimensions that are used to classify and analyse such complexes, while revealing some of the research insights that have been gained. A subsequent section focuses on one of the main defining features of global governance through complexes of institutions: their propensity to continuously evolve and re-configure. The authors examine the drivers and processes of this evolution, in addition to its implications in terms of institutional proliferation or consolidation.

The next chapters, focusing on specific sectors, reveal what complexity in contemporary global governance looks like in practice, while reflecting on its origins and evolution. First, four chapters engage in detailed mappings of the global governance complexes working on cybersecurity, trade, investment and finance. Two of these complexes both lack a central governing institution, yet are very different in their composition. These mappings, in turn, uncover insights into the origins of the complexes, the role of domestic actors in their evolution, and challenges related to their configurations. The chapter on global trade governance, which does have a central governing institution, the WTO, also displays a complex landscape of global formal and informal organisations, regional organisations like the EU, and private actors whose actions may complement but also contradict each other.

While there is considerable literature mapping the range of actors involved in particular global governance complexes, often less attention is paid to the origin of such complexes and the actors and approaches that determine their structure. The chapter on 'Global cybersecurity governance' by Marie Vandendriessche provides interesting insights into the developments of global governance architectures. She shows that global cybersecurity governance – one of the newer global governance complexes – is marked by a high level of diversity of actors in terms of type, membership, legal status, and authority. This diversity is partially driven by different perspectives on how to govern cybersecurity. Vandendriessche details how the bedrock of global cybersecurity governance originated in the space and tradition of the geographical location where the internet itself emerged, namely the United States, and to a lesser extent, Europe. However, the transnational, private-led, and technical origins of the complex were quickly complemented by public actors that have entered the field, partially driven by the diverging governance preferences of the so-called 'sovereigntist states'. Layered over the initially private base of the complex is an array of governance initiatives by regional organisations, as well as governance efforts – and ongoing struggles over them – in formal global intergovernmental arenas such as the United Nations. Simultaneously, private and self-regulatory initiatives have continued to grow. Based on an original dataset of the global governance complex for cybersecurity, Vandendriessche shows the diversity of the complex and describes how the succession of regulatory initiatives has shaped its current topography.

A second chapter focuses on the global governance of trade, which is also characterised by a very diverse number of actors at different levels, from IOs, such as the World Trade Organization (WTO) to the United Nations Conference on Trade and Development (UNCTAD), the Organisation for Economic Co-operation and Development (OECD), and regional organisations like the European Union (EU), to informal bodies like the G7 and G20, and a variety of private actors. Jan Wouters considers each of these actors in order to better understand their respective contributions, strengths, and weaknesses, and their mutual interactions. He thereby indicates how these actors can complement each other, but also how they can contradict one another. 'Complementary' institutions and rules are those for which an interaction enables global governance institutions to better achieve the intended governance objective(s) than they would have achieved without the interaction. 'Contradictory', or antagonistic, institutions and rules are those for which the interaction produces effects that diminish the ability of one or both to achieve the intended governance objective(s). The main challenge for global trade governance seems to be to make sure that all actors strive for complementarity rather than contradictions, which, however, is far from evident in a world where, next to traditional cleavages such as the North–South divide in the UN, geopolitical and geostrategic tensions and contestation (Egan et al., 2023) have recently further politicised trade policies, leading to a weakening of multilateral regimes and a strong rise of bilateralism and unilateralism (Hegde, Wouters, & Raina, 2021).

The chapter by David Levi-Faur, Ilana Blumsack, and Dalit Flaiszhaker on 'Global financial governance: public good under fragmentation' focuses on the finance sector. The authors attempt to identify factors that influence the nature and structure of global governance architectures through a detailed case study of the financial sector. The current regulatory architecture of global financial governance is highly fragmented, in the sense that there is no single actor that fully and formally supervises global finance. Moreover, different IOs (IMF), countries, clubs (G7/G20), and technical bodies (Bank for International Settlements, Financial Stability Board) are active in this space. In addition, global financial governance is informal in the sense that it is typically not based on international treaties: it largely relies on soft law commitments and private guidelines that are often developed by technical and professional experts. In their analysis, Levi-Faur et al. show that domestic politics and central banks determine, to a degree, how finance is governed globally. Powerful actors such as the United States and the EU play an important role, sometimes fuelled by domestic financial interests – and this, in turn, limits the powers of the global financial regulatory regime. In this context, the veto power of some domestic actors is very significant: it determines how the global governance complex is structured and which goals and priorities are important. This explains why the overriding and most prominent issue in global financial regulation is financial stability. Stability – rather than development, access, fairness, antitrust, or consumer affairs – is the driving force behind the structure of global financial governance. Domestic institutional structures, traditions of financial governance, a normative approach to finance, markets, and governments, variations in the size of financial markets and the economy, and financial capacities (including governance capacity) all define the interests of the actors and the extent to which they promote informal or formal global financial institutions and policies.

The next chapter expands on the finance sector and captures a specific driver of global governance complexity, namely statecraft. Catalina Espinosa Notrica, Pablo Nemiña, and Diana Tussie's contribution on 'The Chinese path to a global financial statecraft strategy: between challenge and adaptation to the global financial governance system' explores how China, as a rising power, is reconfiguring global governance by developing new institutions. China's economic might began to increase in an international financial order that systematically under-represented emerging economies. In this context, it was theorised that Beijing could either act as a status quo power, accepting the order as it was, or engage in radical change of the complex. The authors seek to understand which path was chosen and why. They argue that China does not intend to destroy the pre-existing order or drastically change existing global governance institutions. Instead, it aims to revise the regime complexes for finance and development by seeking reforms in existing institutions, but mainly by adding new and parallel institutions. Over the past 20 years, Beijing has become the world's largest bilateral creditor through the powerful Chinese Development Bank, and it has initiated the creation of two multilateral development banks, the New Development Bank (also called the 'BRICS Bank') and the Asian Infrastructure Investment Bank (AIIB). China has thus acted as a revisionist power, in that it did not intend to substitute the existing order of international development finance but rather complement it by putting in place new institutions with norms, rules, and institutions more aligned with its strategic interests. This mixture of defensive and offensive statecraft, in turn, has further increased the complexity of the global governance of development finance.

2.4 Dealing with Complexity: Coordination and Orchestration

The aforementioned chapters illustrate how complex, diverse, and fragmented global governance architectures can be. This is in line with other studies focusing on regime complexes and the literature described by Vandendriessche et al. (Chapter 5 in this book), which try to capture this phenomenon. A key issue is how these architectures operate, and how their distinct levels of complexity, density, and fragmentation affect their performance (Biermann et al., 2009; Biermann & Kim, 2020; Eilstrup-Sangiovanni, 2022; Zelli, 2011; Zürn & Faude, 2013). While research on the effects of complexity is ongoing, it is clear that in complex global governance contexts, ordering mechanisms play an important role in dealing with a multiplicity of actors holding different functions (Eilstrup-Sangiovanni, 2022; Zürn & Faude, 2013). Literature on how coordination challenges can be addressed on a global level has focused, among other things, on the capacity of IOs to perform the role of a central coordinator or orchestrator (Abbott et al., 2015). In this book, several chapters contribute to the study of ordering mechanisms in the context of complexity, through case studies that consider the formats, possibilities, and limitations of coordination and consolidation.

The chapter by Yoram Haftel and Tomer Broude on 'Fiddlers on the roof? International organisations in the international investment agreement regime as traditional global governance' delves into this question and empirically investigates the potential for orchestration in the case of the regime complex dealing with investment. This highly decentralised global governance complex consists of more than 300 international investment agreements and several ad hoc investor-state dispute settlement tribunals. However, a handful of IOs participate in the complex, striving to shape its rules and direction. The chapter seeks to assess the IOs' role in this context, taking into account recent theoretical insights on flexible and informal modes of global governance, such as orchestration. After mapping several modes of governance, Haftel and Broude examine and compare the role of two UN bodies, the UNCTAD and the UN Commission on International Trade Law (UNCITRAL), in the global investment regime. They find that UNCTAD and UNCITRAL play important roles, though mostly in their traditional IO capacities, such as information collection and dissemination, policy advice, training and technical assistance, and as forums for inter-state negotiations and consensus-building. When it comes to orchestrating and aligning the many global governance actors in this complex, their contribution is smaller. As a result, the complex remains decentralised and non-hierarchical. Haftel and Broude raise questions on the possibilities and limitations of orchestration by IOs in addressing fragmentation in global governance and achieving a certain degree of order.

The chapter by Julia Kreienkamp and David Coen on 'Global climate governance under the Paris Agreement: mobilising collective action at multiple scales' also delves into how coordination can be achieved through a detailed case study of global climate governance. Their focus is not on the role of a specific IO in performing the role of a coordinator, but on a new mechanism to achieve coordination: a kind of global experimentalist design (Sabel & Zeitlin, 2012; De Búrca, Keohane, & Sabel, 2014) that links lower-level climate commitments to higher-level monitoring and benchmarking. The chapter starts from the observation that although there is no central authority regulating interactions between different actors in global climate governance, the 2015 Paris Agreement under the UN Framework Convention on Climate Change provides an important overarching framework for cooperation and goal alignment. The Paris Agreement departs significantly from previous attempts to govern climate change through legally binding negotiated commitments. While its shift towards a more bottom-up logic has secured almost universal participation, its success crucially relies on an iterative pledge-and-review process to stimulate ever-increasing ambition among the contracting parties and propel them to put these voluntary commitments into practice. With current ambition levels much too low to keep global temperature rises to 1.5°C – the aspirational temperature goal set by the Paris Agreement – the viability of this mode of governance remains an open question. The authors frame this pledge-and-review mechanism in a mapping of the actors involved in global climate change governance, highlighting the opportunities and limitations presented by an increasingly polycentric and multi-scalar regime complex. One of the key limitations related to the pledge-and-review process is that the enforcement of commitments remains very weak. The approach is built on the idea that naming-and-shaming, through comparing and benchmarking, will push countries to perform better. However, it remains to be seen whether this mechanism truly provides incentives to make progress.

The chapter by Kyle Herman and David Coen on 'The integration of private actors in the global climate regime: targeting the symptoms rather than the disease?' builds on the previous chapter and delves into the role of private actors in influencing the priorities in a global governance regime, *in casu* the carbon governance regime, and in this way adding complexity to coordination efforts. Herman and Coen start by observing that since the 2015 Paris Climate Agreement, private actors have significantly expanded their influence within the global climate governance framework. Their chapter examines their role and demonstrates that their efforts are predominantly focused on carbon emissions management as a response to climate change – a trend referred to as carbon-centric climate governance. However, despite the substantial resources allocated to this approach, greenhouse gas emissions continue to rise. They argue that this governance model, driven by carbon-focused private actors and related measurement protocols, requires a fundamental re-evaluation. A shift is needed to address the root cause – dependence on fossil fuels – rather than merely mitigating the symptoms through emission controls. Their chapter nicely illustrates that private actors often have a significant impact on the direction of a global governance regime and actually complicate coordination and orchestration.

The difficulties of coordination and orchestration are further explored in three detailed case studies that consider the formats, possibilities, and limitations of coordination and consolidation. The first chapter brings together norm contestation, the role of states and IOs in this respect, and international human rights. Ebetürk and Tokhi analyse Türkiye's withdrawal from the Istanbul Convention, an international treaty adopted within the Council of Europe aimed at preventing and combating violence against women, and the EU's reactions thereto. Their chapter provides an important case study of how states may resort to exiting an international treaty as part of political and ideological contestation, and how an IO like the EU reacted to this withdrawal with strong public condemnation and efforts to stigmatise Türkiye's decision. The authors point to the fact that the EU's reaction may have been a missed opportunity as it ultimately reinforced the civilisational tension narrative that Türkiye sought to exploit by exiting the Convention.

Another new mechanism for decentralised coordination is governing by goals. The adoption, in 2015, of the UN Sustainable Development Goals (SDGs) is a key example of this form of global governance. A goal-setting model uses common objectives, instead of rules and norms, to steer actors' behaviour. It is seen as a middle way between rule-making and norm-setting, as it provides more flexibility than rule-making but is equipped with more monitoring mechanisms to track progress than norm-setting. For this reason, a goal-setting model tends to have broad goals and a loose institutional arrangement (Biermann, Kanie, & Kim, 2017; Marx et al., 2021), where lower formalisation may facilitate coordination. The chapter by Sukmawani Bela Pertiwi, Axel Marx, Charline Depoorter, Kari Irwin Otteburn, Tirta Nugraha Mursitama, and Lili Yulyadi Arnakim on 'The challenges of governing sustainable development through goals: prioritization and coordination in Europe and Southeast Asia' analyses global governance through goals as a mechanism to coordinate and make progress on sustainability. The authors introduce and explore this new form of global governance specifically from the perspective of tackling coordination. They find that it generates two new problems regarding the implementation of the goal-setting model and the achievement of global public goals. First, broad goals pose challenges for countries with limited capacities to meet them (Forestier & Kim, 2020), which force such countries to prioritise certain goals to the detriment of others. A loose institutional arrangement characterised by the absence of a central authority and binding mechanisms enables differing policy interpretations and goal prioritisation among actors, resulting in weak enforcement. This finding aligns with the insights of Kreienkamp and Coen (Chapter 11) on enforcement challenges in new forms of global governance. Second, broad goals require not only partnership but also policy coherence among actors at all levels. The involvement of many actors in the typically loose institutional arrangement of the goal-setting model, however, makes coordination a common problem. The success of goal-setting depends on the collective ability to deal with the two aforementioned problems, or, in other words, on the ability to maintain a balance between accommodating national contexts while ensuring policy coherence. The chapter discusses the challenges of goal prioritisation and coordination in the case of the SDGs by empirically focusing on two regions, namely Europe through the EU, and Southeast Asia through the Association of Southeast Asian Nations (ASEAN).

The following chapter focuses on how coordination can be achieved through soft law instruments such as global compacts (GCs) and the relocation of actors within a global governance complex. In their chapter on 'Orchestration in global governance: the Global Compacts on migration and refugees', Andrea C. Bianculli, Miriam Bradley, Robert Kissack, and Juan Carlos Triviño-Salazar look into these changes in global migration governance. Their starting point is, on the one hand, the adoption by the UN General Assembly of two complementary GCs, one on Refugees and the other on Safe, Orderly and Regular Migration in 2018. Both GCs are soft law frameworks that reiterate existing relevant, binding, hard law obligations and establish new non-binding commitments for international cooperation on a range of issues relating to population movements, refugees, and other migrants. On the other hand, a few years earlier, the International Organization for Migration (IOM) joined the UN system as a related organisation, triggering a significant change in the migration regime complex. The authors examine to what extent the GCs have served to reshape global migration governance and, specifically, how the incorporation of global-level institutions has affected pre-existing regional migration governance and the functioning of the regime complex as a whole. It does so through two steps. First, it discusses the incorporation of IOM into the UN system and analyses the process through which the GCs were created, explaining how these developments fit within the wider migration regime complex. Second, it draws on original empirical evidence on the governance of the migration of Venezuelans across South America and of Central Americans through Mexico to the US in order to assess to what extent the incorporation of the IOM into the UN system has affected the regional governance of migration in Latin America, and how the GCs have been used, interpreted, and implemented by governance actors in the region.

3. CONCLUSION

International politics and world affairs are undergoing significant shifts. Global governance, as a concept, emerged in a post-Cold War 'end of history' era, where international cooperation beckoned as a promising avenue to address global challenges. A proliferation of transnational initiatives – public and private, formal and informal – ensued, with the aim of tackling security, environmental, economic, and many other challenges. This explosion of international institutions has resulted in complex global governance arrangements in nearly every issue area. Over the past decades, these have been studied intensively within the growing discipline of global governance.

In this book, we take stock of important developments in global governance research and contribute to some of the key research lines that are now developing. These relate to understanding the role and centrality of IOs in contemporary global governance, the driving forces behind the development of global governance architectures, and how complex global governance systems can be governed. To do so, the chapters in this book draw both on the academic research on and practice of global governance. With analysis taking place either at the level of specific types of international institutions or at the level of full configurations of variegated institutions working on a specific issue area, the book furthermore utilises qualitative and quantitative methods to offer new empirical insights.

Through these insights, we aim to prepare the ground for new research on global governance that is not only relevant for academic debates but also for policy-makers. In a fraught geopolitical environment, governments around the world are confronted with preparing for the future. In this context, discerning how global governance may evolve in the future is of key importance.

REFERENCES

Abbott, K. W., & Faude, B. (2021a). Choosing low-cost institutions in global governance. *International Theory, 13*, 397–426.

Abbott, K. W., & Faude, B. (2021b). Hybrid institutional complexes in global governance. *The Review of International Organizations, 17*, 263–291.

Abbott, K. W., Genschel, P., Snidal, D., & Zangl, B. (2015). Orchestration. In B. Zangl, D. Snidal, K. W. Abbott, & P. Genschel (Eds.), *International Organizations as Orchestrators* (pp. 3–36). Cambridge University Press.

Abbott, K. W., Green, J., & Keohane, R. O. (2016). Organizational ecology and institutional change in global governance. *International Organization, 70*(2), 247–277.

Abbott, K. W., & Snidal, D. (2009). The governance triangle: Regulatory standards institutions and the shadow of the state. In W. Mattli & N. Woods (Eds.), *The Politics of Global Regulation* (pp. 44–88). Princeton University Press.

Aiyar, S., & Ilyina, A. (2023, February 23). Charting globalization's turn to slowbalization after global financial crisis. IMF-blog. https://www.imf.org/en/Blogs/Articles/2023/02/08/charting-globalizations-turn-to-slowbalization-after-global-financial-crisis.

Alter, K. (2014). *The New Terrain of International Law: Courts, Politics, Rights*. Princeton University Press.

Barnett, M., & Finnemore, M. (2004). *Rules for the World: International Organizations in Global Politics*. Cornell University Press.

Barnett, M., Pevehouse, J., & Raustiala, K. (2021). *Global Governance in a World of Change*. Cambridge University Press.

Bauer, M. W., & Ege, J. (2016). Bureaucratic autonomy of international organizations' secretariats. *Journal of European Public Policy, 23*(7), 1019–1037.

Benvenisti, E. (2014). The Law of Global Governance (Volume 368). In *The Hague Academy Collected Courses Online / Recueil des cours de l'Académie de La Haye en ligne*. Brill–Nijhoff.

Biermann, F., Kanie, N., & Kim, R. E. (2017). Global governance by goal-setting: The novel approach of the UN Sustainable Development Goals. *Current Opinion in Environmental Sustainability*, 26–31.

Biermann, F., & Kim, R. E. (2020). Architectures of earth system governance: Setting the stage. In F. Biermann & R. E. Kim (Eds.), *Architectures of Earth System Governance* (pp. 1–34). Cambridge University Press.

Biermann, F., Pattberg, P., Van Asselt, H., & Zelli, F. (2009). The fragmentation of global governance architectures: A framework for analysis. *Global Environmental Politics*, *9*(4), 14–40.

Coen, D. & Pegram, T. (2018). Towards a third generation of global governance scholarship. *Global Policy*, *9*(1), 107–113.

De Búrca, G., Keohane, R. O., & Sabel, C. (2014). Global experimentalist governance. *British Journal of Political Science*, *44*, 477–486.

Egan, M., Raube, K., Wouters, J., & Chaisse, J. (Eds.). (2023). *Contestation and Polarization in Global Governance: European Responses*. Edward Elgar Publishing.

Eilstrup-Sangiovanni, M. (2022). Ordering global governance complexes: The evolution of the governance complex for international civil aviation. *Review of International Organizations*, *17*, 293–322.

Forestier, O., & Kim, R. (2020). Cherry-picking the Sustainable Development Goals: Goal prioritization by national governments and implications for global governance. *Sustainable Development*, *28*, 1269–1278.

Fuchs, D. A. (2004). The role of business in global governance. In S. A. Schirm (Ed.), *New Rules for Global Markets: Public and Private Governance in the World Economy* (pp. 133–154). Palgrave Macmillan.

Hegde, V., Wouters, J., & Raina, A. (2021). Is the rules-based multilateral trade order in decline? Current practices, trends and their impact. *Cambridge International Law Journal*, *10*, 32–53.

Jordana, J. (2017). Transgovernmental networks as regulatory intermediaries: Horizontal collaboration and the realities of soft power. *The ANNALS of the American Academy of Political and Social Science*, *670*(1), 245–262.

Jordana, J., Holesch, A., & Trivino-Salazar, J. C. (2022). Trans-governmental regulatory networks and the European Union's involvement in global governance: An occasional instrument. *Journal of European Integration*, *44*(5), 677–693.

Kahler, M. (2018). Global governance: Three futures. *International Studies Review*, *20*, 239–246.

Kingsbury, B., Krisch, N., & Stewart, R. B. (2005). The emergence of global administrative law. *Law and Contemporary Problems*, *68*(3–4), 15–62.

Lall, R. (2023). *Making International Institutions Work: The Politics of Performance*. Cambridge University Press.

Lenz, T. (2021). *Interorganizational Diffusion in International Relations: Regional Institutions and the Role of the European Union*. Oxford University Press.

Lobel, O. (2004). The renew deal: The fall of regulation and the rise in governance in contemporary legal thought. *Minnesota Law Review*, *89*, 342–470.

Lobel, O. (2012). New governance as regulatory governance. In D. Levi-Faur (Ed.), *The Oxford Handbook of Governance* (pp. 65–82). Oxford University Press.

Marx, A., Depoorter, C., Fernandez de Cordoba, S. F., Verma, R., Araoz, M., Auld, G., Bemelmans, J., Bennett, E. A., Boonaert, E., Brandi, C., Dietz, T., Fouilleux, E., Grabs, J., Gulbrandsen, L. H., Harrison, J., Heilmayr, R., Hernandez, A., Hoekman, B., Lambert, S. R., Lambin, E., Li, L., Maertens, M., Mortara Batistic, P., Michida, E., Nakagawa, J., Negi, A., Pérez-Pineda, J., Ponto, S., Rueda, X., Schleifer, P., Thorstensen, V., & Van der Ven, H. (2024). Global governance through voluntary sustainability standards: Developments, trends and challenges. *Global Policy*, *15*(4), 708–728.

Marx, A., Pertiwi, S. B., Depoorter, C., Hoornick, M., Mursitama, T. N., Otteburn, K., & Arnakim, L. Y. (2021). What role for regional organizations in goal-setting global governance? An analysis of the role of the European Union and ASEAN in the Sustainable Development Goals. *Global Public Policy and Governance*, *1*, 421–445.

Marx, A., & Westerwinter, O. (2022). An ever more entangled union? The European Union's interactions with global governance institutions. *Journal of European Integration*, *44*(5), 597–615.

Mikler, J. (2018). *The Political Power of Global Corporations*. Polity Press.

Pattberg, P., Biermann, F., Chan, S., & Mert, A. (2012). Introduction: Partnerships for sustainable development. In P. Pattberg, F. Biermann, S. Chan. & A. Mert (Eds.), *Public–Private Partnerships for Sustainable Development* (pp. 1–18). Edward Elgar Publishing.

Pauwelyn, J., Wessel, R. A., & Wouters, J. (Eds.). (2012). *Informal International Lawmaking*. Oxford University Press.

Pauwelyn, J., Wessel, R. A., & Wouters, J. (2014). When structures become shackles: Stagnation and dynamics in international lawmaking. *European Journal of International Law*, *25*(3), 733–763.

Pevehouse, J. C., Nordstrom, T., McManus, R. W., & Jamison, A. S. (2020). Tracking organizations in the world: The Correlates of War IGO Version 3.0 datasets. *Journal of Peace Research*, *57*(3), 492–503.

Rhodes, R. (2012). Waves of governance. In D. Levi-Faur (Ed.), *The Oxford Handbook of Governance* (pp. 33–48). Oxford University Press.

Roger, C. B. (2020). *The Origins of Informality: Why the Legal Foundations of Global Governance Are Shifting, and Why It Matters*. Oxford University Press.

Rosenau, J. N. (1995). Governance in the twenty-first century. *Global Governance*, *1*(1), 13–43.

Sabel, C., & Zeitlin, J. (2012). Experimentalist governance. In D. Levi-Faur (Ed.), *The Oxford Handbook of Governance* (pp. 169–184). Oxford University Press.

Saz-Carranza, A., Maggetti, M., Yesilkagit, K., & Coen, D. (2023). Mapping and unpacking global governance bodies: A cross sectional and cross organizational analysis. *International Studies Quarterly*, *67*(3), sqad040.

Saz-Carranza, A., Rueda-Sabater, E., Vandendriessche, M., Moreno, C., & Jordana, J. (2023). The future(s) of global governance: A scenarios exercise. *Global Policy*, *15*, 149–165.

Slaughter, A.-M. (2000). *A New World Order*. Princeton University Press.

Slaughter, A.-M., & Zaring, D. (2006). Networking goes international: An update. *Annual Review of Law and Social Science*, *2*(1), 211–229.

Stone, D. (2019). *Making Global Policy*. Cambridge University Press.

Stone, D., & Moloney, K. (2019). The rise of global policy and transnational administration. In D. Stone & K. Moloney (Eds.), *Oxford Handbook On Global Public Policy And Transnational Administration* (pp. 3–22). Oxford University Press.

Trubowitz, P., & Burgoon, B. (2023). *Geopolitics and Democracy: The Western Liberal Order from Foundation to Fracture*. Oxford University Press.

Vabulas, F., & Snidal, D. (2013). Organization without delegation: Informal intergovernmental organizations (IIGOs) and the spectrum of intergovernmental arrangements. *The Review of International Organizations*, *8*(2), 193–220.

Van den Bossche, P., & Zdouc, W. (2021). *The Law and Policy of the World Trade Organization: Text, Cases and Materials*. Cambridge University Press.

Westerwinter, O. (2021). Transnational public–private governance initiatives in world politics: Introducing a new dataset. *The Review of International Organizations*, *16*, 137–174.

Westerwinter, O. (2022). Transnational governance as strategy? Mapping and explaining the European Union's participation in transnational public–private governance initiatives. *Journal of European Integration*, *44*(5), 695–713.

Wouters, J. (2024). The quiet revolution of global governance law. In M. Accetto, K. Škrubej, & J. H. H. Weiler (Eds.), *Law and (R)Evolution 1920–2020: Past Experiences, Future Challenges* (pp. 137–150). Routledge.

Zelli, F. (2011). The fragmentation of the global climate governance architecture. *Wiley Interdisciplinary Reviews: Climate Change*, *2*(2), 255–270.

Zürn, M. (2018). *A Theory of Global Governance: Authority, Legitimacy, and Contestation*. Oxford University Press.

Zürn, M., Binder, M., & Ecker-Ehrhardt, M. (2012). International authority and its politicization. *International Theory*, *4*(1), 69–106.

Zürn, M., & Faude, B. (2013). On fragmentation, differentiation, and coordination. *Environmental Politics*, *13*(3), 119–130.

2. The evolution of global governance research

Charles Roger, Adam Holesch, Jacint Jordana and Lewin Schmitt

1. INTRODUCTION

Global governance research has grown significantly. At the start of the 1990s, 'governance' was everywhere in practice, but the term itself was hardly in use. Today, things have changed remarkably. 'Global governance' is now a major field of inquiry, uniting researchers from many disciplines: international relations (IR) and international law, sociology, business studies, public administration, history, and more. Each year, hundreds of books and articles are published on the topic by authors located in virtually every part of the world. Universities offer PhDs and master's degrees, undergraduate courses on global governance are increasingly common, and an ever-growing number of workshops, conferences, and events are regularly organised. These developments – along with an expanding set of research programmes, academic centres, schools, and think tanks that orient their work around the idea – collectively attest to a high level of interest in the subject and offer evidence of the field's growing institutionalisation (Jordana, Schmitt, & Holesch, 2020).

In this chapter, our aim is to describe these developments, charting the rise of global governance research from academic obscurity to global celebrity. In doing so, we take a different approach than most other studies of a similar nature. It is safe to say that the broad contours of this history are fairly well understood already. Numerous scholars, from Alice Ba and Matthew Hoffmann to Rorden Wilkinson and Thomas Weiss, have documented the uptake of the concept and offered interpretations of the field's current state (Ba & Hoffmann, 2005; Weiss & Wilkinson, 2019). For the most part, however, their depictions of global governance research have been impressionistic, focusing on a few major writers and some of the most notable works. While undoubtedly useful and in no way wrong in their interpretations, they provide us with a necessarily incomplete understanding of how this field has grown and changed over time. Ultimately, their studies focus on a few prominent trees within a vast forest of scholarly activity.

We offer a more encompassing perspective by using an updated version of our database of global governance research (Roger et al., 2022). The database covers journal articles published between 1975 and 2022 and includes all those that employ 'global governance', or a domain-specific variant of the term, in their titles, abstracts, or lists of keywords.[1] The idea behind this approach is that articles using the term in these places are likely to be ones where global governance is either the focus of an analysis – constituting an article's main object of inquiry – or where the concept serves as a dominant framing device, constituting a lens through which an author analyses world politics. These are two of the dominant ways in which the idea has been used (Rosenau, 1995a; Ba & Hoffmann, 2005; Dingwerth & Pattberg, 2006). While some work is inevitably left out using this approach – for instance, books, studies that solely rely on cognate terms ('world order', 'transnational governance', etc.), or work published in languages that are not well documented in the underlying sources – the database offers a broadly representative picture of all the articles published to date.

With this dataset, we can track trends across the field. The overarching story it tells is one of immense growth. As shown in Figure 2.1, while only a handful of articles had been published on the topic in 1990, there were over 6,500 in total in 2022. While in the 1990s only a dozen or so articles appeared each year, in the 2020s, scholars produced around 600. It has not been a straightforward path, however. In our previous analysis, we identified three distinct stages in the evolution of global governance research: a first, formative stage running from 1975 to 1999; a second occurring between 2000 and 2008; and a third running from 2009 to 2022. In important respects, this periodisation corresponds with patterns identified in earlier accounts. David Coen and Tom Pegram (2015), for instance, divided up global governance research into several 'generations' of scholarship – a first wave that laid down key concepts and set the agenda, as well as a second that picked up and applied these ideas across a range of issue areas and institutions. However, our approach allows us to unpack the dominant trends in each in a more systematic way.

In this chapter, we use this periodisation, along with additional data that has been collected, to explore the key dynamics within each of these 'waves'. In Section 2, we describe the birth of global governance research through an article-by-article examination of key authors, academic venues, and the core

---

1 By 'domain-specific variant' we mean terms like 'global climate governance' or 'global economic governance'. Further details about the database can be found in Roger et al. (2022).

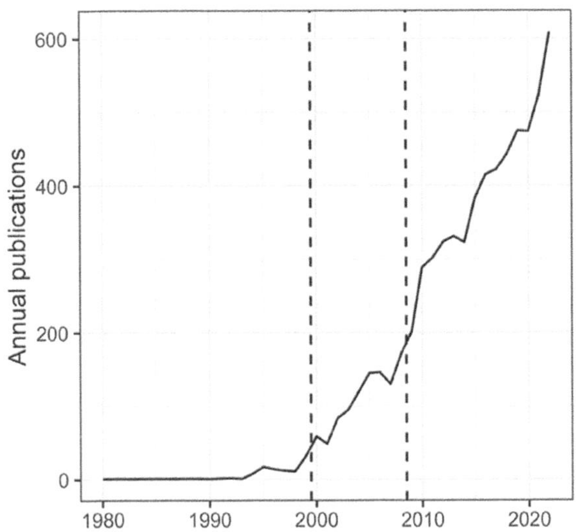

Source: Author's own compilation.

Figure 2.1 *The growth of global governance research*

issues that motivated early work. Such a detailed analysis is possible at this point because the number of articles published in this period is fairly small (100 in total). The section also, correspondingly, has a qualitative flavour, similar to other accounts. It highlights, first, the importance of the World Order Models Project (WOMP). The initial uses of the term, we find, all appear in work by WOMP-affiliated scholars and in associated journals. Second, it emphasises the role of key individuals from the policymaking world, like Willy Brandt, Ingvar Carlsson, and Sir Shridath Ramphal, who boosted the term at the start of the 1990s and led scholars who had become involved in their work to sharpen its meaning – notably, James Rosenau. Finally, during this period, we see the value of the new spaces for academic research on the topic that were created by these early proponents.

The debates that played out within these venues laid the foundations for the second wave of research we focus on. At this point, the number of academic articles explodes and our analysis shifts into a more quantitative mode, zooming out to capture broader patterns of scholarly activity. In Section 3, specifically, we examine how key global governance concepts and ideas were unevenly transposed into a variety of literatures and national contexts. We show that global governance research has expanded significantly to cover several core research areas but has made fewer inroads into others. Similarly, we document several geographical shifts in the uptake of the concept, as the central locus of research initially moved across the Atlantic to Europe and as research has grown more recently in Asia. Finally, in Section 4, our focus turns towards developments at the heart of the most recent, third wave of studies, exploring the growing body of work on inter-institutional interactions – employing new concepts like regime complexity, fragmentation, and polycentricity – and approaching the study of global governance with new methodological rigour.

In the conclusion, we discuss outstanding issues. While remarkable strides have been made over the years, our analysis suggests that there are areas where progress can be made. First, we argue that much research still occurs within subfield journals. Debates often unfold in a fragmented fashion across small academic niches, and opportunities for cross-fertilisation are, accordingly, frequently missed. Second, despite decades of research, very few studies have entered the top IR journals. This may be, in part, because of the historically limited attention to methods that has characterised research on the topic. But as this changes, future possibilities may open up. Finally, and perhaps most importantly, there are still major geographical disparities in publishing. Making global governance research a genuinely global endeavour, we argue, requires sustained attention to this issue.

2. THE BIRTH OF GLOBAL GOVERNANCE RESEARCH

International relations has long been concerned with dynamics of international cooperation. The academic study of international organisation is one of the oldest fields of IR research, dating to the start of the twentieth century (Reinsch, 1911; Potter, 1922; Rochester, 1986). The term 'international organisation', as used by its first advocates, was employed in a manner that was similar to the way 'global governance' is at present. Much of their work, therefore, anticipated, speaks to, and laid the groundwork for what today 'counts' as global governance research. Interestingly, however, it was not until the 1970s that the term 'global governance' emerged, principally in work by researchers associated with the WOMP who challenged the model of IR scholarship that generally prevailed at the time. The earliest written uses of the term appear in the writings of Saul Mendlovitz, the director of the WOMP and head of the New York-based Institute for World Order (IWO).[2] Many other early uses of

---

[2] See, for instance, Mendlovitz (1975a and 1975b). The IWO was created in 1972 by merging two closely related organisations with strong roots in the world federalist movement: the Association for Education in World Government/ Institute for International Order, established in 1948, and the World Law Fund,

the term, mainly in the 1980s, appear in writing associated with the WOMP as well. Virtually all the earliest articles in the database appeared in *Alternatives*, the official WOMP journal.

The emergence of global governance in the writings of WOMP scholars may be attributable to the fact that it aimed to promote novel, normatively orientated thinking about the global system. Through a pioneering transnational dialogue and research programme involving scholars from the Americas, Europe, Asia, and Africa – including luminaries like Johan Galtung, Richard Falk, Rajni Kothari, and Ali Mazrui – its objective was to diagnose global problems, articulate a set of plausible 'preferred worlds', and undertake research on 'transition strategies' with some prospect of achieving them. Its basic assumption was that the existing world order was flawed, and that dominant realist thinking could not provide a way forward. This did not imply, in turn, a single-minded focus on the need for world government. Instead, members embraced a range of alternative approaches, or models, 'below' and 'beyond' the nation-state, and this focus led to studies of an enormous variety of transnational issues and movements, from women's activism, vegetarianism, and alternative lifestyles, to nuclear weapons, global environmentalism, and the New International Economic Order. This orientation led those involved to experiment with a variety of new terms.

That said, within the research of WOMP scholars, the term 'global governance' was not carefully defined, and it did not achieve any special prominence. If anything, 'humane governance' and 'geo-governance' – principally promoted by Kothari (1987) and Falk (1995b) – were more widely employed. But its use rapidly grew over these alternatives after it was picked up by prominent practitioners. By far, the most important was Willy Brandt, the former chancellor of the German Federal Republic (1969–1974), leader of the Social Democratic Party of Germany from 1964 to 1987, and president of the Socialist International (SI) (1976–1992). In the latter capacity, Brandt had in the mid-1980s become involved in leading high-level consultations with the new leadership that had appeared in the Soviet Union. As chancellor, he had been instrumental in developing Germany's Ostpolitik, and as the chairman of the SI he looked for new models of cooperation that could involve the Soviet Union in global problem-solving to a greater extent, helping to break the Cold War deadlock at the end of the 1980s.

---

created in 1961 and founded by Henry Hollins, a banker, the American diplomat and Treasury Secretary C. Douglas Dillon, and Grenville Clark, lawyer and coauthor (with Louis Sohn) of *World Peace through World Law* (1958). In 1982, the IWO changed its name to the World Policy Institute, which published the *World Policy Journal*, a major outlet for geopolitical analysis at the end of the Cold War.

Brandt was highly motivated by the changing conditions within the Soviet Union. In 1985, Mikhail Gorbachev became General Secretary of the Communist Party, and he brought on board a number of forward-thinking policy advisors.[3] Among other things, they injected new ideas – reflected in a new non-Marxist policy language encompassing 'interdependence', 'global problems', 'mutual security', and even 'global government' – that transformed Soviet foreign policymaking at the time (Checkel, 1993; Larson & Shevchenko, 2003). Brandt developed a close relationship with Gorbachev and was impressed by his many conversations with him. Following a meeting in 1988 with Gorbachev and his advisors, where Brandt was accompanied by the German and Dutch politicians Egon Bahr and Jan Pronk, he saw a unique opportunity to bridge the gap between the Cold War powers and reform major global institutions at a time when cross-border problems – poverty, nuclear proliferation, HIV/AIDS, drug trafficking, and so on – were multiplying (Rother & Schmidt, 2006, p. 93; Soviet News, 1988).

Brandt's aim was more political than academic. He imagined a 'Cancún-style' meeting, along the lines of the North–South summit he had organised in 1980 but with wider representation (Thérien, 2005; Rother & Schmidt, 2006, pp. 94–96, pp. 465–468). At that meeting, he was stung by the USSR's refusal to take part. This time, in contrast, it was the Americans – specifically, Brent Scowcroft, national security advisor to President Bush – who rebuffed his proposal. But Brandt was undeterred. At a conference in Königswinter in 1990 – officially a ten-year follow-up to the North–South Report, attended by politicians and members of other independent Commissions – he persuaded participants that opportunities were opening up to renew global cooperation and, given the severity of global problems, they should not be missed (Rother

---

3 Among them was Georgi Shakhnazarov, one of the most prominent Soviet IR theorists. Gorbachev had been attracted to his writing, which centred on the idea of global order and world 'governability' (*upravlyayemosti mira*) (Brown, 2020, pp. 40–41; for key works, see Shakhnazarov, 1984, 1988). Shakhnazarov was made a full-time advisor in 1988 and was thereafter closely associated with Gorbachev's foreign policy revolution. Interestingly, Shakhnazarov had read WOMP studies, sympathised with their aims, and took a leading role in its Global Civilization Project around the same time (Falk, 1995b). Some of his writing was also republished in *Alternatives* under the title 'Prospects of Global Governance' (Shakhnazarov, 1989). This raises the fascinating – although inevitably speculative – possibility that the term came into Brandt's orbit via his association with Gorbachev and advisors like Shakhnazarov. If so, its attractiveness may have derived from the fact that it was already embraced by prominent Soviet officials and was simultaneously new and vague enough, with few prior associations, to fit the moment and avoid putting off the Americans.

& Schmidt, 2006, pp. 483–485). This led to the formation of a working group, comprising Swedish Prime Minister Ingvar Carlsson, former Commonwealth Secretary-General Sir Shridath Ramphal, and Pronk, to outline possibilities for global action. A larger group was later assembled in Stockholm, in April 1991, at which point a comprehensive set of proposals was published, mainly focused on UN reform. This document, the *Stockholm Initiative on Global Security and Governance*, was circulated by Swedish embassies to a range of governments and made extensive use of the term, representing its most high-profile appearance (Mouat, 1991). Ultimately, the effort had little impact, and the term may well have been forgotten. However, the last of its 28 recommendations had some lasting significance: its call for 'an independent International Commission on Global Governance' (Stockholm Initiative, 1991, p. 135).

Brandt passed away the following year, but his initiative was carried forward by Carlsson and Ramphal, whom he had invited to become co-chairs of the new commission. Offices were established in London and Geneva, an executive director (Peter Hansen) was appointed, and deliberations began, with the aim of publishing a detailed report and renewing Brandt's political initiative on firmer intellectual foundations in 1995, coinciding with the UN's fiftieth anniversary (Knight, 2005).[4] This stimulated the first serious attempts to develop the concept. As the central notion and title of the new commission, it was necessary to grapple with its meaning. These efforts initially occurred within meetings under the Commission and in the papers presented at them by scholars like Emma Rothschild, Jorge Castañeda, Georges Abi-Saab, Peter and Ernst Haas, Johan Galtung, and, perhaps most importantly, James Rosenau (for a sample, see Commission on Global Governance, 1995). Their ideas began to filter beyond these venues as well via the efforts made by Carlsson and Ramphal to promote the commission's work in both the popular press and in academic journals like *Security Dialogue*, where pieces by them appeared along with other efforts to 'conceive' global governance (Ramphal, 1992; Carlsson, 1992; Senghaas, 1993).

Following publication of the Commission's report, *Our Global Neighbourhood*, in 1995, the discourse broadened. In line with Brandt's original goals, Carlsson convened a group of 16 prime ministers and heads of state that leveraged the momentum and ideas it generated to push for UN reform (Carlsson, 1995). But the many events that sprang up around the report

---

4 Contemporaneously, the Centre for the Study of Global Governance – the first research institute explicitly focused on the topic – was founded at the London School of Economics, in 1992, with support from the Maurice Laing and Rufford Foundations. Headed by Meghnad Desai until 2004, its later directors included Mary Kaldor, David Held, and Danny Quah.

testified to its wider resonance (e.g., Hays & Morgante, 1995) and, in academia, its proposals stimulated considerable debate. Simai (1997) advanced an alternative approach grounded in earlier work by Harlan Cleveland (1979), for instance, and Falk (1995a), Knight (1995), Baxi (1996) and Massicotte (1999), among others, critiqued the commission's work (also see Harris and Yunker, 1999). The journal *Global Governance* was also launched under the aegis of the Academic Council of the United Nations System and the United Nations University. In its pages, the idea grew in sophistication. Rosenau's (1995b) agenda-setting piece in the first issue gave the idea academic cache and the analytic bite that it previously lacked. It was followed by works that reckoned with his ideas. In the same issue, Robles (1995) offered a perspective informed by French and German approaches to the study of regulation and regimes, while Finkelstein (1995), Smouts (1998), and Murphy (2000) published thoughtful criticism.

Early evidence of the concept's value can be found in its emerging use in applied research. Special issues appeared on the 'pluralization of global governance' and 'UN task-sharing', unpacking the role of non-state actors in traditional international organisations (Gordenker & Weiss, 1995; Smith & Weiss, 1997). Global civil society also became a major focus of many articles. Several studies called attention to the governance-like activities of non-governmental organisations, expert communities, and 'private organisations' comprising multinational corporations (Lipchutz, 1999; Kennedy, 1999; Ronit & Schneider, 1999). Most of this work, still, had a very general orientation. It was largely concerned with shifts in global authority and documenting the new types of global governors that were appearing. Some researchers did apply these emerging ideas to understand patterns of governance in specific issue areas like the environment, security, and social policy (Wapner, 1997; Nossal, 1999; Yeates, 1999). But it was in the period after 2000 – when the literature clearly moved beyond the agenda-setting phase – that this trend really took off.

3. THE CHANGING LANDSCAPE OF GLOBAL GOVERNANCE RESEARCH

The first wave of global governance research comprised relatively few publications. An enterprising scholar can read virtually all the articles published between 1975 and 1999, and develop a picture of what was said and done. Many can be found in a narrow range of journals – *Alternatives*, *Security Dialogue*, *Third World Quarterly*, and *Global Governance* – and, in terms of their topics, a disproportionate number are classified in our dataset as 'general', meaning either that they have no specific issue area focus – and are either purely conceptual or theoretical in nature – or draw on examples from a diverse array of issue areas. This emphasis largely reflects the early state of the literature, as a small group of scholars pioneered a new 'perspective' on world politics and defined its central objects of inquiry (Dingwerth & Pattberg, 2006). In the period after, this all changed: the number of publications grew immensely, the range of topics they focused on expanded, and the locus of scholarly publishing began to shift in important ways.

To track these shifts in the terrain of global governance research, our approach in this section shifts from telling a largely qualitative story about the individual articles that appear in the database to a quantitative analysis of the patterns that emerge across them. Consider, first, the data presented in Figure 2.2 where articles are grouped into several broad categories. In it, we can clearly see a trend towards greater diversity. During the first wave, as noted, 'general' articles were the most common. When studies did apply the ideas that had been developed to specific issues, they largely focused on the economy and environment, though these were comparatively few in number. In the second wave, issue-specific research expands considerably. Studies on these topics became much more common, and new ones were explored that had not been extensively studied before – human rights, global health, security, and so on. A complementary picture emerges if we consider how the number

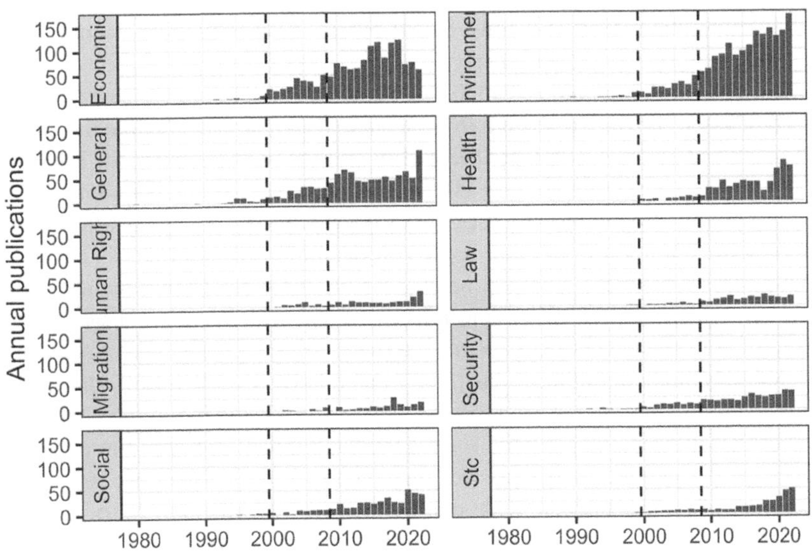

Source: Own compilation.

Figure 2.2 *Global governance articles, by subject, 1975–2022*

of 'domain-specific' versions of the term has changed over time. Whereas 'global governance' was the principal term used in the first wave of scholarship, researchers subsequently adapted it to characterise over 120 varieties: from 'global climate governance' to 'global migration governance' to 'global security governance' and beyond.

What was once a relatively unified conversation playing out among a small group of researchers, therefore, appears to fragment into a complex of issue-specific conversations. However, as Figure 2.2 also demonstrates, the depth of these emerging conversations has varied, reflecting some unevenness in the research landscape. When we look across different categories, research on the governance of economic and environmental issues soon became (and largely remains) the most prominent overall. Throughout the second wave of research, these two categories jointly accounted for around half of all the studies published each year. More recently, work on global health has joined the leading ranks. But, elsewhere, global governance ideas made fewer inroads. Research on international security, in particular, has been surprisingly limited. Within the field of IR, it has been one of the most frequently studied topics; within the literature on global governance, however, it has constituted a comparatively modest part of total publications (Maliniak et al., 2011). Its share has also diminished over time, as research on health and social issues has grown. In other areas, such as human rights and migration, while research has increased from a low base, they still rank below others, despite the importance that scholars regularly ascribe to them.

Clearly, then, the value of global governance as a frame for research on specific issues proved to be high in some areas – including some like the environment and global health that have traditionally been neglected in the broader IR literature (see Green & Hale, 2017) – but much less so in other contexts. It also appears, as we can see in the case of international security, that there has been some variation over time, perhaps reflecting changes in the underlying issue areas. Research on global health, for instance, has been punctuated at several points – first, in 2011, and followed by a more sustained surge in the aftermath of the Covid-19 pandemic. Research on the governance of science, technology, and communications (STC) was relatively limited for some time. But recently it has been a growth area, possibly reflecting mounting concerns about the internet and artificial intelligence. Curiously, the opposite appears to be true when it comes to research on economic issues. There, we see some evidence of waning interest. Although the area grew significantly in the 2000s, and it remains prominent overall, a degree of stagnation can also be seen from the mid-2010s onwards.

Beyond subject matter, the other way in which global governance research diversified relates to the authors involved. As shown in Figure 2.3, the vast majority of publications in the first wave of studies were by scholars based

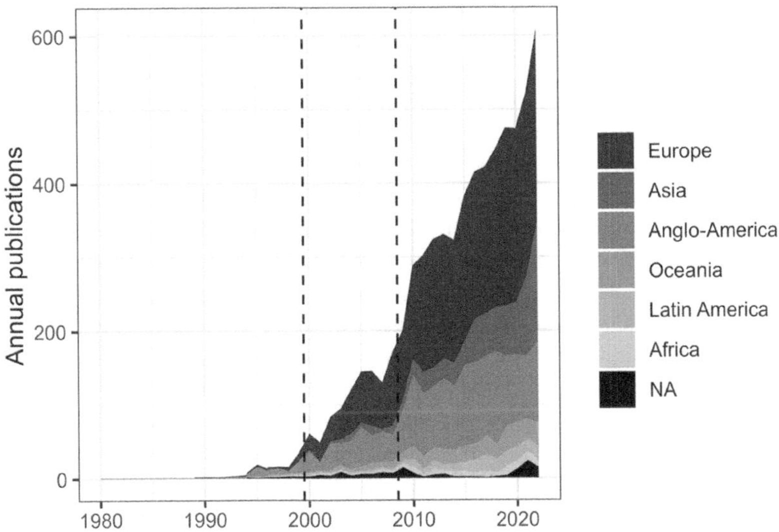

Source: Author's own compilation.

Figure 2.3 *First author locations, by world region, 1980–2022*

in the United States (US). While the WOMP and Commission on Global Governance were both genuinely transnational – albeit largely American- and European-led – initiatives, involving participants from all parts of the world, the majority of publications in the 1990s were by Americans. Scholars like James Rosenau, John Ruggie, Thomas Weiss, Craig Murphy, and Richard Falk – all based at American universities – were among the most important for showing how broader shifts in global authority were challenging prevailing thinking in IR. Their work during this period laid the earliest conceptual foundation for the academic study of global governance. But even beyond these prominent pioneers, research was heavily concentrated in the US (and, to a degree, Canada as well). Between 1995 and 2000, Anglo-American scholars authored over 60 per cent of all publications, on average.

However, their prevalence waned during the second wave. Between 2000 and 2008, the number of Anglo-American publications dropped to around 30 per cent, on average, and dipped as low as 20 per cent in 2008. Their place was taken by Europeans. From 2000 onwards, scholars from Europe have contributed over half of the annually published articles, culminating in a substantial overall lead. Still, in the mid-2020s, the US remains the largest single-country producer of research, accounting for just about 19 per cent of all publications

– hardly an insignificant share. However, it is nearly matched by the United Kingdom. Today, scholars in the UK have produced approximately 16 per cent of all the global governance publications in our dataset. And when we consider Europe as a whole, states there have been responsible for nearly half (49.7 per cent) of the entire body of published research. Accordingly, as we have observed elsewhere, it is fair to say that while IR may have begun (and, to a degree, remains) an American social science, the study of global governance is now largely a European one (Kristensen, 2015; Roger et al., 2022).

This picture has only started to change in the third phase of research, which we focus on next, with major growth in output from academics based in Asia, particularly China. While its contribution up until 2008 was minor, Asia's share of publications since then has grown significantly, and in 2022 the total publications from Asia exceeded Anglo-America's output for the first time – making it the second largest world region. This heralds a notable shift in the overall composition of publications that stands in stark contrast to what is perhaps the most consistent pattern in the dataset: the otherwise limited involvement from academics in the Global South. Although the absolute number of publications by African and Latin American scholars has grown over the last decade, the overall share has remained consistently low. And, overall, despite Asia's recent growth, scholars from the Global South, representing the majority of the world's population, have still collectively authored less than a quarter (24 per cent) of all publications in the dataset. This underscores the restricted set of worldviews and experiences reflected in current discussions.

4. THE MATURATION OF GLOBAL GOVERNANCE RESEARCH

By 2005 – in the midst of the second wave – Michael Barnett and Raymond Duvall (2005, p. 1) could confidently assert that the idea of global governance had 'attained near-celebrity status'. Already, in their eyes, it had become 'one of the central orienting themes in the practice and study of international affairs'. Today, as publications skyrocket, its celebrity status has been consolidated. Between 2000 and 2008 – during the second wave of scholarship – researchers produced roughly 110 publications per year. In the third, which ran from 2009 to 2022, they averaged over 400. In just two years (2021 and 2022), in fact, over 1,100 studies of global governance were published – nearly as many as appeared in the entire decade in which Barnett and Duvall were writing. Of course, during this period, academic publications increased significantly across the board. So, this growth may not be so surprising on its own. But, if we compare the global governance research, as we define it in this chapter, with studies that use related terms like 'international organisation', 'international regimes', or 'world order', it does appear to have grown significantly in relative terms (Roger et al., 2022, p. 495).

The exploding number of publications in the third wave of research provides a strong indication of the continuing value of ideas forged in the first. But, apart from the enormous growth of studies, what is distinctive about research in this most recent period? In this final section, we do not aim to provide a comprehensive analysis of these trends. Instead, we explore two main ideas about the scholarly dynamics at work. The first relates to a *substantive* shift in the nature of the research: from a micro-level focus on individual types of institutions and macro-level changes in the *composition* of governing actors – the shift from public to private authority, for instance – to analyses of meso-level *interactions* between global governors. The second relates to a *procedural* shift in the way that global governance research has been conducted: the degree to which scholars have embraced rigorous methods, whether quantitative or qualitative, to understand the issues and phenomena they are concerned with. Both trends have been widely observed – and, to a degree, may be interconnected – yet, at present, current assessments largely rest on anecdotal impressions. The extent of their reach also remains something of an open question.

The reason for focusing on these two changes is because they each speak, in different ways, to the maturation of the field. The growing focus on inter-institutional interactions, networks of institutions, and regime complexity represents, in our view, one of the notable advances in global governance research that gives substance to concerns that have been central to the field from its earliest days. From the outset, researchers had been aware that institutions exist alongside each other, interact in complex ways, and that these interactions can have important consequences for the way problems are governed. In the 1990s, work by Rosenau (1995a, 1995b), Oran Young (1999), Vinod Aggarwal (1998), and others, called attention to institutional proliferating, the types of relationships between institutions (task-sharing, clustering, embedding, nesting, etc.), and the different strategies actors adopt within varying structures. The refinement of concepts to capture these ideas – from the notions of forum shopping and regime complexity to orchestration and organisational ecology – and the growth of sophisticated research programmes around them appears to offer something new, however, reflecting a progressive shift in the phenomena scholars are concerned with.

To the degree that we indeed find evidence of this, such patterns would illustrate one of the ways in which empirical analyses have matured over time. A shift in methods would offer evidence of a different kind of maturation. Frequently, those immersed in global governance research have lamented the literature's relative lack of methodological rigour. Much of it, especially in the early stages, was accused of being 'too descriptive', focusing on demonstrating the existence and relevance of new actors and processes rather than testing theories about them (see Drezner, 2007, for example). Studies may have looked at world politics in a different way but did not pay careful attention to problems of causal inference – a fact which may explain the limited number that appeared in top IR journals. If so, this was rare and researcher-specific rather than a notable characteristic of the field as a whole. More recently, however, some have argued that this has changed. Roger and Dauvergne (2016, p. 417), for instance, claim that we have seen important areas of global governance research 'shifting onto more rigorous methodological ground, utilising a range of small-n, medium-n, and large-n approaches that support stronger descriptive and causal inferences'. After having laid foundations for the field in earlier periods, they argue, researchers have begun to approach their subject with greater sophistication.

To evaluate the extent of these two shifts, we employ an automated approach similar to the kind of analyses conducted in our earlier work (Roger et al., 2022). Specifically, we use information in the abstracts, titles, and keywords of articles in the dataset to track patterns across publications. To gauge the growth of research on inter-institutional interactions and regime complexity, we compiled a list of unique words utilised by this literature – 'overlap', 'interplay', 'complexity', 'architecture', 'linkage', and so on – including both older and newer terms, and assess whether they are present in these places.[5] Finding evidence of them signals that these ideas constitute a major focus of, or theme within, a study. We can then pool this data to observe overall trends. To gauge methods, we adopt a similar approach, drawing on a comprehensive list of method-specific words – 'process tracing', 'qualitative analysis', 'case study', and so on – and assessing whether they are present as well. Finding them in these places may not tell us how well these methods are used in practice. But they indicate, at least, that methods are discussed explicitly and prominently at the outset of a study.

What does our analysis reveal? First, consider the data in Figure 2.4 showing the number of papers (in both absolute and relative terms) that focus on inter-institutional interactions. It demonstrates that research with such an orientation was comparatively limited during the first and second waves of global governance research. From 1995 to 2008, only about 10–15 per cent of articles appeared to have interactions as an explicit thematic focus. The total number of articles rose over this period but only gradually and without any significant

[5] In this regard, we take care to account for the fact that some – 'regime complex' and 'orchestration', for instance – only appeared in the second period of global governance research (Raustiala & Victor, 2004; Abbott & Snidal, 2009). We include, therefore, a range of related terms, like 'task-sharing', 'cluster', 'overlap', and 'nest', which were proposed in the first stage by scholars like Smith and Weiss (1997), Young (1999) and Aggarwal (1998).

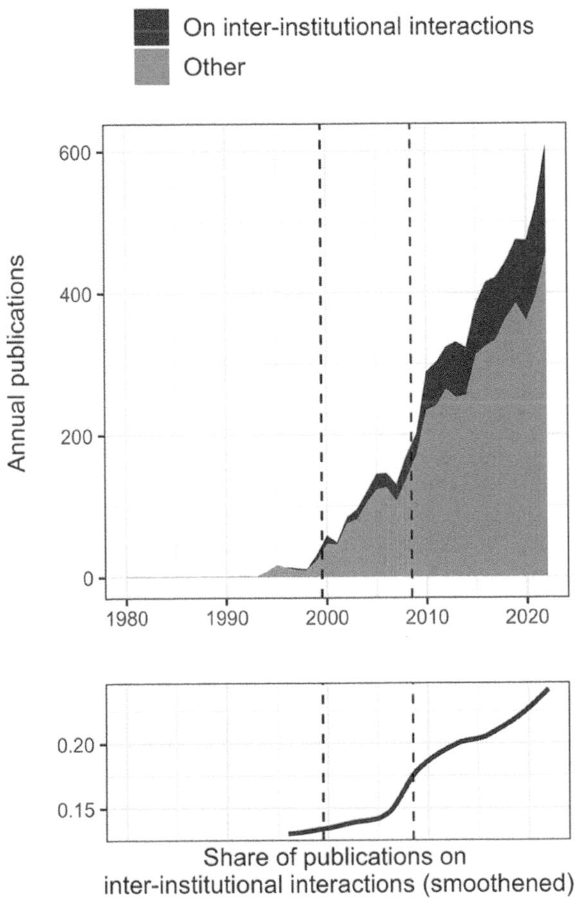

Source: Author's own compilation.

Figure 2.4 *Research on inter-institutional interactions, 1980–2022*

gain in overall share. This changed in the period afterwards, however. Towards the end of the second wave, the number of articles focused on inter-institutional interactions began to grow considerably, and its upward trajectory continued throughout the third phase of research. In the most recent years for which we have data, inter-institutional interactions of various kinds appear as a central theme in 20–25 per cent of all articles, and their growth shows little sign of slowing down. It is safe to say, therefore, that while such a focus was not absent from the first two waves, it has become a particularly distinctive feature of the third, providing evidence of a progressive development in the overall global governance research programme.

Next, consider Figure 2.5 showing how the number of articles that make explicit reference to research methods has changed across the three waves of research. What is particularly striking is the extremely low number of articles that refer to any kind of method at all in earlier periods. On average,

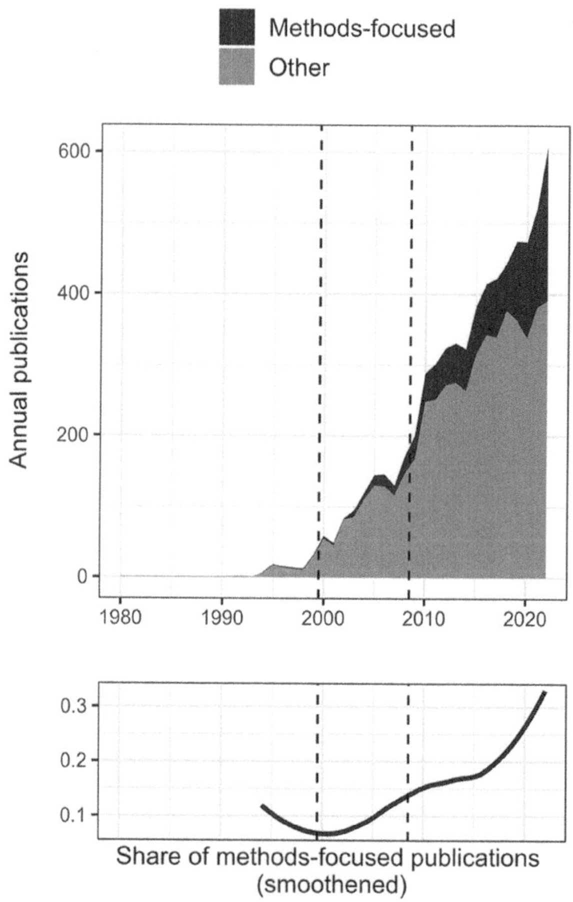

Source: Own compilation.

Figure 2.5 Methods and global governance research, 1980–2022

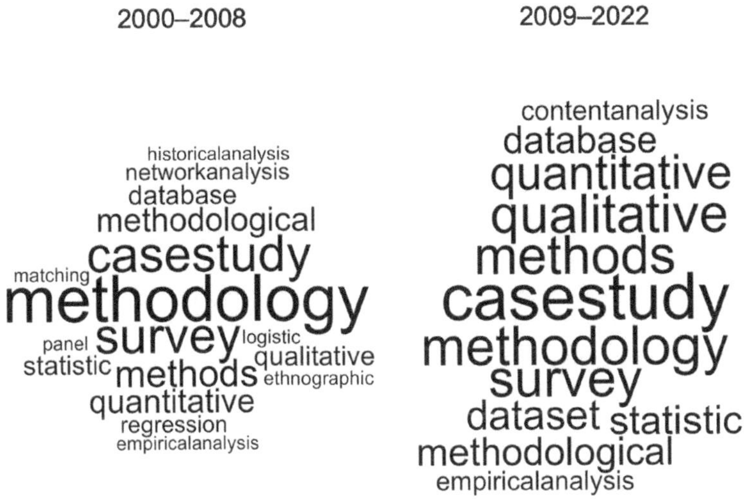

Source: Author's own compilation.

Figure 2.6 Word cloud: key research methods over two decades

during the first two waves of studies, only about 10 per cent of articles did so. Broadly speaking, this confirms long-standing impressions regarding the lack of methodological rigour compared to other areas of research.[6] In the third wave, though, there has been a marked increase in the number of papers that make explicit reference to research methods. At this point, the share rises to an average of 20 per cent and to as much as one-third of all the articles published in more recent years. This suggests that there has indeed been a shift towards more rigorous testing of causal claims, as Roger and Dauvergne and others have asserted, that is likely to have implications for the validity of findings. That said, it is important to observe that the share of methodologically framed articles can still be regarded as low overall, and it remains to be seen whether the changes observed are sustained over time.

What methods have been used? In this case, we delve into the underlying patterns at the heart of this shift by checking for the most frequent methods-related terms, as illustrated in Figure 2.6. Here, we only look at the second

6 Although it is difficult to make sharp inferences given our different approaches to measurement, a comparison with data collected by Sprinz and Wolinsky-Nahmias (2004) and Maliniak et al. (2011) on the use of research methods in the broader field of IR suggests that global governance research is indeed behind trend.

and third waves due to the smaller numbers in the first, which skew the results considerably. What is striking about this comparison is, first of all, the consistency of the most prominent terms across both periods: there are many unspecific mentions of 'methods' and 'methodology' while 'case study' and 'survey' are the most frequently mentioned tools in each. At the same time, there does appear to be a relative change in the types of methods embraced across the two periods. Specifically, while terms like 'regression' and 'logistic' can be found in the second wave (2000–2008), they are much less common in comparison. In the third, by contrast, terms like 'statistic', 'quantitative', 'database', 'dataset', and so on, are more prominent. It appears, then, that in addition to greater overall attention to methodological issues in the literature, there has also been a subtle shift in global governance research towards data-driven and statistical methodologies that mirror what has been happening in many other parts of IR.

5. CONCLUSIONS

Global governance research has made tremendous strides since the term emerged in the mid-1970s. The language of global governance has been taken up by and has informed the work of scholars from virtually all regions of the world and has been transposed to a wide range of issues and institutions; debates about these issues and institutions have evolved over time, shifting towards the exploration of inter-institutional interactions and paying greater attention to issues of causal inference. Despite these signs of progress, however, there are several ways in which the promise of global governance research remains unfulfilled, and where improvements can be made. Our research has revealed, for instance, that the field began with a remarkable degree of unity. Debates played out among a fairly small group of scholars and centred on a limited number of general issues, beginning with how we can conceptualise global governance in the first place and what this new perspective brings to the table in both positive and normative terms. In the ensuing periods, however, this debate fractured into a multitude of conversations as global governance ideas were applied to different fields. This development offered a strong, early indication of their relevance. Yet, as insights have been gained in separate areas, there is a risk that some of the larger lessons and benefits of a more unified dialogue have been lost.

Finding ways to overcome the 'boxed-up' nature of scholarly conversations by fostering communication between scholars working in different issue areas and with different backgrounds therefore offers one important path forward for the field. Further promoting the move towards more rigorous research constitutes another. After several decades of research, improvements on this front have been relatively recent, as seen above. This is a promising development. But attention to methodological issues is still quite low and likely remains out of step with developments in the broader discipline of IR and political science more generally. This means that, ultimately, many findings may rest on theoretical rather than on empirical foundations, and, as noted, this may partly explain the relatively limited number of publications that have historically featured in top political science journals like *International Organization*, *American Political Science Review*, and *World Politics*. The progress we have recorded on methods should not be discounted, certainly, but it also reveals how far the field needs to go in order to catch up with other areas.

Finally, major improvements can still be made towards reducing the geographical disparities we see (Roger et al., 2022). In important respects, our research has shown that global governance research may well be somewhat more diverse than IR as a whole. Despite the prominence of scholars from the US during the first wave of scholarship, Europeans have become leaders in their own right and, more recently, the rise of research from Asia represents an especially welcome development. But while the locus of scholarship has shifted over time, it remains firmly located in the mid-Atlantic overall. Voices from the Global South are notably absent. This means that despite the progress that has undoubtedly been made, debates about global governance remain one-sided and cannot do justice to the enormous diversity of views that must certainly exist. Thus, as in IR, there is much that editors, researchers, conference organisers, and so on, can do to promote diversity within the community of global governance researchers.

REFERENCES

Abbott, K. W., & Snidal, D. (2009). Strengthening international regulation through transnational governance: Overcoming the orchestration deficit. *Vanderbilt Journal of Transnational Law, 42*, 501–578.

Aggarwal, V. K. (1998). *Institutional designs for a complex world: Bargaining, linkages, and nesting.* Cornell University Press.

Ba, A. D., & Hoffmann, M. J. (2005). *Contending perspectives on global governance: Coherence, contestation, and world order.* Routledge.

Barnett, M., & Duvall, R. (2005). *Power in global governance.* Cambridge University Press.

Baxi, U. (1996). 'Global neighborhood' and the 'universal otherhood': Notes on the report of the Commission on Global Governance. *Alternatives, 21*(4), 525–549.

Brown, A. (2020). *The human factor: Gorbachev, Reagan, Thatcher and the end of the Cold War.* Oxford University Press.

Carlsson, I. (1992). A New International Order through the United Nations. *Security Dialogue, 23*(4), 7–11.

Carlsson, I. (1995). Roles for the UN in International Security after the Cold War. *Security Dialogue, 26*(1), 7–18.

Checkel, J. (1993). Ideas, institutions, and the Gorbachev foreign policy revolution. *World Politics, 45*(2), 271–300.

Clark, G., & Sohn, L. B. (1958). *World peace through world law*. Harvard University Press.

Cleveland, H. (1979). The internationalization of domestic affairs. *The Annals of the American Academy of Political and Social Science*, *442*(1), 125–137.

Coen, David and Tom Pegram (2015). Wanted: A Third Generation of Global Governance Research. *Governance*, *28*(4), pp. 417–420.

Commission on Global Governance. (1995). *Issues in global governance: Papers written for the Commission on Global Governance*. Kluwer Law International.

Dingwerth, K., & Pattberg, P. (2006). Global governance as a perspective on world politics. *Global Governance*, *12*, 185–203.

Drezner, D. (2007). *All politics is global: Explaining international regulatory regimes*. Princeton University Press.

Falk, R. (1995a). Liberalism at the global level: The last of the independent commissions? *Millennium: Journal of International Studies*, *24*(3), 563–576.

Falk, R. (1995b). *On humane governance*. Pennsylvania State University Press.

Finkelstein, L. S. (1995). What is global governance? *Global Governance*, *1*(3), 367–372.

Gordenker, L., & Weiss, T. G. (1995). Pluralising global governance: Analytical approaches and dimensions. *Third World Quarterly*, *16*(3), 357–387.

Green, J. F., & Hale, T. N. (2017). Reversing the marginalization of global environmental politics in international relations: An opportunity for the discipline. *PS: Political Science & Politics*, *50*(2), 473–479.

Harris, E. E., & Yunker, J. A. (1999). *Toward genuine global governance: Critical reactions to 'Our Global Neighborhood'*. Praeger.

Hays, M., & Morgante, A. (1995). *A people's response to Our Global Neighbourhood: Dialogues on the report of the Commission on Global Governance*. Boston Research Center for the 21st Century.

Jordana, J., Schmitt, L., & Holesch, A. (2020). Mapping the global governance research landscape. *GLOBE Blog*. https://www.globe-project.eu/en/mapping-the-global-governance-research-landscape_8683.

Kennedy, D. (1999). The underlying politics of global governance. *Harvard International Review*, *21*(3), 52–57.

Knight, W. A. (1995). Beyond the UN system? Critical perspectives on global governance and multilateral evolution. *Global Governance*, *1*, 22–47.

Knight, W. A. (2005). Equivocating on the future of the world: The Commission on Global Governance. In R. Thakur, A. F. Cooper, & J. English (Eds.), *International commissions and the power of ideas* (pp. 99–122). United Nations University Press.

Kothari, R. (1987). On humane governance. *Alternatives*, *12*(3), 277–290.

Kristensen, P. M. (2015). Revisiting the 'American social science': Mapping the geography of international relations. *International Studies Perspectives*, *16*(3), 246–269.

Larson, D. W., & Shevchenko, A. (2003). Shortcut to greatness: The new thinking and the revolution in Soviet foreign policy. *International Organization*, *57*(1), 77–109.

Lipchutz, R. D. (1999). Members only? Citizenship and civil virtue in a time of globalization. *International Politics*, *36*(2), 203–233.

Maliniak, D., Oakes, A., Peterson, S., & Tierney, M. J. (2011). International relations in the US academy. *International Studies Quarterly*, *55*(2), 437–464.

Massicotte, M. J. (1999). Global governance and the global political economy: Three texts in search of a synthesis. *Global Governance*, *5*(1), 127–148.

Mendlovitz, S. H. (1975a). *On the creation of a just world order: Preferred worlds for the 1990's*. Free Press.
Mendlovitz, S. H. (1975b, December 23). World government in year 2000: By cataclysm, drift or design. *Carroll Daily Times Herald*.
Mouat, L. (1991, May 30). Global commission urges reform of United Nations. *Christian Science Monitor*, 24.
Murphy, C. N. (2000). Global governance: Poorly done and poorly understood. *International Affairs*, *76*(4), 789–804.
Nossal, K. R. (1999). International sanctions as instruments of global governance. *Global Society*, *13*(2), 125–137.
Potter, P. B. (1922). *An introduction to the study of international organization*. The Century Company.
Ramphal, S. (1992). Globalism and meaningful peace: A new world order rooted in international community. *Security Dialogue*, *23*(3), 81–87.
Raustiala, K., & Victor, D. G. (2004). The regime complex for plant genetic resources. *International Organization*, *58*(2), 277–309.
Reinsch, P. S. (1911). *Public international unions: Their work and organization*. Ginn and Company.
Robles, A. C. (1995). Global governance and political economy: German and French perspectives. *Global Governance*, *1*(1), 99–117.
Rochester, J. M. (1986). The rise and fall of international organization as a field of study. *International Organization*, *40*(4), 777–813.
Roger, C. B., & Dauvergne, P. (2016). The rise of transnational governance as a field of study. *International Studies Review*, *18*(3), 415–437.
Roger, C., Jordana, J., Holesch, A., & Schmitt, L. (2022). Global governance research: Exploring patterns of growth, diversity, and inclusion. *Global Governance: A Review of Multilateralism and International Organizations*, *28*(4), 486–508.
Ronit, K., & Schneider, V. (1999). Global governance through private organizations. *Governance*, *12*(3), 243–266.
Rosenau, J. N. (1995a). Organizational proliferation in a changing world. In Commission on Global Governance (Ed.), *Issues in global governance: Papers written for the Commission on Global Governance*. Kluwer Law International.
Rosenau, J. N. (1995b). Governance in the twenty-first century. *Global Governance*, *1*(1), 13–43.
Rother, B., & Schmidt, W. (2006). *Willy Brandt: Berliner Ausgabe, Band 8: Über Europa: Hinaus Dritte Welt Und Sozialistische Internationale*. Verlag J.H.W. Dietz Nachf. GmbH.
Senghaas, D. (1993). Global governance: How could it be conceived? *Security Dialogue*, *24*(3), 247–256.
Shakhnazarov, G. (1984). *The coming world order* (M. Light, Trans.). Progress Publishers.
Shakhnazarov, G. (1988). Governability of the world. *International Affairs*, *34*(3), 16–24.
Shakhnazarov, G. (1989). Dialogue: On the prospects of global governance. *Alternatives*, 14(2), 245–257.
Simai, M. (1997). The changing state system and the future of global governance. *Global Society*, *11*(2), 141–163.
Smith, E. M., & Weiss, T. G. (1997). UN task-sharing: Towards or away from global governance? *Third World Quarterly*, *18*(3), 595–619.

Smouts, M. C. (1998). The proper use of governance in international relations. *International Social Science Journal*, *50*(155), 81–89.
Soviet News. (1988, April 6). Mikhail Gorbachev receives Willy Brandt. *Soviet News*.
Sprinz, D. F., & Wolinsky-Nahmias, Y. (2004). *Models, numbers, and cases: Methods for studying international relations*. University of Michigan Press.
Stockholm Initiative. (1991). The Stockholm Initiative on Global Security and Governance. *Pakistan Horizon*, *44*(4), 89–139.
Thérien, J. P. (2005). The Brandt Commission: The end of an era of North–South politics. In R. Thakur, A. F. Cooper, & J. English (Eds.), *International commissions and the power of ideas* (pp. 287–319). United Nations University Press.
Wapner, P. (1997). Environmental ethics and global governance: Engaging the international liberal tradition. *Global Governance*, *3*(2), 213–231.
Weiss, T. G., & Wilkinson, R. (2019). *Rethinking global governance*. Polity Press.
Yeates, N. (1999). Social politics and policy in an era of globalization: Critical reflections. *Social Policy and Administration*, *33*(4), 372–393.
Young, O. (1999). *Governance in world affairs*. Cornell University Press.

PART I

International organizations and complexity in global governance

3. Global governance and intergovernmental organizations: features and developments of authority beyond the nation state

Alexandros Tokhi, İrem Tuncer Ebetürk and Michael Zürn

1. INTRODUCTION

Global governance comprises diverse institutional arrangements, multi-level processes, and a multitude of actors that seek to address trans-boundary challenges.[1] Not least because of the somewhat fuzzy subject matter itself, both the concept and relevant debates about it have undergone several transformations. While earlier works have successfully delimited the field of study and broadened the analytical toolkit and empirical scope by extending their analyses to non-state actors or informal institutions, efforts at systematizing key concepts and formulating a common research agenda emerged only with the third generation of global governance scholarship (Coen & Pegram, 2015). What distinguishes recent contributions from earlier ones is the assumption that global governance represents a political system *sui generis* and not just a set of diverse institutional arrangements and actors that span nation states.

A central component of the global governance system is 'the exercise of authority across national borders as well as contested norms and rules beyond the nation state' (Zürn, 2018, pp. 4–5). In this chapter, we focus on the development of international authority exercised by International Organizations (IOs). Being formalized institutions with a headquarters, IOs can be subjects of authority and hence an integral part of the global governance system. A closer scrutiny of their authority helps uncover key developments and trends, which

[1] For helpful comments and suggestions, we thank the editors of this book and our GLOBE colleagues. For editing assistance, we thank Claudius Deppe.

might inform further inquiries into the institutionalization of world politics. Accordingly, we seek to understand how IOs exercise authority within and across key issue areas in global governance. This inquiry allows us to compare and qualify the relative authoritativeness of certain issue areas and organizations over others, while still identifying general patterns in the exercise of authority across IOs and issue areas.

To do so, we draw on the International Authority Database (Zürn et al., 2021). Our data offer information on the exercise of formal IO authority as defined in legal texts and mandates for 34 IOs from 1919 to 2013. We assess different features of the exercise of authority beyond the nation state by considering macro-historical dynamics, the relative distribution of authority across regionally confined versus globally active IOs, the thematic issue areas in which IOs operate, and the types of authority exercised by IOs that may inform their legitimation strategies.

We proceed in the following way. First, we briefly provide a definition of international authority and our measurement of the evolution of the contemporary global governance system. Next, we review the exercise of authority across time, organizations, across issue areas, and different types of authority. The chapter concludes with a discussion of notable patterns and dynamics and the challenges that lie ahead of IOs.

2. AUTHORITY IN GLOBAL GOVERNANCE

Historically, the currently contested global governance system emerged in the 1990s, building on certain normative principles and institutions that had been developed long before (Zürn, 2018, p. 126). Two such normative principles, the global common good and the rights of individuals, provide the normative basis for global governance today. Almost all international agreements explicitly involve, at least rhetorically, the promotion of global common goods (e.g., a clean environment or international peace) for the benefit of a larger, global community, and not for individual states. Starting with the Universal Declaration of Human Rights in 1948, the rights and duties of individuals and societal actors developed into the second foundational normative principle. Not only are non-state actors recognized as subjects in their own right, but states are expected to respect individuals' entitlements. The second normative pillar has brought analysts to label this global governance system a 'liberal international order' (Ikenberry, 2010, 2018; Lake et al., 2021). To be implemented, these two normative principles require the allocation of resources and responsibilities to actors who produce policies and regulations. This, in turn, nurtures a belief in the possibility of authority beyond the nation state and a need for institutions that channel actors' inputs and produce policies.

Thus, it comes as little surprise that the world has witnessed, since the 1990s and the early 2000s, a remarkable rise in international institutions across all substantive issue areas, including the maintenance of international peace or arms control, global public health or mitigating climate change, and financial stability or cybersecurity, to name just a few. This quantitative growth has also transformed world politics qualitatively. International institutions formulate policy agendas and generate substantive expertise or propose and monitor rules of conduct between states and other global actors to further the provision of public goods for a more encompassing, even, and global community. Such institutional practices often limit state discretion in important ways. In this sense, international institutions exercise authority over states, as well as other actors in the global governance system.

International authority, however, differs from authority relationships within nation states. First, authority in the global realm is reflexive and based on voluntary subordination. States and other addressees of global policies constantly reflect on and check the worthiness of international authority holders. States voluntarily defer to international agents when they recognize their limitations in achieving public goods; they are seldom forced to join and obey international institutions. As a result, international authorities request and recommend policies, rather than issuing enforceable commands.

Second, international authority is typically issue area specific. For example, the World Bank exercises authority in development financing, but not in international security. Moreover, there is no meta-authority that would coordinate sector-specific authoritative institutions, especially in cases of conflict. Indeed, given the growing significance of regime complexes, normative regulatory conflicts are very likely to emerge and impact the exercise of authority and the provision of global public goods (Kreuder-Sonnen & Zürn, 2020; Alter & Raustiala, 2018; Gehring & Faude, 2013; Alter & Meunier, 2009; Orsini et al., 2013). Climate change, for example, affects all aspects of human life and thus might generate regulatory and normative conflicts across a series of distinct issue areas (Keohane & Victor, 2011). Lacking a central arbiter of conflicts, institutions therefore either compete, where some institutions try to expand their influence at the expense of others, or they cooperate, where institutions from different issue areas mutually adjust their policies.

In the global governance system, IOs are the most important carriers of international authority (Abbott & Snidal, 1998; Haftel & Thompson, 2006; Hawkins et al., 2006; Hooghe & Marks, 2015; Lake, 2003; Zürn et al., 2012). Networks of transnational non-governmental actors (NGOs) and some private actors are important for purposes of coordination. And some of those even exercise international authority, with Amnesty International and rating agencies as two noteworthy examples (Hall & Biersteker, 2002; Mattli & Büthe, 2005; Green, 2013). However, as formalized entities with headquarters, it is mainly IOs who embody institutionalized relations of super- and subordination between an international agent and states, among states within an institution, and even with respect to individuals. An analysis of political developments and challenges in the global governance system has therefore to carefully scrutinize IO authority. Accordingly, in the next section, we seek to understand how and to what extent IOs exercise authority within and across key issue areas in the global governance system.

3. MEASURING IO AUTHORITY

Several contributions have argued and shown that states have endowed formal IOs with more policy discretion and autonomy since the end of the Cold War (Abbott & Snidal, 1998; Haftel & Thompson, 2006), delegate more and more encompassing competences to them (Hawkins et al., 2006; Hooghe et al., 2016), and increasingly rely on IOs to overcome political conflicts and provide public goods (Hooghe et al., 2019; Oneal & Russett, 2001; Zürn, 2018). Indeed, IOs exercise authority in their own right, not only in the form of adopting decisions that may be against the short-term interests of their member states (Zürn et al., 2012; Cooper et al., 2008; Hooghe et al., 2019), but also by shaping and diffusing norms, knowledge, and information (Barnett & Finnemore, 1999).

Despite the growing attention to authority beyond the nation state, it is important to distinguish international authority from national authority. Unlike the domestic realm, in world politics, states' subordination to authoritative institutions is voluntary and reflexive, as states depend on—without being forced or persuaded to do so—an international agent that produces policies for the provision of public goods. States, thus, endow international agents with certain rights and competences to perform a set of functions, thereby recognizing the authority of those agents. The legal mandate and competences of an IO therefore encapsulate formal authority relationships in international politics. This legal-formal foundation delimits the boundaries of what an IO can and cannot do, hence influencing the exercise of formal IO authority. An organization becomes more authoritative to the extent that it can issue more binding decisions and competent judgments vis-à-vis its member states.

The conceptual discussions about the role and authority of IOs inspired several projects that produce data on various aspects of IO authority, such as their independence, their mandates and scope, or their degree of pooling and delegation (Haftel & Thompson, 2006; Boehmer et al., 2004; Haftel & Hofmann, 2017; Hooghe et al., 2016). Building upon these works, the measure of IO authority we use in this chapter proposes a single indicator that captures the formal exercise of IO authority over states when designing, adopting, implementing, and reviewing substantive policies. In other words, it measures the extent of formal authority IOs have over states in international policymaking.

Our measure is built on two institutional features constitutive of IO authority. The first feature is IO's autonomy. To have some level of authority over states, an IO must act with a certain degree of autonomy from its member states (Abbott & Snidal, 1998; Haftel & Thompson, 2006). International courts or IO secretariats typically represent highly autonomous IO bodies, followed by an organization's governing body when a subset of states makes decisions on behalf of the entire membership (e.g., UN Security Council). The less a member state can veto policy decisions and actions of an IO, the more autonomous the IO is. Hence, we focus on the organizational body and its decision-making rules (e.g., unanimity, qualified majority, simple majority voting) to determine the extent of autonomy. The second institutional feature constitutive of IO authority is the extent to which an IO can bind its member states. To exercise authority, IOs should be able to limit states' policy discretion and commit them to a particular course of action (Cooper et al., 2008; Zürn et al., 2012). The policies, decisions, or interpretations of IOs can bind states legally or politically. Legal bindingness refers to the legal costs put on states, while political bindingness captures the sovereignty and reputational costs that IOs are entitled to impose upon states, such as different sanction types in cases of non-compliance. Importantly, both dimensions are necessary and jointly sufficient for authority. An IO has authority only when it holds a minimum level of autonomy and bindingness. If either of the two dimensions scores zero, we consider an IO to be not authoritative.

International organizations exercise authority across a set of policy functions that states task them to perform (Avant et al., 2010; Bradley & Kelley, 2008). These include: the initiation and setting of policy agendas (agenda-setting); the debate, design, and adoption of rules and policies (rule-making); the monitoring of rule compliance and state performance (monitoring); the interpretation of treaty norms and dispute settlement (norm interpretation); the sanctioning of non-compliant behavior (enforcement); the production and dissemination of knowledge and expertise relevant to the substantive regulatory problem (knowledge generation); and, finally, the evaluation of IO-internal practices and procedures. These functions produce substantive policies and regulations. We measure the degree of autonomy and bindingness for each of these seven policy functions by hand-coding all relevant legal documents of an IO, such as founding constitutions, their amendments, or rules of procedures. We then aggregate the resulting scores to obtain a unique measure of authority per IO and year.[2]

---

[2] We report the details of the measurement and aggregation process elsewhere (Zürn et al., 2021). In brief, we use the geometric mean to combine the autonomy and bindingness scores per policy function. For our purposes, we obtain the geometric mean by taking the square root of the product of autonomy and bindingness.

4. THE EXERCISE OF AUTHORITY BEYOND THE NATION STATE

Having discussed our concept and measurement, this chapter now inspects authority patterns in global governance. In particular, we consider the development of authority over time, discuss the distribution of authority across regional and global IOs, present the exercise of IO authority across substantive issue areas of world politics, and engage the different types of authority—epistemic and political—that IOs can have.

4.1 The Authority of IOs Over Time

Several contributions have highlighted a trend of increasing IO authority in world politics (Cooper et al., 2008; Hooghe et al., 2019; Lake, 2003; Zürn et al., 2012). From the end of World War II until today, IOs have gained more competences, regulatory power, and influence in global politics. Using the International Authority Database, which details the levels and changes of an IO's authority from the year of its creation until 2013, we can systematically examine these claims.[3] Our data clearly shows that IO authority has, overall, grown considerably and it reached unprecedented levels by the 2010s (in line with the number of IOs). However, its growth trajectory has not always been steady. Periods of slow growth, or even stagnation, follow periods of substantial and immediate growth in IO authority.

Figure 3.1 plots the cumulative percentage change of authority for the IOs in our sample over time. We take the year 1945 as a baseline and compare the development of authority in terms of percentage changes to that point in time. Over almost 60 years, starting in 1945, IO authority has grown by a remarkable 300 percent. The first substantial rise happened at the end of World War II. It is the time where the UN, along with the Bretton Woods institutions, were created. All these organizations are characterized by high degrees of authority in the form of the UN Security Council's veto power system or the International Monetary Fund's (IMF) qualified majority voting, for example.

During the ensuing Cold War period from 1949 until 1991, authority grew in total by 150 percent, resulting in an annual growth rate of about 2.15 percent. This stands in stark contrast to the considerable expansion of IO authority after the end of the Cold War. Between 1992 and 2013, IO authority grew annually

We sum all such policy-function scores of an IO to obtain a single measure of IO authority.

[3] The 'oldest' IO in our sample is the International Labour Organization (ILO), created in 1919.

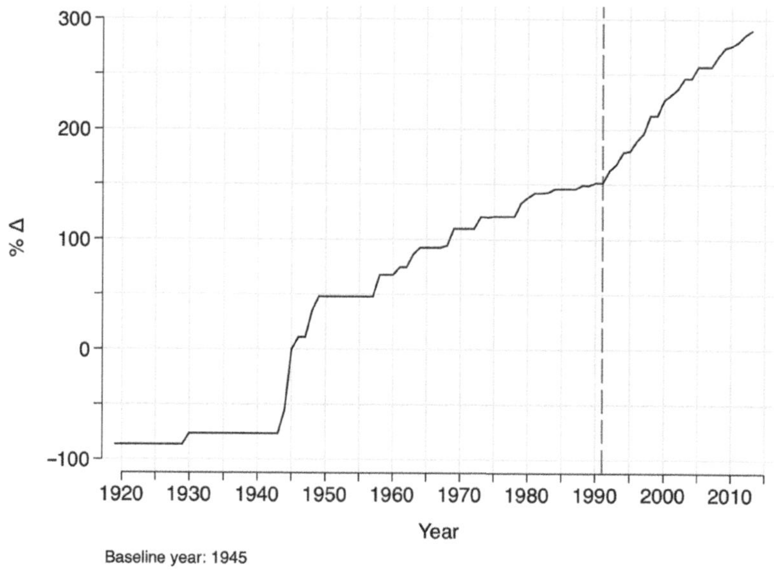

Note: The vertical dotted line in 1991 indicates the end of the Cold War.
Source: Author's own compilation.

Figure 3.1 *Cumulative percentage change of IO authority*

by about 4.25 percent—that is, at a double rate than in the preceding Cold War period.[4] The creation of new and influential IOs in the 1990s, such as the World Trade Organization (WTO) or the International Criminal Court (ICC), as well as the expansion of already existing IO mandates (e.g., Maastricht Treaty), contributed to this strong growth phase.

To further explore the importance of this change in global governance, we regressed changes in authority levels on a post-Cold War indicator and the lagged number of IOs. Indeed, in the post-Cold War period, IOs have on

4 Note that we use the geometric mean to calculate the percentage growth rates. Specifically, we obtain these annual percentage growth rates with the following equation: $\left(\left(Cumulative\ proportion+1\right)^{1/t}\right)-1$, where t is the total years being evaluated. For the post-Cold War period, t=22, and hence: $\left(1.5+1\right)^{1/22}=0.0425*100=4.25\%$.

average more authority than in preceding periods.[5] These patterns suggest an important change in the international system beginning in the mid-1990s: a global governance system built around IOs that wield more authority over states than in any other period of recent history.

Overall, and particularly since the start of the new millennium, IOs have become fundamental pillars of global governance. Not only has their number grown over time, but IOs also became more authoritative, having at their disposal formal-legal instruments and competences to relatively autonomously design policies and implement them by binding states, at least to some extent, to the agreed course of action. This development, however, is not linear and smooth. The authority of IOs seems to grow particularly strongly after major systemic changes, such as the new power distribution emerging after the end of World War II or the breakdown of bipolarity in 1991. More recent contributions have indicated that the growth of IOs, and relatedly their authority, levels off after 2015 (Hooghe et al., 2019; Pevehouse et al., 2020). While few, if any, new IOs are created, the 'stock' of authoritative IOs that has accumulated over time is substantial, forming the normative and regulatory basis for producing and implementing global policies.

4.2 The Authority of Regional and Global IOs

The temporal macro-dynamics have clearly demonstrated a substantial growth of IO authority. However, this does not mean that all IOs are equally authoritative. Quite to the contrary, our data show remarkable cross-IO variation in the extent of authority. Our sample counts 34 IOs that are geographically and thematically representative of the larger population of IOs.[6]

When we consider the sample average of IO authority, we find that overall, IOs tend to be rather moderately authoritative with a mean of 0.25 (standard deviation of 0.18). This suggests that the majority of IOs in our sample cluster at the lower end of the authority range (ranging from 0 to 1). However, there

---

5 The post-Cold War indicator is 1 for all the years after 1991 and 0 before. On average, IO authority after 1991 is by 0.11 points higher than before (standard error: 0.039). The difference is statistically significant at the 1% level with an estimated t-value of $|t|=2.77$. Estimates calculated from time-series regression on differenced cumulative sum of authority as dependent variable and differenced cumulative sum of IOs. N = 94.

6 In brief, we draw a stratified random sample from a relevant population of IOs defined by Sommerer and Tallberg (2017). This population counts 174 organizations and comprises IOs that are independent and intergovernmental, that have at least three member states, and that are active as of 2012 in the sense of convening regularly and producing some output.

Table 3.1 *Estimated population means, after the year 2000*

Data	Mean	95% confidence interval
Global	0.19	0.16, 0.23
Regional	0.23	0.20, 0.26
Total	0.21	0.19, 0.24

Note: N = 407, weighted data.
Source: Own compilation.

is considerable variation in authority between IOs. Some IOs have very high levels of authority, such as the European Union or the IMF, while others, such as the Commonwealth Secretariat (Commsec), score zero on authority.

In an attempt to better understand the sources of this variation, we consider the geographic mandate of IOs. In other words, do global or regional IOs wield more authority? Recent scholarship on IOs and their authority has highlighted the role of shared communities of states that facilitate the delegation of competences, and ultimately authority, to IOs (Haftel, 2013; Hooghe et al., 2016, 2019). Geographic proximity and shared governance challenges are more likely to first occur in specific regions and therefore make it easier for states in a region to agree on the transfer of authority than in purely global settings, where states and their preferences are more heterogeneous and where it is harder to reach an agreement. On the other hand, one could argue that the challenges to coordinate a diverse set of states and advance effective common policies are more likely to be overcome through global IOs with authority. Because they address almost all states of the world (e.g., United Nations or World Health Organization), endowing them with more competences could help solve governance challenges more readily.

To explore this question, we estimate the average authority of global and regional IOs. In terms of regions, our sample comprises IOs from five different regions, following the UN's world region classification: Africa, the Americas, Asia, Europe, and the World.[7] As we intend to capture contemporary patterns, we focus on the period after 2000. Table 3.1 presents the estimated population means for global and regional IOs as well as the overall mean.[8] The overall

[7] We include Oceania, the fifth UN world region, into Asia. Thus, we obtain as the fifth region the 'World' for all global IOs.

[8] Because our sample includes some better-known IOs, such as the European Union, we construct sampling weights to further enhance the representativeness with respect to IO prominence. To do so, we measure IO prominence by using

estimated average authority of IOs is 0.215, representing rather moderate levels when judged from the theoretically possible maximum value (which is 1).

Regional organizations tend to be more authoritative than global ones, as the former have higher average authority levels than the latter (0.23). This pattern is commensurate with recent findings on the growing importance of regional integration (Söderbaum, 2015; Rüland & Carrapatoso, 2022). The African Union (0.39), the Andean Community (0.55), and of course the European Union (0.71) are all influential organizations, all scoring above the estimated mean of regional IOs. Importantly, they have become important institutions that not only represent a shared community, but that can leverage their influence beyond their region, particularly in the case of the European Union (Bradford, 2020). Going beyond those prominent cases of authoritative regional organizations, we find several low-authority IOs in different world regions. In North America, for example, NAFTA (0.08) has extremely low authority scores, while ASEAN in Southeast Asia scores only a little higher (0.10). It seems that regional IOs in Africa, Europa and Latin America indeed display higher levels of authority than global IOs, while IOs in Asia and North America have very little authority. The enormous variation on the regional level leads to the outcome that global IOs are average in authority.

Perhaps this pattern also drives the second notable finding from Table 3.1: that the difference in authority levels between regional and global IOs is not statistically significant. The overlapping confidence intervals imply that the differences in authority are not systematic. In other words, regional and global IOs can be equally (non-) authoritative.[9] And within either category, the variation in authority is quite pronounced, with few highly authoritative organizations, and many moderately authoritative ones.

Google Scholar hits per IO (with an IO being prominent with more than 500 hits) and combine it with a score on the relative frequency of thematic and regional IOs in the population. The resulting sampling weights enhance the representativeness of our data with respect to prominence, geography, and issue area and allow us to draw broader conclusions regarding the population of IOs.

[9] When estimating the mean authority level of regional organizations before the 2000s, it is below that of global IOs. The pre-2000 mean of regional IOs is 0.13 with a 95% confidence interval of [0.11, 0.15], while the one for global IOs is 0.21 with a 95% confidence interval of [0.20, 0.23]. As the confidence intervals in square brackets do not overlap, regional organizations used to be less authoritative than global ones before the 2000s. When compared to the estimates post-2000, regional IOs became more authoritative over time, while global ones did not change in their authority levels.

4.3 Authority Across Issue Areas

We next discuss the distribution of IO authority across substantive issue areas of global governance and over time. The issue area-specific authority helps us understand how many formal-legal competences states transfer to organizations for tackling distinct regulatory problems.

We begin with a presentation of the authority scores of 13 IOs selected from our sample. These 13 IOs overlap between our sample and the IOs studied within the GLOBE project. Figure 3.2 plots the mean authority score per IO. The World Trade Organization (WTO) and the World Bank (WB) represent trade and development organizations, respectively. NATO, the Organization for Security and Cooperation in Europe (OSCE), and the Shanghai Cooperation Organisation (SCO) are security IOs. The two financial IOs on which we focus are the IMF and the Bank for International Settlement. Finally, IOs increasingly take on a range of distinct issues and are only rarely confined to one specific thematic mandate. The best example is the United Nations, which is not only a central security organization, but also a crucial organizational hub

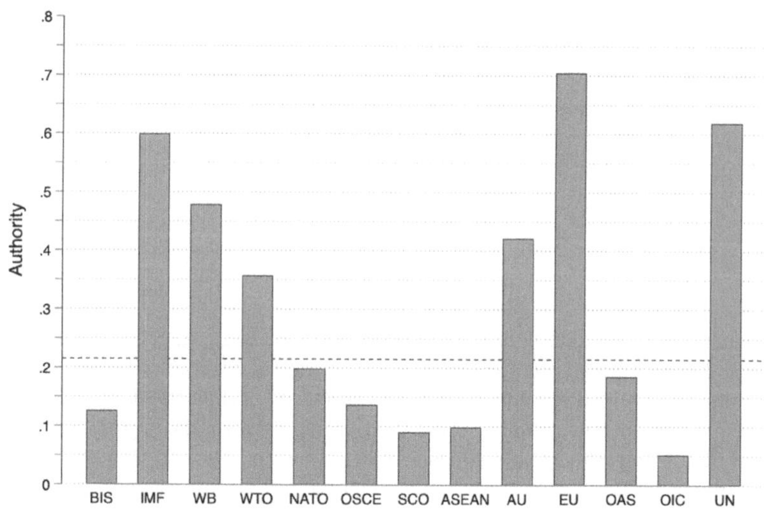

Note: Mean authority in the last five years of our data (2009–2013). Dotted horizontal line indicates the estimated population average of authority.
Source: Author's own compilation.

Figure 3.2 Distribution of authority in selected IOs from the GLOBE project

in global climate change governance, global development, and many more issues. Likewise, the European Union is a multi-issue organization involved in any one of the four issue areas of the GLOBE issue-specific studies. The same holds true for other regional organizations, such as the African Union or ASEAN. Accordingly, we also consider the authority of these multi-issue IOs.[10]

Apart from some multi-issue organizations, trade and development IOs (the WTO and the World Bank) have high levels of formal authority. Their respective averages are above the estimated population average (horizontal dotted line in Figure 3.2). Moreover, the authority of the World Bank is not dramatically less than the WTO's authority. In the finance cluster, by contrast, the IMF and the BIS strongly deviate in their respective levels of authority, as noted and explained in the chapter on international finance in this book: international finance is characterized by one formal authoritative IO, the IMF, and a series of informal arrangements that facilitate consultations between central banks and domestic financial institutions across countries (Levi-Faur, Blumsack, & Flaiszhaker, Chapter 9 in this book). The organizations created through the Bretton Woods Conference, of which the WTO is a late offspring, arguably enjoy high levels of formal-legal authority over their member states. Part of that formal authority stems from qualified majority voting in the World Bank and the IMF, where members' voting power depends on their financial contributions to these institutions and not on the 'one-state-one-vote' principle. This effectively gives a few states a large influence on the policies and rules of the organization to which other states adhere. To little surprise, the authority and influence of the World Bank and the IMF have been politicized by both state and non-state actors (Stephen & Zürn, 2019).

Only broad multi-issue IOs—the UN and the EU—wield higher levels of regulatory competences and policymaking influence over states. Finally, the security organizations in our sample (NATO, OSCE, SCO) have authority levels below the estimated average. Even when counting the UN as a security-only IO, this statistic does not change much.[11] States are reluctant to cede sovereignty and delegate authority to security IOs. Rather, they seek to retain the final say over these IOs' policies and decisions, reflected in the unanimous decision rules. The striking imbalance in the authority levels of security IOs and organizations regulating the global economy corresponds to expectations and qualitative empirical accounts in the early cooperation literature (Keohane, 1984; Jervis, 1982; Keohane & Nye, 1977).

---

10 The multi-issue IOs comprise ASEAN, the AU, the EU, and the OAS, the OIC, and the UN.

11 More precisely, the average authority of the UN, NATO, OSCE, and SCO is 0.24, while the average of the World Bank and the WTO is 0.30.

Do the described patterns apply more generally to the other IOs in relevant issue areas of world politics? To shed light on this question, we now turn to an evaluation of the distribution of IO authority across issue areas. We focus on four broad and encompassing issue areas: the 'economy', 'human rights', 'security', and 'multi-issue'. The first issue area is 'economy' and includes all IOs that foster and regulate markets or economic transactions more generally between states and/or societies. The 'economy' thus comprises trade, development, financial, or commodity IOs. Organizations that protect and promote human lives, livelihoods, and liberties, including a clean environment and cultural self-determination, form the second issue area, which we label 'human rights'. The ICC appears in that issue area, but also labor rights organizations, such as the International Labour Organization (ILO), or UNESCO.[12] 'Security' organizations demarcate the third issue area, comprising formal alliances (e.g., NATO), disarmament and non-proliferation IOs (e.g., IAEA), or human security organizations. Finally, we categorize all IOs that engage in at least two distinct issue areas as 'multi-issue' IOs, such as the UN, the EU, or the African Union (AU).

Figure 3.3 presents the estimated population means of IO authority per issue area. Using sampling weights to enhance representativeness in terms of geography, issue area, and IO prominence, we can draw broader conclusions from our sample to the relevant population of IOs.

Organizations tasked with regulating multiple issues have the highest average authority, around 0.31, exceeding the estimated population average (horizontal dotted line). The 'economy' follows with an average estimated authority level of 0.25. The averages of the two issue areas do not differ much, yet are still enough to be significantly different from each other at the 10 percent level. 'Security' and 'human rights' have considerably less authority than the other two issue areas. In fact, 'human rights' scores lowest in terms of the authority of IOs in that area. The differences between all estimates are statistically significant, allowing us to clearly identify and rank those issue areas with the highest degree of formal-legal authority.

As the estimates suggest, states endow multi-issue IOs with the highest levels of delegated formal authority. One possible reason could be the desire to generate the institutional structures needed to address a variety of distinct global governance tasks, ranging from climate change, to human development, to classic state security and global non-proliferation efforts. Another explanation is that multi-issue IOs provide public goods for a political community, however defined, and therefore differ in their formal institutional design, and

[12] Note that we categorize the OSCE as a 'human rights' organization as the larger share of its mandate is to protect human rights.

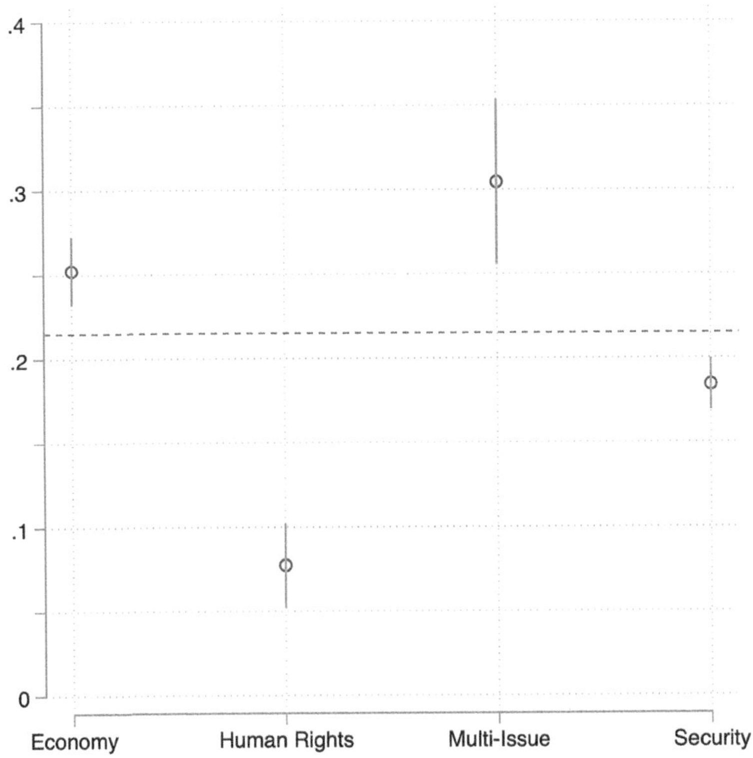

Notes: Horizontal dotted line indicates average IO authority. Vertical gray bars around mean estimates are 95% confidence bands. The multi-issue and economy issue areas differ significantly from each other at the 10% significance level. $t>1.86$, $p<0.063$. Weighted data.
Source: Author's own compilation.

Figure 3.3 Estimated average population authority per issue area

thus authority, from more task-specific, thematically narrower IOs (Lenz et al., 2014). While multi-issue IOs exhibit the highest average authority, it is not, however, their exclusive feature. Economic organizations that can be considered task-specific have similar levels of authority.

The low estimated average authority in 'human rights' should not conceal the trend that in the last 20 years, this issue area has witnessed the biggest relative growth in its authority. Between the creation of the OSCE in 1975 until

2013, the authority of human rights IOs grew by an astonishing 350 percent. Authority in the economy, by contrast, grew during that same period by about 100 percent. Starting in the mid-1970s, the rise of authoritative human rights institutions accelerated even more after the end of the Cold War, expanding and deepening the global institutions that protect individual rights. This development set the normative foundations of the contemporary global governance system.

4.4 Types of IO Authority

Having discussed the over-time growth of IO authority, its distribution across organizations, and the issue areas with the highest degrees of institutionalization and international authoritative policymaking, we now examine what types of authority IOs exercise. The types of authority exercised can influence the identity and the perception of IOs by both their staff, states, and citizens. The identity of an IO, formed by its dominant type of authority exercise, can shape, in turn, the (self-)legitimation practices of IOs and ultimately influence their perceived legitimacy (Tallberg & Zürn, 2019; Von Billerbeck, 2020).

Given the authority IOs wield, they come under pressure to justify it, either with references to common goods, general normative principles, or other criteria of legitimation (e.g., technocratic expertise). The legitimation strategies IOs adopt are therefore likely to vary and depend on the specific set of functions they perform and consequently have to justify (Zürn, 2018). It is therefore important to more closely inspect the type of authority IOs perform, as this may give some indication about the likely self-understanding of IOs and their ensuing legitimation strategies.

Our data allow us to differentiate between different types of authority exercised by IOs. These may delineate different self-understanding that feeds into IOs' legitimation strategies. We focus on two types of authority: political and epistemic, which are formally exercised by IOs to varying degrees (Zürn et al., 2012). Political authority rests on the assumption that someone should be entitled to make binding decisions in order to advance a common good. Epistemic authority is based on having special knowledge or moral expertise. It implies that the views expressed by an individual or an institution are recognized as trustworthy.

Operationally, we measure an IO's political authority by summing the scores on three policy functions: agenda-setting, rule-making, and enforcement. Norm interpretation, monitoring, evaluation, and knowledge generation can be considered as epistemic functions of IOs. Accordingly, we sum the scores on these four functions and obtain a measure of formal epistemic authority. Both scores are normalized to range between 0 and 1. To assess the extent to which either type of authority is prevalent in IOs, we calculate the

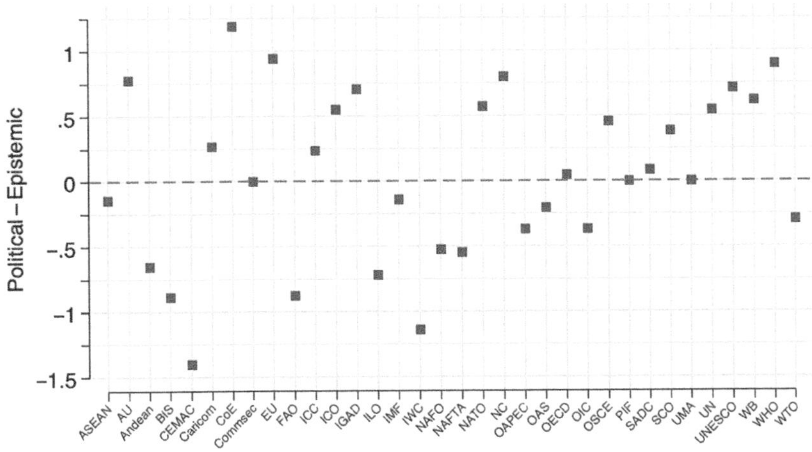

Notes: Negative values indicate that IOs exercise more epistemic authority than political authority, while positive values indicate that IOs exercise more political than epistemic authority. The value zero (dotted horizontal line) indicates that both types of authority are balanced in an IO.
Source: Authors' own compilation.

Figure 3.4 Relative distribution of types of IO authority across IOs

difference between political and epistemic authority per IO and plot the resulting distribution in Figure 3.4.

We can discern strong differences regarding the types of authority across IOs. Some IOs, such as Central African Economic and Monetary Community (CEMAC) or the Bank for International Settlements (BIS), exercise predominantly formal epistemic authority, while others, such as the EU or the Nordic Council (NC), exercise mainly political authority. With the exception of the Commonwealth Secretariat and the Arab Maghreb Union (UMA) that score zero on both types, the OECD, Southern African Development Community (SADC), and the Pacific Island Forum (PIF) exercise both types to equal degrees. The prevalence of either type of authority, together with an IO's overall authority score, can be used to analyze how an IO perceives itself and how that might matter for its (self-)legitimation narratives. For example, recent contributions have shown that NATO sees itself as an organization at the service of its member states (Von Billerbeck, 2020). Figure 3.4 shows that NATO exercises more political than epistemic authority. Moreover, NATO exercises its political authority on a comparatively low level, as its overall authority score of 0.19 suggests. Taken together, this can limit NATO's needs and scope of self-legitimation claims and reinforce its self-perception as a facilitator of inter-state cooperation.

By contrast, the Food and Agriculture Organization (FAO), which exercises predominantly epistemic functions with an above-average overall authority score (0.49), can more easily claim to be an authoritative—and perhaps neutral—expert in its substantive issue area than less authoritative IOs with a similar prevalence of epistemic authority, such as the ILO with its lower authority score of 0.27 (Busch et al., 2022). Finally, the United Nations exercises an almost equal degree of epistemic and political authority, which may suggest that it needs to more intensely legitimize itself to reconcile its different policy responsibilities and aspirations to develop and implement diverse, and often conflicting, policy objectives.

The types of authority exercised can not only shed some light on the likely self-legitimation strategies that IOs might adopt, but also indicate which IOs could be the object of societal and state-driven politicization. The European Union or the Council of Europe, for example, exercise predominantly political authority and are increasingly contested by alliances between state and non-state actors. For example, many backsliding democracies within the Council of Europe challenge its human rights norms and obstruct the work of both its Parliamentary Assembly and that of the European Court of Human Rights. A similar and even more pronounced pattern holds in the case of the European Union. Being a highly politically authoritative IO, it has become the object of fierce contestation and challenges from within, through authoritarian populist parties, different civil society organizations, and transnational movements. By contrast, IOs with a predominantly epistemic task profile are considerably less, if at all, politicized. Few go out on the street to lambast the Bank for International Settlements or the International Whaling Commission (IWC).

5. CONCLUSION: DISCUSSING TRENDS AND CHALLENGES

We can distil four key trends from our analysis of global authority patterns. First, over time, the aggregate authority of IOs has grown remarkably, with the end of the Cold War marking the beginning of a qualitatively new period for global governance. Not only are more IOs created, but the authority of IOs, both new and existing ones, grows at a double rate compared to previous periods. Second, our data reveal that IOs are, on average, only moderately authoritative, while considerable variation exists across organizations. Some achieve extremely high authority scores, while others are weak or not authoritative. Comparing the distribution of authority across regional and global IOs from 2000 onwards, we found no systematic differences, despite expectations in the literature that regional IOs would wield more influence over their member states than global ones. This finding reflects the strong differences between different regions in the world. Third, concerning the thematic mandate of IOs, our data demonstrate that multi-issue IOs tend to enjoy the highest authority levels, closely followed by IOs active in the 'economy'. While 'human rights' IOs score lowest in their average authority levels, they have witnessed the most significant increase in their authority, accelerated by the end of the Cold War and the increasing global need to safeguard fundamental freedoms and rights. Fourth, IOs differ in terms of the types of authority they exercise. Some almost exclusively exercise political authority, while others are mainly tasked with epistemic practices. These different task profiles have implications for the likelihood of societal contestation of IOs. They may feed into the (self-)legitimation strategies IOs employ vis-à-vis states and civil society actors.

The patterns and developments described foreshadow some of the most notable challenges IOs (will) face in global governance. One challenge is that the distribution and growth dynamic of IO authority appears to be halted. Our data ended in 2013, yet many signs and indications suggest that the authority of IOs 'froze'. In the last couple of years, the growth in the number of IOs has slowed down, and it also appears that the competencies of existing IOs have not been deepened in significant ways (Pevehouse et al., 2020). This suggests that the formal-legal authority that states have endowed IOs with has not changed much since its peak in the early 2000s. As a result, the status quo of international authority is relatively stable in formal-institutional terms and cements the comparatively high authority levels of multi-issue and economic IOs at the expense of security and human rights organizations. This is not without problems, as economic IOs, in particular, face severe challenges, such as the now-defunct WTO. At the same time, the demand for more protection of individual freedoms and effective multilateral security cooperation, even if only regionally organized, grows. The existing institutional fabric does not catch up with these political and societal challenges that become more prevalent. This impedes adequate actions and reactions of global governance institutions with potentially significant implications for their legitimacy. Moreover, the types of authority exercised and the related legitimation strategies will be essential elements in the strategies of IOs to address the growing contestation and politicization they now face. Populist parties and governments in established democracies, powerful authoritarian states, and declining trade and global economic activity undermine authoritative international organizations' normative and political foundations. The attacks of populists and authoritarian states on IOs and the liberal international order these primarily represent have become more forceful and frequent, leading to the withdrawal of resourceful states from IOs (e.g., Brexit), threats to stop funding, or the open denial of IOs' epistemic output and analyses. Despite much debate about IOs and their eventual deficiencies, the current level of authority in terms of the formal-legal features of international organizations seems relatively stable. However, this relative stickiness or steadiness in terms of formal features may become an important problem for global governance because it is uncertain to which extent these may adjust to demands for trans-boundary regulation.

REFERENCES

Abbott, K. W., & Snidal, D. (1998). Why States Act Through Formal International Organizations. *Journal of Conflict Resolution*, 42(1), 3–32.

Alter, K. J., & Meunier, S. (2009). The Politics of International Regime Complexity. *Perspectives on Politics*, 7(1), 13–24.

Alter, K. J., & Raustiala, K. (2018). The Rise of International Regime Complexity. *Annual Review of Law and Social Science*, 14(1), 329–349.

Avant, D. D., Finnemore, M., & Sell, S. K. (2010). Who governs the globe? In D. D. Avant, M. Finnemore, & S. K. Sell (Eds.), *Who Governs the Globe?* (pp. 1–34). Cambridge University Press.

Barnett, M., & Finnemore, M. (1999). The Politics, Power, and Pathologies of International Organizations. *International Organization*, 53(4), 699–732.

Boehmer, C., Gartzke, E., & Nordstrom, T. (2004). Do Intergovernmental Organizations Promote Peace? *World Politics*, 57(1), 1–38.

Bradford, A. (2020). *The Brussels Effect: How the European Union Rules the World*. Oxford University Press.

Bradley, C. A., & Kelley, J. (2008). The Concept of International Delegation. *Law and Contemporary Problems*, 71(1), 1–36.

Busch, P.-O., Heinzel, M., Kempken, M., & Liese, A. (2022). Mind the Gap? Comparing De Facto and De Jure Expert Authority of International Public Administrations in Financial and Agricultural Policy. *Journal of Comparative Policy Analysis: Research and Practice*, 24(3), 230–253.

Coen, D., & Pegram, T. (2015). Wanted: A Third Generation of Global Governance Research. *Governance*, 28(4), 417–420.

Cooper, S., Hawkins, D., Jacoby, W., & Nielson, D. (2008). Yielding Sovereignty to International Institutions: Bringing System Structure Back in. *International Studies Review*, 10(3), 501–524.

Gehring, T., & Faude, B. (2013). The Dynamics of Regime Complexes: Microfoundations and Systemic Effects. *Global Governance: A Review of Multilateralism and International Organizations*, 19(1), 119–130.

Green, J. F. (2013). *Rethinking Private Authority: Agents and Entrepreneurs in Global Environmental Governance*. Princeton University Press.

Haftel, Y. Z. (2013). Commerce and Institutions: Trade, Scope, and the Design of Regional Economic Organizations. *The Review of International Organizations*, 8(3), 389–414.

Haftel, Y. Z., & Hofmann, S. C. (2017). Institutional Authority and Security Cooperation Within Regional Economic Organizations. *Journal of Peace Research*, 54(4), 484–498.

Haftel, Y. Z., & Thompson, A. (2006). The Independence of International Organizations. *Journal of Conflict Resolution*, 50(2), 253–275.

Hall, R. B., & Biersteker, T. J. (Eds.). (2002). *The Emergence of Private Authority in Global Governance* (1st ed.). Cambridge University Press.

Hawkins, D. G., Lake, D. A., Nielson, D. L., & Tierney, M. J. (Eds.). (2006). *Delegation and Agency in International Organizations*. Cambridge University Press.
Hooghe, L., Lenz, T., & Marks, G. (2019). *A Theory of International Organization*. Oxford University Press.
Hooghe, L., & Marks, G. (2015). Delegation and Pooling in International Organizations. *The Review of International Organizations*, 10(3), 305–328.
Hooghe, L., Marks, G., Schakel, A. H., Niedzwiecki, S., Chapman Osterkatz, S., & Shair-Rosenfield, S. (2016). *Measuring Regional Authority. A Postfunctionalist Theory of Governance, volume I*. Oxford University Press.
Ikenberry, G. J. (2010). The Liberal International Order and its Discontents. *Millennium: Journal of International Studies*, 38(3), 509–521.
Ikenberry, G. J. (2018). The End of Liberal International Order? *International Affairs*, 94(1), 7–23.
Jervis, R. (1982). Security Regimes. *International Organization*, 36(2), 357–378.
Keohane, R. O. (1984). *After Hegemony*. Princeton University Press.
Keohane, R. O., & Nye, J. S. (1977). *Power and Interdependence: World Politics in Transition*. Little, Brown.
Keohane, R. O., & Victor, D. G. (2011). The Regime Complex for Climate Change. *Perspectives on Politics*, 9(1), 7–23.
Kreuder-Sonnen, C., & Zürn, M. (2020). After Fragmentation: Norm Collisions, Interface Conflicts, and Conflict Management. *Global Constitutionalism*, 9(2), 241–267.
Lake, D. A. (2003). The New Sovereignty in International Relations. *International Studies Review*, 5(3), 303–323.
Lake, D. A., Martin, L. L., & Risse, T. (2021). Challenges to the Liberal Order: Reflections on International Organization. *International Organization*, 75(2), 225–257.
Lenz, T., Bezuijen, J., Hooghe, L., & Marks, G. (2014). *Patterns of International Organization. Task Specific vs. General Purpose*. Robert Schuman Centre for Advanced Studies (RSCAS) Research Paper No. 128.
Mattli, W., & Büthe, T. (2005). Global Private Governance: Lessons from a National Model of Setting Standards in Accounting. *Law and Contemporary Problems*, 68(3/4), 225–262.
Oneal, J. R., & Russett, B. (2001). *Triangulating Peace: Democracy, Interdependence, and International Organizations*. Norton.
Orsini, A., Morin, J.-F., & Young, O. (2013). Regime Complexes: A Buzz, a Boom, or a Boost for Global Governance? *Global Governance: A Review of Multilateralism and International Organizations*, 19(1), 27–39.
Pevehouse, J. C., Nordstrom, T., McManus, R. W., & Jamison, A. S. (2020). Tracking Organizations in the World: The Correlates of War IGO Version 3.0 Datasets. *Journal of Peace Research*, 57(3), 492–503.
Rüland, J., & Carrapatoso, A. (Eds.). (2022). *Handbook on Global Governance and Regionalism*. Edward Elgar Publishing.
Söderbaum, F. (2015). *Rethinking Regionalism*. Palgrave Macmillan.
Sommerer, T., & Tallberg, J. (2017). Transnational Access To International Organizations 1950–2010: A New Data Set. *International Studies Perspectives*, 18(3), 247–266.
Stephen, M. D., & Zürn, M. (2019). *Contested World Orders: Rising Powers, Non-governmental Organizations, and the Politics of Authority Beyond the Nation-state*. Oxford University Press.

Tallberg, J., & Zürn, M. (2019). The Legitimacy and Legitimation of International Organizations: Introduction and Framework. *The Review of International Organizations*, 14(4), 581–606.
Von Billerbeck, S. (2020). 'Mirror, Mirror On The Wall': Self-legitimation By International Organizations. *International Studies Quarterly*, 64(1), 207–219.
Zürn, M. (2018). *A Theory Of Global Governance: Authority, Legitimacy, and Contestation*. Oxford University Press.
Zürn, M., Binder, M., & Ecker-Ehrhardt, M. (2012). International Authority and its Politicization. *International Theory*, 4(1), 69–106.
Zürn, M., Tokhi, A., & Binder, M. (2021). The International Authority Database. *Global Policy*, 12(4), 430–442.

4. Designed for different times? Institutional challenges of international organisations and the rise of informality

Kari Irwin Otteburn and Axel Marx

1. INTRODUCTION

The idea that international governance is facing greater challenges in recent years has firmly taken hold and has only been reinforced by increasing polarisation, contestation, and tension between states. Emblematic of this 'gridlock' (Hale, Held, & Young, 2013) is the increasing perception that treaty-based intergovernmental organisations (IOs) – as the traditional and most formal forms of intergovernmental cooperation and often the principal leaders of global governance – are confronted with growing contestation (Wiener, 2014), ceding authority to other actors (Grigorescu, 2020) and are in decline (Debre & Dijkstra, 2023) or are ill-equipped to fulfil their own mandates (Klabbers, 2017).

It seems that, more than ever, IOs are confronted with different dynamics that affect their authority and legitimacy on the one hand (Zürn, Tokhi & Binder, 2021, Tokhi, Ebetürk, & Zürn, Chapter 3 in this book) and performance in achieving their governance goals on the other (Lall, 2023). In parallel and more recently, a variety of informal institutions and processes have arisen to address governance challenges across a range of issue areas (Roger, 2020). States have increasingly turned towards establishing more informal international organisations (IIOs) that can be formed quickly, flexibly, and with fewer costs, as they typically lack a foundational treaty with rules for participation, a permanent secretariat, or major funding commitments. Alongside this – and often as an outcome of IIO negotiations – international policy-making is increasingly taking on an informal character, through memoranda of understanding (MoUs), guidelines, declarations, and other non-binding instruments. While this rise in informality in international cooperation is multifaceted and is driven by different forces, it is by some considered to be a response to challenges IOs face (Pauwelyn, Wessel & Wouters, 2014).

In recognition of these dynamics, recent literature presents a vast variety of potential explanations for why IOs appear to be under pressure. A vast majority of the explanations put forth in recent years point to external dynamics that relate to but are ultimately beyond the control of IOs and their member states, such as increasing multipolarity, recent manifestations of nationalism and populism in domestic politics (Trubowitz & Burgoon, 2023), or the emergence and proliferation of many other global governance institutions that provide alternatives to pursue international affairs (Abbott & Snidal, 2009). Less attention is paid to internal institutional features of IOs. We contend that external dynamics exert greater pressure on IOs because their mandates, internal governance processes, and resources are not fully able to accommodate changes in the external environment. Many IOs were established in a vastly different world order. Their design, procedures, and *modus operandi* were aligned with that external environment. Much of classical organisational sociological research shows that organisations can only perform if they 'fit' with their external environment (Carroll & Hannan, 2004). When the external environment changes, many organisations face difficulties adjusting, largely due to their design.

This misalignment between environment and institutional structure is likely why we observe similar institutional challenges across IOs in different issue areas and a key reason informal and alternative governance arrangements have gained prominence in recent years (Abbott, Green, & Keohane, 2016). But the institutional challenges that contribute to the loss of authority, legitimacy, and performance of IOs are not fully understood. As a result, it is not clear whether informal policy-making and IIOs are likely to fill the gaps in global governance. This chapter seeks to explore these questions by identifying some of the internal factors that prevent IOs from achieving their governance goals. This identification is based on a comparative analysis of mapping reports in six policy issue areas – trade, security, climate change, migration, development, and finance (Coen, Kreienkamp & Pegram, 2020; Levi-Faur & Blumsack, 2019; Marx et al., 2019; Sánchez Cobaleda et al., 2020). It then assesses whether informal organisations are better equipped to operate in the current global order.

This chapter begins with setting the stage by engaging with recent literature on the role and functioning of IOs in global politics. In section 3, we identify and analyse a set of overarching challenges for IOs. In section 4, we introduce informal lawmaking and IIOs and consider the extent to which these newer formats of global governance (may) succeed in overcoming the institutional challenges of IOs. A conclusion follows.

2. SETTING THE SCENE: INTERNATIONAL ORGANISATIONS IN GLOBAL POLITICS

Whereas two decades ago, Susan Strange (1998) famously asked why 'international organisations never die' and functionalist approaches to international relations usually take for granted that IOs will do their jobs (Lall, 2017), recent scholarship has focused on the stagnation and death of IOs (Gray, 2018; Eilstrup-Sangiovanni, 2018; Hooghe, Lenz, & Marks, 2019b; Hale, Held, & Young, 2013; Cohen, 2018), challenges to IOs' governance capacity, and variation in IOs' performance (Lall, 2017, 2023). This literature suggests numerous factors are responsible for IOs' declining capacity to meet their governance goals. Scholarship on the purpose and design of IOs spans decades (Nye & Keohane, 1971; Ruggie, 1993). In more recent years, research has focused on questions of IOs' legitimacy and authority (Zürn, 2018; Hooghe et al., 2017; Dellmuth, Scholte, & Tallberg, 2019) and to a more limited extent on their performance and efficacy (Lall, 2017, 2023; Gutner & Thompson, 2010). Additionally, scholars are increasingly exploring how geopolitical shifts and global political trends of populism and nationalism influence IOs (Copelovitch & Pevehouse, 2019).

Because this chapter aims to understand IO's internal challenges, we make some assumptions. First, we assume that IOs are set up by states to address a global problem that is presumed to be improved through cooperation (for a challenge of this assumption, see Davis, 2023). We also assume that although states design institutions rationally (Koremenos, Lipson, & Snidal, 2001), they do so with imperfect knowledge about *inter alia* future events, each other's preferences, and even the full extent of the problem or governance context (i.e., bounded rationality) and that international agreements (including those that establish IOs) are the outcomes of bargaining and ultimately represent a compromise. Once established, IOs develop agency and autonomy independent of their member states (Guzman, 2013; Barnett & Finnemore, 2004), and interactions between member states and IOs can have significant implications for governance processes (Cortell & Peterson, 2022). In other words, IOs as both autonomous governance actors and as instruments for member states can and do achieve governance objectives, but because they are not perfect, the extent to which they are able to do so varies considerably and there is often room and cause for reform. Finally, we also assume that path dependency and institutional design choices limit IOs' ability to reform, and change is therefore slow and rarely substantial (Hanrieder, 2014).

Another set of assumptions pertains to the evolving governance context in which IOs operate. Though recent scholarship explores challenges to IOs resulting from geopolitical changes – with some wondering if multilateralism can withstand a shift to multipolarity (Cohen, 2018) – we assume that the 'global order' has never been static and geopolitical evolution is ever-present. Although their interests will change over time, member states will consistently attempt to pursue these interests within IOs (Davis, 2023). Moreover, due to globalisation, increased economic interdependence, urgent global threats like climate change, and power shifts, global governance problems have intensified in recent times (Hale, Held, & Young, 2013).

Against this backdrop, this chapter first focuses on leading IOs to gain a more thorough understanding of the structural aspects of IOs that prevent them from meeting new and harder challenges posed by today's governance context. We then consider a phenomenon that is partly driven by the inability of IOs to address global challenges: the increasing relevance and use of informal law-making and IIOs. In doing so, we assess how the turn to informality addresses institutional limitations observed within IOs.

3. INSTITUTIONAL CHALLENGES FOR IOS IN GLOBAL GOVERNANCE

When establishing or reforming IOs, states negotiate a number of institutional features that have consequences for how IOs can fulfil their purpose(s), including the features identified by Koremenos, Lipson, and Snidal (2001) in their classic work on institutional design: membership rules, scope of mandate, centralisation of tasks, rules for controlling the institution, and flexibility of arrangements. Practical decisions, too, like an IO's budget, headquarters, and management (see Lall, 2017; Gray, 2018), are a product of negotiation. Other institutional features, like an organisation's culture and development of shared norms (Hooghe, Lenz, & Marks, 2019a), are partly a product of these decisions but also develop organically. Moreover, many institutional features evolve over time, and IOs – to varying degrees – make autonomous decisions that impact their institutional dynamics (Gutner & Thompson, 2010; Gray, 2018). The next sections identify key challenges with which IOs are confronted and which are linked to their institutional design and procedures.

3.1 Approach

Existing research identifies many of the main challenges facing IOs across issue areas (Marx et al., 2019; Sánchez-Cobaleda et al., 2019; Levi-Faur & Blumsack, 2019; Coen, Kreienkamp, & Pegram, 2020). While these challenges are frequently presented as specific to a particular IO, we can identify similar challenges across issue areas. To arrive at the primary institutional challenges for IOs, we first identified key challenges facing IOs according to existing literature in six key governance areas that were analysed: trade, development, security, climate, migration, and finance. Based on this comparative cross-issue analysis we identify three key institutional challenges:

1. IOs face difficulties balancing the needs of a diverse set of stakeholders and members due to inappropriate decision-making rules or inflexibility of governance structures;
2. IOs' mandate hampers action and policy autonomy;
3. IOs lack sufficient resources to fulfil their functions, primarily due to lack of support from their member states.

Combined, these challenges create increased inertia (Shanks, Jacobson, & Kaplan, 1996) within IOs, limiting their capacity to meet governance goals and respond to new challenges. We elaborate on each of these limitations in this section.

3.2 Inflexible Decision-Making and Governance Processes

Many of the commonly shared challenges faced by IOs in our analysis relate to governance processes, embodied in IOs' decision-making procedures. Decision-making can be set up in diverse ways, from giving every member state one vote and making decisions by consensus (requiring unanimity) or by majority voting, or to various forms of weighted voting, whereby some states' votes count more than those of other states. Each of these systems has inherent drawbacks, which will be more or less pronounced depending on other factors, such as number of members or the IO's scope. There are two primary trade-offs (see Figure 4.1). First, a tension exists between ensuring responsiveness to the greatest number of member states (egalitarian) versus ensuring responsiveness to the most powerful member states (asymmetric). Second, there is a tension between ensuring all members agree (consensus) versus ensuring that decisions are made (voting).

Different examples in the mapping reports (Coen, Kreienkamp & Pegram, 2020; Levi-Faur & Blumsack, 2019; Marx et al., 2019; Sánchez-Cobaleda et al., 2019) identify these trade-offs and tensions within specific IOs. The World Trade Organization (WTO), for example, failed to reach a consensus on the Doha development agenda after nearly 20 years of negotiations, which is widely seen as a major setback for the organisation (Mavroidis, 2011). Because the WTO rules are made through consensus, reaching decisions on important rules has been difficult due to fundamental divisions between member states. Accordingly, many member states have sought out bilateral and plurilateral arrangements instead, which, while not necessarily at odds with a multilateral approach, may reduce its priority for some states.

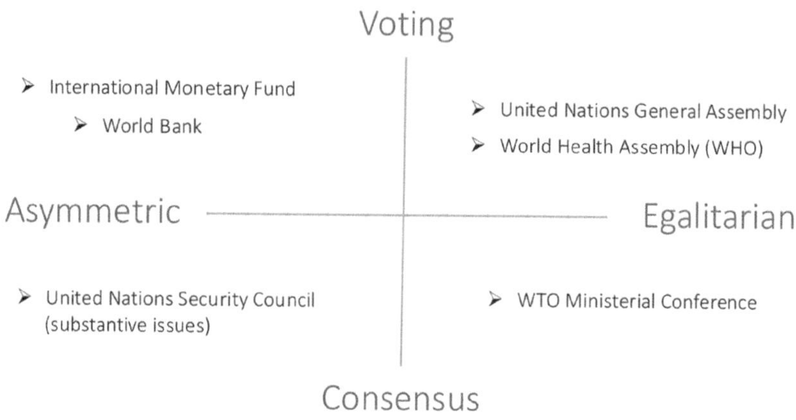

Source: Author's own compilation.

Figure 4.1 Trade-offs in decision-making rules

Hence, while decision-making by consensus may appear to offer the most equal level of representation for all members, granting the IO a certain level of participatory legitimacy (Schneider & Urpelainen, 2012), IOs with large memberships, like the WTO, often struggle to reach decisions (Koremenos, Lipson, & Snidal, 2001; Lall, 2017). If the IO can reach a decision at all, the outcome may not be as robust as some members would like since it may represent a lowest common denominator decision. Additionally, states may use their vote to extract incentives from other members – as Woods describes: 'Even the smallest state can hold the others to ransom' (Woods, 1999, p. 49; see also Schneider & Urpelainen, 2012).

In contrast, some IOs grant extra voting privileges (such as veto power or votes with more weight) to a particular member or set of members in order to gain their support (Koremenos, Lipson, & Snidal, 2001) or in light of greater financial contributions. This arrangement may be rejected by less powerful members as unrepresentative, particularly when voting arrangements remain static while the relative positions of member states change within the organisation (Hallaert, 2020). For example, despite the significant increase in membership to the United Nations (UN), the permanent members of the UN's Security Council (UNSC) – China, France, Russia, the UK, and the US – have not changed since the council's establishment after the Second World War. Because the UN Charter gives each of the five permanent UNSC members a veto right (Art 27.3), in practice it 'ensures that the system of collective security cannot be used against the P5 [permanent members] or their closest allies' (Sánchez-Cobaleda et al., 2019, p. 31). While this veto right was established to ensure the support of these states due to their importance in the war's aftermath, the UNSC has long been criticised for unrepresentative decision-making (Hurd, 2007; Binder & Heupel, 2015).

Similar criticisms are made of the decision-making rules of the International Monetary Fund (IMF). Because votes are based on quotas determined by financial contributions and major decisions require a supermajority of 85%, the US enjoys an automatic veto due to its share of 16% of votes (Eichengreen & Woods, 2016). The composition of the IMF's executive board has also been criticised since only a handful of powerful members (the US, Japan, France, Germany, the UK, Russia, Saudi Arabia, and China) have their own representative, while other members must share representatives. Though quotas and board representation criteria are updated every five years, the decision-making structure has enabled the US to refuse to increase certain members' quotas (US Treasury, 2019; see also Henning, 2020), thereby allowing certain powerful states to 'shape IMF governance according to their national interests' (Eichengreen & Woods, 2016, p. 31).

Similarly, the World Bank's decision-making structures give excessive power to advanced Western economies due to weighted voting based on financial contributions, despite various reform attempts (Wang, 2017; Wouters & Odermatt, 2014; Ocampo, 2016; Vestergaard & Wade, 2015). The bank's slow and uneven response to some stakeholders' needs – especially developing countries – surrounding the 2008 financial crisis (Culpeper, Griffith-Jones, & Titelman, 2016) may be demonstrative of these power imbalances and the limited reach of reforms.

The issue of representativeness and divisions between developed economies and developing and emerging economies surfaced across all the issue areas covered in our analysis. Recent scholarship has likewise paid much attention to contestation at the multilateral level by emerging powers and developing countries, which has been linked to shifts of global power and growing multipolarity (Glaser, 2019; Hallaert, 2020; Hooghe, Lenz, & Marks, 2019b; Kahler, 2013). Of note has been the slowness – or unwillingness – of many IOs to adjust to 'states' growing (or ebbing) power' (Koremenos, Lipson, & Snidal 2001, p. 762). As Hale, Held, and Young (2013) point out, 'it is the interplay between emerging multipolarity and institutional inertia that illuminates the current shortfalls and failings of the UN system: namely that dominant powers continue to bolster their interests and resist emerging powers, resulting in deadlock in key negotiations' (p. 228).

Member states that feel they do not have an appropriate level of 'voice' within an institution may engage in contestation within the IO, threaten to exit, or establish new (potentially competing) institutions. China's establishment of the Asian Infrastructure and Invest Bank (AIIB) in 2016 is largely seen as a response to the World Bank's insufficient attention to the needs of developing countries, especially concerning infrastructure finance (Wang, 2017). At the WTO, incumbent powers see bloc voting by emerging economies (namely, Brazil, Russia, India, China, and South Africa) as a form of contestation. The other side of the same coin is that emerging powers see resistance to change by member states benefitting from the status quo as a lack of attention to the needs of less powerful members. Overall, dissatisfaction with decision-making rules may be held by both powerful and less powerful states and is a 'prominent driver for delegitimation' among IOs (Tallberg & Zürn, 2019, p. 593).

An IO's failure to adequately adjust to the evolving needs of its stakeholders is likely to negatively impact its legitimacy. Indeed, IOs have long been understood to be slow to adjust to changes in global conditions, often going through long periods of inertia punctuated by rare and inconsistent moments of quick reform and change (Manulak, 2020). Negotiations can be slow and difficult procedures even with a small number of parties – as membership increases, negotiation processes can become increasingly complex and drawn out.

Much of this concerns path dependency. Importantly, the extent to which IO's internal reform is hampered by path dependency and inflexibility will have much to do with the institutional design choices, especially decision-making rules, made at the time of the IO's establishment and to handle challenges particular to that context. The initial design of the institution typically privileges the most powerful members at the time of establishment – a trade-off often seen as justified to gain the buy-in of a powerful state – and is not designed to be responsive to future shifts of power without damage to the institution (Hale, Held, & Young, 2013; Davis, 2023). As the context within which the IO operates changes (often radically) over time, the rigidity of original structures may lead to new and more pressing challenges for an IO, including increasing politicisation and declining support. In some cases, such as when it has few competitors, an IO's inflexibility may not greatly affect its standing. In other cases, such as when other institutions or forms of global governance for a particular issue area are available, an IO's rigidity can be a major source of the delegitimation processes that render it obsolete (Lipscy, 2017; Debre & Dijkstra, 2023).

3.3 Misaligned Mandate and Lack of Autonomy

We define an IO's mandate as the activities and functions it has been granted authority to carry out, including the degree of independence with which it can make decisions and set the agenda (Zürn, Tokhi & Binder, 2021).

An IO's mandate may be too narrow and therefore not allow the organisation to undertake necessary activities to achieve certain goals nor grant the IO enough autonomy to respond flexibly to changing global conditions. On the other hand, it might be seen as too broad, giving rise to questions of its legitimacy or the inability to meet objectives (Lawrence, 2008; Heldt & Schmidtke, 2017).

In climate change governance, inadequate mandates have been a significant challenge for the UN Framework Convention on Climate Change (UNFCCC), the UN Environment Programme (UNEP), and the Intergovernmental Panel on Climate Change (IPCC). The mandates of all three IOs are rather narrow, significantly reducing their scope of action and autonomy to develop initiatives – likely reflecting the political sensitivity surrounding climate change governance (Coen, Kreienkamp, & Pegram, 2020). For example, the IPCC's design as a bridge between scientists and policy-makers has reduced its role to one that is 'purely advisory' (Coen, Kreienkamp, & Pegram, 2020, p. 24). The IPCC does not carry out independent research, and its outputs require approval from member states, which prevents the IPCC from generating new knowledge and suggesting necessary, potentially politically unpopular, policy (Haas & Stevens, 2011, as cited in Coen, Kreienkamp, & Pegram, 2020), thereby undermining its policy autonomy and inhibiting effective global action.

Indeed, some IOs' mandates are designed to be deliberately narrow – states often and deliberately avoid granting too much autonomy or too expansive of a mandate in order to ensure the IO's future activities and decisions will not encroach upon the member states' sovereignty (Guzman, 2013).

However, the different GLOBE mapping papers also showed that IOs across issue areas frequently engage in activities beyond those articulated in their mandates. This confirms previous research which finds that over time IOs rarely stick within the confines of their mandate but expand their missions and take on new activities, a process sometimes referred to as 'mission creep' (see, e.g., Lawrence, 2008). This mission creep can result in tensions between the governance structure of an IO and the goals it pursues. For example, the World Bank and the IMF have been criticised for expanding their mandates beyond their original mandates, without a sufficient parallel reform of decision-making procedures. As Stiglitz explains regarding the IMF: 'Given the wide impact of IMF programs and the steady expansion of its operations into the areas of development and poverty alleviation, it does not seem appropriate that the IMF should just reflect the views of representatives from finance ministries and central banks' (2010, p. 208).

This expansion of mandates might result in a form of reprisal that further impedes an IO in carrying out its activities. For example, in trade governance, the US increasingly finds its interests to be at odds with decisions of the WTO's dispute settlement mechanism, the Appellate Body, which it has accused of overstepping its mandate through 'judicial overreach' (Kerremans, 2020; Ihara, 2018). As a result, the US has unilaterally sought to undermine the WTO by blocking appointments and renewals of Appellate Body members, thereby bringing the dispute settlement system to a halt (Marx et al., 2019).

Finally, linked to the mandate, a lack of IO autonomy might create challenges for IOs. The degree of autonomy of IOs is important due to the 'time inconsistency' problem (Lall, 2017): when an IO is first established, its rules and legal structure usually represent 'equilibrium expectations' (Stone, 2011, p. 12), though these are undoubtedly tipped in favour of the most powerful members. But after establishment, the global context and member states' interests might change, and states may seek to influence outcomes in favour of their national interests. This can go at the expense of the IO's autonomy and ability to achieve its goals (Lall, 2017, p. 253). In other words, IOs are relatively path-dependent, inert and cannot easily adapt to a changed environment, which creates new challenges in fast-changing geopolitical contexts. Some authors suggest that an IO's lack of policy autonomy appears to be a primary cause of poor performance (Lall, 2017) and loss of vitality (Gray, 2018).

When IOs are perceived to be operating too autonomously or to be making decisions outside of their mandate, they may face criticism for overstepping their mandate. Member states that perceive an IO to overstep its bounds are likely to reduce support for the IO, renegotiate its commitments, threaten withdrawal, or engage in another form of contestation (Daßler & Heinkelmann-Wild, 2021).

3.4 Lack of Resources

Finally, a lack of resources – including funding, staff, information, and feedback from member states – is a major challenge for IOs across issue areas. Access to resources has obvious and immediate impacts on an IO's ability to function, and by extension, on its legitimacy and performance (Heldt & Schmidtke, 2017; Ege & Bauer, 2017; Gray, 2018). Nevertheless, many IOs 'simply lack adequate personnel and resources to perform well' (Gutner & Thompson, 2010, p. 238). For example, the UNEP is hampered by severe budget and staff constraints due to its reliance on voluntary contributions, which make up 95% of its income (UN Environment, 2017). These resource limitations have generated doubts as to whether the organisation can meet its governance goals (Nanda & Pring, 2012).

Staff members' level of expertise and experience also matters; an IO's ability to provide competitive compensation and attractive career opportunities impact its ability to attract and retain high-quality staff. The ability to attract top staff is not solely dependent on an IO's financial resources. Gray (2018) shows that something as seemingly innocuous as the choice of location for an IO's headquarters is a key determinant of the quality of IO's permanent staff and the organisation's overall vitality, including the impression of its importance in the global debate on a particular issue area (Coen, Kreienkamp, & Pegram, 2020). The UNEP headquarters in Nairobi, away from the centres of international political activity, have constrained the IO's capacity 'to assert itself as the central actor in global environmental issues and to attract and retain the most high-quality policy staff' (Ivanova, 2008, p. 161).

There are several – often obvious – reasons why IOs frequently face resource shortages. As we saw in previous sections, states reduce support for IOs over frustration with existing decision-making structures or decisions that adversely affect them, or because the IO is simply seen to not be doing its job. When members do not meet their financial commitments, IOs often lack capacity to ensure their performance. Additionally, there are other factors in play. In some cases, a member state may find that it can enjoy the benefits of membership without making sufficient financial commitments ('freeriding'). Additionally, one member state's lack of (or reduction of) support for an IO may trigger other member states to reconsider their own support, for political or practical reasons. In this way, reduced support can be self-perpetuating. For example, the US' perception that some NATO member states were not contributing enough led the US – NATO's biggest funder – to reconsider its own support (Sánchez Cobaleda et al., 2019; *The Guardian*, 2019). Moreover, as states limit resources, an IO is increasingly unable to fulfil its roles and is likely to face further difficulties in garnering sufficient support.

Additionally, an IO's scope, which encompasses its governance objectives and operational issue areas, can significantly influence the support it garners from member states. An IO's scope may be broad, covering many issue areas, such as the UN, or narrowly confined to a specific topic. Furthermore, an IO's issue area may range from technical or specialised matters, which often lack public awareness, to more general concerns well known to citizens, which are more likely to be politicised. IOs with a more politicised scope are more susceptible to challenges posed by worldwide trends of nationalism and populism (Hooghe, Lenz, & Marks, 2019b; Bearce & Jolliff Scott, 2019; Eilstrup-Sangiovanni, 2018) or by shifting power of domestic parties, which may result in declining support and resources for certain IOs. The UNFCCC, for example, has been affected by the system-wide decrease of US financial support for international cooperation on climate change (Coen, Kreienkamp, & Pegram, 2020).

Relatedly, in recent decades, citizens of many member states have perceived some IOs as unresponsive to their needs or, worse, culpable for the uneven distributional effects of economic globalisation (Bearce & Jolliff Scott, 2019; Hooghe, Lenz, & Marks, 2019b). Accordingly, support for IOs has diminished among some groups of citizens over time – especially those who feel that their state's participation in an IO has a negative impact on their own interests (Bearce & Jolliff Scott, 2019) – resulting in political cleavages among electorates and domestic political contestation of state involvement in IOs. This contestation at the domestic level can translate to contestation within and against the IO (Copelovitch & Pevehouse, 2019; Buisseret & Bernhardt, 2018; Ecker-Ehrhardt, 2014; Trubowitz & Burgoon, 2023).

Finally, besides a decrease in funding and resources one can also observe a shift in funding from general funding of IOs to earmarked funding. Earmarked funding is specific funding from donors to IOs to develop and implement specific projects. In some cases, earmarked funding adds to the budget of IOs but more often it leads to a re-allocation from general funding to project-specific funding which might affect the efficiency and longer-term strategies of IOs (Reinsberg, 2023; Heinzel, Cormier & Reinsberg, 2023). It also affects the flexibility and autonomy of IOs to adjust to a changing environment (Metcalfe-Hough et al., 2021).

4. INCREASING INFORMALITY

4.1 Rise of Informality

The challenges facing IOs, including reaching new agreements, is one of the most probable reasons states have increasingly turned to the establishment of more IIOs (Vabulas & Snidal, 2013) and the development of more informal types of global policy-making. Recent decades have witnessed a rapid rise in the prominence of IIOs (Roger, 2020) and the increased reliance on informal international policy or lawmaking (Terpan, 2015; Pauwelyn, Wessel, & Wouters, 2014).

Regarding the former, states and regional organisations participate in a variety of arrangements and forums for intergovernmental cooperation that cannot be considered formal organisations, such as the Visegrad Four, the Financial Stability Board or, most famously, the 'G groups'.

While IIOs vary in terms of formality and function, we draw on the definitions put forth by Charles Roger (2020, pp. 26–28) and Vabulas and Snidal (2013, p. 197) and define IIOs as organisations that are: (1) formed by states or those representing states; (2) are established by non-binding agreements or shared understandings that cannot be considered traditional sources of international law, such as an MoU rather than a treaty; and (3) lack formalised and/or permanent structures of institutionalisation such as a dedicated secretariat or permanent headquarters and staff.

IIOs can often avail of certain looser policy-making mechanisms such as peer review, monitoring, dialogue, and capacity building. Despite the informality, member states nevertheless often have an incentive to comply with decisions – less influential member states because they risk losing their seat at the table, and more influential member states because their non-compliance would undermine the system (Wouters & Odermatt, 2014, p. 67). Though decisions reached by IIOs are not formally binding, consensus reached through an IIO is often reaffirmed through a formal IOs' decision-making procedures and follow-up measures are often delegated to a formal IO relevant to the issue area, such as, for example, the OECD following up on agreements reached in the G20 (Pauwelyn, Wessel, & Wouters, 2014; Vabulas & Snidal, 2013).

4.2 Impact of IIOs on IOs and Global Governance

While IIOs lack institutional structures, specific rules, enforcement mechanisms and formal (treaty-based) authority, these informal institutions nevertheless have several advantages and a unique role to play in global governance (for an overview of limitations of IIOs, see Roger, 2020).

First, IIOs offer states a forum for dialogue and consensus-building that are less restrictive of state sovereignty. As such, states have a greater incentive to participate (Wouters & Odermatt, 2014). In other words, informal arrangements can solve collective action problems (Bradford, 2010). Further, informal cooperation and non-binding instruments can be more flexible and nimbler in responding to crises or abrupt changes (Vabulas & Snidal, 2013; Wouters & Odermatt, 2014; Roger, 2020), in addition to being able to take on a wider variety of topics that might fall outside the mandate of a formal IO.

Recognising these advantages, several IOs and regional organisations like the EU seek to engage IIOs in partnerships and are even major contributors of IIO funding (Roger, 2022). In addition, IOs frequently work with a range of instruments and are themselves key sources of informal rule-making. Indeed, IOs have increasingly made use of instruments and practices that do not lead to a binding treaty or other traditional source of international law, but instead rely on its normative weight for compliance (Pauwelyn, Wessel, & Wouters, 2014). Examples include declarations, MoUs, international regulatory standards, goals, and guidelines. Because these instruments – sometimes referred to as 'soft law' – do not lead to legal obligations in a strict sense, the bargaining costs are lower, making them a 'decisively cheaper means of agreement-making' (Brummer, 2010, p. 631). This can be particularly useful in certain areas of governance that may be more politically sensitive or intrusive into states' autonomy, and we therefore see greater use of informal lawmaking in the governance of climate change, finance (see Brummer, 2010), and corporate responsibility. Consider, for example, the United Nations Guiding Principles on Business and Human Rights, which remains a significant international instrument in the governance of business and human rights despite its non-binding nature. Moreover, some instruments contain both formal and informal approaches, such as the Paris Agreement, which contains both binding obligations and non-binding commitments.

Nevertheless, several potential challenges related to the rise of informal international cooperation have been identified in the literature. First, the establishment or persistence of informal law or IIOs sometimes serves to prevent, delay, or pre-empt binding cooperation (Roger, 2020). In some cases, this is a result of undemocratic forces, such as protecting elite interests. At other times, this occurs because a powerful state (or set of states) prefers a non-binding approach in an issue area where their view is at odds with other states and uses their weight to block negotiations for formal cooperation (Roger, 2020). Relatedly, the rise of informality is often attributed to inertia in cooperation on a binding agreement that reflects a lack of political will to solve a problem. In these cases, the establishment of informal arrangements is not done to take advantage of the best features of informality to best solve a global problem, but rather to stall or redirect progress on an issue. Finally, the use of informal law and informal organisations may (intentionally or not) create an illusion of action in a governance area, curbing further cooperation on the issue (Roger, 2020).

Second, the establishment and growth of IIOs can contribute to greater complexity within governance regimes (see Vandendriessche, Jordana & Marx, Chapter 5 in this book). IIOs' mandates frequently overlap with mandates of formal IOs, and they can initiate other types of global governance institutions, such as public–private partnerships (Marx & Westerwinter, 2022) or 'economic corridors' (Brunner, 2013). Moreover, IIOs themselves often cover multiple issue areas, expanding their scope as global governance actors (Vabulas & Snidal, 2013; see also Vandendriessche, Jordana & Marx, Chapter 5 in this book).

Some other issues relate to the features of their informality. With limited compliance mechanisms, they can fail to provide the necessary degree of certainty and may be insufficient for brokering or enforcing decisions they make. Occasionally, agreements reached through IIOs may need to be reinforced through a formal agreement carried out by a formal IO (Sauer, 2019). Informality can also lead to (perceptions of) an accountability deficit, leading member states to contest actions taken by an IIO on their behalf (Roger, 2020).

While not discounting the advantages and disadvantages of informal cooperation described above, it remains uncertain whether informal cooperation presents a solution for the institutional limitations and challenges identified in Section 3. We consider these next.

Where states are unable to reach a formal agreement, informal institutions or instruments may provide a pathway out of stalled decision-making. However, informal arrangements are not always designed to ensure compliance, and, accordingly, may fail to resolve the governance problem at hand. For example, while recognising that the G20 has delivered significant global governance solutions, especially during the Covid pandemic, there are rising concerns that the G20 will not be able to continue to deliver in a multi-polar world with opposing blocs and in which economic decoupling and fragmentation become more prevalent (Bertoldi, Scherrer & Stanoeva, 2023).

A similar observation can be made concerning informality as a solution for IOs' often rigid governance structures, particularly concerning membership and voting. While informality seems to be more flexible, decision-making can also be hampered by diverging interests of the members of the IIO, as is illustrated by the failure to reach a consensus-based final statement following the G20 summit in Buenos Aires (2018). The US then refused to sign a joint statement on climate change.

Because IIOs are flexible, they can be quickly adapted, contracted, or expanded based on the interests of states and governance needs. This can eliminate some challenges stemming from a mandate that is too narrow or not dynamic, which can hamper the performance of some IOs, as described above. An IIO is also unlikely to be accused of 'overstepping' its mandate since it does not engage in formal rule-setting. In several IIOs, like transnational regulatory networks, it is often not official political state representatives who are involved but representatives from state administrations, ministries, or public agencies. They have some degree of autonomy in decision-making but cannot make strong political commitments. Moreover, many IIOs lack independent autonomy from the states that form them since they have no secretariat. Without a degree of independence to pursue its mandate, IIOs lack enforcement capacity and other means to ensure progress in achieving jointly formulated goals.

Concerning a lack of resources, IIOs can be confronted with similar challenges compared to IOs since many informal organisations lack consistent funding and other institutional resources like a permanent secretariat and staff. Hence, informality is unlikely to overcome this particular limitation of IOs and is in fact likely to face greater difficulties in this regard. Contributions are likely to be earmarked for specific purposes, which may further contribute to a lack of autonomy.

5. CONCLUSION

International organisations have to operate in a changing geopolitical and global governance context, which presents a number of challenges for them. This chapter aimed to identify some general challenges that international organisations of a public nature face across different issue areas, both formal and informal. They frequently share three primary institutional limitations: (1) IOs face difficulties balancing the needs of a diverse set of stakeholders and members due to inappropriate decision-making rules or inflexibility of governance structures; (2) IOs' mandates often do not grant the IO sufficient policy autonomy or scope of action to meet its goals; (3) IOs' frequently lack the necessary resources, including funding, staff, and access to information and a shift in funding from general funding to earmarked funding. These limitations create 'friction' between developments in the external environment of IO and their capacity to govern in this changed environment.

Importantly, our analysis and examples demonstrate that the challenges may not necessarily be inherent, but rather a result of a combination of incompatible institutional features or institutional design decisions that are no longer compatible with a multi-polar world. Moreover, our analysis suggests that these structural institutional limitations are not likely to be fully resolved through increased informality in certain issue areas. Whereas informal policy-making and institutions may provide a way out of decision-making gridlock and rigid governance structures, they are likely to face greater problems related to autonomy and resources, while bringing in additional challenges related to enforcement. Given the potential downsides of informality – including increased regime complexity and the pre-emption of binding cooperation – greater attention should be paid to when and where informal arrangements are likely to succeed and how more traditional IOs can be reformed to perform in a changing world.

Moreover, the analysis triggers a reflection on the future of IOs and decision-making in IOs. In a fragmented geopolitical world, it becomes increasingly difficult to find a consensus among a large membership, and veto-players can paralyse an organisation. This creates a continued 'gridlock' (Hale, Held, & Young, 2013). How to overcome this gridlock is a major challenge. In some cases, different forms of 'differentiated integration' or plurilateral agreements embedded in multilateral agreements might be a way forward. This would allow an IO to make progress on some topics with a more limited number of members. This way of moving forward might address challenges 1 (accommodating the needs of stakeholders) and 2 (expanding mandate and autonomy). However, this can create a situation in which IOs progress at multiple speeds and this may increase the risk of leaving some members behind and not engaged in the dynamics of global governance. The latter might not be a preferable outcome. Hence the pros and cons of this strategy should be carefully assessed, and the applicability might differ between IOs. Addressing challenge 3 (resources) will be very difficult in the short term. All indications on funding indicate that member states are less likely to invest and fund IOs and are shifting their funding from general funding to earmarked funding, which gives more exposure to donors but less autonomy to IOs to develop and implement longer-term strategies.

REFERENCES

Abbott, K. W., Green, J. F., & Keohane, R. O. (2016). Organizational ecology and institutional change in global governance. *International Organization*, *70*(2), 247–277.

Abbott, K. W., & Snidal, D. (2009). Strengthening international regulation through transnational new governance: Overcoming the orchestration deficit. *Vanderbilt Journal of Transnational Law*, *42*, 501–578.

Barnett, M., & Finnemore, M. (2004). *Rules for the world: International organizations in global politics*. Cornell University Press.

Bearce, D. H., & Jolliff Scott, B. (2019). Popular non-support for international organizations: How extensive and what does this represent? *The Review of International Organizations*, *14*(2), 187–216.

Bertoldi, M., Scherrer, H., & Stanoeva, G. (2023). *The G20@15: Can it still deliver?* European Commission. https://economy-finance.ec.europa.eu/system/files/2023-11/eb076_en.pdf, DOI: 10.2765/653583.

Binder, M., & Heupel, M. (2015). The legitimacy of the UN Security Council: Evidence from recent General Assembly debates. *International Studies Quarterly*, *59*(2), 238–250.

Bradford, A. (2010). International antitrust cooperation and the preference for nonbinding regimes. In A. T. Guzman (Ed.), *Cooperation, comity, and competition policy* (pp. 319–344). Oxford University Press.

Brummer, C. (2010). Why soft law dominates international finance – and not trade. *Journal of International Economic Law*, *13*(3), 623–643.

Brunner, H. P. (2013). What is economic corridor development and what can it achieve in Asia's subregions? *ADB Working Paper Series on Regional Economic* Integration. https://aric.adb.org/pdf/workingpaper/WP117_Brunner_What_is_Economic_Corridor_Development.pdf.

Buisseret, P., & Bernhardt, D. (2018). Reelection and renegotiation: International agreements in the shadow of the polls. *American Political Science Review*, *112*(4), 1016–1035.

Carroll, G. R., & Hannan, M. T. (2004). *The demography of corporations and industries*. Princeton University Press.

Coen, D., Kreienkamp, J., & Pegram, T. (2020). Working paper: Mapping of climate change governance and narratives. *GLOBE Report*. https://www.globe-project.eu/mapping-global-climate-change-governance_10120.pdf.

Cohen, H. G. (2018). Multilateralism's life cycle. *American Journal of International Law*, *112*(1), 47–66.

Copelovitch, M., & Pevehouse, J. C. W. (2019). International organizations in a new era of populist nationalism. *The Review of International Organizations*, *14*(2), 169–186.

Cortell, A. P., & Peterson, S. (2022). Autonomy and international organisations. *Journal of International Relations and Development*, *25*(2), 399–424.

Culpeper, R., Griffith-Jones, S., & Titelman, D. (2016). Multilateral development banks. In J. A. Ocampo (Ed.), *Global governance and development* (pp. 168–190). Oxford University Press.

Daßler, B., & Heinkelmann-Wild, T. (2021). International authority, democracies, and exit from international organizations. Paper prepared for the Political Economy of International Organization (PEIO) online seminar, 9 February.

Davis, C. L. (2023). *Discriminatory clubs: The geopolitics of international organizations*. Princeton University Press.

Debre, M. J., & Dijkstra, H. (2023). Are international organisations in decline? An absolute and relative perspective on institutional change. *Global Policy*, *14*(1), 16–30.

Dellmuth, L. M., Scholte, J. A., & Tallberg, J. (2019). Institutional sources of legitimacy for international organisations: Beyond procedure versus performance. *Review of International Studies*, *45*(4), 627–646.

Ecker-Ehrhardt, M. (2014). Why parties politicise international institutions: On globalisation backlash and authority contestation. *Review of International Political Economy*, *21*(6), 1275–1312.

Ege, J., & Bauer, M. W. (2017). How financial resources affect the autonomy of international public administrations. *Global Policy*, *8*, 75–84.

Eichengreen, B., & Woods, N. (2016). The IMF's unmet challenges. *Journal of Economic Perspectives*, *30*(1), 29–52.

Eilstrup-Sangiovanni, M. (2018). Death of international organizations: The organizational ecology of intergovernmental organizations, 1815–2015. *The Review of International Organizations*, *15*(2), 339–370.

Glaser, C. L. (2019). A flawed framework: Why the liberal international order concept is misguided. *International Security*, *43*(4), 51–87.

Gray, J. (2018). Life, death, or zombie? The vitality of international organizations. *International Studies Quarterly*, *62*(1), 1–13.

Grigorescu, A. (2020). *The ebb and flow of global governance: Intergovernmentalism versus nongovernmentalism in world politics*. Cambridge University Press.

Gutner, T., & Thompson, A. (2010). The politics of IO performance: A framework. *The Review of International Organizations*, *5*(3), 227–248.

Guzman, A. (2013). International organizations and the Frankenstein problem. *European Journal of International Law*, *24*(4), 999–1025.

Haas, P. M., & Stevens, C. (2015). Organized science, usable knowledge, and multilateral environmental governance. In R. Lidskog & G. Sundqvist (Eds.), *Governing the air: The dynamics of science, policy, and citizen interaction* (pp. 125–161). The MIT Press.

Hale, T., Held, D., & Young, K. (2013). Gridlock: From self-reinforcing interdependence to second-order cooperation problems. *Global Policy*, *4*(3), 223–235.

Hallaert, J. J. (2020). The tragedy of international organizations in a world order in turmoil. *ECIPE Policy Briefs*, *6*. ECIPE. https://ecipe.org/publications/tragedy-of-international-organizations.

Hanrieder, T. (2014). The path-dependent design of international organizations: Federalism in the World Health Organization. *European Journal of International Relations*, *21*(1), 215–239.

Heinzel, M., Cormier, B., & Reinsberg, B. (2023). Earmarked funding and the control–performance trade-off in international development organizations. *International Organization*, *77*, 475–495.

Heldt, E., & Schmidtke, H. (2017). Measuring the empowerment of international organizations: The evolution of financial and staff capabilities. *Global Policy*, *8*(5), 51–61.

Henning, C. R. (2020). Regional financial arrangements and the International Monetary Fund: Sustaining coherence in global financial governance. *CIGI*. https://www.cigionline.org/publications/regional-financial-arrangements-and-international-monetary-fund-sustaining-coherence.

Hooghe, L., Lenz, T., & Marks, G. (2019a). *A theory of international organization.* Oxford University Press.

Hooghe, L., Lenz, T., & Marks, G. (2019b). Contested world order: The delegitimation of international governance. *The Review of International Organizations, 14*(4), 731–743.

Hooghe, L., Marks, G., Schakel, A. H., Niedzwiecki, S., Chapman Osterkatz, S., & Shair-Rosenfield, S. (2017). *Measuring international authority: A postfunctionalist theory of governance (Vol. III).* Oxford University Press.

Hurd, I. (2007). *After anarchy: Legitimacy and power in the United Nations Security Council.* Princeton, NJ: Princeton University Press.

Ihara, J. (2018). WTO dispute settlement body: Developments in 2017. *World Trade Organization.* https://www.wto.org/english/tratop_e/dispu_e/ihara_17_e.htm.

Ivanova, M. (2008). UNEP as anchor organization for the global environment. In F. Bierman, B. Siebenhüner, & A. Schreyögg (Eds.), *International organizations in global environmental governance* (pp. 151–173). Routledge.

Kahler, M. (2013). Rising powers and global governance: Negotiating change in a resilient status quo. *International Affairs, 89*(3), 711–729.

Kerremans, B. (2020). Dispute settlement and multilateral trade governance: A tale of short-term paralysis and systemic frustrations. *GLOBE Case Study on the WTO.* https://www.globe-project.eu/case-study-on-the-world-trade-organization.

Klabbers, J. (2017). Reflections on role responsibility: The responsibility of international organizations for failing to act. *European Journal of International Law, 28*(4), 1133–1161.

Koremenos, B., Lipson, C., & Snidal, D. (2001). The rational design of international institutions. *International Organization, 55*(4), 761–799.

Lall, R. (2017). Beyond institutional design: Explaining the performance of international organizations. *International Organization, 71*(2), 245–280.

Lall, R. (2023). *Making international institutions work: The politics of performance.* Cambridge University Press.

Lawrence, R. Z. (2008). International organisations: The challenge of aligning mission, means and legitimacy. *World Economy, 31*(11), 1455–1470.

Levi-Faur, D., & Blumsack, I. (2019). Mapping of global financial institutions. *GLOBE Report.* https://www.globe-project.eu/mapping-global-financial-institutions.

Lipscy, P. Y. (2017). *Renegotiating the world order: Institutional change in international relations.* Cambridge University Press.

Manulak, M. W. (2020). A bird in the hand: Temporal focal points and change in international institutions. *The Review of International Organizations, 15*(1), 1–27.

Marx, A., Otteburn, K., Deciancio, M., Peixoto, J., Pertiwi, B., Singh Bal, C., Hegde, V., Nemiña, P., Yulyadi, L., Nugraha Mursitama, T., Gao, W., Van der Loo, G., Wouters, J., & Qingmin, Z. (2019). Mapping of the trade and development global regimes and institutions. *GLOBE Report.* https://www.globe-project.eu/mapping-of-the-trade-and-development-global-regimes-and-institutions_9714.pdf.

Marx, A., & Westerwinter, O. (2022). An ever more entangled union? The European Union's interactions with global governance institutions. *Journal of European Integration, 44*(5), 597–615.

Mavroidis, P. C. (2011). Doha, Dohalf or Dohaha? The WTO licks its wounds. *Trade Law and Development, 3*(2), 367–381.

Metcalfe-Hough, V., Fenton, W., Willitts-King, B., & Spencer, A. (2021). *The grand bargain at five years: An independent review.* ODI. https://odi.org/en/publications/the-grand-bargain-at-five-years.

Nanda, V. P., & Pring, G. (2012). *International environmental law and policy for the 21st century: 2nd revised edition*. Martinus Nijhoff.
Nye, J. S. Jr., & Keohane, R. O. (1971). Transnational relations and world politics: An introduction. *International Organization*, *25*(3), 329–349.
Ocampo, J. A. (2016). Global economic and social governance and the United Nations system. In J. A. Ocampo (Ed.), *Global governance and development* (pp. 3–31). Oxford University Press.
Pauwelyn, J., Wessel, R. A., & Wouters, J. (2014). When structures become shackles: Stagnation and dynamics in international lawmaking. *European Journal of International Law*, *25*(3), 733–763.
Reinsberg, B. (2023). Earmarked funding and the performance of international organizations: Evidence from food and agricultural development agencies. *Global Studies Quarterly*, *3*(4), 1–14.
Roger, C. B. (2020). *The origins of informality: Why the legal foundations of global governance are shifting, and why it matters*. Oxford University Press.
Roger, C. B. (2022). The coral reefs of global governance: How formal IOs make informality work. *Journal of European Integration*, *44*(5), 657–675,
Ruggie, J. (1993). *Multilateralism matters: The theory and praxis of an institutional form*. Columbia University Press.
Sánchez Cobaleda, A., Kouliopoulos, A., Kissack, R., Bradley, M., & Badell Sánchez, D. (2020). Mapping of global security threats and the global security architecture. *GLOBE Report*. https://www.globe-project.eu/mapping-of-global-security-threats-and-the-global-security-architecture.
Sauer, T. (2019). The role of informal international organizations in resolving the Iranian nuclear crisis (2003–15). *Journal of Common Market Studies*, *57*(5), 939–955.
Schneider, C. J., & Urpelainen, J. (2012). Accession rules for international institutions: A legitimacy–efficacy trade-off? *Journal of Conflict Resolution*, *56*(2), 290–312.
Shanks, C., Jacobson, H. K., & Kaplan, J. H. (1996). Inertia and change in the constellation of international governmental organizations, 1981–1992. *International Organization*, *50*(4), 593–627.
Stiglitz, J. E. (2010). *The Stiglitz Report: Reforming the international monetary and financial systems in the wake of the Global Crisis*. The New Press.
Stone, R. W. (Ed.). (2011). A theory of international organization. In *Controlling institutions: International organizations and the global economy* (pp. 11–32). Cambridge University Press.
Strange, S. (1998). Why do international organisations never die? In B. Reinalda & B. Verbeek (Eds.), *Autonomous policymaking by international organizations* (pp. 213–221). Routledge.
Tallberg, J., & Zürn, M. (2019). The legitimacy and legitimation of international organizations: Introduction and framework. *The Review of International Organizations*, *14*(4), 581–606.
Terpan, F. (2015). Soft law in the European Union: The changing nature of EU law. *European Law Journal*, *21*(1), 68–96.
The Guardian (2019). Trump re-election could sound death knell for Nato, allies fear, 2 December. http://www.theguardian.com/world/2019/dec/02/nato-donald-trump-second-term.
Trubowitz, P., & Burgoon, B. (2023). *Geopolitics and democracy: The Western liberal order from foundation to fracture*. Oxford University Press.

UN Environment. (2017). *Status of Contributions | UNEP – UN Environment Programme*. Available at: https://www.unep.org/about-un-environment/funding-and-partnerships/check-your-contributions (Accessed: 19 June 2025).

United States Department of the Treasury. (2019). Report to Congress from the Chairman of the National Advisory Council on International Monetary and Financial Policies. April 2019.

Vabulas, F. and Snidal, D. (2013). Organization without delegation: Informal intergovernmental organizations (IIGOs) and the spectrum of intergovernmental arrangements. *The Review of International Organizations, 8*(2), 193–220.

Vestergaard, J., & Wade, R. H. (2015). Protecting power: How Western states retain their dominant voice in the World Bank's governance. In D. Lesage & T. Van de Graaf (Eds.), *Rising powers and multilateral institutions* (pp. 175–196). Palgrave Macmillan.

Wang, H. (2017). New multilateral development banks: Opportunities and challenges for global governance. *Global Policy, 8*(1), 113–118,

Wiener, A. (2014). *A theory of contestation*. Springer.

Woods, N. (1999). Good governance in international organizations. *Global Governance, 5*(1), 39–61.

Wouters, J., & Odermatt, J. (2014). Comparing the 'four pillars' of global economic governance: A critical analysis of the institutional design of the FSB, IMF, World Bank, and WTO. *Journal of International Economic Law, 17*(1), 49–76.

Zürn, M. (2018). *A theory of global governance: Authority, legitimacy, and contestation*. Oxford University Press.

Zürn, M., Tokhi, A., & Binder, M. (2021). The international authority database. *Global Policy, 12*(4), 430–442.

5. Beyond the formal intergovernmental organization: studying the complexity of global governance

Marie Vandendriessche, Jacint Jordana and Axel Marx

1. INTRODUCTION

Global governance today encompasses a tangle of institutions of different types and compositions. In the quarter-century following World War II, multilateral institutions, such as the World Bank and United Nations, became the main global governance actors (Henning & Pratt, 2023). These entities – chiefly formal intergovernmental organizations based on treaties – remain important actors in global governance today, as outlined in Chapter 3. Following the end of the Cold War, new transnational rule-making actors emerged on the global stage. The growth in the number of formal intergovernmental organizations (FIGOs) slowed, while new types of global governance institutions emerged (Marx & Westerwinter, 2022), including informal intergovernmental organizations (Roger, 2020; Vabulas & Snidal, 2013), private transnational regulatory organizations (Abbott et al., 2016), transnational public–private governance initiatives (Westerwinter, 2021) and transnational regulatory networks (Jordana et al., 2022).

A series of contextual trends facilitated the surge in the density and diversity of global governance institutions. These trends include the spread of globalization and the appearance of transnational issues that required governance, such as cybersecurity and climate change (Alter & Raustiala, 2018; Kahler, 2020); a decrease in the costs of organizing transnationally, partially related to technological developments (Abbott & Faude, 2021; Eilstrup-Sangiovanni, 2022); an increase in the influence and agency of domestic interest groups (Keck & Sikkink, 1998; Mikler, 2018); the emergence of new private governance initiatives (Alter & Raustiala, 2018; Eilstrup-Sangiovanni, 2022); and a shift towards multipolarity in world politics (Alter & Raustiala, 2018; Morse &

Keohane, 2014; Pratt, 2021). The landscape of global governance that emerged as a result is undoubtedly complex. Most global issues today are not governed by a single, monolithic institution but instead by a set of varied institutions (often collectively termed a "complex" or architecture), which overlap, complement, substitute, and antagonize each other to varying degrees.

In spite of this empirical reality, until about two decades ago, most scholarship on global governance retained a narrow focus on just one component of these complexes of institutions: the most formal of them all, regimes and formal intergovernmental organizations. Many of these studies aimed to explain institutional design and its effects based on problem structure, that is, the characteristics of the governance problem and the actors involved in it (Alter & Meunier, 2009, p. 21). This line of scholarship offered important insights; however, it largely neglected the wider ecosystem of alternative institutions and therefore only considered one piece of the puzzle. Additionally, these studies often departed from the premise that regimes were created on a blank slate – yet the rich institutional context surrounding them clearly could, and did, play a role (Alter & Meunier, 2009, p. 21).

It was scholars of international environmental politics, foremost, who initially became concerned with the wider institutional context and its implications for international institutions. As Gómez-Mera et al. (2020) explain, this was triggered by empirical observations and concerns about the effectiveness of global governance. On the one hand, global environmental governance was very dense (with multiple institutions active at any one time) and highly fragmented. On the other hand, since many transnational environmental problems persisted and even worsened, it was often deemed ineffective. This led researchers to study, among other things, spillovers between global governance institutions and to consider how institutions could better keep up with rapid changes in biophysical and socio-economic systems. As such, global environmental governance arguably formed the initial breeding ground for studies of global governance complexity. The scholarship in this field thus progressed from focusing on distinct international *institutions* to studying larger institutional *configurations*, and individual institutions *within* those configurations.

This chapter sheds light on extant scholarship on complexes of global governance institutions, focusing on the lenses that are used, the main dimensions under study, and significant debates in the field. It starts with an examination of five of the frameworks that have been used in this research, including an analysis of their defining features and key debates. This overview also provides insights into the main dimensions that are used to classify and analyze such complexes, while revealing some of the research insights that have been gained. In a subsequent section, the chapter focuses on one of the main defining features of global governance through complexes of institutions: their propensity to continuously evolve. This section examines the drivers and processes of evolution, in addition to its results: the implications for institutional proliferation or consolidation, as well as current findings on general long-term patterns of evolution in global governance complexes. The chapter concludes with reflections on the direction of travel in the research field.

2. FRAMEWORKS TO ANALYZE THE MESO-LEVEL OF GLOBAL GOVERNANCE

Over the past 20 years, multiple frameworks have been developed to study the complexity of global governance at the meso-level. They all focus their analysis on the institutional level that is a step higher than individual international institutions, but lower than global governance as a whole. This perspective facilitates a structural view, which can help untangle the effects of institutional configurations on discrete institutions and on the outputs and outcomes of global governance (Biermann & Kim, 2020; Kim & Morin, 2021). Yet beyond the shared premise that the institutional context matters, divergences appear between the frameworks. While many rightly suggest it is time to move forward from conceptual debates to squarely concentrate research efforts on explanatory questions (Alter, 2022; Alter & Raustiala, 2018; Drezner, 2009), definitions are critical: in the end, how a framework is defined determines the populations of institutions it can study.

Following a seminal study by Raustiala and Victor (2004), the first, prolific line of research focused on *regime complexes* and regime complexity. While this literature yielded and continues to yield fruitful scholarship covering many issue areas, it has also faced criticism. On the one hand, it has been critiqued for focusing excessively on formal intergovernmental organizations, to the detriment of other institutional forms (Abbott & Faude, 2022, p. 265; Eilstrup-Sangiovanni & Westerwinter, 2022). On the other hand, scholars have questioned the basic premise that regime complexes lack hierarchy (Orsini et al., 2013). Consequently, in the past decade in particular, new terms and frameworks like *global governance complexes* (Eilstrup-Sangiovanni & Westerwinter, 2022) and *hybrid institutional complexes* (Abbott & Faude, 2022) have been put forward to study global governance in its full density and diversity and offer a more complete understanding of configurations across issue areas. In addition, in parallel with the research on regime complexes, a set of scholars has engaged with the meso-level of global governance through the lens of *global governance architectures* (Biermann et al., 2009), and more recently, *superclusters* and *supercluster complexes* (Kim & Morin, 2021). The latter frameworks have often been used to examine the causes and effects of fragmentation among institutions within complexes. The following section delves into these five frameworks, exposing their defining characteristics and main conceptual debates while placing them in the broader research context.

2.1 Regime Complexes: a Prolific Research Strand Rife with Definitional Debates

The first framework proposed to move past classic regime and international organization studies was that of *regime complexes*. Born at the crossroads between international law and international relations studies (Alter & Raustiala, 2018), regime complex literature departed from the reflection that despite widespread observations of institutional proliferation and increasing density in global governance, scholars largely continued to focus on individual international institutions in isolation from their context. In 2004, Raustiala and Victor proposed the analytical framework of regime complexes to move beyond these studies of distinct regimes.

Raustiala and Victor believed that governance through regime complexes, initially defined as "an array of partially overlapping and nonhierarchical institutions governing a particular issue-area" (2004, p. 279), was likely much more prevalent than observed up to then by the scholarly literature. The complexes were defined as comprising multiple international legal agreements, termed "elemental regimes" (Raustiala & Victor, 2004, p. 279), which functionally overlap but without an agreed upon hierarchy to address potential conflicts between rules. These features, Raustiala and Victor (2004, pp. 279–280) suggested, would lead to distinctive dynamics within a complex – including path-dependent development, forum shopping, the existence of legal inconsistencies, and specific dynamics in domestic policy implementation.

From this point on, empirical research on regime complexity developed rapidly, with a modulating focus over time. Initial studies produced detailed mappings of global governance in specific issue areas (for example, climate change (Keohane & Victor, 2011), human rights (Hafner-Burton, 2009), or trade (Gómez-Mera, 2015)) and on the *origins* or *causes* of complexity. In 2011, for example, Keohane and Victor proposed a model to explain why some issues become governed through regime complexes rather than through regimes. They suggested that three forces would determine the design of the institution(s) governing an issue area: the distribution of interests among states, in function of states' power; the level of uncertainty on the issue; and the scope for linkages with other issues.

Towards the end of the 2000s, scholars increasingly began to call for studies pushing beyond mapping regime complexity and its causes, and towards political and analytical questions on the *consequences* of regime complexity. The base argument was that the structural characteristics of international regime complexity – defined at this stage by Alter and Meunier as "the presence of nested, partially overlapping, and parallel international regimes that are not hierarchically ordered" (2009, p. 13) – were unlikely to have clear causal consequences for global governance outcomes. However, these structures could create "a political environment that alters the behavior and political salience of states, IOs, and sub-state actors", which, in itself, could be consequential (Alter & Meunier, 2009, p. 21).

In parallel to the developing body of empirical research, however, the term *regime complexes* found itself in a process of continuous recharacterization, which has generated a "bewildering" array of definitions (Eilstrup-Sangiovanni & Westerwinter, 2022, p. 236). In 2011, for example, Keohane and Victor (2011, p. 8) more flexibly defined regime complexes as "loosely coupled sets of specific regimes", which they situated at the center of a continuum between fully integrated regulatory institutions with "comprehensive, hierarchical rules" and "highly fragmented collections of institutions with no identifiable core and weak or non-existent linkages between regime elements". The concept's constant redefinition stems from a series of academic debates about the defining characteristics of regime complexes – *inter alia*, on hierarchical relations within regime complexes and the nature of actors involved in the complex.

The role of *hierarchy* is a first point of significant contention. The original definition of regime complexes, by Raustiala and Victor in 2004, clearly highlighted the non-hierarchical nature of these institutional configurations. Subsequent iterations of the concept by Alter and Meunier (2009) repeated this affirmation, and a comprehensive review by Alter and Raustiala in 2018 highlighted "an absence of hierarchy among institutions and rules" as "the key political feature of a regime complex" (p. 332). Yet the first generation of empirical research on regime complexes questioned this affirmation, observing that some form of hierarchy or order can be present within complexes. Orsini et al. (2013, p. 31), for example, deemed hierarchy to be an "ambiguous and unnecessary feature of the former definition" of regime complexes, and proposed a definition that replaced the condition of non-hierarchical relations with a requirement of interaction between the components of the complex. Alter and Raustiala (2018) countered, however, that the lack of hierarchy in the initial definitions did not necessarily suggest an absence of *order* within the regime complex. Instead, the original definitions highlighted an absence of hierarchy to clearly distinguish regime *complexes* from the individual regimes that were studied before them.

Regardless, the current trend in research on global governance complexity, whether through the lens of regime complexes or other frameworks (explored later in this chapter), is to avoid setting *ex ante* requirements for the level of hierarchy in a complex. Henning and Pratt (2023), for instance, replace this constraint with an exploration of *relationships of authority* within regime complexes, which can either be hierarchical, non-hierarchical, or situated between these two poles. Eilstrup-Sangiovanni and Westerwinter (2022, p. 244), meanwhile, agree that in complexes of global governance institutions, there is no classic hierarchy in the sense of one "peak" institution holding official responsibility for taking political decisions which require follow-up by institutions that are lower down on the ladder (Powell, 1990; Williamson, 1975). Yet they argue that elements of formal and informal hierarchy can be present in a complex and the degree of *vertical differentiation* among institutions can be used as one of the axes that co-define the shape of a complex.

A second important debate is on *diversity*, namely the extent to which research on regime complexity has focused excessively on state-based institutions – and in particular, formal intergovernmental organizations – or has included other forms of global governance institutions. Many have noted that empirical studies of regime complexity have focused heavily, and often solely on formal, state-based arrangements (Abbott & Faude, 2022, p. 265; Alter, 2022, p. 379; Eilstrup-Sangiovanni & Westerwinter, 2022). When it comes to the definition of regime complexes, Alter (2022) explains that the original concept did not preclude institutional forms beyond formal intergovernmental agreements (Alter & Meunier, 2009; Alter & Raustiala, 2018; Keohane & Victor, 2011; Raustiala & Victor, 2004). Yet at the same time, Alter and Raustiala (2018, p. 336) do emphasize the "largely formal, legal nature of the elemental units" in a regime complex, as well as their "public nature", in order to differentiate regime complexes from networks or transnational legal orders.

Regardless of whether the focus on formal intergovernmental organizations in research on regime complexes stemmed from definition or practice, the critique of this bias has led to redefinitions and the emergence of new analytical lenses. On the one hand, newer definitions of the regime complex concept often more explicitly consider institutions such as informal intergovernmental organizations and private transnational regulatory organizations (Henning & Pratt, 2023). On the other hand, new lenses such as *global governance complexes* (Eilstrup-Sangiovanni & Westerwinter, 2022) and *hybrid institutional complexes* (Abbott & Faude, 2022) were developed in part to circumvent the definitional debates surrounding regime complexes and offer more "neutral" frameworks capable of analyzing the full range of shapes a complex could take. These two frameworks are explored in the next section.

2.2 Global Governance Complexes and Hybrid Institutional Complexes: Bypassing Definitional Debates and Highlighting Diversity

2.2.1 Global governance complexes

To enable rigorous studies of complexes of global governance institutions while cutting through overall terminological confusion[1] and the lengthy conceptual debates described above, Eilstrup-Sangiovanni and Westerwinter (2022) recently proposed a meta-term: *global governance complexes.* Defined as "system[s] of governance composed of at least three international or transnational institutions or actors whose mandates, functions and memberships overlap, and that jointly address a specific policy problem" (p. 238), global governance complexes differ from regime complexes in three ways.

First, as discussed above, whether deliberately or not, research using the framework of regime complexes largely remained focused on public, state-based, formal international institutions. The definition of global governance complexes, in contrast, does not give pre-eminence to state-based institutions and instead is open to the full range of institutional authority and diversity in global governance. Second, in global governance complexes, similarly to regime complexes, there is no "formal authority empowered to resolve rule conflicts" (Eilstrup-Sangiovanni & Westerwinter, 2022, p. 237). However, while regime complexes are generally defined as non-hierarchical, global governance complexes may be hierarchically or non-hierarchically ordered. Third, relations between institutions in a global governance complex can run the full range between conflict and cooperation. This contrasts with some scholarship on regime complexes, which often presupposed that overlapping institutions within a complex must be in conflict (Alter & Raustiala, 2018, p. 345; Gehring & Faude, 2013; Orsini et al., 2013, p. 28).

From the definitions above, it follows that there are no prior assumptions regarding the shape that a global governance complex will take. Likewise, it is not presumed that relations between the institutions in a complex will play out in any specific way. Each global governance complex can take a unique form, which can be defined through its position on two axes: systemic dimensions and mechanisms for ordering relations (Eilstrup-Sangiovanni & Westerwinter, 2022). By offering a framework that can encompass complexes

[1] In addition to the frameworks discussed in this chapter, other frameworks, such as institutional complexes and polycentric governance, were put forward. Space constraints do not allow for an in-depth exploration of all frameworks in this chapter – however, see Oberthür and Pozarowska (2013) and Jordan et al. (2018) to understand institutional complexes and polycentric global governance, respectively.

of global governance institutions of any shape and type, along with measurable dimensions, Eilstrup-Sangiovanni and Westerwinter explicitly aim to enhance the "commensurability of terminology, data and findings" in research on institutional complexity (2022, p. 235).

When it comes to the first (systemic) axis, the structures of global governance complexes can vary along three dimensions: scale, diversity, and density. Scale refers to the number of units, diversity refers to the heterogeneity among the units (for example, whether they are formal or informal, comprising state or non-state members), and density covers the number and diversity of ties between units (for example, overlaps between membership, functions, and mandates or shared personnel and sources of funding). On the second axis, ordering mechanisms, a global governance complex is determined by its level of vertical differentiation (hierarchy), horizontal differentiation (task differentiation, i.e., the division or duplication of labor among competences such as agenda-setting, rule-making, monitoring, implementation, and enforcement), and mechanisms to manage complexity, such as orchestration, creation of cross-cutting institutions, or redesign of existing institutions. Varying configurations of the three systemic dimensions of a complex may generate different global governance outcomes.

2.2.2 Hybrid institutional complexes

The global governance complex is just one of the terms that was recently introduced in the literature. Driven by the need to engage with theoretical and empirical realities of institutional diversity in studies of global governance complexity, Abbott and Faude (2022) proposed yet another analytical lens: *hybrid institutional complexes*. Pointing to the definitional debate on diversity (see section 2.1, above), Abbott and Faude highlight that the literature on regime complexes considers elemental regimes to be "all interstate institutions – treaties and treaty-based FIGOs" (2022, p. 268). They juxtapose regime complexes with *hybrid institutional complexes*. The latter are marked by a high degree of diversity among the entities that comprise them, in membership, legal shape, and authority (Alter, 2022). These "heterogenous interstate, infra-state, public–private and private transnational institutions, formal and informal" (Abbott & Faude, 2022, p. 264) interact continuously to address governance problems through one or more governance functions.

When compared with regime complexes, the higher levels of heterogeneity in hybrid institutional complexes lead to two distinctive characteristics. On the one hand, functional differentiation tends to be higher in hybrid institutional complexes, and overlapping claims to authority are therefore less frequent. On the other hand, similarly to regime complexes, formal hierarchy is typically lacking in hybrid institutional complexes – but informal hierarchy is a recurrent ordering mechanism. Although Abbott and Faude (2022) deal with regime complexes and hybrid institutional complexes as separate concepts to provide comparative insights, they acknowledge that they are not mutually exclusive. In fact, regime complexes could actually be seen as "low-diversity hybrid institutional complexes" (Abbott & Faude, 2022, p. 268). Similarly, when it comes to global governance complexes (where the level of diversity in the complex is not predefined), hybrid institutional complexes could in fact be considered high-diversity global governance complexes.

The state-based bias of the regime complex as an analytical lens was one of the reasons why Abbott and Faude (2022) turned the spotlight on hybrid institutional complexes. However, they also underlined the *empirical* reality that most global governance today does not take place through sets of formal intergovernmental organizations or a single institution on its own (2022, p. 264): it occurs in configurations of highly diverse global governance institutions. And in most cases, these hybrid institutional complexes in fact represent an evolution of incumbent regime complexes, which diversified as new institutional types became more prevalent. Given that hybrid institutional complexes govern "most issue areas in world politics today", Abbott and Faude (2022, p. 264) argue that these configurations merit specific investigation.

The unique characteristics of hybrid institutional complexes lead the authors to a series of conjectures on interinstitutional ordering, as well as on the complexes' substantive and political fit with governance problems and the outcomes for the global governance of these problems. When global governance takes place through hybrid institutional complexes a series of benefits and risks emerges (Abbott & Faude, 2022). Hybrid configurations may for instance facilitate certain mechanisms of coordination: founders of new institutions may explicitly design their new institutions to *avoid* overlap with existing ones (a mechanism known as contextual design (Reinsberg & Westerwinter, 2019)). Yet hybrid institutional complexes do not guarantee a pre-eminence of coordination: sometimes, founders of new institutions may deliberately choose to *bypass* incumbent institutions, generating unproductive overlaps.[2]

Overall, through their proposal of this new analytical lens, Abbott and Faude (2022) hope to initiate an empirical research agenda on the specific characteristics and results of governance through hybrid institutional complexes, given their prevalence in contemporary global governance. They posit that certain governance problems could more effectively be addressed through hybrid institutional complexes (Abbott & Faude, 2022, p. 278). These complexes may be better suited to govern diverse problems with multiple sub-issues, since they

[2] Abbott and Faude (2022, p. 284) remark, nevertheless, that they expect the latter type of power-based strategies to be as prevalent in hybrid institutional complexes as they are in regime complexes.

require multifaceted solutions, which can be provided by the diversity of actors that constitute the complex. In addition, when non-state actors lie at the root of the governance problems, an institutional complex involving those very actors – a hybrid institutional complex – can be useful in finding solutions.

2.3 Global Governance Architectures and Supercluster Complexes: Frameworks Related to Fragmentation

2.3.1 Global governance architectures

Another frequently used framework in global governance research is *global governance architectures*. Though the term began to circulate in the literature in the early 2000s, its first common definition was laid out by Biermann et al. in 2009. Metaphorically speaking, global governance architectures could be described as "buildings with copious rooms, lavish apartments, winding staircases and meandering corridors, all part of one interrelated system while keeping independent roles and spaces" (Biermann & Kim, 2020, p. 2). More concretely, global governance architectures were defined as "the overarching system of public and private institutions that are valid or active in a given issue area of world politics", including "organizations, regimes, and other forms of principles, norms, regulations and decision-making procedures" (Biermann et al., 2009, p. 15). In terms of scope, they were demarcated as lying between international regimes (which are component parts of global governance architectures) and the overarching international order (which "reflects the organization of the entire system of international relations" (Biermann et al., 2009, p. 16), rather than of individual issue areas of global governance).

Importantly, Biermann et al. (2009) offered this first definition of global governance architectures in an article on fragmentation in global governance. At the time, institutional fragmentation[3] was a growing object of study in global governance and international law literature. Scholars had observed that fragmentation was prevalent and growing, making it "an inherent structural characteristic of international relations" (Zelli & van Asselt, 2013, p. 3) and international law (Koskenniemi, 2007). This observation led to questions on the ensuing material and functional overlaps between institutions, as well as potential dysfunctionalities (Zelli & van Asselt, 2013). Biermann et al. in fact highlighted that they "advance the notion of global governance architecture

---

[3] Fragmentation is defined broadly by Biermann et al. (2009), who state that "[m]any policy domains are … marked by a patchwork of international institutions that are different in their character (organizations, regimes, and implicit norms), their constituencies (public and private), their spatial scope (from bilateral to global), and their subject matter (from specific policy fields to universal concerns)" (p. 16).

in particular … *because* it allows for [the understanding of fragmentation]" (2009, p. 16, emphasis added). The original definition of the concept emphasizes that all global governance architectures are fragmented to some degree, partially because of their origins: global governance architectures typically emerge in a decentralized and unplanned fashion, without a central "architect". While non-fragmented architectures could exist in theory, empirically these situations are difficult to find (Biermann et al., 2009).

However, fragmentation was not studied uniquely through the prism of global governance architectures: research on regime complexes, a tightly related concept,[4] also focused on locating collections of institutions working on a single issue on a continuum between integration and fragmentation. Both the causes of fragmentation and its consequences for global governance remain an important object of study today (Gómez-Mera et al., 2020; Henning & Pratt, 2023).

2.3.2 Supercluster complexes

More recently, scholars have called into question whether global governance is indeed as fragmented as some would argue, and whether institutional proliferation necessarily leads to increased fragmentation (Kim, 2020, p. 913). As Kim and Morin (2021) note, global governance architectures (which they also call *superclusters*) have largely been studied as *de facto* independent entities, and change within the entities is largely considered a function of endogenous processes. However, recent empirical observations demonstrate that exogenous influences may also play a role (Morin et al., 2018). Moreover, institutions have been observed to develop links with other institutions outside their policy domains. All of this suggests that the boundaries of global governance architectures or superclusters may be more porous than previously assumed (Kim & Morin, 2021, p. 29).

Kim and Morin (2021) introduce the concept of *supercluster complexes* to capture these developments and study them. Supercluster complexes are

---

[4] The original definition of global governance architectures, articulated by Biermann et al. in 2009, does not explicitly differentiate the framework of global governance architectures from that of regime complexes, and indeed, the two concepts describe very similar realities (Zelli & van Asselt, 2013, p. 6). Later, in 2020, Biermann and Kim highlighted that individual global governance architectures may consist of one or more regime complexes. In some cases, therefore, regime complexes and global governance architectures would overlap; in others, a global governance architecture could contain multiple regime complexes. The level of analysis employed by both frameworks, nevertheless, is relatively similar, remaining above the level of regimes and individual institutions, and under the overarching level of global order.

defined as "massive institutional structures", the "largest known institutional structures before considering global governance as a whole, with all its policy domains". They consist of "two or more interlocking governance superclusters that exert a measurable influence on each other's course of development" (Kim & Morin, 2021, p. 29). To probe their existence, Kim and Morin study the trade and environment governance architectures through a network of networks approach, based on citations between international agreements as a proxy. In doing so, they identify the contours of a supercluster complex in which trade and environment are embedded.

The authors thus hypothesize that we may be experiencing a gradual convergence of at least some superclusters. This suggests a wider finding for global governance: that institutional proliferation may not necessarily be leading to greater fragmentation. Instead, it may be giving rise to some sort of flexible, polycentric order across policy domains. Through the introduction of a new framework, therefore, Kim and Morin (2021) push for a new frontier in research on global governance, studying the emergence, consequences, and policy implications of supercluster complexes.

2.4 Different Frameworks, Similar Research Objectives

The frameworks outlined above were all conceived to study the same level of global governance: the meso-level, where clusters of institutions govern one or more related issues. Their unit of analysis therefore lies between the micro-level, which comprises individual institutions, and the macro-level, which covers global governance as a whole, or the global order. Targeting this meso-level allowed researchers to begin teasing out the effects of the structural context and to overcome the premise that individual institutions are developed or operate in a vacuum.

Why then, do so many different frameworks – including, but not limited to, the five described previously – exist to study the same meso-level? In some cases, new frameworks were developed to remedy definitional issues related to preceding ones: this is arguably the case for global governance complexes. In others, frameworks were created in parallel, as scholars focused on specific aspects of global governance complexity: the lens of global governance architectures, for example, was developed in the context of research on fragmentation. And yet in other cases, the frameworks explicitly define complexes with specific characteristics or scales: hybrid institutional complexes, for instance, can only describe collections of highly diverse institutions working on an issue area (see Figure 5.1); whereas supercluster complexes have a larger scope, spanning multiple issue areas, by definition.

One key explanation for the sometimes-perplexing range of frameworks is the fact that there is still no common analytical framework to study the

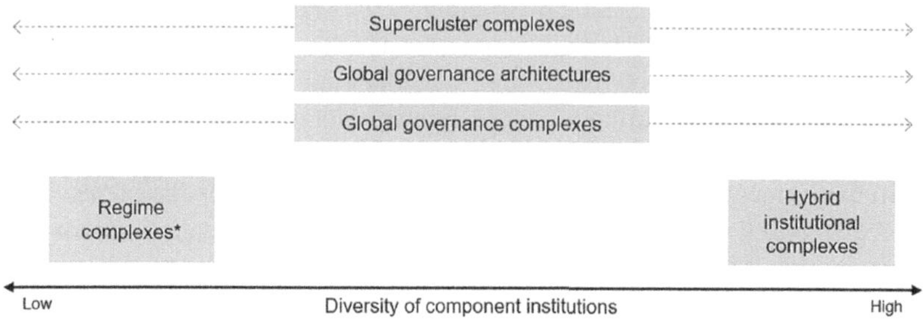

Note: * It is an object of extensive debate whether the low diversity of regime complexes derives from the definition of the framework or from reseach practice.
Source: Author's own elaboration.

Figure 5.1 Level of diversity among component institutions in the five frameworks

structural characteristics of the ecosystem of global governance institutions (Abbott et al., 2016; Kim, 2020).[5] Nevertheless, after two decades of research, a trendline is arguably emerging: scholars are defining existing and new frameworks more comprehensively, and to some extent, in a more neutral or commensurable fashion. See Section 4 for a discussion of this direction of travel.

Regardless of the framework they use, scholars in this field share an interest in improving the understanding of the origins, shape, evolution, and effectiveness of global governance through complexes of institutions. To do so, in essence, they take a similar approach. First, they identify the governance issue (or issues, in the case of supercluster complexes) that is or needs to be addressed. Second, they identify the units – institutions – that compose the complex governing this area. When identifying these units, they typically study both the number of institutions that are active ("scale", as termed by Eilstrup-Sangiovanni & Westerwinter (2022)), and the diversity among them. Importantly, scholars of complexes of global governance institutions analyze these units as a set, rather than as individual institutions (Gómez-Mera et al., 2020). Third, scholars research how the institutions are connected. The main questions are: to what extent do the institutions overlap, or are they disconnected (which is sometimes discussed through the lenses of fragmentation,

5 Kim (2020) reviews research based on the concepts of fragmentation, polycentricity, and complexity, arguing that these concepts were imported from other fields to study the meso-level of global governance, but that each came with their own assumptions and biases.

integration, or differentiation); and what authority relations (sometimes termed hierarchy, or order) exist among them? From this point on, some scholars go on to study, for example, the effectiveness of global governance through these configurations, or how these complexes evolve and why they follow a certain trajectory over time. This final critical point – evolution – is discussed in the next section.

3. ANALYZING EVOLUTION IN COMPLEXES OF GLOBAL GOVERNANCE INSTITUTIONS

When global governance takes place through complexes of institutions, it is marked by an important feature: instability and a resultant tendency towards further evolution (Abbott et al., 2016). As Raustiala and Victor (2004, p. 280) originally argued, this is due to "inconsistency at the 'joints'" between institutions. Moreover, whatever evolution takes place will necessarily be path-dependent to some extent, given the institutional structure that is already in place. Over the past two decades, the evolution of regime complexes has become the object of important research. This section examines the drivers and processes of evolution first, focusing on contextual and structural drivers that spark evolutionary processes on the one hand, and models that aim to explain institutional choices in a context of complexity on the other. It then turns to the results of these processes, covering implications for institutional proliferation or consolidation, as well as recent findings regarding patterns of evolution in global governance complexes.

Once a complex of global governance institutions exists, what contextual or structural factors may incentivize its evolution? First, exogenous contextual trends that lie at the origins of global governance complexity (including globalization, new technologies, new actors relying on decreased organizational costs, and a shifting interstate power balance) remain in place once a regime complex has been established and can therefore continue to spark evolution. Second, the (understanding of a) governance problem can change, sparking the need for a concurrent change in its governance. Third, the shape of the global governance complex itself can generate pressures that stimulate evolution.

Locking into this final point, Henning and Pratt (2023) focus on structural features. They posit that regime complexes that are more fragmented (that is, where the levels of hierarchy and differentiation are low – a characteristic inherent to younger regime complexes) will be fundamentally competitive, which sparks further evolution. Abbott et al. (2016) and Morin (2020), meanwhile, have worked at the level of populations of organizations, drawing on theories of organizational ecology. According to these streams, when organizational density increases, resource scarcity ensues. This scarcity, in turn, can incentivize changes in (and in between) populations of organizations. Certain populations, for example, may specialize in niches, thereby ultimately reducing functional overlap in the complex. Finally, Eilstrup-Sangiovanni (2022) highlights that institutional overlap within regime complexes may lead to undesired consequences – and this may drive certain actors to actions that change the complex further. For the principals of the institutions caught up in the overlap, additional administrative burden may ensue; and for international organizations themselves, the overlap can increase competition for scarce resources.

Multiple contextual, issue-based, and structural drivers can thus incentivize evolution within global governance complexes. But endogenous institutional choices made by states and other actors can also lead the complex to evolve. These institutional choices may be linked to the contextual and structural factors described earlier or motivated by other factors. The following paragraphs examine how states and other actors take existing regime complexes into consideration when creating new institutions (or reforming and even dissolving existing ones).

Jupille et al. (2013) propose a theory of boundedly rational institutional choice, bringing together rationalist and historical institutionalist streams, to analyze what drives states in their choices to create new institutions, modify existing ones, or retain the status quo (and by extension, modify a regime or regime complex). This theory holds that in the absence of full information, and taking into account the existing institutional architecture, states are unlikely to create new institutions to address a governance problem. Before generating a new institution (with the high costs this implies), they will display "satisficing" behavior and consider all other options first, choosing the least costly one that provides sufficient benefits. This implies running through a choice ladder of using an existing focal institution directly, selecting among different existing institutions, or changing a present institution – all before deciding to create a new one.

Colgan et al. (2012) also consider satisficing behavior and path dependency when explaining change in a regime complex. According to their model, change will only take place when states are sufficiently dissatisfied with the status quo – and when dissatisfaction is high enough, the shape of the innovation in the regime complex will be determined by the level of homogeneity of preferences among major actors (states) in the complex. If solution preferences are relatively homogeneous, path-dependent innovation is expected – for example, through reform of an existing institution. If they are heterogeneous, however, this can either lead to gridlock and therefore no innovation; or *de novo* innovation – for example, the creation of a new institution. State dissatisfaction is also at the heart of the power-based argument put forward by Pratt (2021), who argues that states dissatisfied with their level of representation at existing institutions may create new institutions to gain control – despite the rule inconsistency this can generate. In this context, more recently, scholars have noted that states may also choose to establish informal intergovernmental organizations (Roger, 2020) and other low-cost institutions[6] (Abbott & Faude, 2021; Westerwinter et al., 2021) rather than classic formal intergovernmental institutions. Low-cost institutions may offer distinct benefits to pursue global governance strategies, such as lower transaction and coordination costs between the actors involved.

Yet it is not only states that can make active choices that shape the evolution of a regime complex. Eilstrup-Sangiovanni (2022), for example, builds a hypothesis that when institutional density is on the rise, and states choose not to engage in a top-down restructuring of the complex, international organizations and bureaucrats may drive a process of bottom-up adaptation. In this process, organizations may actively seek niches to avoid competition and therefore specialize in particular tasks and functions (see also Abbott et al., 2016; Morin, 2020). Organizations and the bureaucrats that manage them could also, however, pursue task expansion more aggressively, to capture a share of other organizations' resources or take a more cooperative approach, exchanging and pooling resources among themselves to adapt to resource scarcity.

Many of the theories above can clarify why states create new institutions. Overall, this may lead to the impression that states tend to foster institutional *proliferation* and possibly fragmentation – but research from multiple theoretical streams reveals a more intricate reality. Johnson and Urpelainen (2012), for instance, created a testable theory based on spillovers. According to their functional theory, which is supported by empirical analysis, states will choose to integrate or separate regimes depending on whether spillovers between those regimes are negative or positive. When a spillover is negative – that is, when cooperation in one issue area hinders governance in another – states will work to integrate regimes. However, when it is positive – when cooperating in one issue area simultaneously advances outcomes in another – states do not actively seek further integration. The authors point to a trade-off to explain this choice: when regimes are separate, subgroups of states choose to invest fully in the "pet projects" of their preference (Johnson & Urpelainen, 2012, p. 672). This situation leads, collectively, to larger benefits for all states than an integrated regime – where all states would be forced to invest in multiple projects and might be more hesitant to do so.

---

[6] Abbott and Faude (2021, p. 399) introduced the term low-cost institutions to refer to a common class of diverse institutional forms, including informal intergovernmental organizations, transgovernmental networks, and transnational public–private partnerships. The authors treat these diverse organizational types as a group, in juxtaposition to treaty-based institutions, to enhance the theoretical parsimony and generalizability of research on these institutions.

Recent research has pointed to further drivers of regime complex *consolidation* or defragmentation. According to Eilstrup-Sangiovanni (2022), states may choose to restructure regime complexes when increasing density and overlap generate excessive governance costs. At that point, the principals can engage in a top-down process, for example, by dissolving existing institutions or creating cross-cutting institutions for coordination. Another route to defragmentation is contextual design: when principals add new institutions, they may consider the existing institutional landscape, making design choices that avoid conflictual overlap (Reinsberg & Westerwinter, 2019). These outcomes are more likely when state preferences align. Recently, Kim and Morin (2021) also detected a trend towards integration, driven by a multitude of uncoordinated and microscopic efforts to coordinate institutions and mitigate negative spillovers between policy domains (p. 39). In their empirical research on the trade and environment superclusters, they identified new institutions that were generated with cross-domain links.

Scholars have furthermore produced findings on major patterns in the evolution of complexes of global governance institutions. Rather than evolving along a smooth, gradual path, complexes often display patterns of "punctuated equilibrium" (Krasner, 1984), where periods of stasis are followed by periods of innovation and change. Exogenous shocks or dissatisfaction among sets of principals can determine the moments of change between periods (Colgan et al., 2012; Eilstrup-Sangiovanni, 2022). In the case of global energy governance, for instance, Colgan et al. (2012) argued that dissatisfaction with oil prices led to innovation within the regime complex. Relatedly, Manulak (2023) has investigated the role of so-called "temporal focal points": at these key moments for global governance complexes, a significant number of institutional changes take place in a brief and intense burst, leading to the realization of accumulated incentives for change.

Research has additionally shown that, rather than evolving linearly in a single direction, complexes of institutions tend to fluctuate over time. Building on an empirical study of the governance of health, labor, and technical standards, for example, Grigorescu (2020) demonstrates that global governance of particular issue areas ebbs and flows between intergovernmentalism and non-governmentalism.[7] Similarly, the global governance complex for civil aviation has been demonstrated to vary between order and disorder (Eilstrup-Sangiovanni, 2022).

---

[7] He finds that the domestic preferences of powerful states are important determinants of the direction of the flow: when powerful states increase their domestic activism, intergovernmentalism increases (Grigorescu, 2020).

In spite of the recurrent fluctuations described above, scholars have recently argued that the long-term, overall trend in global governance complexity is towards more stability and less fragmentation. Henning and Pratt (2023), for example, posit that following the Cold War, regime complexes working on new issues initially take on a fragmented shape, displaying low hierarchy and low differentiation. However, given the inherent competition within these fragmented architectures, they expect these regime complexes to evolve towards stronger hierarchy and/or differentiation over time. Similarly, drawing on findings from network analysis, Kim (2020, p. 913) states that the general long-term trend in global governance is towards defragmentation. Finally, Kim and Morin's (2021) findings on the trade-environment supercluster complex suggest that the idea of global governance being highly fragmented may not hold as true as expected.

4. CONCLUSION: DIRECTION OF TRAVEL

Today, most issues are governed through complexes of international institutions, as opposed to the monolithic multilateral organizations that emerged just after World War II.[8] Following the Cold War, global governance institutions proliferated, leading to increasing density. Simultaneously, diversity increased as well, with the institutional landscape broadening to include institutions with differing membership types (private, public and hybrid) and levels of formality.

Two decades ago, scholars began to examine global governance on the level of institutional configurations rather than single institutions, initially termed regime complexes (Raustiala & Victor, 2004). The research stream has been prolific and has offered important insights into how complexes of global governance institutions operate. Collectively, this scholarship has contributed to what some call a "structural theory of global governance" (Biermann & Kim, 2020; Kim & Morin, 2021), which considers individual institutions in their wider context and reflects on the origins and effects of these structural contexts. The now-extensive research in this field incorporates insights from different disciplines, including international law, international relations, public administration theory, and complexity science. A wide range of frameworks have furthermore been applied in interpretative efforts, including functional, structural, organizational, principal–agent and power-based theories. Yet 20 years on, there is still no single common theoretical framework to study complexes of global governance institutions (Gómez-Mera et al., 2020; Kim,

---

8 For a more nuanced assessment of this pattern, see Grigorescu (2020).

2020; Kim & Morin, 2021).[9] In addition, some highlight that while the study of institutional density has advanced, research continues to lag when it comes to truly considering the full spectrum of institutional diversity (Abbott & Faude, 2022).[10]

In recent years, however, three clear trends have emerged in the study of global governance complexity. First, attention to diversity is visibly increasing (Abbott et al., 2016; Abbott & Faude, 2021, 2022). Second, there is a strong push to move past the conceptual disagreements that have to some extent dominated the field in the past. Recent contributions have proposed concepts and frameworks that are more "neutral", and therefore able to capture the full scope of complexes of global governance institutions through clear and commeasurable dimensions (examples include global governance complexes (Eilstrup-Sangiovanni & Westerwinter, 2022) and a recent redefinition of regime complexes (Henning & Pratt, 2023)). Third, and relatedly, an effort is underway to create general theoretical frameworks with robust explanatory power (Alter, 2022; Eilstrup-Sangiovanni & Westerwinter, 2022; Henning & Pratt, 2023; Kim, 2020). After two decades of productive scholarship on the most prevalent shape of global governance today, this research field therefore continues to hold significant promise for further study.

REFERENCES

Abbott, K. W., & Faude, B. (2021). Choosing low-cost institutions in global governance. *International Theory*, *13*, 397–426.

Abbott, K. W., & Faude, B. (2022). Hybrid institutional complexes in global governance. *The Review of International Organizations*, *17*, 263–291.

Abbott, K. W., Green, J. F., & Keohane, R. O. (2016). Organizational ecology and institutional change in global governance. *International Organization*, *70*(2), 247–277.

Alter, K. J. (2022). The promise and perils of theorizing international regime complexity in an evolving world. *Review of International Organizations*, *17*(2), 375–396.

Alter, K. J., & Meunier, S. (2009). The politics of international regime complexity. *Perspectives on Politics*, *7*(1), 13–24.

Alter, K. J., & Raustiala, K. (2018). The rise of international regime complexity. *Annual Review of Law and Social Science*, *14*, 329–349.

Biermann, F., & Kim, R. E. (2020). Architectures of earth system governance. In *Architectures of Earth System Governance* (pp. 1–34). Cambridge University Press.

---

[9] This is partially evidenced by the discussion of frameworks in Section 2 of this chapter.

[10] In part, this may be due to what Alter (2022, p. 389) calls "measurement predilection": the inclination to study what can more easily be measured – in this case, formal state-based institutions.

Biermann, F., Pattberg, P., van Asselt, H., & Zelli, F. (2009). The fragmentation of global governance architectures: A framework for analysis. *Global Environmental Politics*, *9*(4), 14–40.

Colgan, J. D., Keohane, R. O., & van de Graaf, T. (2012). Punctuated equilibrium in the energy regime complex. *Review of International Organizations*, *7*(2), 117–143.

Drezner, D. W. (2009). The power and peril of international regime complexity. *Perspectives on Politics*, *7*(1), 65–70.

Eilstrup-Sangiovanni, M. (2022). Ordering global governance complexes: The evolution of the governance complex for international civil aviation. *Review of International Organizations*, *17*, 293–322.

Eilstrup-Sangiovanni, M., & Westerwinter, O. (2022). The global governance complexity cube: Varieties of institutional complexity in global governance. *The Review of International Organizations*, *17*, 233–262.

Gehring, T., & Faude, B. (2013). The dynamics of regime complexes: Microfoundations and systemic effects. *Global Governance*, *19*(1), 119–130.

Gómez-Mera, L. (2015). International regime complexity and regional governance: Evidence from the Americas. *Global Governance*, *21*, 19–42.

Gómez-Mera, L., Morin, J.-F., & Van De Graaf, T. (2020). Regime complexes. In F. Biermann & R. E. Kim (Eds.), *Architectures of Earth System Governance: Institutional Complexity and Structural Transformation* (pp. 133–157). Cambridge University Press.

Grigorescu, A. (2020). *The Ebb and Flow of Global Governance: Intergovernmentalism Versus Nongovernmentalism in World Politics*. Cambridge University Press.

Hafner-Burton, E. M. (2009). The power politics of regime complexity: Human rights trade conditionality in Europe. *Source: Perspectives on Politics*, *7*(1), 33–37.

Henning, C. R., & Pratt, T. (2023). Hierarchy and differentiation in international regime complexes: A theoretical framework for comparative research. *Review of International Political Economy*, *30*(6), 2178–2205.

Johnson, T., & Urpelainen, J. (2012). A strategic theory of regime integration and separation. *International Organization*, *66*, 645–677.

Jordan, A., Huitema, D., van Asselt, H., & Forster, J. (Eds.). (2018*). Governing Climate Change: Polycentricity in Action?* Cambridge University Press.

Jordana, J., Holesch, A., & Triviño-Salazar, J. C. (2022). Trans-governmental regulatory networks and the European Union's involvement in global governance: An occasional instrument? *Journal of European Integration*, *44*(5), 677–693.

Jupille, J., Mattli, W., & Snidal, D. (2013). *Institutional Choice and Global Commerce*. Cambridge University Press.

Kahler, M. (2020). The arc of complex global governance. From organization to coalition. *APSA Annual Meetings, 10–13 September.*

Keck, M. E., & Sikkink, K. (1998). *Activists Beyond Borders: Advocacy Networks in International Politics*. Cornell University Press.

Keohane, R. O., & Victor, D. G. (2011). The regime complex for climate change. *Perspectives on Politics*, *9*(1), 7–23.

Kim, R. E. (2020). Is global governance fragmented, polycentric, or complex? The state of the art of the network approach. *International Studies Review*, *22*(4), 903–931.

Kim, R. E., & Morin, J. F. (2021). Massive institutional structures in global governance. *Global Environmental Politics*, *21*(3), 26–48.

Koskenniemi, M. (2007). The fate of public international law: Between technique and politics. *Modern Law Review*, *70*(1), 1–30.

Krasner, S. D. (1984). Approaches to the state: Alternative conceptions and historical dynamics. *Politics*, *16*(2), 223–246.

Manulak, M. W. (2023). *Change in Global Environmental Politics: Temporal Focal Points and the Reform of International Institutions*. Cambridge University Press.

Marx, A., & Westerwinter, O. (2022). An ever more entangled Union? The European Union's interactions with global governance institutions. *Journal of European Integration*, *44*(5), 597–615.

Mikler, J. (2018). *The Political Power of Global Corporations*. Polity Press.

Morin, J. F. (2020). Concentration despite competition: The organizational ecology of technical assistance providers. *Review of International Organizations*, *15*(1), 75–107.

Morin, J. F., Dür, A., & Lechner, L. (2018). Mapping the trade and environment nexus: Insights from a new data set. *Global Environmental Politics*, *18*(1), 122–139.

Morse, J. C., & Keohane, R. O. (2014). Contested multilateralism. *Review of International Organizations*, *9*(4), 385–412.

Oberthür, S., & Pozarowska, J. (2013). Managing institutional complexity and fragmentation: The Nagoya Protocol and the global governance of genetic resources. *Global Environmental Politics*, *13*(3), 100–118.

Orsini, A., Morin, J.-F., & Young, O. (2013). Regime complexes: A buzz, a boom, or a boost for global governance? *Global Governance*, *19*(1), 27–39.

Powell, W. M. (1990). Neither market nor hierarchy: Network forms of organization. *Research in Organizational Behavior*, *12*, 295–336.

Pratt, T. (2021). Angling for influence: Institutional proliferation in development banking. *International Studies Quarterly*, *65*(1), 95–108.

Raustiala, K., & Victor, D. G. (2004). The regime complex for plant genetic resources. *International Organization*, *58*(2), 277–309.

Reinsberg, B., & Westerwinter, O. (2019). The global governance of international development: Documenting the rise of multi-stakeholder partnerships and identifying underlying theoretical explanations. *The Review of International Organizations*, *16*, 59–94.

Roger, C. (2020). *The Origins of Informality: Why the Legal Foundations of Global Governance Are Shifting, and Why it Matters*. Oxford University Press.

Vabulas, F., & Snidal, D. (2013). Organization without delegation: Informal intergovernmental organizations (IIGOs) and the spectrum of intergovernmental arrangements. *Review of International Organizations*, *8*(2), 193–220.

Westerwinter, O. (2021). Transnational public–private governance initiatives in world politics: Introducing a new dataset. *The Review of International Organizations*, *16*(1), 137–174.

Westerwinter, O., Abbott, K. W., & Biersteker, T. (2021). Informal governance in world politics. *The Review of International Organizations*, *16*(1), 1–27.

Williamson, O. E. (1975). *Markets and Hierarchies: Analysis and Antitrust Implications*. Macmillan Publishers.

Zelli, F., & van Asselt, H. (2013). Introduction. The institutional fragmentation of global environmental governance: Causes, consequences, and responses. *Global Environmental Politics*, *13*(3), 1–13.

PART II

Sector-specific analysis

6. Global cybersecurity governance: a hallmark of heterogeneity?

Marie Vandendriessche

1. INTRODUCTION[1]

According to the International Telecommunications Union (2023), nearly 70% of the world's population currently use the internet. Internet connections form the backbone of the contemporary global economy, facilitating trade, travel, energy systems, education, (government) services, and many other pillars of economic systems. With this connectivity, however, come cybersecurity risks, such as viruses, data breaches, and cyberattacks on physical infrastructure. Prominent examples include the Stuxnet virus physically disrupting Iran's nuclear centrifuge programme in 2010 (Nye, 2017, p. 48), interruptions to the power distribution systems in Ukraine starting from 2015 (DeNardis, 2020, p. 5), and scores of ransomware attacks – some on critical infrastructure, such as the cyberattack on the Colonial oil pipeline in the US in 2021.

While governance of the internet and its predecessors commenced more than half a century ago (initially in a light-touch, technical mode), efforts to govern cybersecurity developed more recently. As such, cybersecurity – a subdomain of internet governance – constitutes one of the newer areas of global governance. Over the past three decades, this field has become fiercely contentious, and institutions of many different types have become involved. The resulting configuration of institutions has been termed a 'hybrid institutional complex'

[1] This chapter builds partially on research conducted in the context of the GLOBE project, including an original dataset on global cybersecurity governance and a working paper related to this dataset (Kouliopoulos et al., 2020). Excellent data collection and research assistance was provided by Athanasios Kouliopoulos, Anna Fonts Picas, Clara Martén, Cristina de Esperanza and Laia Serrano i Sorroca. The author would also like to acknowledge Andreas Dür and Markus Gastinger, organisers of the *Workshop on International Organizations Beyond IGOs* (Paris Lodron University of Salzburg, Austria, September 9, 2022), as well as the workshop participants, for helpful suggestions on research in progress.

(Abbott & Faude, 2022), that is, a complex marked by a high level of diversity in membership, legal shape, and authority. Complexes of this hybrid type are highly prevalent in contemporary global governance (see also Chapter 5 in this book), meaning that cybersecurity is to some extent demonstrative of how most global problems are governed today.

This chapter begins by discussing cybersecurity as a governance problem. Thereafter, it provides a systematic overview of the global governance of cybersecurity. First, the chapter builds on secondary literature to describe how internet and cybersecurity governance developed over the past three decades, focusing on specific organisations and institutional forms that have been active over time. Second, the chapter draws on primary empirical data to provide a meso-level analysis of the global governance complex for cybersecurity. This exploration provides insights on the overarching characteristics of the complex, the institutions that populate it, and their diversity. A conclusion draws both strands together.

2. CYBERSECURITY AS A GOVERNANCE PROBLEM

The first instance of networked package-switching[2] computers can be traced back to 1969, when researchers at UCLA tried to log into a computer at Stanford (Singer & Friedman, 2014, pp. 16–17). The effort was part of a project named ARPANET, funded by the US Department of Defense, whose initial aim was to allow academics to make use of idle computers across the USA at a moment when demand for computer time at many universities exceeded supply (Abbate, 2000, p. 37; Singer & Friedman, 2014, p. 17). This connection constitutes the world's first steps into the internet and cyberspace era (Nye, 2014, p. 5).

For two decades following the initial connection, the internet was primarily used for academic and non-commercial purposes. In the 1980s, the for-profit sector in the US began to take an interest. Still, it took until 1990 for a researcher at CERN in Switzerland to create a new networking interface combining a HyperText Transfer Protocol (HTTP) and URLs (a complementary system to identify the associated documents), thereby 'inventing' the world wide web as we know it today (Nye, 2014, p. 5; Singer & Friedman, 2014, p. 20). These steps, coupled with other inventions – including web browsers – ultimately led to the popularisation of the internet.

[2] Package-switching refers to the exchange of small 'envelopes of data'. This differs from earlier telegraph and telephone networks, which operated based on circuit-switching (Singer & Friedman, 2014, p. 17).

In 1988, the internet was exposed to its first worm, but reactions to this initial security breach were relatively muted.[3] According to Zittrain (2008, p. 42), the mildness of this response can be ascribed to the ethos of the community that originally developed the internet. The internet was intentionally designed as an open network that could be accessed and further contributed to by third parties – the underlying assumption was that those third parties would operate with benign intentions.[4] For the first few decades, this assumption largely held, as internet usage was confined to academic and non-commercial spheres. It was in the transition from the research use-dominated beginnings of the internet to its privatisation and popularisation that cyber risks increased in frequency and in significance (Nye, 2014, p. 6).

While some cyberattacks thus took place in the late 1980s and early 1990s, it was not until the mid-1990s and particularly the twenty-first century that concern about these threats escalated (DeNardis, 2014, p. 88; Dunn Cavelty, 2008, p. 2; Maurer, 2011; Stiennon, 2015, p. 9). Today, cybersecurity is a pervasive concern for both private and public actors. It is a multifaceted problem (Abbott & Faude, 2022; Finnemore & Hollis, 2016, p. 427; Nye, 2014) that never ceases to evolve as global levels of connectivity continue to increase (Dunn Cavelty, 2014; Verhelst & Wouters, 2020).

As attention to cybersecurity has grown, so has interest in its governance. It is important, at this point, to shed light on the relation between internet governance and cybersecurity governance. Ever since the days of ARPANET in the late 1960s, the internet and its predecessors have been subjected to some form of governance: for many years, engineers and private actors coordinated the distribution of domain names and established standards for interoperability

[3] The Morris worm, launched by a Cornell University graduate student, infected 5–10% of all machines with an internet connection at the time; however, it did not affect the data or information contained in the devices (DeNardis, 2014, pp. 88–89; Zittrain, 2008, p. 37). The episode led to a brief reaction in the mainstream media and to the establishment of the first computer emergency response team (CERT) at Carnegie Mellon University (DeNardis, 2014, pp. 89–90). Yet much of the technical community developing the internet were unworried and regarded the worm as a 'fun challenge' to solve – a curiosity, rather 'than a call to arms' (Zittrain, 2008, pp. 38–39).

[4] The internet was built as a 'generative system' that was purposefully incomplete and open to third-party contributions (Zittrain, 2008, pp. 26–35). The reasons for this flexible design were twofold: on the one hand, it was assumed that problems in the network could be solved later and possibly by others; and on the other, it was presumed that users and designers of the network could be trusted to modify it with a benign intent only (Zittrain, 2008, p. 31). In other words, the internet's basic design was based on trust, and focused on providing fertile terrain for innovation, rather than security.

between devices, among others (DeNardis, 2014, p. 18). Despite the pre-existence of this governance in *practice*, however, the *term* 'internet governance' did not come into widespread usage until the 1990s (DeNardis, 2014, p. 18; Hofmann et al., 2017). This timing was no coincidence: internet governance came under greater scrutiny from the moment internet adoption started to spread vertiginously, and as its commercialisation accelerated[5] (Bradshaw et al., 2015, pp. 8–9; DeNardis, 2014, p. 222).

In 2005, *internet governance* was defined by the UN World Summit on the Information Society as 'the development and application … of shared principles, norms, rules, decision-making procedures and programmes that shape the evolution and use of the Internet' (WGIG, 2005). This extensively used definition is broad, focusing on all aspects that keep the internet and internet-connected world operational (DeNardis, 2014, p. 6; Mueller, 2017, p. 415; Raymond & DeNardis, 2015; van Eeten & Mueller, 2012, p. 721). *Cybersecurity governance*, in contrast, captured the attention of policymakers and academics slightly later than internet governance. It arguably has a narrower scope (Raymond & DeNardis, 2015, p. 588), and as per the Working Group on Internet Governance (WGIG) definition mentioned above, it is a subdomain of internet governance (Mueller, 2017, pp. 415–416).

However, the scope of cybersecurity as a governance problem is disputed (Futter, 2018; Urgessa, 2020). Some argue that the choice between terms is a question of framing, with internet governance being used primarily by a civilian transnational community; and cybersecurity being invoked by actors focusing on national security, geopolitics and conflicts between nation-states (Mueller, 2017, p. 417). Others find that in recent decades, the use of the term cybersecurity has eclipsed internet governance, even though discussions under the *label* cybersecurity often in fact cover the *substance* of internet governance (Mueller, 2017; van Eeten & Mueller, 2012, p. 727). Definitions of cybersecurity furthermore vary as to whether protection of the referent object extends

---

5 As Bradshaw et al. (2015, p. 8–9) explain, during the period where the internet was used primarily for academic and non-commercial purposes, its governance was primarily technocratic, and the issues that required attention were relatively simple coordination problems with limited distributional concerns. From the 1990s on, when internet usage and connectivity became more widespread, many of these coordination problems were exacerbated, partially because the number of players increased while the homogeneity between them decreased. In addition, cooperation problems – where parties have incentives to cheat – began to emerge. Contention thus increased, and concern about internet and cybersecurity governance grew. Bradshaw et al. (2015, p. 9) furthermore highlight that cooperation problems are the clearest when it comes to state security, for example the acquisition of offensive cyber capabilities.

only to information *technologies* (see, for example, Finnemore & Hollis, 2016, p. 431), or beyond this, to the entities or persons *impacted* by cybersecurity issues or breaches (von Solms & van Niekerk, 2013).

In this chapter, cybersecurity governance will be considered a subdomain of internet governance (following DeNardis, 2014, p. 88; Mueller, 2010; Pernice, 2018, p. 133; Raymond & DeNardis, 2015, p. 588; and WGIG, 2005, among others) that focuses on protecting networks, computers, programs and data from unauthorised access and breaches of confidentiality, integrity and availability (Kouliopoulos et al., 2020, p. 11). The next section draws on secondary literature to trace the development of internet and cybersecurity governance over time.

3. THE DEVELOPMENT OF GLOBAL CYBERSECURITY GOVERNANCE

3.1 Technical, Transnational and Private-Led Beginnings

As discussed above, in its first decades, the internet was predominantly used by academics and for non-commercial purposes. It was organised through principles of open access so that local information networks could link with the global infrastructure, and to provide space for continuous development of the network (Bradshaw et al., 2015, p. 13; Farrell & Newman, 2021, p. 336; Zittrain, 2008, pp. 26–35). Some forms of light-touch, technical governance of the internet and its predecessors already existed from 1969 onwards. But it was not until the 1990s – a period in which information technology and flows continued to mature and spread, and cyber risks gradually began to grow – that interest in internet governance, and slightly later, cybersecurity governance, began to grow.

At the outset, internet and cybersecurity governance did not emerge within existing or new multilateral bodies like the International Telecommunications Union (ITU), the United Nations' specialised agency for information and communication technologies. Instead, it was initially US-based (reflecting, in part, the US' involvement in the early development of the internet in the 1970s (Hofmann & Pawlak, 2023, p. 2131)) and private actor-led.[6] Emblematically, the internet's domain name system was regulated by a private non-profit organisation established under Californian law: the Internet Corporation for

[6] According to Hofmann et al. (2017, p. 1408), the initial governance model for the internet matched the 'regulatory zeitgeist' of the late 1990s, which favoured self-regulation by markets over public command-and-control models.

Assigned Names and Numbers (ICANN), created in 1998 (Farrell & Newman, 2021, p. 336).

3.2 The Role of States and Formal Intergovernmental Organisations

In the 2000s, this bottom-up, private-led governance model came under increasing scrutiny. On the one hand, the implosion of the dot-com bubble led to calls for stronger regulation (Flonk et al., 2020, p. 369). On the other hand, cleavages between the preferences of states – and, relatedly, the policy frames they employed (Hofmann & Pawlak, 2023) – spilled into the open. Conflicts over norms and institutions ensued. These cleavages are variably labelled as a split between liberals and sovereigntists (Flonk et al., 2020), liberal and illiberal states (Farrell & Newman, 2021), or state preferences for either multistakeholderism or multilateralism (Chen & Yang, 2022).

The crux of the debate relates to the role of states and state sovereignty. One side supports a largely bottom-up, transnational governance model including a diversity of different actors (including private ones), with a smaller role for the state, while the other prefers a more intergovernmental model with strong involvement of the state and a smaller role for private actors. The coalitions of states supporting either side are neither completely monolithic, nor are state preferences on either side of the divide wholly aligned or fixed in time. Traditionally, however, the US leads the first camp, which the EU is also a part of – though its views are not always entirely aligned with the US'; Russia and China fall within the second camp.[7]

[7] The situation is of course more complex than a simple dichotomy. Hofmann and Pawlak (2023), for example, highlight differences between the policy frames of the US (preferring a multistakeholder approach to ensure technological and political stability for the internet – an engine of economic growth – while retaining control over the internet's critical resources), the EU (taking a human-centric approach to regulation to protect competitiveness, security, economic growth and human rights), Russia (highlighting an information security frame and sovereignty to ensure control over the security of its information infrastructure), China (aiming to conserve sovereignty in cyberspace in function of order, social stability, and regime legitimacy), and India, Brazil and South Africa (stressing the internet's potential to boost human development and reduce poverty while simultaneously emphasising the importance of sovereignty, human rights protection, and the multistakeholder model). Chen and Yang (2022) also point to the importance of pushing past a pure West versus non-West dichotomy, focusing on regional cyber governance models by the EU and ASEAN.

This divide was highly visible during a series of summits in the early 2000s. Following a proposal made by the ITU within the UN system in 1998,[8] a first World Summit on the Information Society (WSIS) took place in Geneva in 2003 (Klein, 2004). At and before this summit, a group of states and civil society organisations challenged the central role of ICANN and the US dominance over this critical piece of the governance architecture. Furthermore, the multilateralist camp tried to shift internet and cybersecurity governance to formal intergovernmental organisations at the global level – the ITU, in particular. Many of these states also pushed for an understanding of internet governance that was broader than its purely technical origins. When the disagreements proved too thorny to overcome at the 2003 WSIS (Kleinwächter, 2004), a Working Group on Internet Governance was created to smooth the terrain.

In the end, 2005 saw the emergence of a compromise, which was reflected in a report by the WGIG and at the second WSIS in Tunis. First, the definition of internet governance was broadened from purely technical aspects to include many other policy domains, including content regulation and cybersecurity (Mueller, 2017, p. 416). Second, a multistakeholder model for internet governance was reaffirmed, legitimising the existing institutions and recognising the important roles of private actors and civil society. Yet at the same time, the Tunis Agenda confirmed that states retain sovereign rights over public policy in internet-related issues (Flonk et al., 2020, p. 373).

The role of the state in cybersecurity and its governance has remained a central question to this day. Two main points stand out: the responsibility of the state in the creation of cyber risks (such as cyberattacks) and the responses to them; and state control over information. When it comes to the first point, the late 2000s saw an increase in cyberattacks committed both by state and non-state entities (van Eeten, 2017, p. 430). In 2007 and 2008, respectively, for example, Estonia and Georgia experienced 'politically-motivated' Distributed Denial of Service (DDoS) cyberattacks (Georgieva, 2020, p. 38),[9] which most scholars signal as the start of the age of cyberwarfare (Stiennon, 2015, p. 16).[10]

---

[8] It was also in 1998 that cyber norms were first placed on the agenda of the First Committee of the United Nations General Assembly (Raymond, 2016, p. 123).

[9] In the case of Estonia, the massive cyberattacks against its banking, telecom and government infrastructure followed a government decision to move a statue of a Soviet soldier from the centre of Tallinn to the outskirts. In the case of Georgia, cyberattacks started the month before Russia's use of military force against the country, targeting Georgian networks, banks, and governmental websites (Stiennon, 2015, pp. 17–20).

[10] Stiennon (2015, p. 8) defines cyberwarfare as 'an extension of policy by actions taken in cyberspace by state actors (or by non-state actors with significant

In the same period, it also became evident that despite how critical cybersecurity was to the world's economies and services, nation-states' roles in incidence response were minimal at best (Mueller et al., 2013). The Conficker botnet incident of 2008–2009 was revealing: when malware was used to exploit a flaw in the Microsoft Windows operating system, the main line of response was generated by an ad-hoc virtual working group composed of individuals that 'happened to be responsible for some parts of the [i]nternet due to their professional roles … or voluntarily contributed their time independently of their occupational duties and roles' (Mueller et al., 2013, p. 96). From this moment on, governments began to increase their involvement in the networks of technical communities that handled cyber incident response (Greiman, 2015, p. 8).

Additionally, state control over information became a major point of contention around this period. On the one hand, when the 2013 Snowden revelations showed that the US had been leveraging its position of privilege to obtain information about its own citizens as well as citizens and governments around the world (Farrell & Newman, 2021, p. 345), it ignited calls for change in global cybersecurity governance – both by the 'sovereigntist' camp and from within the 'liberal' one. Brazil, for example, attempted to overhaul the US' dominance of the internet and cybersecurity governance by creating the NETmundial Initiative, a new multistakeholder governance forum (Flonk et al., 2020, p. 380). Meanwhile, the EU – in particular France and Germany – pushed for a restructuring of ICANN (Greiman, 2015, p. 7) away from the US' singular influence, which ultimately led to the US relinquishing its stewardship of the Internet Assigned Numbers Authority (IANA) in 2016 (Mueller, 2017, p. 417).

On the other hand, struggles persist over freedom of expression and information flows. China and Russia, for instance, strive to retain control over 'information security' at the domestic level (Hofmann & Pawlak, 2023, p. 2132). And at the international level, information techniques have been deployed for offensive purposes. Examples include hacking related to the 2016 US presidential election and Brexit referendum, as well as Russia-sponsored flooding and domestic disinformation campaigns in and related to Ukraine (Farrell & Newman, 2021, p. 348).

Divergent state views on information freedom and security have played out at the UN, among other fora. The UN's Governmental Group of Experts (GGE) on Advancing Responsible State Behaviour in Cyberspace in the

---

state direction or support) that constitute a serious threat to another state's security, or an action of the same nature taken in response to a serious threat to a state's security (actual or perceived)'.

Context of International Security,[11] for example, was established in 2004 and came together multiple times through to 2021. The GGE produced a landmark report in 2013, confirming agreement among states (including the US and China) that international law and the UN Charter in particular applied in cyberspace (Greiman, 2015, p. 1), and in 2015, a GGE report managed to introduce 11 voluntary principles on responsible state behaviour for an 'open, secure, stable, accessible and peaceful ICT environment' (Chen & Yang, 2022, p. 53). Yet consensus began to crumble from 2015 onwards. By 2018, a Russian initiative led to the establishment of a parallel UN working group, with an identical mandate to the GGE: the Open-Ended Working Group (OEWG) on Developments in the Field of ICTs in the Context of International Security.[12;13] Progress on these matters at the UN level remains rocky.

3.3 Regional Governance Initiatives

A great deal of media, policymaking and scholarly attention has gone towards the cybersecurity-related struggles and stalemates between nation-states in global multilateral institutions. In parallel, however, and partially in response to the gridlock at the UN level, global cybersecurity governance continued to develop through different institutional channels: regional and private, among others.

When it comes to regional governance, the EU was a frontrunner: already in 1990, the Commission of the European Communities published a proposal for a Council Decision in the field of information security, followed by a data protection directive (1995) and specific telecommunications and data privacy directive (1997) (Urgessa, 2020, p. 4). By 2004, the EU had set up its Agency for Network and Information Security (ENISA) (Pernice, 2018, p. 126), and

---

11 The group was originally named the UN GGE on Developments in the Field of Information and Telecommunications in the Context of International Security.

12 Though the US and EU initially opposed the OEWG, they ultimately engaged in it to defend some of the consensus points already adopted at the GGE (Hofmann & Pawlak, 2023, p. 2141).

13 The OEWG is due to be replaced in 2025 by a new and permanent regulatory dialogue at the UN: the Programme of Action (PoA) to Advance Responsible State Behaviour in the Use of Information and Communications Technologies in the Context of International Security. This initiative was proposed by France through a UN General Assembly resolution to avoid the OEWG becoming the only venue at the UN addressing cyberspace governance, with a predominance of the sovereignty policy frame. By highlighting cyber capacity-building as central in the PoA, developing countries were more inclined to lend their support to the proposal for this new body (Hofmann & Pawlak, 2023, p. 2142).

by 2013, it had developed a Cybersecurity Strategy. The EU has continued to expand its cybersecurity-related governance capacities since, including through a cyber diplomacy toolbox and a framework on countering hybrid threats (Pawlak & Biersteker, 2019, p. 31). Another regional actor of note is ASEAN, which has been engaging with cybersecurity through its various configurations since the mid-2000s, and which some argue might play a brokerage role between the US and Chinese approaches to cyber governance (Chen & Yang, 2022; Van Raemdonck, 2021).

Certain regional intergovernmental organisations have also generated legal initiatives, occasionally reaching beyond their original membership. In 2001, the Council of Europe developed the Budapest Convention on Cybercrime, the first international treaty on internet crimes. With 69 parties to date, including the US and 24 other non-members of the Council of Europe, the Convention is often seen as a model for harmonisation – yet it is far from universal, and has limitations in terms of applicability (Greiman, 2015, p. 6; Nguyen & Golman, 2021). In 2014, the African Union furthermore adopted a Convention on Cyber Security and Personal Data Protection (also known as the Malabo Convention), bringing together elements of electronic commerce, personal data protection, and the promotion of cybersecurity. Nevertheless, its ratification process has been slow, with Mauritania becoming the fifteenth state to ratify the convention in 2023, thereby finally allowing its entry into force.

3.4 (Self-)Regulation by Private Firms

Amid this fragmented global governance landscape, private regulation has also continued to develop, with an important role for self-regulation by large private firms (Raymond & DeNardis, 2015, p. 603). Farrell and Newman (2021) describe this as companies 'filling in the vacuum' in the face of the ITU's state of 'drift', by building private international orders (p. 345). Interestingly, this has meant that the true governance of transborder information flows was built by large private companies based primarily in US or Western countries – and thus again, *not* in so-called sovereigntist or illiberal states (Farrell & Newman, 2021, p. 345). In addition, this implies that the model of 'true multistakeholderism' affirmed by the 2005 WGIG report 'was increasingly confined to ICANN and technical standards, while self-regulation by firms provided most of the rest of the governance architecture' (Farrell & Newman, 2021, p. 345).

Yet with global governance at the interstate level remaining gridlocked, recent years have even seen private firms clamouring for or trying to generate multistakeholder governance initiatives of their own. One example is Microsoft's 2017 call to create a Digital Geneva Convention, which would bind governments to protect civilians from nation-state cyberattacks during peacetime – with active assistance by technology companies – and to avoid 'cyber-attacks that target the private sector or critical infrastructure or the use of hacking to steal intellectual property' (Smith, 2017). Mixed models have also started to emerge, such as the 2018 Paris Call for Trust and Security in Cyberspace, which is open to endorsement by both state and non-state actors, and aims to realign 'fragmented discussions of norms that have been scattered across multiple fora' (Eggenschwiler, 2019, p. 9).

4. GLOBAL CYBERSECURITY GOVERNANCE: A MAP OF THE COMPLEX

The developments described above have resulted in a hybrid institutional complex (Abbott & Faude, 2022) governing cybersecurity, comprising a multitude of institutions that are heterogenous in their membership, authority and legal base. The following section provides a meso-level analysis of this complex, based on a dataset initially built in the context of the Horizon 2020 project GLOBE.[14]

In this dataset, cybersecurity is defined as 'a set of technologies, processes and practices designed to protect networks, computers, programs and data from unauthorised access and breaches of confidentiality, integrity, and availability' (Kouliopoulos et al., 2020, p. 11). This definition closely follows Dunn Cavelty (2014, p. 702), but adds emphasis on the so-called CIA 'triangle' or 'triad' of confidentiality, integrity and availability, the three primordial objectives of security in an information environment (Singer & Friedman, 2014, pp. 35–36). When it comes to the debate on the referent object of cybersecurity (see Section 2), the dataset focuses on the security of processes, technologies and information, while remaining agnostic as to content-related matters (see also DeNardis, 2014, p. 21; Finnemore & Hollis, 2016, p. 431). Finally, the inclusion of unauthorised access means this definition limits itself to cyber risks that are generated intentionally (similarly to the approach taken by Finnemore and Hollis (2016, p. 431)). Therefore, only wilful breaches are covered; unintentional human errors or programming mistakes are not considered.

Drawing on Keohane and Nye (2000), global cybersecurity governance is defined in the dataset as the collection of 'institutions that guide and restrain collective global activities related to cybersecurity' (Kouliopoulos et al., 2020, p. 12). More concretely, this refers to institutions that are membership-based[15] and have a minimum of three members in at least two different states. The

[14] The dataset contains information on the institutions' membership, institutional design, governance functions and year they commenced working on cybersecurity issues, among others.

[15] Note that this excludes organisations like ICANN from the dataset: according to Article 23 of its by-laws, ICANN does not have members.

membership of these institutions can be public, private, or hybrid; legally, the institutions may be based on treaties, contracts, or they may lack a written constitutive document altogether. Each of the institutions performs at least one governance function related to the provision of cybersecurity.

By 2021, the global governance complex for cybersecurity was made up of 83 institutions. Geographically speaking, the institutions are predominantly transcontinental – that is, they have members that are based in at least two different UN-designated regions. Fewer than one quarter have members from just one region. Revealingly, among the transcontinental institutions, a large majority are headquartered in the US or EU. In addition, institutions composed solely of private members are overwhelmingly headquartered in the US. It would seem, then, that the geographical spread of headquarters corresponds to some degree with the development of the global governance complex described in Section 3: it reflects the US' unique position at the origins of the internet and the role of (often US-based) private firms in regulation. In contrast, treaty-based institutions are slightly more evenly spread in terms of their headquarters. This is partially because a number of them are regional by definition: the African Union, East African Community, and Caribbean Community and Common Market (CARICOM) are examples.

The data furthermore shows that governance functions and institutional forms relate in interesting ways in the complex (see Figure 6.1, below). First, information-sharing and capacity-building are common functions across all institutional forms, regardless of formality or membership (although institutions without a written constitutive document are comparatively less likely to engage in capacity-building). Second, norm-setting is primarily executed by formal intergovernmental organisations, as well as those that have public members (regardless of their legal base). Technical standard-setting, finally, is a function most commonly held by contract-based institutions, as well as institutions whose membership is hybrid or private-only.

Regarding the overall shape of the complex, global cybersecurity governance has been labelled a hybrid institutional complex, where heterogeneity is the defining characteristic (Abbott & Faude, 2022). This variety is apparent when it comes to the legal shape of the institutions. Classic treaty-based organisations comprise over a third of the institutions; contract-based organisations, such as the Anti-Phishing Working Group and Internet Society, make up roughly half of the complex; and under a fifth of the institutions lack a written constitutive document (examples include informal intergovernmental organisations such as the G7).

The membership of the institutions is also heterogeneous. Despite the private-led beginnings of internet governance (and hence cybersecurity governance), however, public members are surprisingly present across the complex. Close to one-third of the institutions are made up solely of private members,

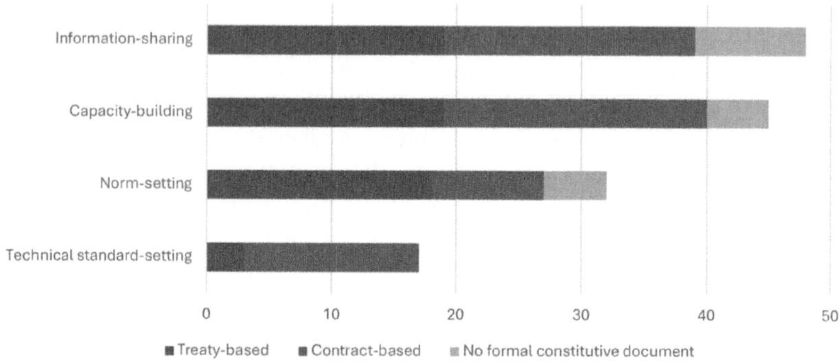

Source: Author's own elaboration.

Figure 6.1 Prevalence of governance functions related to institutions' legal bases in global cybersecurity governance

but the rest of the institutions (70%) contain public members, such as national governments, substate agencies, or intelligence agencies. In addition, the membership of just over half of the institutions in the complex is purely public. In other words, despite the bottom-up, transnational origins of global cybersecurity governance, the current shape of the complex reveals the significant interest that public actors have taken in this governance problem. This leads to two reflections – one on the evolution of the complex, and one on multistakeholderism.

First, *today*, public actors are extremely widespread in cybersecurity governance, and treaty-based intergovernmental organisations occupy over a third of the complex. However, a look at the *evolution* of the complex confirms that the institutions that began working on cybersecurity[16] prior to the 1990s were all contract-based. It was only from the 1990s onwards that treaty-based, formal intergovernmental institutions made their first forays into global cybersecurity governance. Later, in the 2000s, regional intergovernmental organisations began to engage with the governance problem. Finally, the trend towards increasing informality (Roger, 2020; Vabulas & Snidal, 2013) discussed in Chapter 4 of this book is also reflected in the complex. Institutions

16 The year an institution begins working on cybersecurity is defined in the dataset as the year in which each institution first engaged in a governance function related to the provision of cybersecurity. This initial engagement is detected based on the first concrete output or commitment emitted by the institution in relation to this governance function.

that have joined the complex in recent years (an example is the Paris Call for Trust and Security in Cyberspace), for instance, often lack institutionalisation. These empirical observations thus match the technical, bottom-up, and private beginnings of the complex described in Section 3. They also show that the global governance of cybersecurity did not begin as an interstate matter: interest by nation-states came later on. This goes against the notion that hybrid institutional complexes – of which global cybersecurity governance is a prime example – most often emerge as transmutations of incumbent interstate regime complexes (Abbott & Faude, 2022, p. 264).

Second, as described in Section 3, in 2005, states reached consensus that internet governance was by definition a multistakeholder endeavour, with roles for governments, the private sector and civil society (WGIG, 2005, p. 4). Scholars have pointed out, however, that discourse and praxis may differ when it comes to this definition. Raymond and DeNardis (2015, p. 588), for example, used three case studies to show that many areas of internet governance are not, in fact, governed through multistakeholderism.[17] Similarly, the global governance of cybersecurity only takes on multistakeholder forms to a limited degree (Kouliopoulos et al., 2020, p. 23). 70% of the institutions governing cybersecurity have just one type of member, and two-thirds of these single-membership institutions contain governmental members only. It is possible that this predominance of public members is related to the frame of cybersecurity, which is often associated with national security (DeNardis, 2014, p. 104; Mueller, 2017, p. 417). However, when it comes to the *practice* of global cybersecurity governance, the mere *presence* of states (though overwhelming) may not be an effective guarantee of the actual provision of cybersecurity. Van Eeten (2017, p. 433), for instance, suggests that control in cybersecurity may still lie with 'distributed, private forms of governance'.

5. CONCLUSION

Cybersecurity is one of the newer areas in global governance, and a critical one given the singular importance of the internet in contemporary society. The configuration of the institutions engaged in cybersecurity governance has been labelled as representative of how most global governance takes place today, namely through hybrid institutional complexes containing highly diverse institutions in membership and formality (Abbott & Faude, 2022, p. 264). As shown in this chapter, global cybersecurity governance may only

[17] They define multistakeholderism as 'two or more classes of actors engaged in a common governance enterprise concerning issues they regard as public in nature, and characterised by polyarchic authority relations constituted by procedural rules' (Raymond & DeNardis, 2015, p. 573).

have commenced in the mid-1980s, but it has seen important shifts over the past four decades. These successive changes have produced a complex of a particular hybrid shape.

As was the case for internet governance, the bedrock of global cybersecurity governance originated in the space and tradition of the geographical location where the internet itself emerged: the United States, and to a lesser extent, Europe. These foundations are transnational, technical and private-led. Layered over this base, however, are an array of governance initiatives by regional organisations, as well as governance efforts – and ongoing struggles over them – in formal global intergovernmental arenas such as the UN. Global cybersecurity governance would, then, seem to be provided through a multitude of channels and institutions, many of which are public. Yet private initiatives and self-regulation are also rife and growing. Some argue that these initiatives have emerged precisely as a reaction to governance gaps: while states may engage with cybersecurity in multiple fora, this does not guarantee actual delivery of cybersecurity (Farrell & Newman, 2021; Raymond & DeNardis, 2015, p. 603).

An exploration of an original dataset on the global governance complex for cybersecurity (see Section 4) revealed that the succession of shifts described above have shaped its topography. The geographical spread of the institutions' headquarters, for instance, reflects the historical origins of the internet and its initial governance in the US and Europe. Furthermore, taking a meso-level perspective, the diversity of the governance initiatives described in Section 3 has indeed translated into a heterogeneous collection of institutions – a hybrid institutional complex. Interestingly however, this complex did not develop as a transmutation of an existing interstate regime complex (as suggested by Abbott and Faude (2022, p. 264)); rather, the roots of the complex lie in contract-based institutions.

The institutions of the complex are diverse in their legal shape. In terms of membership, however, public members are more prevalent than perhaps would be expected when considering the complex' private and technical origins. It would seem, then, that the multistakeholder model that was theoretically set out for internet governance through the 2005 WGIG also did not materialise in the case of cybersecurity governance. In other words, multistakeholderism may be more common in discourse than in practice (Raymond & DeNardis, 2015). An alternative explanation for the prevalence of public members is that nation-states take a greater interest in cybersecurity than in more technical areas of internet governance (Mueller, 2017, p. 417), and are hence more present. Still, it remains questionable whether the mere fact of states *debating* the global governance of cybersecurity in a range of fora translates to real influence or impact on the actual *delivery* of cybersecurity (van Eeten, 2017).

Discerning the impact or performance of the individual members and institutions in the complex remains beyond the scope of this chapter, and merits further study.

REFERENCES

Abbate, J. (2000). *Inventing the internet.* MIT Press.

Abbott, K. W., & Faude, B. (2022). Hybrid institutional complexes in global governance. *The Review of International Organizations, 17,* 263–291.

Bradshaw, S., DeNardis, L., Osler Hampson, F., Jardine, E., & Raymond, M. (2015). *The emergence of contention in global internet governance.* Global Commission on Internet Governance Paper No. 17.

Chen, X., & Yang, Y. (2022). Different shades of norms: Comparing the approaches of the EU and ASEAN to cyber governance. *International Spectator, 57*(3), 48–65.

DeNardis, L. (2014). *The global war for internet governance.* Yale University Press.

DeNardis, L. (2020). *The Internet in everything.* Yale University Press.

Dunn Cavelty, M. (2008). *Cyber-security and threat politics: US efforts to secure the information age.* Routledge.

Dunn Cavelty, M. (2014). Breaking the cyber-security dilemma: Aligning security needs and removing vulnerabilities. *Science and Engineering Ethics, 20*(3), 701–715.

Eggenschwiler, J. (2019). *International cybersecurity norm development: The roles of states post-2017.* EU Cyber Direct; Research in Focus, April. https://perma.cc/7PR4-C72T

Farrell, H., & Newman, A. L. (2021). The janus face of the liberal international information order: When global institutions are self-undermining. *International Organization, 75*(2), 333–358.

Finnemore, M., & Hollis, D. B. (2016). Constructing norms for global cybersecurity. *American Journal of International Law, 110*(3), 425–479.

Flonk, D., Jachtenfuchs, M., & Obendiek, A. S. (2020). Authority conflicts in internet governance: Liberals vs. sovereigntists? *Global Constitutionalism, 9*(2), 364–386.

Futter, A. (2018). 'Cyber' semantics: Why we should retire the latest buzzword in security studies. *Journal of Cyber Policy, 3*(2), 201–216.

Georgieva, I. (2020). The unexpected norm-setters: Intelligence agencies in cyberspace. *Contemporary Security Policy, 41*(1), 33–54.

Greiman, V. A. (2015). Cybersecurity and global governance. *Journal of Information Warfare, 14*(4), 1–14.

Hofmann, J., Katzenbach, C., & Gollatz, K. (2017). Between coordination and regulation: Finding the governance in internet governance. *New Media and Society, 19*(9), 1406–1423.

Hofmann, S. C., & Pawlak, P. (2023). Governing cyberspace: Policy boundary politics across organizations. *Review of International Political Economy, 30*(6), 2122–2149.

International Telecommunications Union. (2023). *Internet use.* Facts and Figures 2023. https://www.itu.int/itu-d/reports/statistics/2023/10/10/ff23-internet-use/.

Keohane, R. O., & Nye, J. S. (2000). Governance in a globalizing world. In J. S. Nye & J. D. Donahue (Eds.), *Governance in a globalizing world* (pp. 1–41). Brookings Institution Press.

Klein, H. (2004). Understanding WSIS: An institutional analysis of the UN World Summit on the information society. *Information Technologies and International Development, 1*(3–4), 3–13.

Kleinwächter, W. (2004). Beyond ICANN vs ITU? How WSIS tries to enter the new territory of Internet governance. *Gazette: The International Journal for Communication Studies*, *66*(3–4), 233–251.

Kouliopoulos, A., Vandendriessche, M., & Saz-Carranza, A. (2020). *Case study of cyber governance*. https://www.globe-project.eu/case-study-of-cyber-governance_11363.pdf.

Maurer, T. (2011). *Cyber norm emergence at the United Nations: An analysis of the UN's activities regarding cyber-security*. Belfer Center for Science and International Affairs, Science, Technology, and Public Policy Program; Discussion Paper, Issue 11. https://www.belfercenter.org/publication/cyber-norm-emergence-united-nations-analysis-uns-activities-regarding-cyber-security.

Mueller, M. (2010). *Networks and states: The global politics of internet governance*. The MIT Press.

Mueller, M. (2017). Is cybersecurity eating internet governance? Causes and consequences of alternative framings. *Digital Policy, Regulation and Governance*, *19*(6), 415–428.

Mueller, M., Schmidt, A., & Kuerbis, B. (2013). Internet security and networked governance in international relations. *International Studies Review*, *15*(1), 86–104.

Nguyen, D. C. Le, & Golman, D. W. (2021). Diffusion of the Budapest Convention on cybercrime and the development of cybercrime legislation in Pacific Island countries: 'Law on the books' vs 'law in action'. *Computer Law and Security Review*, *40*, 105521.

Nye, J. S. (2014). The regime complex for managing global cyber activities. *Global Commission on Internet Governance*, *1*. https://www.cigionline.org/sites/default/files/gcig_paper_no1.pdf.

Nye, J. S. (2017). Deterrence and dissuasion in cyberspace. *International Security*, *41*(3), 44–71.

Pawlak, P., & Biersteker, T. (2019). *Guardian of the galaxy: EU cyber sanctions and norms in cyberspace*. EU Institute for Security Studies; Chaillot Paper 155.

Pernice, I. (2018). Global cybersecurity governance: A constitutionalist analysis. *Global Constitutionalism*, *7*(1), 112–141.

Raymond, M. (2016). Managing decentralized cyber governance: The responsibility to troubleshoot. *Strategic Studies Quarterly*, *10*(4), 123–149.

Raymond, M., & DeNardis, L. (2015). Multistakeholderism: Anatomy of an inchoate global institution. *International Theory*, *7*(3), 572–616.

Roger, C. (2020). *The origins of informality: Why the legal foundations of global governance are shifting, and why it matters*. Oxford University Press.

Singer, P. W., & Friedman, A. (2014). *Cybersecurity and cyberwar: What everyone needs to know*. Oxford University Press.

Smith, B. (2017, February 14). *The need for a digital Geneva Convention*. Microsoft. https://blogs.microsoft.com/on-the-issues/2017/02/14/need-digital-geneva-convention/#sm.001vmxlx4fckfcd11ci132tpwpta8.

Stiennon, R. (2015). A short history of cyber warfare. In J. A. Green (Ed.), *Cyber warfare: A multidisciplinary analysis* (pp. 7–32). Routledge.

Urgessa, W. G. (2020). Multilateral cybersecurity governance: Divergent conceptualizations and its origin. *Computer Law and Security Review*, *36*, 105368.

Vabulas, F., & Snidal, D. (2013). Organization without delegation: Informal intergovernmental organizations (IIGOs) and the spectrum of intergovernmental arrangements. *Review of International Organizations*, *8*(2), 193–220.

van Eeten, M. (2017). Patching security governance: An empirical view of emergent governance mechanisms for cybersecurity. *Digital Policy, Regulation and Governance*, *19*(6), 429–448.

van Eeten, M., & Mueller, M. (2012). Where is the governance in internet governance? *New Media and Society*, *15*(5), 720–736.

Van Raemdonck, N. (2021). *Cyber diplomacy in Southeast Asia*. EU Cyber Direct; Digital Dialogues.

Verhelst, A., & Wouters, J. (2020). Filling global governance gaps in cybersecurity: International and European legal perspectives. *International Organisations Research Journal*, *15*(2), 105–124.

von Solms, R., & van Niekerk, J. (2013). From information security to cyber security. *Computers & Security*, *38*, 97–102.

WGIG. (2005). *Report of the Working Group on Internet Governance*. https://www.wgig.org/docs/WGIGREPORT.pdf.

Zittrain, J. (2008). *The future of the internet and how to stop it*. Yale University Press.

7. Global trade governance: between antagonism and complementarity

Jan Wouters

1. INTRODUCTION

The global governance of trade is characterised by a very diverse number of actors at different levels, from states and international organisations (IOs), such as the World Trade Organization (WTO), the United Nations Conference on Trade and Development (UNCTAD), the Organisation for Economic Co-operation and Development (OECD), and regional organisations like the European Union (EU), informal bodies like the G7, G20 and BRICS, and a variety of private actors. The present chapter considers each of these actors in order to better understand their respective contributions, strengths and weaknesses, and their mutual interactions.

We start at the global level, focusing second on (cross-) regional actors and dynamics, and third on private actors. A silver thread throughout the chapter will be the finding that the two most prominent challenges for global trade governance are: (i) revitalising the global multilateral system by strengthening the WTO, and (ii) making sure that all actors strive for complementarity rather than antagonism.

This is, however, far from evident in a world where traditional cleavages, such as the North–South divide in the United Nations (UN), geopolitical and geostrategic tensions and contestation, have recently further politicised trade policies, triggering a weakening of multilateral regimes and a strong rise in bilateralism and unilateralism.

2. ACTORS AT GLOBAL LEVEL

2.1 World Trade Organization

Having been set up in 1995 as a successor to the General Agreement on Tariffs and Trade (GATT), the WTO is a relatively young global organisation. In terms of membership, it has grown impressively ever since: from 128 (including the EU) at the time of its creation to 166 today. All major trading powers (including China since 2001 and Russia since 2012) are part of it, representing over 98% of global trade and global GDP. In its first years, the WTO saw several successful breakthroughs, notably in areas such as financial services and public procurement (WTO, 2015). The launch of the 'Doha Development Agenda' (DDA) in November 2001 should have given new momentum for a major trade round where developing countries would be given priority attention. However, more than 20 years later, the DDA has not delivered, and the WTO is in a state of crisis. Except for the Trade Facilitation Agreement, which entered into force in 2017, and the Agreement on Fisheries Subsidies adopted at the 12th Ministerial Conference on 17 June 2022, the WTO has not been able to adopt new multilateral trade agreements (Winn & Rai, 2019). Moreover, the 'crown jewel' of the WTO, its dispute settlement system, has been severely damaged: because of the opposition by the United States (US), the Appellate Body is effectively defunct since December 2019, as its members have reached the end of their mandates and vacant positions have not been filled. To overcome this, an alternative mechanism has been set up, the 'Multi-Party Interim Appeal Arbitration Arrangement' (MPIA), consisting of 10 arbitrators who hear appeals of WTO panel reports (Pauwelyn, 2023). Currently, 54 WTO Members have accepted this arrangement. At the 13th Ministerial Conference in Abu Dhabi, members reaffirmed their commitment to finding an agreement to restore a fully functioning dispute settlement system by the end of 2024, but that goal was not reached. To overcome its regulatory deadlock, the WTO currently experiments with 'Joint Initiatives' (JIs) by groups of like-minded members. While JIs only bind those members who commit to them, the benefits are extended to all WTO members in accordance with the most-favoured nation principle. However, India and South Africa oppose JIs (for other criticism, see Kelsey, 2022). Currently JIs have been concluded on Services Domestic Regulation and on Investment Facilitation for Development, while discussions are continuing on JIs for e-commerce and micro, small, and medium-sized enterprises (Peres, 2024).

2.2 United Nations and United Nations System

After its coming into being in 1995, the WTO has largely overshadowed the original UN initiatives in global trade governance. The original Havana Charter, creating the International Trade Organization (ITO), had been developed under the auspices of the UN, in accordance with the purpose laid down in the UN Charter that the organisation would 'achieve international co-operation in solving international problems of an economic … character' (Art 1(3)). In the face of US opposition to a too powerful ITO, the contracting parties decided to only make provisional application of the GATT, an annex to the ITO Charter (Wouters & De Meester, 2007). This lasted for 47 years, until the WTO was set up. In the meantime, the UN General Assembly had created UNCTAD in 1964 in order to promote the interests of the quickly rising number of developing countries. Among UNCTAD's main achievements, one can mention the Generalised System of Preferences, which promotes the export of manufactured goods from developing countries by offering tariff reductions or eliminations, and a variety of commodity agreements which aimed at stabilising world prices in the interest of developing countries (UNCTAD, 1985). In the 1970s and 1980s, UNCTAD became involved with the New International Economic Order (NIEO) project, which developing countries had launched with a view to achieving a more equitable and equal international economic system. Partly as a consequence thereof, Western powers became increasingly disenchanted with UNCTAD and pursued the creation of an IO outside the UN system, which was to become the WTO (Rajagopal, 2009).

The wider UN system of specialised agencies naturally also has a bearing on international trade. The International Monetary Fund (IMF) and the World Bank develop policies that directly affect international trade relations – hence the GATT's Uruguay Round, launched in 1986, inter alia sought to ensure coherence between the work of the Bretton Woods institutions and of the future WTO. Other specialised agencies, such as the UN Food and Agriculture Organization (FAO), have a strong impact on trade in agriculture and fisheries products, especially through its regulatory policies and the work of the Codex Alimentarius Commission, which it created in 1961. The Codex Alimentarius, a collection of internationally recognised standards, codes of practice, guidelines, and recommendations relating to food, food production, food labelling, and food safety, plays a fundamental role in global food trade: WTO agreements like the SPS Agreement (on sanitary and phytosanitary standards) recognise its authoritative force (Arcuri, 2015).

The UN has tried a number of times to regain the initiative on international trade, but largely in vain. For instance, various UN General Assembly (UNGA) resolutions have been adopted on 'international trade and development' which speak out on a number of challenges for the multilateral trading system and try to give back a more central role to UNCTAD (see e.g., UNGA, 2018). General Assembly resolutions have also frequently highlighted the need for a more equitable international economic system and from time to time still refer to the older NIEO initiative (see e.g., UNGA, 2022).

2.3 Informal Bodies

The oldest informal body in the area of international trade is the Group of Seven, or G7, established initially as G6 in Rambouillet in 1975 by the major industrialised countries: the US, the United Kingdom, France, Germany, Japan, and Italy. Soon after, they were joined by Canada and the then European Economic Community (EEC). In 1998, Russia was admitted to the G7, except for certain financial and economic affairs, forming the G8 (Dobson, 2007). However, Russia's membership was suspended in the spring of 2014 following its annexation of Crimea. Originally, the G7 was an exclusive economic club. Its genesis is specifically connected with the collapse of the Bretton Woods system of fixed exchange rates, the oil crisis, and the subsequent economic recession in the 1970s (Fioretos, 2019). Later the G7 started to emphasise more strongly its political mission – spreading the 'market democracy' model. After the fall of the Berlin Wall, attention shifted to the post-communist transition, the reform of international institutions, and global issues such as democratisation, the environment, drugs, and terrorism. The G7 operates on the basis of annual summits of the heads of state and government of its members. Around these meetings, a system of ministerial meetings to discuss and build consensus on specific challenges in various domains has been formed. Thus, the G7 ministers of trade, finance, and foreign affairs meet at least annually. While the lack of institutionalisation of the G7 has proven to be a strength, the period of the first Trump administration showed its vulnerability to worsening personal relations between its leaders (Andrione-Moylan & Wouters, 2023), with a revival and new dynamics appearing during the Biden administration (Kirton, 2023).

One of the criticisms regularly voiced to the G7 is that it is a non-representative Western 'rich men's club'. One can see the rise, since 1999, of the Group of Twenty (G20) in that light. The G20 was first conceived in reaction to the G7's perceived failure to adequately respond to the financial crisis that hit East Asia in the late 1990s. The G20 finance ministers and Central Bank governors convened for the first time in Berlin on 15–16 December 1999 (Hajnal, 2019). The group brings together the systemically most important economies worldwide: it comprises 19 countries and the EU, and, since the 2023 New Delhi Summit, the African Union. G20 meetings were lifted to the level of heads of state and government with the Washington Summit in 2008, in response to the (Western) financial crisis. Since then, a G20 Leaders' Summit has been held annually (initially, during the crisis, twice a year), whereas the G20 finance ministers and Central Bank governors meet twice a year. Since the 2009 Pittsburgh Summit, the G20 has called itself 'the premier forum for our international economic cooperation' (G20, 2009b). Depending on the topics under debate, the G20 Chair may also invite other States to attend the G20 Leaders' Summits. In addition, a number of heads of international institutions (IMF, World Bank, WTO, International Labour Organization, OECD) are usually also represented at G20 Summits. In economic terms, the G20 membership represents five continents, 66% of the world's population, approximately

85% of global GDP, and approximately 75% of international trade. Like the G7, the G20's activities are not governed by an underlying founding document or charter. The G20 does not impose any formal membership conditions, nor does it employ any formal rules or mechanisms with respect to voting, decision-making, or dispute resolution. At its core, the G20 is designed as an international forum for debate and consensus-seeking on all matters related to global economic governance. The informality that characterises the G20 also applies to its decision-making, as the outcome does not amount to a legally binding commitment for its members. The G20 has taken great care to avoid any institutionalisation of its structure. There is strong cooperation between the G20 and other formal IOs, such as the IMF, WTO, and OECD. The G20 also works in cooperation with the Financial Stability Board, which it created at its London Summit in April 2009 (Wouters & Odermatt, 2014), and the Basel Committee on Banking Supervision.

The BRICS has become another important informal body in international economic governance. Originally created as a group of four emerging economies (Brazil, the Russian Federation, India, and China) in 2009, it quickly expanded to include South Africa in 2010. Its initial goal was to discuss proposals to improve the global economic situation, reform of financial institutions, and foster cooperation and coordination for the future, with a view to making changes to global governance (Mostafa & Mahmood, 2015). The BRICS has discussed a variety of topics and, most importantly, founded the New Development Bank (NDB) as an alternative to the World Bank and the IMF. While its original members are all G20 members, in 2023, the BRICS expanded to include Egypt, Ethiopia, Iran, and the United Arab Emirates (BRICS+). With that, BRICS+ has increasingly become a geopolitical bloc that rivals the G7 and challenges the Western-dominated world order in cooperation with countries from the Global South, striving for an alternative international system based on multipolarity and non-interference (see Section 6). Apart from initiatives rivalling the World Bank, such as the creation of the NDB in 2014, monetary cooperation (including the 2015 Contingent Reserve Arrangement) is high on the agenda to make BRICS countries less dependent on the US dollar. Combined, BRICS members today represent 45% of the world population and more than 37% of world GDP (Haans & Thomas, 2023).

3. ACTORS AT (INTER-) REGIONAL LEVEL

3.1 OECD

The OECD was established in 1960 in Paris as a successor to the Organisation for European Economic Co-operation (OEEC), which was founded with 18 Western European countries in 1948 to administer the Marshall Plan. From its original 20 member countries, the US, Canada, and 18 European states, it has gradually expanded geographically. It now counts 38 member countries, making it a truly inter-regional organisation: Japan, Australia, New Zealand, Mexico, Chile, Israel, Colombia and Costa Rica are among the most recent accessions. On 25 January 2022, the OECD Council decided to take the first step in accession discussions with six candidate countries – Argentina, Brazil, Bulgaria, Croatia, Peru, and Romania. Meanwhile, accession talks have also started with Thailand and Indonesia. The accession process for Russia, which began in 2007 and was suspended in 2014, has been formally closed following its aggression against Ukraine. The OECD describes itself as 'a community of nations committed to the values of democracy based on rule of law and human rights, and adherence to open and transparent market-economy principles' (OECD, 2011). It aims to maximise the promotion of economic growth, employment, and living standards in a stable financial climate, as well as further liberalisation of world trade. To achieve these aims, its activities focus on information exchange, consultations, and conducting studies. The Council, which operates based on consensus, may make binding decisions, issue recommendations, and adopt conventions. Under the supervision of the Council, around 250 specialised committees, working groups, and expert groups operate, in which member countries develop ideas and evaluate progress in specific policy domains, such as trade, science, work, education, financial markets, or the economy.

The OECD makes many contributions to global trade governance, from important work on international taxation (Transfer Pricing Guidelines, Model Tax Convention, Base Erosion and Profit Shifting work in follow-up to the G20 initiative, etc.) to Guidelines for Multinational Enterprises (MNEs), statistical databases, agriculture and fisheries, foreign direct investment, financial markets, capital markets, corporate governance, and competition, typically through the use of soft law mechanisms and peer review. From time to time, a 'hard' law approach is also chosen, such as in the case of the OECD antibribery convention.

An important feature of the OECD is that it works closely with other bodies, such as the G7, the G20, UNCTAD, and the WTO (Wouters & Van Kerckhoven, 2011) (see Section 6). Typically, the OECD provides evidence-based analysis, data, and expertise to these other bodies. In many cases, it has been instrumental in supporting new policy initiatives. For example, the OECD played an important role in the fight against money laundering and terrorist financing, as it contributed to the 1989 G7 decision to establish the Financial Action Task Force, which is located within the OECD. In the G7, the OECD also contributes, among other areas, to dynamics on international taxation, climate change, sustainable development, and artificial intelligence (AI). In the G20, the OECD offers expertise, but also monitors commitments (such as the G20's 2008 commitment to not revert to protectionist measures, which the OECD monitors together with UNCTAD and the WTO) and has brought innovative approaches and standards to the G20 playbook, such as the OECD/G20 Base Erosion and Profit Shifting Project and the G20 AI Principles. The European Commission is a full participant in its work and a member of its Development Assistance Committee (Wouters, 2024b).

3.2 EU

The EU's contribution to global trade governance is unique and diverse. As the world's most important regional integration organisation with unique supranational features, currently consisting of 27 member states, the EU has exclusive powers – meaning that only it can act, and not its member states – for a customs union (its oldest achievement, completed in 1966), an external trade policy (the 'Common Commercial Policy'), establishing the competition rules for its internal market, and conducting monetary policy – with the Euro as a single currency – for the 20 member states that belong to the Euro area. Pursuant to its own founding treaty, as confirmed in various policy documents (see, recently, European Commission and High Representative, 2021), the EU is strongly committed to multilateralism as a mode of international cooperation: the Treaty on European Union (TEU) stipulates that the Union 'shall promote multilateral solutions to common problems' and that it 'shall work for a high degree of cooperation in all fields of international relations, in order to … promote an international system based on stronger multilateral cooperation and good global governance' (Art 21(2) first paragraph and subheading, TEU). As a founding Member of the WTO, the EU has traditionally been deeply engaged in all multilateral trade activities conducted there, from negotiations for new agreements to the peer review processes in the Trade Policy Review Mechanism and has a very active role in the WTO's dispute settlement system.

Still, disillusionment with the WTO has set in since the failed Cancún Ministerial Conference in 2003. The European Commission redefined the priorities of EU trade policy with its 2006 communication *Global Europe: Competing in the World* (European Commission, 2006). Henceforth, while it remained committed to the WTO and the DDA, the EU prioritised deep and preferential trade agreements with its strategic partners. According to the Commission:

> Free Trade Agreements (FTAs), if approached with care, can build on WTO and other international rules by going further and faster in promoting openness and integration, by tackling issues which are not ready for multilateral discussion and by preparing the ground for the next level of multilateral liberalisation. Many key issues, including investment, public procurement, competition, other regulatory

> issues and IPR [intellectual property] enforcement, which remain outside the WTO at this time can be addressed through FTAs. (European Commission, 2006, p. 8)

This new approach has resulted in an unprecedented flurry of deep and comprehensive preferential trade agreements with a great number of countries, from Korea, Canada, Singapore, and Japan to Chile, Mexico, New Zealand, and MERCOSUR, with many more in the pipeline. Still, it would be wrong to conclude that the EU has given up on the WTO. When the Appellate Body ceased to function in December 2019 (see Section 2.1), the EU took the lead alongside several partners in proposing the aforementioned MPIA as a temporary backstop mechanism. The Commission has also made various contributions to the debate on WTO reform (Wouters & Hegde, 2022). Despite this multilateral engagement, the last years have seen the EU adopting a significant number of unilateral initiatives in the area of international trade and environment, some of which have been criticised as not being fully in line with international law. This applies in particular to the new Carbon Border Adjustment Mechanism (EU, 2023a): the jury is still out on its compatibility with WTO rules (Bacchus, 2021) and the Paris Agreement (Quick and Das, 2023). The EU Deforestation Regulation (EU, 2023b) caused so much controversy that the Commission proposed delaying its date of application to October 2024. Last but not least, the EU's increasing 'weaponisation' of its trade policy and recently adopted unilateral trade instruments such as the Anti-Coercion Instrument (EU, 2023c), the Foreign Subsidies Regulation (EU, 2022) and the Enforcement Regulation (EU, 2021), tread a delicate line in terms of their compatibility with international and WTO law (Crochet & Gustaffson, 2021).

3.3 Other Regional Developments

Other regions in the world have seen important regional dynamics in the field of trade. In Africa, the African Union brokered the African Continental Free Trade Area (AfCFTA) in 2018, which currently has 43 parties, making it the world's largest free trade area, spanning 1.3 billion people. AfCFTA is aimed at making intra-Africa trade easier, inter alia by creating a single African market for goods and services, removing non-tariff barriers, building African expertise in intellectual property, investment, competition and e-commerce, and lowering taxes and tariffs between the parties (Ofori-Amoah, 2024).

Remarkable dynamics have also taken place in the Pacific. The Trans-Pacific Partnership (TPP) was signed in 2016 but never entered into force, as the US withdrew under the first Trump administration. Under the leadership of Japan, the Comprehensive and Progressive Agreement for Trans-Pacific Partnership (CPTPP) was agreed upon in January 2018. It is a separate treaty that incorporates, by reference, the provisions of the TPP, with the exception of a number of suspended provisions (Huerta-Goldman & Gantz, 2022). Eleven countries have signed up to it (Australia, Brunei, Canada, Chile, Japan, Malaysia, Mexico, New Zealand, Peru, Singapore and Vietnam), with the United Kingdom (UK) on its way to accede to it. With combined economies of 13.4% of global GDP, the CPTPP is one of the largest free trade areas in the world, next to the US–Mexico–Canada Agreement, the EU's internal market, and another important recent agreement in Asia-Pacific, the Regional Comprehensive Economic Partnership (RCEP). The RCEP constitutes the largest trading bloc in the world today, as it brings together 15 countries (Australia, Brunei, Cambodia, China, Indonesia, Japan, South Korea, Laos, Malaysia, Myanmar, New Zealand, the Philippines, Singapore, Thailand and Vietnam), accounting for 30% of the world's population and 30% of global GDP. It was conceived at a 2011 ASEAN summit and signed on 15 November 2020, entering into force on 1 January 2022 for the first 10 countries.

Latin America and the Caribbean present probably the most complex trade governance structures, with four customs unions at different stages – MERCOSUR, the Andean Community, the Central American Common Market, and CARICOM – and a great diversity of preferential trade agreements (see, for options for change, Rosales & Herreros, 2021).

4. PRIVATE ACTORS

In the field of transnational trade, there has always been 'normative' action by private actors: this is how the '*lex mercatoria*' came about (Wouters, 2020). A well-known modern example is the work of the International Chamber of Commerce, which was created as an association under French law in 1919 and represents more than 45 million companies. Its Incoterms are among the most important worldwide standards for the sale of goods (Coetzee, 2020).

Over the past decades, a variety of other private bodies have emerged whose regulatory or other activities have an increasingly important impact upon global trade governance. Initiatives for 'voluntary sustainability standards' have skyrocketed in a variety of sectors, particularly in the food sector (Wouters, 2020). Such standards have not been drafted by legislatures or regulatory authorities but have instead been formulated by non-governmental entities, such as, in the example of the food sector, supermarket chains, retail consortia, manufacturers, producers, and trade cooperatives. A prominent example is GlobalG.A.P., the 'Global Partnership for Good Agricultural Practice' (until 2007 EurepGAP), which is a business-to-business private standard-setting initiative of the food industry. Food retailers, producers, and suppliers that agree to the terms of reference of the organisation are all eligible for membership. More than 200,000 food producers from all over the world are certified by GlobalG.A.P. Interestingly, the whole GlobalG.A.P. legal design rests on purely private law mechanisms. Its ownership and day-to-day administration are in the hands of FoodPlus GmbH, a private limited company based in Cologne, which is subject to German company law. The shareholders are the supermarket chains, food producers, retailers, and so on. Since GlobalG.A.P. is a private initiative, it is not subject to traditional democratic control and accountability mechanisms, raising multiple questions in terms of accountability and democratic legitimacy (Hachez & Wouters, 2011; Wouters, 2024a). A second example of private law-based governance is forest certification. In the absence of a binding legal instrument under international law, a variety of forest law enforcement and private governance initiatives have emerged. These are aimed at tackling sensitive issues related to illegal logging and promoting sustainable forest management worldwide through certification. Private actors set and enforce standards for the management of forests, also referred to as 'forest certification' (Marx, Bécault, & Wouters, 2012). A famous example of such an initiative is the Forest Stewardship Council (FSC). Launched in 2003, the FSC is a widely recognised system of forest certification that has often been praised for being an innovative and properly functioning global 'soft' governance mechanism. Its environmental and sustainability standards benefit a global network of businesses, organisations, and communities (Gil et al., 2019). Similarly to GlobalG.A.P., FSC is run by a German, non-profit legal entity based in Bonn, FSC Global Development GmbH.

The aforementioned initiatives question state sovereignty as they operate without the involvement of public authorities and often develop much higher labour, environmental, and health/sanitary standards than what public international authorities, like the Codex Alimentarius Commission (see Section 2.2), are able to produce (Marx & Wouters, 2018). They are not without their critics, though (see Section 6).

5. COMPLEMENTARY INTERACTIONS

'Complementary' interactions between global governance institutions and rules are those that enable better achievement of intended governance objective(s) than would have been achieved without the interaction. Examples of this include the interactions between the OECD and the EU, as well as the close cooperation of the OECD with the G7 and, more recently, with the G20 (Wouters & Van Kerckhoven, 2011). As to the former, the EU takes place as a full participant in most of the OECD's work and is even a full member of the Development Assistance Committee (Vlastou-Dimopoulou, 2019). Members of the EU Delegation in Paris, along with councillors and experts from the European Commission, EU agencies, and the European Central Bank, actively engage in regular dialogue through the OECD technical committees on issues such as taxation, agriculture, health, statistics, trade, investment, climate, digitalisation, education, employment, social affairs, innovation, development cooperation, and many other areas. The EU benefits from the statistical data and economic studies of the OECD, which include surveys of EU policies and the Euro zone. OECD policy and standard-setting initiatives often find their way into EU legislation, such as the 2016 and 2017 anti-tax avoidance directives, which implement in EU law the OECD recommendations against base erosion and profit shifting to ensure that profits of MNEs are taxed where the economic activities generating those profits are performed and value is created. Additionally, the 2022 Council Directive – on ensuring a global minimum level of taxation for MNE groups and large-scale domestic groups in the Union – carries out in EU law the OECD's 2021 Model Rules ('Tax Challenges Arising from the Digitalisation of the Economy – Global Anti-Base Erosion Model Rules Pillar Two') (Wouters, 2024b).

Concerning the OECD's interactions with the G7 and G20, the following can be noted. Historically, the OECD has cooperated intensively with the G7, whose members are all OECD member countries. The OECD has performed as a *de facto* secretariat for the G7 by responding to specific requests for work or by providing intellectual foundations for the G7's work (Woodward, 2007). The OECD has often fulfilled the task of maintaining momentum and keeping track of developments between G7 meetings. It has been invited to the G7/G8 meetings since 2007. Also, with the G20, there is a considerable overlap in membership: 11 members of the G20 are members of the OECD, and thanks to the inclusion of the EU, 22 member countries are also indirectly represented in the G20. The involvement of the same countries in both bodies is a strong asset for their growing cooperation. In addition, the limited membership of the OECD is an advantage for its efficiency vis-à-vis other IOs. Substantively, the OECD has a lot to offer to the G20 in terms of experience and knowledge, while the G20 can provide a high-level political commitment to the OECD's agenda, increasing the relevance of the OECD within the global economic governance architecture.

The following examples illustrate, in a non-exhaustive manner, some of the complementary interactions between the G20 and OECD. At the first G20 Leaders meeting in Washington in mid-November 2008, the OECD was encouraged to continue its work on the promotion of the exchange of information on tax. At its London Summit in April 2009, the G20 welcomed the publication of a blacklist of tax havens by the OECD; at this meeting, combating tax havens became a priority for the G20 (G20, 2009a). From the September 2009 Pittsburgh Summit onwards, the OECD Secretary-General has been invited to the G20 summits, indicating the growing interaction between both bodies. At the Pittsburgh Summit, the OECD was urged to further its work on energy subsidies. Moreover, to prevent illicit capital outflow, the G20 called for the adoption of the OECD Anti-Bribery Convention by all the G20 members and non-members, once more drawing upon the work and expertise of the OECD on the matter. The G20 further welcomed OECD assistance in the fields of employment policy and international trade. At the June 2010 Summit in Toronto, the G20 called upon the OECD to monitor and report on trade and protectionism, in collaboration with the WTO and UNCTAD. The foregoing amply demonstrates the complementary dynamics between the G20 and the OECD, which are linked to the evolution of the G20: after initially dealing with the single issue of organising an urgent internal coordinated response to constrain the negative impact of the 2007–2009 global financial crisis, its issue coverage has expanded to a diverse set of more structural global issues, in particular international tax reform (see OECD, 2024).

6. ANTAGONISTIC INTERACTIONS

'Antagonistic' or contradictory interactions between global governance institutions and rules are those which diminish the ability to achieve intended governance objective(s). Examples are the aforementioned dynamics of the BRICS+ as opposed to the G7 (see Section 2.3), and the mixed reactions of states and IOs to the aforementioned private governance initiatives or voluntary sustainability standards (see Section 4). Thus, in 2005 St. Vincent and the Grenadines complained in the WTO SPS Committee about GlobalG.A.P. requirements restricting its ability to export bananas to the EU (Halabi, 2016).

The BRICS+ dynamics are very interesting, as they constitute an example of an expanding group of non-Western countries that are vying for changes to the international economic order. A common theme is the complaint that the G7 and Western countries restrain the development of BRICS+ countries through unilateral sanctions and protectionist measures and that they fail to respect the principles of sovereignty and non-intervention. The latest BRICS+ developments show a willingness to decouple from the US dollar and establish their own reserve currency (Maihold, 2024).

As to voluntary sustainability standards, they receive mixed signals in the international community. The EU from time to time relies on private governance schemes, for instance in its food regulation (Havinga, 2018) and deforestation legislation, although shortcomings have been found in voluntary sustainability schemes, which have not always addressed the EU's latest regulatory adaptations (Cosimo et al., 2024). More mixed responses, oscillating between endorsement, concerns, and outright criticism, can be found at the WTO. Concerns have arisen, especially in respect to developing countries, that these standards may create unjustified and unnecessary obstacles to trade. The WTO's Committee on Sanitary and Phytosanitary Measures (SPS Committee) has become one of the fora in which the relationship between public international (WTO) rules and private food standards is being discussed (Du, 2018; Wouters & Geraets, 2012).

7. CONCLUDING THOUGHTS

In this chapter, we have seen that the global governance of trade is characterised by a very diverse number of actors at different levels, from states and a disparate set of IOs, such as the WTO, UNCTAD, OECD, and the EU, to informal bodies like the G7, G20 and BRICS, and a variety of private actors. The two most prominent challenges for global trade governance seem to be: (i) to revitalise the global multilateral system by strengthening the WTO (inter alia through the adoption of new multilateral or plurilateral trade agreements and repairing the dispute settlement system), and (ii) to make sure that all public and private actors work towards complementarity rather than contradictions. This is, however, far from evident in a world where, next to traditional cleavages, such as the North–South divide in the UN, geopolitical and geostrategic tensions and contestation further politicise trade policies, triggering a weakening of multilateral regimes and a renewed rise of bilateralism and unilateralism.

REFERENCES

Andrione-Moylan, A., & Wouters, J. (2023). Populists at the G7 and G20: Informal cooperation in turbulent times. In M. Egan, K. Raube, J. Wouters, & J. Chaisse (Eds.), *Contestation and polarization in global governance: European responses* (pp. 124–142). Edward Elgar Publishing.

Arcuri, A. (2015). Global food safety standards: The evolving regulatory epistemology at the intersection of the SPS Agreement and the Codex Alimentarius Commission. In P. Delimatsis (Ed.), *The law, economics, and politics of international standardisation* (pp. 79–103). Cambridge University Press.

Bacchus, J. (2021). Legal issues with the European carbon border adjustment mechanism. *CATO Briefing Paper*, (125), August 9.

Coetzee, J. (2020). CISG and Incoterms: Reviving the traditions of the lex mercatoria. In A. Hutchinson & F. Myburgh (Eds.), *Research handbook on international commercial contracts* (pp. 159–180). Edward Elgar Publishing.

Cosimo, L. H. E., Masiero, M., Mammadova, A., & Pettenella, D. (2024). Voluntary sustainability standards to cope with the new European Union regulation on deforestation-free products: A gap analysis. *Forest Policy and Economics*, *164*, 103235.

Crochet, V., & Gustaffson, M. (2021). Lawful remedy or illegal response? Resolving the issue of foreign subsidization under WTO law. *World Trade Review*, *20*(3), 343–366.

Dobson, H. (2007). *Group of 7/8*. Routledge.

Du, M. (2018). WTO Regulation of transnational private authority in global governance. *International and Comparative Law Quarterly*, *67*(4), 867–902.

European Commission (2006). Communication to the Council, the European Parliament, the European Economic and Social Committee and the Committee of the Regions. *Global Europe: Competing in the world.* European Commission.

European Commission and High Representative of the European Union for Foreign Affairs and Security Policy (2021). *Strengthening the EU's contribution to rules-based multilateralism: Joint communication to the European Parliament and the Council.* European Union.

European Union (2021). Regulation (EU) 2021/167 of 10 February 2021 amending Regulation (EU) No 654/2014 concerning the exercise of the Union's rights for the application and enforcement of international trade rules. *Official Journal of the European Union, L49*, 1.

European Union (2022). Regulation (EU) 2022/2560 of 14 December 2022 on foreign subsidies distorting the internal market. *Official Journal of the European Union, L330*, 1.

European Union (2023a). Regulation (EU) 2023/956 of the European Parliament and of the Council of 10 May 2023 establishing a carbon border adjustment mechanism. *Official Journal of the European Union, L130*, 52.

European Union (2023b). Regulation (EU) 2023/1115 of the European Parliament and of the Council of 31 May 2023 on the making available on the Union market and the export from the Union of certain commodities and products associated with deforestation and forest degradation and repealing Regulation (EU) No 995/2010. *Official Journal of the European Union, L150*, 206.

European Union (2023c). Regulation (EU) 2023/2675 of 22 November 2023 on the protection of the Union and its Member States from economic coercion by third countries. *Official Journal of the European Union, L2675*, 2023.

Fioretos, O. (2019). Minilateralism and informality in international monetary cooperation. *Review of International Political Economy, 26*(6), 1136–1159.

G20 (2009a). London Summit - Leaders' statement, 2 April 2009. *G7/G20 Documents.* https://g7g20-documents.org/database/document/2009-g20-united-kingdom-leaders-leaders-language-london-summit-leaders-statement.

G20 (2009b). Leaders' statement: The Pittsburgh Summit, 24–25 September 2009. *OECD G20.* https://www.oecd.org/g20/summits/pittsburgh/G20-Pittsburgh-Leaders-Declaration.pdf.

Gil, A. A., Colonna, T., Hontelez, J., Karmann, M., & Oropeza, A. P. (2019). Forest Stewardship Council: Transforming the global forestry sector. In M. Schmidt, D. Giovannucci, D. Palekhov, & B. Hansmann (Eds.), *Sustainable global value chains* (pp. 481–497). Springer.

Haans, J. F., & Thomas, C. J. (2023). Status competition: The BRICS' quest for influence in global governance. *China Report, 59*(4), 388–401.

Hachez, N., & Wouters, J. (2011). A glimpse at the democratic legitimacy of private standards: Assessing the public accountability of GlobalG.A.P. *Journal of International Economic Law, 14*(4), 677–710.

Hajnal, P. I. (2019). *The G20: Evolution, interrelationships, documentation* (2nd ed.). Routledge.

Halabi, S. (2016, September 12). The battle between public and private food safety standards. *Yale Journal on Regulation Notice & Comment Blog.* https://www.yalejreg.com/nc/the-battle-between-public-and-private-food-safety-standards/.

Havinga, T. (2018). Private food safety standards in the EU. In H. Bremmers & K. Purnhagen (Eds.), *Regulating and managing food safety in the EU: A legal-economic perspective* (pp. 11–37). Springer.

Huerta-Goldman, J. A., & Gantz, D. A. (Eds.). (2022). *The comprehensive and progressive trans-pacific partnership: Analysis and commentary.* Cambridge University Press.

Kelsey, J. (2022). The illegitimacy of joint statement initiatives and their systemic implications for the WTO. *Journal of International Economic Law, 25*(1), 2–24.

Kirton, J. (2023). The G7 alliance's expanding effectiveness. *The Wilson Quarterly, 47*(4).

Maihold, G. (2024). Beyond the status quo: BRICS+ and the challenge to the G7. *EconPol Forum, 25*(1), 18–19.

Marx, A., Bécault, E., & Wouters, J. (2012). Private standards in forestry: Assessing the legitimacy and effectiveness of the Forest Stewardship Council. In A. Marx, J. Swinnen, M. Maertens, & J. Wouters (Eds.), *Private standards and global governance: Economic, legal and political perspectives* (pp. 60–97). Edward Elgar Publishing.

Marx, A., & Wouters, J. (2018). Global constitutionalism and private governance: The discrete contribution of voluntary sustainability standards. In T. Suami, A. Peters, M. Kumm, & D. Vanoverbeke (Eds.), *Global constitutionalism: European and East Asian perspectives* (pp. 496–517). Cambridge University Press.

Mostafa, G., & Mahmood, M. (2015). The rise of the BRICS and their challenge to the G7. *International Journal of Emerging Markets, 10*(1), 156–170.

OECD. (2011). *OECD 50th anniversary vision statement.* Meeting of the OECD Council at Ministerial Level, Paris, 25–26 May. https://www.mofa.go.jp/policy/economy/oecd/vision_statement1105.pdf.

OECD. (2024). *OECD Secretary-General tax report to G20 leaders: G20 Brazil,* November 2024. OECD. https://www.oecd.org/en/publications/oecd-secretary-general-tax-report-to-g20-leaders-g20-brazil-november-2024_99a5b4cf-en.html.

Ofori-Amoah, B. (2024). *The African Continental Free Trade Area: Prospects, problems and challenges.* Springer.

Pauwelyn, J. (2023). The WTO's multi-party interim appeal arbitration arrangement (MPIA): What's new? *World Trade Review, 22*(5), 693–701.

Peres, A. (2024). Transience of (in)formality: The role of the joint initiatives in reforming the WTO negotiations. *World Trade Review, 23,* 385–407.

Quick, R., & Das, I. (2023). The EU's CBAM-Regulation stands in contrast to fundamental EU-obligations under the Paris Agreement. https://ielp.worldtradelaw.net/2023/07/guest-post-the-eus-cbam-regulation-stands-in-contrast-to-fundamental-eu-obligations-under-the-paris-.html.

Rajagopal, B. (2009). *International law from below: Development, social movements and world resistance.* Cambridge University Press.

Rosales, O., & Herreros, S. (2021). 'Multilateralizing regionalism' in Latin America and the Caribbean. World Trade Organization. https://www.wto.org/english/res_e/publications_e/wtr11_forum_e/wtr11_14jun11_e.htm.

United Nations Conference on Trade and Development (1985). *The history of UNCTAD 1964–1984.* United Nations.

United Nations General Assembly (2018). *International trade and development* (Resolution 73/219, adopted on 20 December 2018). United Nations. https://documents.un.org/doc/undoc/gen/n18/459/54/pdf/n1845954.pdf.

United Nations General Assembly (2022). *Towards a new international economic order* (Resolution 77/174, adopted on 14 December 2022). United Nations. https://digitallibrary.un.org/record/3998613?v=pdf.

Vlastou-Dimopoulou, F. (2019). Organisation for Economic Co-operation and Development (OECD): The EU's position as a de facto member. In R. A. Wessel & J. Odermatt (Eds.), *Research handbook on the European Union and international organizations* (pp. 316–337). Edward Elgar Publishing.

Winn, J., & Rai, S. (2019). *Trade facilitation and the WTO.* Cambridge Scholars Publishing.

Woodward, R. (2007). The Organization for Economic Co-operation and Development: Meeting the challenges for the twenty-first century? In S. Lee & S. McBride (Eds.), *Neo-liberalism, state power and global governance* (pp. 231–244). Springer.

World Trade Organization (2015). *The WTO at twenty: Challenges and achievements.* World Trade Organization.

Wouters, J. (2020). Le statut juridique des standards publics et privés dans les relations économiques internationales. *Recueil des Cours de l'Académie de la Haye*, 406.

Wouters, J. (2024). The quiet revolution of global governance law. In M. Accetto, K. Škrubej, & J. H. H. Weiler (Eds.), *Law and (R)evolution 1920–2020: Past experiences, future challenges* (pp. 137–150). Routledge.

Wouters, J. (2025). The European Union and global economic governance institutions: Keeping the flame alive in turbulent times. In C. Kaddous & F. Hoffmeister (Eds.), *The European Union diplomacy in Multilateral Fora.* Hart Publishing.

Wouters, J., & De Meester, B. (2007). *The World Trade Organization: A legal and institutional analysis.* Intersentia.

Wouters, J., & Geraets, D. (2012). Private food standards and the World Trade Organization: Some legal considerations. *World Trade Review, 11*(3), 479–489.

Wouters, J., & Hegde, V. (2022). Reform of global trade governance: The role of the European Union. *Journal of European Integration, 44*(5), 715–730.

Wouters, J., & Odermatt, J. (2014). Comparing the 'four pillars' of global economic governance: A critical analysis of the institutional design of the FSB, IMF, World Bank, and WTO. *Journal of International Economic Law, 17*(1), 49–76.

Wouters, J., & Van Kerckhoven, S. (2011). The OECD and the G20: An ever closer relationship? *George Washington International Law Review, 43*(2), 345–374.

8. Fiddlers on the roof? International organisations in the international investment agreement regime as traditional global governance

Yoram Z. Haftel and Tomer Broude

1. INTRODUCTION

What are the governance roles of IOs in the international investment agreement (IIA) regime? This regime – as a 'set of implicit or explicit principles, norms, rules, and decision-making procedures around which actors' expectations converge' (Krasner 1983, 2) in the area of foreign direct investment (FDI) – is a 'radically decentralised' one. For better or for worse, a multilateral institution that addresses FDI is nowhere in sight. Despite several attempts to advance global regulation, at least since the late 1940s, neither a would-be 'World Investment Organisation' (Bonnitcha, Poulsen, and Waibel 2017, 19–22) nor a multilateral agreement on rules and procedures exists, with the 1990s failure of negotiation of a Multilateral Agreement on Investment serving as a cautionary tale (Muchlinski 2000).

Instead, cross-border investment is addressed by more than 3,000 IIAs, most of which are bilateral investment treaties (BITs).[1] By July 2025, more than 1,400 investment disputes between investors and host states had been launched and adjudicated in an institutionally dispersed system known as investor-state dispute settlement (ISDS). Importantly, IIAs are generally similar to each other in their functions, rules, and structure, yet have significant nuances in their content, often because of ISDS experience gained regarding restrictions that they impose on state regulatory autonomy (Haftel and Thompson 2018; Thompson, Broude, and Haftel 2019; Haftel, Link, and Broude 2023). Nevertheless, over time, several intergovernmental IOs have

[1] Other IIAs are treaties with investment provisions (e.g., free trade agreements).

engaged with this regime in various ways. These include the International Centre for Settlement of Investment Disputes (ICSID), part of the World Bank (WB) Group, and two United Nations (UN) bodies: the UN Conference on Trade and Development (UNCTAD) and the UN Commission on International Trade Law (UNCITRAL).[2]

Investigating the latter two IOs,[3] this chapter utilises primary documents and secondary accounts to examine and compare their roles in the IIA regime. Selecting UNCTAD and UNCITRAL for analysis is useful because both are salient fora for the discussion of norms and rules. UNCTAD, with its broader mandate regarding international development, devotes much of its attention in the field of investment to IIA substantive rules, while UNCITRAL, with its broader mandate in commercial law, focuses on ISDS. Moreover, while UNCTAD lacks a law-making mandate, UNCITRAL is considered the principal trade law-making organ of the UN. Additionally, both have attracted only limited scholarly attention in the context of global investment rules. We aim to fill this gap, adopting a comparative perspective.

Understanding the ways in which these IOs affect international investment policies ideally requires an analytical framework that links IOs to global governance more broadly. Recent writings on global governance identify several 'modes' of such governance and ponder their attributes and implications. We utilise this body of work to examine UNCTAD and UNCITRAL as IOs in a systematic manner. Starting with Abbott, Genschel, Snidal, and Zangl (2015), we can distinguish between 'hard' and 'soft' as well as between 'direct' and 'indirect' modes of governance.

Regarding the first distinction, hard modes of governance refer to the delegation of authority to the purported 'governing' IO. Under these conditions, IOs may set clear obligations, conduct binding dispute settlements, and enforce their rules. Softer modes of governance predominate when IOs do not have

---

2 ICSID played a crucial role in setting up ISDS rules and procedures in the regime's early days (St John 2018) but currently has more of an administrative role (Poulsen 2015). The World Trade Organization (WTO) is also relevant, but its main interaction with the IIA regime is through the Trade-Related Investment Measures (TRIMs) agreement, dealing with narrow aspects of investment rules and hence excluded from the analysis. Interactions also exist with the WTO's General Agreement on Trade in Services (GATS) through 'Mode 3' (Broude 2013), but these have unravelled over the last decade (Alschner 2019). The Organisation of Economic Co-operation and Development also interacts with investment but is excluded due to limited space.

3 While part of the UN system, UNCTAD and UNCITRAL function, in practice, as distinct IOs, sometimes labelled emanations, as we explain in the rest of this chapter.

such powers. Then, they have to rely on inducements, persuasion, and epistemic guidance. When unable to set rules themselves, IOs engage in less intrusive activities, which may be subsumed under 'coordination' or 'centralisation' (Abbott and Snidal 1998; Abbott et al. 2015). These may include such roles as serving as a forum or facilitator for negotiation, the exchange of information and views, the collection and dissemination of information, research, and technical assistance.

The difference between direct and indirect modes of governance pertains to relationships between IOs and other actors in a given international regime. Abbott et al. (2015) are especially interested in what they term 'orchestration', wherein IOs delegate responsibilities to mostly non-state 'intermediaries', rather than interacting directly with states. This is not the only way IOs interact with non-state actors, however. Another possibility is global public–private partnerships (PPPs), defined as 'voluntary agreements between public actors (IOs, states, or sub-state public authorities) and nonstate actors (nongovernmental organizations [NGOs], companies, foundations, etc.) on a set of governance objectives and norms, rules, practices, or implementation procedures and their attainment across multiple jurisdictions and levels of governance' (Andonova 2017, 2).

Adjacent to such 'PPPs' is the concept of 'global experimentalist governance' (henceforth: GXG) (De Búrca, Keohane, and Sabel 2014). This approach underscores a bottom-up, trial-and-error process of policy formulation and implementation. GXG may open the possibility for IOs to learn from more 'localised' non-state actors who experiment with 'outside the box' initiatives and adopt and disseminate them more widely. To be clear, we are not endorsing any of these approaches but do espouse them as a springboard for conceptual and empirical exploration of global investment governance.

Our analysis indicates that neither UNCTAD nor UNCITRAL has the authority to set rules, adjudicate disputes, or enforce compliance. Both bodies therefore must rely on soft modes of governance, perhaps the softest on the spectrum: policy analysis and capacity-building, involving both state and non-state actors (UNCTAD), and similar functions with a more enhanced, yet circumscribed, forum for intergovernmental debates and negotiations (UNCITRAL). One is hard-pressed to identify either orchestration or GXG in the work of either IO. Their capacities are in line with the more traditional, formal roles of IOs, emblematic of the UN more generally, and more consistent with conventional theoretical understandings of IOs as arenas for inter-state interaction and bargaining.

Regarding interaction with other actors, here, too, we uncover little evidence of new modes of governance, such as orchestration or GXG. Both UNCTAD and UNCITRAL are, first and foremost, traditional arenas for inter-state interaction and centralised functions – negotiation, information gathering, research, and technical assistance. We nevertheless identify some elements of partnerships in their activities. UNCTAD collaborates with a wide variety of non-state actors, from regional IOs, to local NGOs, to academic institutions. UNCITRAL, as a forum for the development of ideas in such a diffuse system, engages not only with states but with independent legal and academic experts interested in ISDS reform. Ostensibly, such partnerships compensate for these bodies' lack of 'hard' authority and assist in their 'soft', epistemic authority (Zürn 2018).

Overall, we show that the role of IOs in global investment governance has followed traditional modes, with an absence of governance beyond preservation of their positions as negotiation fora, policy analysers, and capacity-builders. Hence our reference in the title to *Fiddler on the Roof*, where Tevye the Milkman proclaims, 'Here in Anatevka, we have traditions for everything' – a nod to the enduring 'traditions' of IO involvement in governance, which have remained largely unchanged despite their engagement in the dynamic and evolving field of international investment law. This chapter further establishes and substantiates this claim. Each of the next two sections takes a closer look at UNCTAD and UNCITRAL, respectively, as IOs in the IIA regime. The final section ponders the implications of this analysis for global investment rules and governance.

2. UNCTAD IN THE IIA REGIME

2.1 UNCTAD and (Lack of) Formal Authority

Insofar as an international regime reflects specific rules and decision-making procedures, the formal authority and institutional independence of IOs to set them are central to their ability to shape it (Abbott and Snidal 1998; Hooghe, Lenz, and Marks 2019). From this perspective, it would be uncontroversial to argue that member states have delegated no formal authority to UNCTAD in the area of international investment policies. As former UNCTAD Secretary-General Rubens Ricupero lamented in 2000, '[UNCTAD] does not set rules on trade and investment, has no enforcement authority and does not resolve disputes involving the national interests of its members' (cited in Taylor and Smith 2007, 83). Instead, bilateral and regional treaties are the main instruments of rule-making and the provision of frameworks for binding dispute settlement. Ad hoc arbitration bodies and domestic courts are the primary tools to adjudicate investment disputes and enforce their rulings.

This lack of authority dates back to UNCTAD's early days. Formed in 1964, UNCTAD is not a self-standing IO. It is not even a specialised agency of the

United Nations (UN),[4] but rather an emanation of the UN General Assembly (UNGA), depending on it for its budget and staff. Nevertheless, starting as a one-off conference in Geneva (not on international investment), it evolved into a permanent body with several formal organisational features. The most important ones are the Ministerial Conference and the Secretariat. The former serves as a forum to debate policy issues and its output reflects member states' positions on development-related matters. It provides UNCTAD with general direction but rarely makes actual decisions, which is why it is sometimes dubbed 'Under No Conditions Take Any Decision' (Nye 1973, 334; Taylor and Smith 2007, 1–2). In the area of FDI, Ministerial Conferences frequently adopted declarations and resolutions on the role of multinational corporations (MNCs) reflecting the positions of member states.

The Secretariat, for its part, is formally a subordinate part of the UN Secretariat, thereby lacking formal powers and independence. As its name suggests, UNCTAD focused on trade and development in the first three decades of its existence, with only limited interest in FDI, MNCs, and IIAs. Instead, the UN established a separate body – the United Nations Centre on Transnational Corporations (UNCTC) – in 1975. The UNCTC was associated with the agenda of the New International Economic Order (NIEO) and was very critical of MNCs (Fredriksson 2003, 5–6). Only in the 1990s, with the UNCTC shut down and its responsibilities transferred to UNCTAD, did investment become a core UNCTAD mandate (Fredriksson 2003; Fredriksson and Zimny 2004). Since then, the UNCTAD Secretariat serves as the UN's focal point for such issues.

Like in other issue areas, UNCTAD was assigned the responsibility for research, policy analysis, technical assistance, and consensus-building in the areas of MNCs, FDI, and investment policy, with increased attention to IIAs (Fredriksson 2003, 7). UNCTAD's Secretariat started working on IIAs in 1996 within the Division of Investment, Technology, and Enterprise Development (DITE), which was later named the Division of Investment and Enterprise (DIAE). We now take a closer look at these functions.

First, given the decentralised nature of the IIA regime, information on IIAs and ISDS has been scattered across national ministries, regional IOs, and various other public and private bodies. UNCTAD took it upon itself to collect and publicise this information. From 1996, UNCTAD published several compendia of IIAs, launching in 2004 an online database of existing IIAs (UNCTAD 2013, 22), which has increased in coverage and sophistication over

[4] UN specialised agencies are IOs working with the UN in accordance with relationship agreements between each organisation and the UN. Examples include the World Bank and the World Health Organization.

time. Currently, UNCTAD's online database includes a wealth of data on most IIAs and ISDS cases. These efforts made UNCTAD almost a 'one-stop shop' for policymakers, practitioners, and researchers interested in IIAs and ISDS.

Second, UNCTAD's Secretariat engaged in research and policy analysis, most notably through the annual World Investment Report (WIR), published since 1991 (initially under UNCTC auspices). WIR devotes at least one chapter to IIAs, and several of its issues have offered extended analyses of IIA-related matters. Alongside WIR, from the late 1990s, the DIAE published numerous papers and reports on IIAs and related matters. This voluminous body of policy analysis strives to inform decision-makers in member states, especially those from the Global South, about trends in international investment policies.

Third, the UNCTAD staff provides training and technical assistance to mostly low and middle-income countries. With the growing interest in FDI and the lack of a multilateral agreement on its regulation, in the 1990s many of these countries turned to IIAs. In contrast to free trade agreements, however, they had little understanding of IIAs and experience with their negotiation (Fredriksson and Zimny 2004, 132; Poulsen 2015). UNCTAD was probably the first international body to identify and fill this void (Fredriksson and Zimny 2004, 132), from at least the early 2000s, organising a large number of training courses, national seminars, and other events intended to build governments' capacity in the area of IIAs. UNCTAD continued these efforts in the 2010s, with a focus on courses and seminars designed to train IIA negotiators from the Global South and the provision of technical assistance on the management of investment disputes. Finally, UNCTAD officials provided ad hoc assistance to states and regional IOs that negotiated IIAs or developed template agreements, known as 'Model BITs', as well as to those that reviewed their IIA programmes or engaged in the renegotiation or termination of IIAs (e.g., UNCTAD 2017, 26–27).

Fourth, since taking on matters related to FDI, DIAE has served as a forum for consensus-building and discussion among government officials and experts on these issues. In so doing, it encouraged coordination among member states on investment rules and practices. In the 2000s, for example, several meetings were held with the intention of reaching agreement on desirable elements of IIAs and their content (UNCTAD 2002, 21–22). UNCTAD also provided a platform for the exchange of ideas and information among a network of several hundred IIA experts (UNCTAD 2006, 8). The role of this network was further institutionalised and enhanced in 2010 with the establishment of an annual 'IIA Conference', in conjunction with the World Investment Forum (UNCTAD 2010, 41).

In summary, it appears that the UNCTAD Secretariat, and DIAE specifically, is tasked mostly with such traditional duties as the collection of information, coordination of member states' activities, the publication of reports, and so on. These strategies fit more comfortably with Abbott and Snidal's (1998, 9) attribute of 'centralisation', which refers to 'a concrete and stable organisational structure and an administrative apparatus managing collective activities' rather than 'independence'. The UNCTAD administration advanced 'support for state interaction' and 'coordination and norm elaboration' (Abbott and Snidal 1998, 10–16) but had no meaningful formal powers to affect investment policies, set a negotiation agenda, or resolve investment disputes (Haftel and Thompson 2006).

2.2 UNCTAD, Institutional Complexity and Modes of Governance

Looking at UNCTAD and the IIA regime from the perspective of regime complexity, we reiterate that IIAs and ISDS were not part of UNCTAD's original mandate. It only took on FDI in the 1990s and quickly became a focal point for all related issues within the UN system. With the failure of the Mulitialteral Agreement on Investment (MAI), it became clear that IIAs are the main instruments through which member states design international investment rules, and UNCTAD began to offer some systematic analyses of development in this area. As we have seen, UNCTAD has gradually added resources devoted to this matter as well as activities and output. Significantly, it was able to leave its mark on the regime's norms and rules because it encountered little competition from other IOs.[5] Unlike other policy areas, in which UNCTAD's role was secondary – that is, in comparison with the WTO regarding trade and the WB regarding development finance – it was helpful that UNCTAD worked in a relatively institution-free environment with respect to investment. Thus, UNCTAD's scope expansion into the area of investment policies strengthened its broader claim for relevance and legitimacy in global economic governance.

Abbott et al. (2015, 12) underscore the distinction between direct and indirect modes of IO governance. They are especially interested in the combination of soft and indirect governance labelled 'orchestration', and emphasise the presence of intermediaries in the governing process. There is little evidence to suggest that UNCTAD is engaged in orchestration by delegating responsibility to non-state actors. UNCTAD commonly works directly with national governments in such functions as technical assistance, capacity-building, and consensus-building. At the same time, UNCTAD is not shy of working with other non-state actors to advance its agenda and disseminate ideas and information. A glance at DIAE activities indicates that it partnered with global and

[5] ICSID may be a partial exception, but its main focus is on ISDS rather than IIAs.

regional IOs as well as with civil society groups and academic institutions in various activities.

With respect to other IOs, the WTO teamed up with UNCTAD in the early 2000s in order to improve FDI policies in the Global South (Fredriksson and Zimny 2004, 133). Such collaboration has waned since then, presumably because the WTO accepted the position of UNCTAD as a leading IO with respect to IIAs (UNCTAD 2010, 20–21). More recently, the OECD's Directorate for Financial and Enterprise Affairs and the DIAE, which have overlapping mandates and competencies, collaborated in a number of ways. Most prominently, they jointly produce annual reports monitoring investment measures of G20 members for this group's meetings. It should be noted, though, that there is only anecdotal evidence of collaboration with IOs dealing with ISDS more directly (i.e., UNCITRAL and ICSID).

UNCTAD also works together with a large number of regional IOs and NGOs, mostly in training and technical assistance. With respect to the former, from its early years, the DIAE partnered with such organisations in its efforts to reach and train officials in the Global South. This collaboration has continued in the 2010s and into the 2020s. In one example, UNCTAD co-organises an annual workshop with the Islamic Development Bank, and in another, it joined forces with the Caribbean Community to organise a regional training session for officials from the latter's member states. NGOs engage with UNCTAD on capacity-building and technical assistance (Taylor and Smith 2007, 42). One area of collaboration is training NGOs on civil society involvement in international investment. UNCTAD also partnered with NGOs like the International Institute for Sustainable Development to organise workshops on IIAs, ISDS, and their implications. Similarly, the DIAE collaborates with academic institutions and experts, in the context of research and policy analysis, but also in organising training sessions and conferences (Fredriksson 2003, 35; UNCTAD 2018, 88).

This reality fits comfortably with the notion of public–private partnerships (PPPs), mentioned in the introduction. Indeed, UNCTAD appears to be at the centre of PPPs involved in international investment policies, and perhaps their main entrepreneur and 'assembler'. This is in line with Andonova's (2017, 3) observation that 'it is IOs that often lead or provide the forum and normative glue for [PPPs], crafting a political space for the interface between public purpose and private practice in international relations'. Furthermore, UNCTAD's partnerships meet most, if not all, aspects of PPPs (Andonova 2017, 8–10). First, it is a decentralised network with multiple sources of authority pooling various competencies of different actors. This is apparent from UNCTAD's collaboration with diverse actors ranging from global and regional IOs to local

NGOs and academic experts. Its network is flexible and not highly legalised.[6] Some of UNCTAD's partnerships are short-lived but others are more long-lasting, depending on particular goals or circumstances. Importantly, actors self-select into this network. That is, UNCTAD partners with like-minded states and non-state actors. In doing so, it is able to retain, amplify, and disseminate its normative position and the policy prescriptions emanating from it.

From this perspective, one might argue that UNCTAD's collaboration with public and private actors is a manner by which it compensates for its lack of formal authority. That is, by working with other actors who see eye-to-eye on investment rules and practices, UNCTAD boosts its epistemic authority and centrality in this area. Interestingly, this seems to go against one of Andonova's (2017, 42) hypotheses that 'IOs are more likely to engage in the development of global partnerships when they have greater agency autonomy'. The UNCTAD case study is more consistent with her argument that

> as IOs open the doors to greater interaction with advocacy or business entities, they can inadvertently or deliberately augment their autonomy by bringing in external resources and reducing financial dependence on the principals or by increasing their informational advantage. Such collaboration can shift the focal point of policy trajectories toward a more activist direction that is favored by the agency or toward the preferences of some principals compared to others.

PPPs can enhance the autonomy even of IOs that are short on this quality.

Finally, we ponder the possibility that UNCTAD is engaged in GXG (De Búrca et al. 2014). GXG requires the fulfilment of five criteria. First, this framework assumes a broadly shared perception of a common problem. This assumption does not hold for the IIA regime. At least since the mid-2000s, international investment rules have been contested, and one is hard-pressed to identify a broadly shared understanding of a common problem. Second, GXG underscores bottom-up rather than top-down dynamics (Keohane and Victor 2015). While UNCTAD may have borrowed some ideas from national governments, NGOs, or academic experts, it seems that much of its efforts and activities are devoted to educating and assisting other actors.

Third, and perhaps most importantly, GXG assumes that the main cooperation problem is uncertainty about the cost, benefits, and outcome of specific policies. Hence, it relies on the knowledge and experience of local actors and requires routine re-evaluation. In the IIA regime, the main problem is the

---

[6] UNCTAD's collaboration with non-state actors is on the less formal end of PPPs and does not constitute a transnational public–private governance initiative, defined as 'Multistakeholder partnerships that *formally* involve states along with IGOs, nongovernmental organizations, and business actors' (Reinsberg and Westerwinter 2021, 61; emphasis ours).

distribution of costs and benefits rather than uncertainty. It is fairly well understood which sets of rules benefit foreign investors (and perhaps home countries) and which favour the flexibility and policy goals of host countries. The main challenge is to balance these divergent objectives. While some experimentation with respect to specific reforms may occur (e.g., the European Union's (EU) multilateral investment court proposals), it is difficult to argue that this approach is central to UNCTAD's role within the IIA regime and that GXG is the most useful framework to analyse this IO.

3. UNCITRAL IN THE IIA REGIME

3.1 UNCITRAL and (Lack of) Formal Authority

We now turn to UNCITRAL,[7] again taking as a departure point the question of formal authority. Like UNCTAD, UNCITRAL is neither a self-standing IO nor a UN specialised agency, but an emanation of the UNGA, dependent on it for budget and staffing (more so than UNCTAD).[8] UNCITRAL may be stronger than UNCTAD as a member-driven rule-making forum, with the original mandate 'to further the progressive harmonization and unification of the law of international trade', yet its formal authorities and independence are very limited, and one is 'struck by the modesty of [UNCITRAL's] goals when viewed against the totality of problems that beset international trade' (Farnsworth 1972, 316). Its rule-making is non-binding and highly dependent

---

[7] We selected UNCITRAL over ICSID for two reasons. First, because of the prevalent use of UNCITRAL Arbitration Rules in ISDS. Originally intended for international *commercial* arbitration, they are incorporated by many IIAs and applied in one-third (351/1070) of known IIA-based ISDS cases. ICSID rules have been used almost twice as much, though UNCITRAL Rules' share is probably higher, considering unreported cases (e.g., contract-based investment disputes). Second, UNCITRAL has over the last decade been the most significant multilateral forum for ISDS reform (the 2013 Rules on Transparency and Working Group III on ISDS reform, since 2017 (WGIII)). ICSID is also active, though to a lesser extent, in ISDS reform (ICSID 2021).

[8] UNCITRAL's annual budget over the last decade is estimated at 3–4 million USD, with a staff of about 20–25. About only one quarter relates to ISDS. This pales in comparison with UNCTAD, which has an annual overall budget of 68 million USD and a staff of more than 450 (UNCTAD 2021). This underlines the weak formal role of the Secretariat and its reduced independence. In 2001, former UNCITRAL Secretary Gerold Hermann stated publicly – in a different context – that '[t]he Secretariat's lack of resources is a particularly disappointing feature' (Hermann 2001, p. 29).

on subsequent choices made by member states, in domestic legislation and treaties. It has no enforcement powers and does not itself resolve disputes.

UNCITRAL was established in 1966 as a standing UN Commission. It reports to the UNGA through the UN Sixth (Legal) Committee, but the International Trade Law Division (ITLD) of the UN Office of Legal Affairs (OLA) functions as its secretariat.[9] Unlike UNCTAD, UNCITRAL was from its initiation envisioned as a political body partaking in international rule-formation, without binding authority. Article 8 of UNCITRAL's Founding Resolution allows it several modes of action to fulfil its mandate, including coordination and a 'close collaboration' with UNCTAD.

Importantly, among these methods of action is that of 'preparing or promoting the adoption of new international conventions, model laws and uniform laws, and promoting the codification and wider acceptance of international trade terms, provisions, customs and practices, in collaboration, where appropriate, with the organizations operating in this field'. This appears to be the main method in which UNCITRAL has been active and influential. UNCITRAL was envisioned as a 'site' (Cohen 2011) for intergovernmental engagement and negotiation over internationally recognised norms, without a priori binding authority. As a classical UN-styled IO, negotiation in UNCITRAL results in legal texts that states may choose to formally ratify or adopt in domestic legislation. One of UNCITRAL's successes has been the 1980 UN Convention on Contracts for the International Sale of Goods (CISG). The CISG provides uniform rules governing international commercial contracts for the sale of goods, applying between parties whose place of business is in contracting states. The CISG has been ratified by 100 states, indeed reflecting the lion's share of international trade volumes, but with notable exceptions, such as the UK (Moss 2005).

UNCITRAL's central forum is the commission itself, whose members are UN states. These are elected in rotation by the UNGA for staggered six-year terms, observing a distribution among the UN's five regional groupings. Originally composed of 29 elected States (Contini 1968), the commission expanded in 1973 to include 36 members, and in 2003 dramatically increased to 60. Other states may participate in commission proceedings without voting rights. The latest expansion of the commission's membership attests to its role as a rule-making forum. In 1979, a commentator noted that '[T]he success of the Commission and the importance of its work have led to keen competition to obtain and retain membership' (Honnold 1979, p. 207). However, it

---

[9] UNCITRAL's secretary, an experienced commercial and ISDS counsel and arbitrator herself, serves concurrently as director of ITLD, as have her predecessors.

also manifests UNCITRAL's position as a conventional political rule-making forum. UNGA's resolution 57/20 of 21 January 2003 to expand membership carefully noted 'that the Commission is a technical body' and that 'the increase of members has neither budgetary implications …, nor serves as a precedent for the enlargement of other bodies'. The caveats reflect perennial budgetary issues and contemporary pressures to expand representative participation in UN bodies.

While the commission serves as UNCITRAL's main body, and the OLA/ITLD serves as its secretariat, there is a significant additional layer of governance, namely the subsidiary working groups, which 'draft the substantive instruments for specific issue areas' (Kelly 2011). UNCITRAL is composed of six working groups, whose mandates shift over time. UNCITRAL and its secretariat undertake other tasks, albeit not always in the area of international investment.

First, UNCITRAL follows standard UN policies to *collect and publicise* information. It has an online, searchable database on international commercial arbitration – 'Case Law on UNCITRAL Texts' (CLOUT) – on the UNCITRAL Model Law of Commercial Arbitration, in which UNCITRAL has deservedly taken great pride. It focuses, however, quite exclusively on the comparative use of this model law in domestic legal systems and does not relate to investment law. UNCITRAL issues a yearbook which, unlike UNCTAD's research-based WIR, is a report of the commission's work and proceedings.

Second, regarding *research and policy analysis*, UNCITRAL's secretariat, by its own depiction, 'is responsible for preparing working papers for [working group (WG)] meetings, providing administrative services to that [WG] and reporting' (UNCITRAL 2013, 7). Moreover, it drafts 'texts on topics that are being considered for possible future inclusion in the work programme' (UNCITRAL 2013, 9), taking an active role in policy formulation. In the current WGIII ISDS reform discussions, the secretariat has issued a considerable volume of 'Notes from the Secretariat' (e.g., UNCITRAL 2021). Roberts (2018, p. 424), focusing on negotiation dynamics of UNCITRAL members, states that '[a]s an international organisation striving for legitimacy and resources in a world of scarcity, UNCITRAL's secretariat actively scouts promising new topic areas for work'. This is not surprising, given the not uncommon 'entrepreneur' position that the broader UN Secretariat has undertaken (Andonova 2017, ch. 3).

Third, UNCITRAL provides only limited *training and technical assistance*. It has a law library in Vienna for delegates and visitors, holds seminars, and conducts some technical cooperation and assistance activities vis-à-vis its model laws. These activities can only be conducted if funds can be obtained from other sources (UNCITRAL 2013, 27). Fourth, UNCITRAL's major strength is its role in *consensus-building and discussion*. Decisions by the commission are taken by consensus but are not binding (i.e., the adoption of model law texts or revisions to rules, such as the arbitration rules, ultimately depend on the extent to which they will be adhered to and incorporated by states and other parties) (see UNCITRAL 2013, 13–21 on types of UNCITRAL instruments).

Notably, UNCITRAL regularly interacts with non-state actors engaged in its mandate, including ISDS. These include other IOs, NGOs – not without controversy (Kelly 2011) – and individuals, with an emphasis on academic and practical expertise.[10] The current work of WGIII with respect to ISDS has garnered the interest of several global IOs, such as ICSID, UNCTAD, the OECD, and the WTO.[11] UNCITRAL welcomes the participation of observers from regional IOs (UNCITRAL 2013, 6), such as the African Union, the Economic Community of West African States, and the Gulf Cooperation Council. In sum, as an IO, UNCITRAL possesses very little formal authority. In contrast to UNCTAD, its main strength appears to be as a space for consensus-building among its member states, in consultation with non-state actors; but of itself, it has no formal, independent powers.

3.2 UNCITRAL and Modes of Governance

We now generally apply the same framework of analysis employed regarding UNCTAD, in order to discern UNCITRAL's mode (or modes) of global governance. We will not repeat the theoretical dimensions and typologies, which cover a spectrum such as formal IOs (Abbott and Snidal 1998), soft/indirect distinctions including orchestration (Abbott et al. 2015), GXG (De Búrca et al. 2014), and PPP (Andonova 2017). On these, we graft other related observations regarding the governance function of UNCITRAL (albeit not in the area of ISDS), as an IO that engages in 'normative modelling' (Cohen 2011) or 'Inventive Global Governance' (Block-Lieb and Halliday 2017).

In our view, despite these different approaches, UNCITRAL is ultimately a traditional, UN-based intergovernmental IO, much along the lines identified by Abbott and Snidal (1998). As we have seen, this includes an active secretariat, engagement with other organisations, governmental and non-governmental, and inputs from outside the organisation, including agenda-setting. Thus, while elements of other modes of global governance may appear in its work, these do not alter the basic mode pursued since UNCITRAL's establishment in the 1960s. This might be a disappointing conclusion for those seeking

---

[10] UNCITRAL has 'always drawn on the expertise and practical know-how of the businessmen and lawyers whom it is ultimately to serve' (Suy 1981, 140).

[11] The EU is the only IO formally participating in WGIII. As it turns out, it plays a key role in the discussions (Broude and Haftel 2022).

new modes of global governance, both descriptive and prescriptive, but it does have implications for the critique and future development and reform of the IIA regime in general and ISDS in particular – and for global governance more generally.

Following Abbott et al. (2015), UNCITRAL is a governance infrastructure that is both soft (i.e., no or little delegation to the IO) and direct (i.e., acting mainly vis-à-vis states). UNCITRAL's mandate in international trade law may be broad, with ISDS only a fraction of it, but it has no authority that goes beyond the decisions of its membership, taken through the commission or, more importantly, in the WGs. Moreover, these decisions – model laws, legislative guides, or other focal points such as the arbitration rules – are themselves not binding. They cannot constitute an advanced mode of delegation to the organisation for several reasons. First, since the practice is one of consensus, this means that states have not 'let go' and still want strong control over outcomes. Second, as noted, outcomes are not binding. Indeed, most of them are subsequently subject to formal adoption by states that is entirely voluntary. States can choose whether and how to incorporate rules into their legal systems, even when adopted by consensus in UNCITRAL. Third, commercial and investment arbitrations involve private parties, and even when acting within the framework of the arbitration rules, they may choose to adopt procedures that stray from the rules, *ex ante* or *ex post*. Although the arbitration rules are a centrepiece of UNCITRAL's contribution to the IIA regime, UNCITRAL and its secretariat are not involved in actual ISDS proceedings. UNCITRAL is not an appointing authority for arbitrators and does not serve as an administrator for disputes.

Is UNCITRAL nevertheless an 'orchestrator', soft and indirect (Abbott et al. 2015) within its mandate in general and in the area of ISDS reform in particular? Block-Lieb and Halliday (2017, ch. 5) – academics who themselves participated as delegates in UNCITRAL work and hence are not entirely removed from the question, opining on the basis of multimethod research – have noted with respect to (non-ISDS) WGs that '[b]ecause the secretariat employs fewer than a dozen of its own staff, UNCITRAL could not have achieved a fraction of its historic output except through the assistance of volunteer delegates'. They describe the establishment of expert groups by invitation, purportedly at the behest of the secretariat, colloquia, 'inner circles and networks', and 'corridor politics'. For example, with respect to the Academic Forum in WGIII on ISDS Reform, such practices exist also in the IIA regime. This might indicate a degree of 'indirect' governance. However, despite this participation of non-state actors, it is hard to say that they have received delegated responsibility from the IO, or that they act as intermediaries of international law-making. To be sure, the implementation of UNCITRAL outcomes is to a large extent left to governments, non-state actors, commercial entities, lawyers, and arbitrators.

Although very different from UNCTAD, UNCITRAL has some elements similar to the concept of PPP (Andonova 2017), for example, with respect to the UN Secretariat, to which UNCITRAL is related. UNCITRAL has acted as a facilitator, a 'site' (Cohen 2011) or a 'space', an 'assembler' for rule-making, and in this course of action, it has engaged with both state parties, as a matter of course, and a range of non-state actors. That said, while the nature of application of UNCITRAL outcomes is decentralised, as PPP would expect (non-binding, requiring application by states, etc.), it is highly legalised, as a UN-mandated, law-making commission. Moreover, participants in UNCITRAL processes, primarily states, do not self-select: they are elected members of the commission and the WGs. They must gain a mandate from their regional grouping, even when they wish to take on the task. Quite naturally, actors do choose their own modus operandi in negotiations (Block-Lieb and Halliday 2017), such as the composition of the delegation and prior consultation mechanisms.

Can UNCITRAL's work be characterised as GXG, addressing the five criteria posited for this mode of governance (De Búrca et al. 2014)? Regarding the first – an inclusive, participatory, and non-hierarchical process set up for states and other participating units to reflect and identify a broadly shared perception of a common problem – this might be broad enough to include the work of UNCITRAL WGIII, although the process cannot truly be said to be non-hierarchical, given the dominance of states and hierarchies between them. It is also far from clear that there is a broadly shared perception of a common problem, despite the formulation of agenda items by consensus in the WGIII (Roberts 2018).

Second, regarding a 'framework understanding' with open-ended goals, the agenda of WGIII can be seen as a framework, but the goals are restricted (e.g., not including substantive law issues) and contested. Most importantly, regarding the third, fourth, and fifth conditions – leaving implementation to lower-level and contextually situated actors; continuous feedback from local contexts with reporting and monitoring; and routine re-evaluation of goals – as with UNCTAD, it seems that GXG is not a useful way to understand the modalities in which UNCITRAL has engaged with the IIA regime. To some extent, most parts of its work output have been left to states, but the discretion to adapt norms is not very high. UNCITRAL can be considered GXG only if state-driven law-making processes are considered to be 'bottom-up' or 'local' (belying their transboundary nature). Moreover, there is practically no 'experimental' governance in UNCITRAL, unless one considers the facilitation of debate regarding new initiatives, such as the multilateral investment court, as experimental; and there is no overt reporting and monitoring.

Finally, Cohen (2011, 568) uses the term 'normative modelling', 'through which legal norms, principles, and standards for the global political economy are articulated' to describe UNCITRAL's work as a 'site' for negotiation (again, not in the ISDS context). Block-Lieb and Halliday (2017, ch. 10) refer to UNCITRAL's 'inventiveness' and the 'technologies' it has used in its law-making roles. Yet, in sum, we believe that UNCITRAL in general, and with respect to ISDS reform in particular (in WGIII), has been operating over the last years very much in line with traditional intergovernmental IO practices. While it involves Secretariat support, engagement with non-state actors, and elements of innovation and modelling, UNCITRAL ultimately remains a forum for inter-state negotiation aimed at developing – and potentially reforming – rules. These activities may reflect creativity, but they do not amount to a new mode of global governance.

4. CONCLUSION

This chapter examined the role of UNCTAD and UNCITRAL in the rather diffused and decentralised IIA regime. It shows that these two IOs have been working in ways that would have been well recognised decades ago and may therefore be considered 'old fashioned': collecting and disseminating information, writing and publishing policy reports and analyses, and organising members' conferences and meetings. There is little evidence that UNCTAD and UNCITRAL engaged in more 'fashionable' (at least in current research on IOs) modes of governance, such as orchestration and experimentation. Ultimately, *plus ca change, plus c'est la meme chose* (the more things change, the more they stay the same). Tevye the Milkman would have put it differently: tradition.

Taken as a whole, the analysis indicates that these UN emanations do not enjoy much formal authority and, from this perspective, have limited ability to influence global investment rules and policies. Nevertheless, they may have more authority than initially meets the eye, though UNCTAD more so than UNCITRAL. The absence of a focal IO in the IIA regime allowed UNCTAD to position itself as an important player in this issue area and gradually accumulate 'epistemic' authority (Zürn 2018). It was able to establish this by articulating a relatively clear, even if changing, position on the desirable direction of the IIA regime and by working with states and non-state actors to disseminate and advocate for it.

From a broader theoretical perspective, while it examines only two IOs in one issue area, this chapter challenges recent efforts to theorise global governance. Insofar as these two UN bodies' emphasis on traditional IO roles is commonplace, it may be the case that the current theorisation of modes of governance is inapplicable to important issue areas of world politics, such as trade and security. This observation calls for greater attention to the cooperation problems IOs are designed to solve and how that affects their mode of governance and nature of authority.

REFERENCES

Abbott, Kenneth W., Philipp Genschel, Duncan Snidal, and Bernhard Zangl. 2015. Orchestration: Global governance through intermediaries. In Kenneth W. Abbott, Philipp Genschel, Duncan Snidal, and Bernhard Zangl (eds.) *International Organizations as Orchestrators*, 3–36. Cambridge: Cambridge University Press.

Abbott, Kenneth W., and Duncan Snidal. 1998. Why states act through formal international organizations. *Journal of Conflict Resolution* 42 (1): 3–32.

Alschner, Wolfgang. 2019. Heading for divorce? Investment protection rules in free trade agreements. In Manfred Elsig, Michael Hahn and Gabriele Spilker (eds.) *The Shifting Landscape of Global Trade Governance*, 325–358. Cambridge: Cambridge University Press.

Andonova, Liliana B. 2017. *Governance Entrepreneurs: International Organizations and the Rise of Global Public–Private Partnerships.* Cambridge: Cambridge University Press.

Block-Lieb, Susan, and Terence C. Halliday. 2017. *Global Lawmakers: International Organizations in the Crafting of World Markets.* Cambridge: Cambridge University Press.

Bonnitcha, Jonathan, Lauge N. Skovgaard Poulsen, and Michael Waibel. 2017. *The Political Economy of the Investment Treaty Regime.* Oxford: Oxford University Press.

Broude, Tomer. 2013. Investment and Trade: The 'Lottie and Lisa' of International Economic Law? In Roberto Echandi and Pierre Sauvé (eds.) *Prospects in International Investment Law and Policy*, 139–155. Cambridge: Cambridge University Press.

Broude Tomer, and Yoram Z. Haftel. 2022. The growing pains of actorness: The European Union in global investment governance. *Journal of European Integration* 44 (5): 749–768.

Cohen, Edward S. 2011. Normative modeling for global economic governance: The case of the United Nations Commission on International Trade Law (UNCITRAL). *Brooklyn Journal of International Law* 36 (2): 567–604.

Contini, Paolo. 1968. Proceedings of the 1968 Annual Meeting of the American Foreign Law Association – The United Nations Commission on International Trade Law (UNCITRAL) – First Session and Preparatory Work. *American Journal of Comparative Law* 16 (4): 666–680.

De Búrca, Gráinne, Robert O. Keohane, and Charles Sabel. 2014. Global experimentalist governance. *British Journal of Political Science* 44 (3): 477–486.

Farnsworth, Allan E. 1972. UNCITRAL: Why? What? How? When? *American Journal of Comparative Law* 20 (2): 314–322.

Fredriksson, Torbjörn. 2003. Forty years of UNCTAD research on FDI. *Transnational Corporations* 12 (3): 1–40.

Fredriksson, Torbjörn, and Zbigniew Zimny. 2004. Foreign direct investment and transnational corporations. In UNCTAD, *Beyond Conventional Wisdom in Development Policy: An Intellectual History of UNCTAD 1964–2004*, 127–140. New York and Geneva: UN.

Haftel, Yoram Z., Morr Link, and Tomer Broude. 2023. Last year's model? Investment arbitration, learning, and the gap between model BITs and IIAs. *Journal of International Economic Law* 26 (3): 483–499.

Haftel, Yoram Z., and Alexander Thompson. 2006. The independence of international organizations: Concept and applications. *Journal of Conflict Resolution* 50 (2): 253–275.

Haftel, Yoram Z., and Alexander Thompson. 2018. When do states renegotiate investment agreements? The impact of arbitration. *The Review of International Organizations* 13 (1): 25–48.

Hermann, Gerold. 2001. The Role of UNCITRAL. In Ian Fletcher, Loukas Mistelis, and Marisa Cremona (eds.) *Foundations and Perspectives of International Trade Law* (28–33). London: Sweet and Maxwell.

Honnold, John. 1979. The United Nations Commission on International Trade Law: Mission and methods. *American Journal of Comparative Law* 27 (2/3): 201–211.

Hooghe, Liesbet, Tobias Lenz, and Gary Marks. 2019. *A Theory of International Organization*. Oxford: Oxford University Press.

ICSID. 2021. Proposals for Amendments of ICSID Rules. Working Paper #6. https://icsid.worldbank.org/sites/default/files/documents/ICSID_WP_Six.pdf (last visited: January 16, 2022).

Kelly, Claire R. 2011. The politics of legitimacy in the UNCITRAL Working Methods. In Tomer Broude, Marc L. Busch, and Amelia Porges (eds.) *The Politics of International Economic Law*, 106–129. Cambridge: Cambridge University Press.

Keohane, Robert O., and David G. Victor. 2015. After the failure of top-down mandates: The role of experimental governance in climate change policy. In S. Barrett, C. Carraro, and J. de Melo (eds.) *Towards a Workable and Effective Climate Regime*, 201–212. London, UK: CEPR Press.

Krasner, Stephen D. 1983. Structural causes and regime consequences: Regimes as intervening variables. In Stephen D. Krasner (ed.) *International Regimes*, 1–21. Ithaca: Cornell University Press.

Moss, Sally. 2005. Why the United Kingdom has not ratified the CISG. *Journal of Law and Commerce* 25: 483–485.

Muchlinski, Peter T. 2000. The rise and fall of the multilateral agreement on investment: Where now? *The International Lawyer* 34 (3): 1033–1053.

Nye, Joseph S. 1973. UNCTAD: poor nations' pressure groups. In Robert W. Cox and Harold K. Jacobson (eds.) *The Anatomy of Influence: Decision Making in International Organizations*, 334–370. New Haven: Yale University Press.

Poulsen, Lauge N. Skovgaard. 2015. *Bounded Rationality and Economic Diplomacy: The Politics of Investment Treaties in Developing Countries*. Cambridge: Cambridge University Press.

Reinsberg, Bernhard, and Oliver Westerwinter. 2021. The global governance of international development: Documenting the rise of multi-stakeholder partnerships and identifying underlying theoretical explanations. *The Review of International Organizations* 16 (1): 59–94.

Roberts, Anthea. 2018. Incremental, systemic, and paradigmatic reform of investor-state arbitration. *American Journal of International Law* 112 (3): 410–432.

St John, Taylor. 2018. *The Rise of Investor-State Arbitration: Politics, Law, and Unintended Consequences*. Oxford: Oxford University Press.

Suy, Erik. 1981. Achievements of the United Nations Commission on International Trade Law. *The International Lawyer* 15 (1): 139–147.

Taylor, Ian, and Karen Smith. 2007. *United Nations Conference on Trade and Development (UNCTAD).* London: Routledge.

Thompson, Alexander, Tomer Broude, and Yoram Z. Haftel. 2019. Once bitten, twice shy? Investment disputes, state sovereignty and change in treaty design. *International Organization* 73 (4): 859–880.

UNCITRAL. 2013. A Guide to UNCITRAL: Basic facts about the United Nations Commission on International Trade Law. New York: UN. chrome-extension://efaidnbmnnnibpcajpcglclefindmkaj/https://uncitral.un.org/sites/uncitral.un.org/files/media-documents/uncitral/en/12-57491-guide-to-uncitral-e.pdf (last accessed: June 13, 2025).

UNCITRAL. 2021. Possible reform of investor-State dispute settlement (ISDS) Draft Code of Conduct – Note by the Secretariat, 15 September. A/CN.9/WG.III/WP.209, https://undocs.org/en/A/CN.9/WG.III/WP.209 (last accessed: January 25, 2022).

UNCTAD. 2002. Progress Report. Work undertaken within UNCTAD's work programme on international investment agreements between the 10th Conference of UNCTAD, Bangkok February 2000, and July 2002 (UNCTAD/ITE/Misc.58). New York and Geneva: UN.

UNCTAD. 2006. *Division on Investment, Technology and Enterprise Development: Activities Report 2006.* New York and Geneva: UN.

UNCTAD. 2010. *Division on Investment and Enterprise: Activities Report 2010.* New York and Geneva: UN.

UNCTAD. 2013. *International Investment Policymaking in Transition: Challenges and Opportunities of Treaty Renewal.* IIA Issues Note, No. 4 (June). New York and Geneva: UN.

UNCTAD. 2017. *Division on Investment and Enterprise: Results and Impact Report 2017.* New York and Geneva: UN.

UNCTAD. 2018. *UNCTAD Reform Package for the International Investment Regime.* IIA Issues Note, Issue 2. York and Geneva: UN.

UNCTAD. 2021. *UNCTAD at a Glance.* Geneva: UNCTAD.

Zürn, Michael. 2018. *A Theory of Global Governance: Authority, Legitimacy, and Contestation.* Oxford: Oxford University Press.

9. Global financial governance: public good under fragmentation

David Levi-Faur, Ilana Blumsack and Dalit Flaiszhaker

1. INTRODUCTION

Why study the network of actors and institutions that govern global finance? The answer might be simple: it is an opportunity not only to identify those actors and institutions that shape the daily governance of global finance, but it is also an opportunity to identify their goals and their jurisdictions. The task is challenging because finance is complex. The governance of global finance is mainly a matter for informal networks of actors, a highly technical domain where deliberations proceed in closed circles of experts and privileged interests (private and public alike). This chapter examines the architecture of the global financial system which carries much of the responsibility for our financial welfare.

Let us start with the definitions that clarify the scope of our subject. *Finance* is defined in a broad manner as the activities, the institutions, and the actors involved in the production and allocation of money. Finance thus denotes the set of activities and the collection of actors, institutions, regulators, and practices that deal with the creation, management, and distribution of money between creditors and debtors. The financial industry subsumes three major connected fields: the monetary system, banking, capital markets, pensions, and insurance (Moloney et al., 2015; Armour et al., 2016). The administrative governance of these functions and institutions differs between countries in more than one respect (Zysman, 1983). Financial regulation is sometimes integrated and is at times divided between different regulatory institutions. In many cases, central banks supervise the banking sector; capital markets are often supervised by an autonomous agency, and pensions and insurance are governed jointly with the stock exchanges in some countries and independently in others (Jordana & Levi-Faur, 2010; Jordana & Rosas, 2018).

Finance can be categorised also by the type of borrower. The first is public finance: government and sub-government borrowing from different sources of lending institutions while using different forms of finance such as bank loans and bonds. The second area is corporate finance: loans, bonds, and stocks from domestic and international markets for corporations. The third is consumer finance: for instance, mortgages and short-term loans from banks or from alternative lenders or credit cooperatives. This money is governed by governments and their institutional agents and acts as a means of payment, a store of value, and a unit of account. Banks, with the cooperation of the state, are still the cornerstone of the financial system, as they produce money using the loans and the credit-making process which are facilitated by their privileged access to cheap loans from the central bank. While banks play an essential role in our financial system, at the same time they are economic and political actors with private interests. The negative externalities of banking may sometimes inflict disastrous consequences on the financial system, to the detriment of the economy and society at large.

Finance carries some significant public good characteristics and therefore plays a functional role in society. It is the process in which money used as savings or short-term deposits circulates from one entity to another in any domestic or global jurisdiction via financial instruments – for instance, different types of loans or stocks – for various purposes. It is useful to understand that while finance has a social and economic function, it is also an industry with private interests in and of itself, with worldviews and particular ways of self-organisation and norms. While there are some overlaps between the interests of finance and the public good, the extent of these overlaps is highly contested in some circles, although they are a matter of agreement in the closed financial-policy network that composes finance. A pro-market approach to financial regulation – at the global and national levels – seems to be the norm. In practice, the extent to which this approach is manifested varies greatly across different parts of the system, with insurance on the light side compared to the banks, depending on the country, region, size of the institution, era, and type of issue.

Cross-border capital flows have grown substantially in the last three decades. People sometimes assume that this growth in global capital flow goes against the will and the interests or control of the state and other public institutions, as global finance may be perceived as 'free' from institutions (Porter, 2005, p. 25). This unfounded suggestion tends to ignore the interests of some of the most powerful states (or better yet, important financial constituencies in those states) in an era of capital liberalisation. The suggestion also ignores the degree to which this liberalisation rests on a system of rules and institutions that are mainly public. As Tony Porter already observed: 'no one is going to transfer millions of dollars electronically without being confident that the transaction is governed by a wide variety of rules' (Porter, 2005, p. 25). Perhaps most important is the extent to which this liberalisation involves uncertainty and instability, which in turn requires even more controls.

The globalisation of capital thus goes hand in hand with the globalisation of governance institutions and actors. *Governance*, in contrast to the term *government*, represents a paradigmatic shift in the way we think about the social and economic order. Governance – by which we mean order, its scope, intensity, and legitimacy – is made up of more than governments and states. Private and transnational orders co-exist with governmental and intergovernmental orders. Together, they constitute more decentralised, multi-level, and hybrid forms of order than the conventional theory of government suggests (Dingwerth & Pattberg, 2006; Levi-Faur, 2012). By *global financial governance*, we refer to the collection of public and private governance arrangements that compose the incomplete and evolving institutional landscape, which in turn governs both the financial industry and its governing bodies.

As we demonstrate in the following sections, the overriding and most prominent issue that organises the global financial regulation regime is financial stability. Stability – rather than development, access, fairness, antitrust, or consumer affairs – is the driving force behind global financial organisation. Against a backdrop of global regulatory competition, when global financial stability is in question, it is assessed against divergent national interests and the autonomy of the pertinent regulators. Domestic institutional structures; traditions of financial governance; a normative approach to finance, markets, and governments; variations in the size of financial markets and the economy, and financial capacities (including governance capacity) define the interests of the actors and the extent to which actors promote informal or formal global financial institutions and policies.

The rest of this chapter is organised into four parts. The first part deals with global financial regulation as a public good. The second part depicts prominent examples of the institutions and actors that govern finance. The third and penultimate part sets out to assess the architecture of the regulation of global finance, and the fourth part concludes the chapter.

2. GLOBAL FINANCIAL GOVERNANCE AS A GLOBAL GOOD

In highly developed capitalist systems, almost everyone suffers when the financial system is dysfunctional, while everyone benefits when the financial system functions well. We write 'almost everyone' because instability itself is sometimes in the short-term interest of financial interests that can gain from certain degrees of instability and even from a more profound level of instability. Nonetheless, a resilient financial system is a public good. But who should provide a well-functioning and resilient financial system? What is a well-functioning and resilient financial system? Is it stock-market based or bank based? Should it prioritise stability, or flexibility and innovation (Ford, 2017)? How much risk should we allow the financial system to take? How should we value short-term or long-term financial strength? And, how will the short- and long-term benefits of a strong financial system be distributed? All these questions, and more, arise when it comes to the discussion of finance as a global public good. This section discusses finance as a global public policy good, before it introduces financial instability as the major issue composing the supply of global regulation as a public good. The section concludes with a brief discussion of some public goods that the global financial regime does not provide.

2.1 Finance as a Global Public Good

Public goods are goods, including services, institutions, and values, that constitute the community, that is, define its identity, mission, and its boundaries, or benefit from it through practices such as exchange, gift, stability, legitimacy, trust, and efficacy. In other words, public goods are both the institutions that govern society and the goods that are provided for the public. When we say 'public good', we deal both with the constitutive elements of the public and the efficiency aspects.

The distribution of public goods can be done with or without reducing the potential or the actual benefits of others. This distribution can be efficiency-driven or normatively driven. However, this definition of public goods is rather broad. A narrower and more common definition of public goods aims to draw the line between goods that are public by nature and goods that are more private. It confines the term 'public good' to goods that are both non-rivalrous and non-excludable. Financial stability, for example, is a public good. We all enjoy it, though not to the same extent, but at the same time we cannot charge for it or sell it on the basis of personal benefit. What makes public goods unique and interesting for scholars and public policy analysts is that they are prone to undersupply and to free riding. Unlike public goods, private goods are supplied for a fee. Private goods are *private* in the sense that their consumption is excludable (i.e., conditional on a fee or a price).

At the same time, the consumption of private goods makes them scarcer or less available to others. Take for example a financial service such as a loan. Loans are private goods in the sense that their provision is conditional upon repayment. When they are available for one, they are unavailable to others, in particular given the constraints on the risks that loans bear. We would say in such cases that these loans are 'excludable and rivalrous'. Conventional wisdom suggests that the provision of *public* goods is the domain of government action and hierarchies, whereas the provision of *private* goods is the domain of the market. A significant part of the discussion around public goods – at both national and global levels – revolves around the claim that public goods represent a problem of classic collective action. At the same time, the debate has revolved around the actual match between a certain industry and a good as a public or private good. It is perhaps not surprising that few goods are purely private or public (Kaul et al., 1999). In our context, the discussion is about to what extent finance, or its constitutive parts and functions, is a public or a private good. And of course, later on, we should also discuss to what extent it is a national, regional, or global public or private good.

It is useful to distinguish between two hybrid types of goods and services (see Figure 9.1). Given that public and private goods are distinguishable based on their excludability and rivalry, what about situations where only one of the two conditions are met? This introduces a useful conceptualisation of two more types of goods and services, with some examples from the field of finance, that are a mixture between private and public goods. *Club goods* are goods that are non-rivalrous and excludable. Since consumption is non-rivalrous, the 'tragedy of the commons' – that is, overconsumption or the overproduction of goods or services – would hardly be applicable here. An example of a club good is financial education; one can provide it to some members of the club to the exclusion of others. In an ideal world, to get the same financial education as others, one's financial education does not come at the expense of those others.

		Rivalry	
		Rivalrous	**Non-rivalrous**
Excludability	**Excludable**	**Private Good** (e.g., loans, payment systems)	**Club Good** (e.g., financial education)
	Non-excludable	**Common Pool Good** (e.g., sovereign wealth fund)	**Public Good** (e.g., financial stability, deposit insurance)

Source: Author's own compilation.

Figure 9.1 A narrow perspective on public goods

Still, when one's financial education is not one constant or coherent learning event, but rather a process of learning, it might become an instrument of gaining benefits at the expense of others. Common pool resources, on the other hand, are goods that are rivalrous and non-excludable. Here the tragedy of the commons hits forcefully, and it requires some economic, social, or administrative mechanism to limit the depletion of common resources. An example is a sovereign wealth fund that limits present consumption for the benefit of future generations.

It is useful to note that simply because a good is in the public sector does not mean it is a public good (Stiglitz, 2006, p. 150). Sometimes private hierarchies in the form of meta-organisations or trade organisations provide a public good either to everyone or solely to their members. The same holds true for private goods: supply by the private sector does not necessarily make a good private. Economic power, political power, and social norms determine the provision of goods as much as the degree of their rivalry or excludability. It is also important to note that public goods – for example, knowledge – can be turned by government legislation into a private good via procedures, such as a patent.

2.2 Financial Stability as the Global Public Policy Good?

Financial stability is widely considered a virtue. Consequently, financial instability is considered a vice, even if it may carry some positive externalities. Financial instability not only destroys economic assets, it also destroys human lives. In this sense, the stability of financial markets, at the global, regional, and national levels, is priceless. This does not mean that there is full consensus around the desirability of stability; it only means that the issue of global financial stability is the overarching public good that has so far had the largest effect on the shape of global financial governance (Frieden, 2016). Nonetheless, stability – like meals – does not come for free. It has costs, and those costs are not necessarily distributed evenly. To achieve stability, one needs to limit business risks and uncertainty and increase the accountability of the main actors and institutions. This is especially of interest in finance because financial markets are notoriously unstable and subject to periodic crises, with substantial economic and social costs. Financial instability is expressed, for example, in runs on banks; volatility of capital markets; currency and exchange rate crises; over-indebtedness of sovereign states, corporations, or households, and the general instability of the rules of the game, for instance, sudden changes in capital account regimes or interest rates. Table 9.1 provides a summary list of the potential sources of instability. The more economically and financially interdependent countries and regions are, the greater are the effects of instability – and of the measures to reduce the impact of that instability – on other countries and regions. Financial instability is highly transmittable and highly infectious.

Table 9.1 Financial sources of global financial instability

Issue	Potential problems	Elaboration
The stability of the value of money over time	Inadequate or volatile inflation rates	Too high and too low inflation rates are costly for economic growth and therefore for the stability of the financial system
The price of credit	Inadequate or volatile interest on the price of credit	Interest rates that are too high or too low lead to under- or over-borrowing, or to quick changes in the price of credit. This in turn leads to the collapse of countries, corporations, or consumers
Exchange rates (currency crises)	Inadequate or volatile exchange rates	Inadequate exchange rates affect the conditions of trade negatively and may create manipulative capital flight. Volatility in exchange rates is a cost and a source of risk for business, countries, and consumers
Debt problems of corporations, the public sector and consumers	Too much or too little debt by corporations, the public sector and consumers	Sustainable debt for productive and constructive purposes affects the financial and economic system positively. Too much or too little debt is a source of risk (e.g., sovereign defaults)
Saving problems	Too much or too little in savings	Imbalances in trade create instability between over-savers and under-savers
National balance of payments	Consistent surpluses or deficits	Deficits and surpluses have to be recycled through the international system, but this recycling cannot continue without limit
Reckless behaviour of the financial industry	Speculation, high leveraging, asset liability mismatches, creative reporting	Competitive pressures create incentives for reckless behaviour
Problematic regulatory rules, strategies, or institutions	Regulatory failures, regulatory completion, blame shifting, blame avoidance	Regulation adds its own risks to the system even if, on balance, it is necessary and useful
Growing systemic risk	Integration of the financial system and its regulation in one centre creates systemic risks	Integration increases dependency, complexity, and sometimes increases vulnerabilities

Issue	Potential problems	Elaboration
Trust panics	Banking panics, stock market crashes, currency panics, contagion, herd behaviour	Cases where lack of confidence in the financial institutions or their regulators leads to cycles of destructive behaviour by both rational and irrational actors

Source: Author's own compilation.

Against this background, it is widely recognised that measures taken to stabilise the international financial system can benefit all countries and are therefore considered a public good (Kaul et al., 1999, Porter, 2005; Frieden, 2016).

Every financial action has some externalities: both positive and negative. Some externalities are costly, and some are less so. The distribution of the costs and benefits of externalities varies across and between groups, and this adds another dimension to the complex considerations of financial governance. In the provision of financial stability, for example, the positive externality enjoyed by all actors is a more stable economic environment, but when providing too much of this stability, the negative externalities can hit economic growth, for instance, because less funding is available for new industries.

When one moves the concept of public good to the global level, the distribution and scale of the externalities often change, and the structure of incentives, the access to resources, and the ability to enforce agreements and contracts varies. In this context, *globalisation of the public good* means purposeful collective action by international institutions to provide goods and services at the global level. Still, the globalisation of public goods – such as financial stability – may also be the result of unilateral moves of national or domestic actors that have positive or negative effects on other nations. Financial stability in the United States has positive effects on other countries and actors, simply because it is the biggest economy in the world and the major global financial actor. Financial inclusion in one country may lead to a spiral of norms and actions that increase financial inclusion in other countries. Actors – state and corporate alike – cannot confine the effects of their actions to within their borders. For example, the devaluation of the Chinese renminbi directly affects China's trading partners. This means that not only the stability but also the 'efficient' rate of the Chinese currency has some of the characteristics of a global public good. Of course, not all currencies or exchange rates have the same distributive effects. Some are of minor importance in global commerce, even if they have highly significant effects in their domestic environment. In the grand scheme of things, since a certain financial interdependence is accepted as a virtue, the use of regulation to maximise benefits and to minimise costs is ineluctable. The more interdependent the world is, the more important are the problems of positive and negative externalities of financial stability and instability, and the more important it is for the global system to provide the right incentives for maintaining stability.

2.3 Beyond Financial Stability: Mobilising Finance for the Greater Good

Finance and its governance systems can contribute to the greater financial good. They can do this not only with regard to global, national, and regional stability, as explained above, but also in other spheres, such as economic development, social inclusion, sustainability, human rights, security and equality. For now, as our analysis suggests, the ambitions surrounding these other goods are limited, with the exception of security via the global Anti-Money Laundering (AML) regime and Counter Terrorist Finance (CTF). Action for financial development is relatively limited at both the global level (e.g., the World Bank) and the regional level (e.g., the Inter-American Development Bank, the Asian Development Bank). The efforts to coordinate action for financial inclusion at the global level have come about through new financial technologies rather than through international or intergovernmental actions. Progressing at a slow pace, the greening of the economy through the creation of sustainability criteria at the financial level has been modest and sluggish, not unlike the conditionalities with respect to human rights criteria in financial action. In the current normative order – where inequality is growing without an effective response from the rich countries – the probability of concerted global action for re-distributive policies is rather low.

While some examples of important progress do exist, they are marginal to the main interest of the chief players. Take for example the UN's *Guiding Principles on Business and Human Rights*. The guidelines promote, inter alia, good corporate citizenship, but they stop short of determining the responsibility of businesses for working relations with non-conforming businesses or state entities. The relevant guideline puts forth a governance model that eschews not only hard law measures, but it also only stipulates the liability of the actors for their own direct actions. This narrow approach regarding the liability and responsibility of the actors is the rule.

One notable exception is the AML/CTF regime, where banks (and other organisations) have increasingly been held accountable not only for their own business practices, but also for those of their clients. Sanctions have become more and more salient, and the reach of that regime has extended into the global realm. This exception may suggest an interesting avenue for progress, as it demonstrates the mobilisation of the financial system as part of this regime, where banks and other economic actors have been obliged to report suspicious financial activities. Here, the financial system works as an agent against drug trade, terrorist activity, human trafficking, tax evasion, and corruption. Banks and their senior officers are increasingly subject to large fines and criminal prosecution if they fail to meet the growing standards of the institutional regulatory and compliance systems. Thus, a public good that is not directly connected to stability, or even to good financial governance, is achieved by means of the financial system. Banks have become semi-regulators of AML and the foot soldiers in the fight against certain types of crimes and terrorism. On the one hand, banks are now at the front of implementing the AMF/CTF regime, while on the other hand, this regime is not connected (at least not directly) to financial stability.

2.4 Global Financial Governance as a Global Public Good

The primary challenge of global policy for public goods is that despite the widespread benefits they carry for many people as well as across borders, there are no immediate for-profit or not-for-profit actors to produce them. The demand is there, but the supply is less so (Frieden, 2016, p. 34). This is not an issue of negligence or the cost of coordination, but rather a matter of interest. No central global financial institution exists to set and enforce formal global rules on finance. Unlike state-level financial markets, global financial markets – for states, corporations, and individuals – show a weakness of the formal institutional setting to govern them, or of a global sovereign to act as the lender of last resort, or of a bankruptcy option for dealing with financial instability. In the absence of such tools, responsibility has been laid at the feet of the International Monetary Fund (IMF) (Copelovitch, 2010, p. 12), although its mandate is limited. In the language of the public goods literature, we can say that the benefits of financial stability are not *excludable* (we do not charge globally for stability) and that stability is not *rivalrous* (one's benefits do not come at the expense of others). To overcome this challenge, we need to trust governments to identify stability as a good and to balance it against gains and risks. However, at the global level, there is no single clear governor. How should an architecture be designed – one that would solve the problem without leading to some carrying the costs or reaping the benefits at the expense of others? The answer to that question is not that clear, and the US – considering its primary role in the global economy – has not signalled any decisive moves towards a formal stable solution in recent decades. Instead, some narrow regimes and informal institutions have emerged to tackle the issue. Governments' approaches to global financial regulation still differ widely, torn between a hands-off approach (self-regulation) and a 'hands-on approach'. The EU is very active in this domain through its membership of and its participation in informal bodies such as the G20 or the Financial Stability Board (FSB).

3. ACTORS AND INSTITUTIONS IN GLOBAL FINANCIAL GOVERNANCE

This section presents the primary international organisations that operate in the finance sector, together with their tasks. There are three types of actors: (a) formal international organisations; (b) informal international, intergovernmental and transnational organisations; and (c) hybrid and private actors. We will briefly explore the most prominent institution of each type and provide an example to demonstrate the basic characteristics of each one.

3.1 Formal International Organisations

The two formal intergovernmental organisations in the global financial architecture are the IMF, and the World Bank. We will focus on the IMF.

The formal aim of the IMF is 'to foster global monetary cooperation, secure financial stability, facilitate international trade, promote high employment and sustainable economic growth, and reduce poverty around the world'.[1] Striving to enhance overall macroeconomic activity – that is, sustaining stability while allowing for economic growth – the IMF nowadays pushes forward an agenda of open capital markets and 'responsible' fiscal policy via conditionalities imposed on countries in crisis that need its loans (Jensen, 2004; Lipscy, 2015). While membership of the IMF is open and includes 189 countries[2] voting rights are weighted according to the members' gross national product. Additionally, the United States holds veto power on much of the IMF's operation and over its agenda (Weisbrot & Johnston, 2016).

The two main tools of the IMF are surveillance and lending. The goal of surveillance is 'to help head off risks to international monetary and financial stability, alert the institution's member countries to potential risks and vulnerabilities, and advise them of needed policy adjustments'[3] (Moschella, 2012). Using the second tool – lending – the IMF's loans to member countries are for short-term crisis management rather than for purposes of development or welfare. The terms of IMF loans include conditionalities, that is, demands for a commitment from the receiving country to introduce a balanced budget and to implement some austerity measures. As Jensen states (Jensen, 2004), the

---

1 International Monetary Fund. (n.d.). *About the IMF.* Retrieved September 1, 2024, from https://www.imf.org/en/About.

2 International Monetary Fund. (n.d.). *IMF Country Information.* Retrieved September 1, 2024, from https://www.imf.org/en/Countries.

3 International Monetary Fund. (2007). *Bilateral surveillance over members' policies: Executive board decision.* International Monetary Fund.

main focus of these conditions is to control deficits and to encourage market liberalisation.

The IMF does not act – nor does it have the capacities or resources to act – as the global central bank and the global lender of last resort. While the IMF is a highly technical institution, with considerable financial expertise, it is at the same time a highly political institution. The IMF has been criticised, for example, for its policies depending on the interest of not only its largest shareholders, namely the West and America, but also its bureaucrats, both of whom exercise partial but incomplete control over IMF policymaking (Copelovitch, 2010, p. 6). 'The high correlations between voting with the US on the Security Council and the lending decisions of the IMF' attest to the dominance of the US (Vreeland, 2019). Austerity policies and lending conditions have been more demanding when a country was challenging Western and especially US interests.

3.2 Informal Governmental Organisations

An extensive system of informal global institutions lies at the heart of global financial architecture. We will focus on the Bank for International Settlements (BIS), the organisation that provides the platform for much of this informal activity. Yet, other informal regulatory bodies should also be mentioned in this regard, such as The International Organization of Securities Commissions (IOSCO), the international body that brings together the world's securities regulators and sets the global standards for the securities sector. There are also two informal global institutions that provide specific public goods: the FSB – an informal international body that monitors, makes recommendations for, and coordinates standard-setting and implementation regarding the global financial system – and the Financial Action Task Force (FATF), whose goals are to set standards and to promote the effective implementation of legal and operational measures for combating money laundering, terrorist financing, and other threats related to the integrity of the international financial system.

The BIS is one of the most important symbols of the informal institutions of global financial governance. It is often referred to as the 'central bank of central banks' (Seabrooke, 2006; Hughes & Palke, 2019). The BIS aims to serve as a platform for cooperation and information-sharing of central banks and financial regulators in their pursuit of monetary and financial stability (Seabrooke, 2006; Alexander (2009a).

After the 2008 global financial crisis, *macroprudential policy*, which focuses on connected and correlated failures among institutions, became a prominent term in the international financial discourse. As its advocate, the BIS has gained substantial impact on shaping financial policy in various countries (Westermeier, 2018). Moreover, since macroprudential policy focuses on the financial system as a whole, it calls for top-down regulation and supervision, which the BIS has helped to provide (Maes, 2010). Consequently, by utilising its authoritative status and position as an international host, as well as its ability to conduct research and policy analysis, the BIS has gradually increased its influence on senior policymakers, both inside and outside the banking system. Gradually, the BIS has become not only an institution that fosters cooperation, but one that takes an active role in shaping global financial policy (Westermeier, 2018).

Today, the BIS also serves as the host of several highly important and specialised committees in financial oversight. The most important of these committees is the Basel Committee on Banking Supervision (BCBS). The BCBS marks the most significant progress towards global financial governance. It has been seeking to improve the quality of banking worldwide 'by adopting international standards of prudential supervision covering such issues as capital adequacy and consolidated supervision of a bank's cross-border operations' (Alexander et al. 2005, p. 35). Although BCBS regularly disseminates guidance and information to its members on best banking and regulatory practices, its hallmark is the Basel Accords. These Accords are advisory in nature, because the committee has no legal supervisory authority over any country's banking system (Felsenfeld & Bilali, 2004).

In addition, the BIS hosts global institutions that keep independent presence such as FSB and the International Association of Insurance Supervisors (IAIS).

Informal intergovernmental authority in the financial world has also evolved as summit diplomacy in the form of clubs of rich countries and under the label the 'Group of …'. The most important is the smallest of these clubs: The Group of Seven (G7). This is an informal forum of the most industrialised countries that is in charge of a process in which heads of state, finance ministers, and central bankers hold an annual cycle of meetings. The G7 process has no official legal status, no permanent home base, and no secretariat (Baker, 2008, p. 3).

The annual G7 summit is important for the interdisciplinary discussion of political, security, and economic matters, as well as for the formation of a consensus among the leaders of the world's major countries. Developments in this regard have responded to increasing financial globalisation, financial crises, and instability.

Another important informal body is The Group of Twenty (G20) – an intergovernmental forum for international economic cooperation. The G20 brings together the leaders of the largest economies, representing around 80% of the world's economic output. Throughout the year, representatives from the G20 countries gather to discuss financial and socioeconomic issues.

3.3 Hybrid and Private Governance

A typical hybrid body is the Group of Thirty (G30). This group is a non-profit, international body consisting of very senior representatives of the private sector, the public sector, and academia from all countries, including emerging markets (Kenen, 2008; Chiang, 2012; Tsingou, 2015). As the name suggests, it has 30 members at any one time (Tsingou, 2015, p. 235). The G30 aims to deepen the understanding of international economic and financial issues and to explore the international repercussions of decisions taken in the public and private sectors.

In addition to these informal groups, there are numerous private bodies that are relevant to global financial governance, including business and professional institutions. One example is the Institute of International Finance (IIF). The IIF is the global association for the finance industry and has over 400 member organisations in 70 countries. Its mission is 'to advocate for regulatory, financial and economic policies that are in the broad interests of its members and foster global financial stability and sustainable economic growth'.[4] IIF members include commercial and investment banks, asset managers, insurance companies, hedge funds, and central banks. The IIF facilitates member meetings with policymakers and regulators, and it employs a team of economists to conduct independent research on the global financial market. It also organises member-only meetings and conferences.

Another example of a private body that is relevant to global financial governance is the International Swaps and Derivatives Association (ISDA). ISDA is a trade organisation of participants in the market for over-the-counter derivatives (Flanagan, 2001, p. 227). It represents all market participants globally in furtherance of high trading standards and market integrity.[5] Its mission includes the following goals: fostering safe and efficient markets; representing the industry through public policy engagement, education, and communication; enhancing counterparty and market-risk practices, and ensuring a prudent and consistent regulatory capital and margin framework. To achieve these goals, the ISDA supports several committees and conferences on a wide variety of issues in the industry (Morgan, 2008, pp. 645–646). It is also an influential lobbyist on regulatory issues worldwide (Morgan, 2008, p. 649).

The ISDA also attempts to develop standardised documentation globally. This is to pursue legal certainty and maximum risk reduction while advancing practices related to trading in order to enhance the safety, liquidity, and

---

[4] Institute of International Finance. (n.d.). *About the IIF.* Retrieved December 14, 2024, from https://www.iif.com/.

[5] International Swaps and Derivatives Association. (n.d.). *ISDA*. Retrieved December 14, 2024, from https://www.isda.org/.

transparency of global derivatives markets. The best known of these standardised documents is the 'ISDA Master Agreement'.

4. THE ARCHITECTURE OF GLOBAL FINANCIAL GOVERNANCE

'The Western financial system is rapidly coming to resemble nothing as much as a vast casino', wrote Susan Strange in her manuscript *Casino Capitalism* (Strange, 2015 [1986], p. 1). The casino metaphor was as true in the 1980s as it is today. There have been changes of course – many of the financiers have been replaced by fast computer algorithms and high-speed communication networks – but the gambling goes on. The managers and owners of the casino usually win. But perhaps the metaphor is not that useful, since the structure of the system may be resilient, and the price that is paid may be worth it. Who can guarantee that a more robust, centralised, and formalised system can provide better performance? The jury is still out on this question, even if – given the recent financial crisis of 2007 – common sense suggests that financial stability is the victim of excessive risk taking and greed.

One thing is clear, however: the current regulatory architecture of global financial governance is *fragmented*, and it is fragmented in more than one sense. We identify eight characteristics of this fragmentation. It is fragmented in a sense that there is no single financial actor – neither weak nor strong, public or private, formal or informal – that fully and formally supervises global finance. There is no 'World Financial Supervision Organisation' in the same way that, since 1995, we have had the World Trade Organization (WTO) and the General Agreement on Tariffs and Trade (GATT) before it (Singer, 2007; Brummer, 2011). Global financial governance is fragmented also in the sense that different types of public and private organisations act in tandem without appropriate and clear lines of legal or normative accountability. Global financial regulation is furthermore fragmented in the sense that it is not part of the United Nations system of governance in general or economic governance in particular. It is a world in and of itself, with strong boundaries vis-à-vis other arenas of governance. Finally, fragmentation manifests in the existence of three different governance organisations: formal international organisations (such as the IMF), club organisations (G7, G20), and technical pillars (BIS committees). These various dimensions of fragmentation have been sustained and reinforced by fragmented domestic structures of regulatory governance in the US and by split governance and organisations of the financial system in the leading financial countries (Germain, 2010, p. 154).

The second characteristic of global financial governance is that it is highly *informal*. Informality is evident in that the authority to promote global goods and avoid global risks is not ratified by international conventions. In other words, it is not institutionalised. In this sense, the regulation of global finance is a notable exception to the trend of legalisation in world politics (Singer, 2007, p. 9). Of course, this informality – often described as 'soft law' – serves the interests of the major players in the system. But in a highly globalised world, it also allows for flexibility of governance arrangements while safeguarding the priorities of national interests and policy communities. Informality allows technical actors – central bankers and other financial regulators – to avoid or circumvent proper governance. At the same time, informality potentially permits criticism, in theory at least, for a lack of legitimacy. Informal arrangements are not legally binding, and thus compliance and enforcement are left to normative actors and peer pressure and to 'market discipline', when markets work. Informality is apparent in the fact that many of the global regulatory and governance institutions are informal. Such is the case of the informal G7, as well as the publicly obscure BIS with its various committees (Porter, 2005, p. 32; Westermeier, 2018, p. 175). To be more concrete, one can draw on David Zaring's (1998) examples. The founding document of the IAIS is its certificate of incorporation as a non-profit organisation in the state of Illinois. The IOSCO similarly derives its legal existence from a private bill passed by the Quebec National Assembly. The BCBS, unlike IOSCO and IAIS, does not even have a legal existence at a national level; its existence was first marked by a press release issued through the BIS. It is hardly surprising, therefore, that its three Basel Accords do not have a formal status (Zaring, 1998).

Third, global financial governance is dominated by *technical and professional discourse rather than by political discourse*. This is clearly the result of the complexity of the field. It nevertheless also reflects the fact that financial regulators themselves are professional bureaucrats, mostly with degrees and experience in finance rather than in general economic policy. Field issues and policy issues on the agenda rarely get public attention. This is especially the case when issues move to the global arenas (Singer, 2007; Frieden, 2016). Global arenas allow central bankers and the financial community to shape financial regulation and to respond to financial crises. Perhaps paradoxically, rather than diminishing the prominence of central bankers, the global financial crisis has resulted in an increase in the salience of central bankers.

The fourth characteristic of global financial governance is that it is highly *nationally based*, with governments delegating little agency to international organisations. Again, the national character of global financial regulation is expressed in the prominent role of nationally based central bankers and other financial regulators in the global arenas.

Fifth, and following the national character of financial regulation, *domestic politics* – especially of the most powerful nations – counts heavily in the decisions about how much, when, and in what form to migrate regulation to the global level. This suggests that the reluctance of national regulators to delegate upwards to global and regional jurisdictions derives from additional considerations and not only from the protection of their power. Domestic financial interests in the main centres of finance exert influence that limits the powers of the global financial regulatory regime (Porter, 2005, p. 27; Underhill & Zhang, 2008; Donnelly, 2019, pp. 362–363).

Sixth, global financial governance is organised around the *interests of the Western liberal, and often rich, democracies.* It reflects the priorities of the club of rich countries and their dominance in the economic and military spaces at least since the nineteenth century. This means, as observed by Jones and Knaack, that rule-making powers are restricted to a select number of mostly developed economies: 'The Financial Stability Board (FSB) at the apex of international regulatory cooperation includes only 25 jurisdictions, while the Basel Committee on Banking Supervision has 28' (Jones & Knaack, 2019, p. 194). The 'Asian Century' might prove to have a significant effect in the future, but for now, its effect on the direction of global financial regulation is rather modest.

Seventh, global financial governance is more specifically *US-centred.* The US is the pivot and the veto player that exerts the greatest veto role (Posner, 2009). There are nonetheless changes towards more transatlantic cooperation, and the EU is fortifying the European bargaining position vis-à-vis the hegemon.

The final characteristic of global financial regulation – like domestic financial regulation – is that it cannot be captured by the neoliberal narrative of state versus finance (and vice versa). Given the centrality of finance in the economy, the main storyline is state with finance (Helleiner, 1995; Porter, 2005, pp. 18–20). More controls by the state blur the distinction between politics and the economy at the same time that the professional elite of central bankers and financial regulators is more dominant and more powerful than the politicians.

5. CONCLUSIONS

Finance and global financial governance are among the most influential activities in our economies, polities, and societies. *Financialisation* – the embeddedness of financial institutions, ideas, and incentives into our social, economic, and political life – is progressing at both the national and the global level (Epstein, 2005; Krippner, 2005; van der Zwan, 2014). Better regulatory governance at the national, regional, and global level is of great importance, not only because it can bring more stability but also because it can bring more sustainable growth and a fairer, more equal world, while also improving the life chances of millions who live in poverty. This will not be achieved without a political agenda and a shift in priorities of governance in the major polities of the world. It will not come without the collaboration of profit-oriented actors and institutions, but also, it will not come from them. Truly global public-goods policy requires interest-based change as well as ideational change that will lead to both a more comprehensive institutionalisation and formalisation of the current informal institutions. More global financial regulation can allow more stable growth of markets; it can allow markets to grow in a manner that promotes a just and fairer global society. The challenges of slow growth, instability, social and political stagnation and, of course, poverty, climate change, demographic changes, and unsustainable growth can all be tackled by better financial governance. But better financial governance is not likely to come through experts' clubs, insulated technocratic governance, or politically controlled finance. It can be advanced by open dialogue and the better understanding of the world of finance by the attentive elites.

The first part of this chapter suggests the existence of narrower and broader conceptions of global public good. It then identifies global financial instability as the major issue around which the current institutions and actors revolve. Preventive policies around instability dominate the global financial agenda despite the growing challenges of climate change, poverty, and political instability. This should be a major agenda for reforming finance and global financial governance. Moreover, the first part of the chapter identifies global financial governance as a public good. In doing so, it moves beyond the narrow definition of public good that dominates much of the discussion in welfare economics.

The second part focuses on the actors and institutions of global governance. It identifies the relatively marginal role of formal institutions in global financial governance, and the major role of informal organisations. These informal global governance organisations are supported by private organisations, as well as private–public collaborations. The analysis reveals the existence of informal expert-based and industry-based institutionalisation beyond the reach of public scrutiny and democratic control.

The third part of the chapter covers the principles that shape the current regulatory architecture. First, by demonstrating its multiple lines of fragmentation (e.g., no single global regulator and multiple spheres of financial governance). Second, global financial governance is highly informal and is not institutionalised. Third, global financial governance is dominated by technical and professional discourse rather than by political discourse. Fourth, global financial governance is highly nationally based, with governments delegating little agency to international organisations. Fifth, and following the national character of financial regulation, domestic politics – especially of the most powerful nations – counts heavily in the decisions to migrate regulation to the global level. Sixth, global financial governance is organised around the interests of the Western liberal, often rich, democracies. Seventh, global financial governance is more specifically US-centred. Finally, global financial regulation, like domestic financial regulation, cannot be captured by the neoliberal narrative of state versus finance or state versus markets. More state controls blur the distinction between politics and the economy at the same time that the professional elite of central bankers and financial regulators is more dominant and more powerful than the politicians.

In a world of nations, regions, and a global financial industry, the need for global governance ought not to be taken for granted. Functional reasoning around the existence of global and national interdependencies co-exists in conjunction with normative reasoning about global virtues. Still, and with all due respect to functional and normative reasoning, global governance exists to serve the interests of the major actors and their coalitions. Global governance is a product of power and interests entrenched in institutions that are themselves the product of the fusion of interests and norms. The advance and design of particular forms of financial architecture are not shaped only by normative and functional needs but by the peculiarities of historical events and developments, by particular institutional trajectories, and by an impressive mosaic of softer and harder forms of governance.

REFERENCES

Alexander, K. (2009a). Bank for International Settlements. In C. Tietje & A. Brouder (Eds.), *Handbook of transnational economic governance regimes* (pp. 305–318). Brill Nijhoff.

Alexander, K. (2009b). Global financial standard setting, the G10 Committees, and international economic law. *Brooklyn Journal of International Law*, 34(3), 861–882.

Alexander, K., Dhumale, R. & Eatwell, J. (2005). *Global Governance of Financial Systems. The International Regulation of Systemic Risks.* Cambridge University Press.

Armour, J., Awrey, D., Davies, P. L., Enriques, L., Gordon, J. N., Mayer, C. P., & Payne, J. (2016). *Principles of financial regulation.* Oxford University Press.

Baker, A. (2008). The group of seven. *New Political Economy*, 13(1), 103–115.

Borio, E. V. C., & Toniolo, G. (2006). One hundred and thirty years of central bank cooperation: A BIS perspective. *BIS Working Papers*, 197. Bank for International Settlements.

Borowicz, M. (2015). Private and international law: The international swaps and derivatives association. *European Journal of Legal Studies*, 8(1), 46–66.

Brummer, C. (2011). How international financial law works (and how it doesn't). *Georgetown Law Journal*, 99(2), 257–328.

Chiang, C.-C. (2012) Group of Thirty. In G. Ritzer (Ed.), *The Wiley-Blackwell encyclopedia of globalization* (pp. 1053–1056). Wiley-Blackwell.

Copelovitch, M. S. (2010). *The International Monetary Fund in the global economy: Banks, bonds, and bailouts.* Cambridge University Press.

Dingwerth, K., & Pattberg, P. (2006). Global governance as a perspective on world politics. *Global Governance*, 12(2), 185–203.

Donnelly, S. (2019). Financial Stability Board (FSB), Bank for International Settlements (BIS) and financial market regulation bodies. In R. A. Wessel & J. Odermatt (Eds.),

Research handbook on the European Union and international organizations (pp. 360–385). Edward Elgar Publishing.
Epstein, G. A. (Ed.). (2005). *Financialization and the world economy*. Edward Elgar Publishing.
Felsenfeld, C., & Bilali, G. (2004). The role of the Bank for International Settlements in shaping the world financial system. *University of Pennsylvania Journal of International Economic Law*, 25(3), 945–1046.
Flanagan, S. M. (2001). The Rise of a Trade Association: Group Interactions Within the International Swaps and Derivatives Association. *Harvard Negotiation Law Review*, 6, 211–264.
Ford, C. (2017). *Innovation and the state: Finance, regulation, and justice*. Cambridge University Press.
Frieden, J. (2016). The governance of international finance. *Annual Review of Political Science*, 19, 33–48.
Germain, R. (2010). *Global politics and financial governance*. Macmillan International Higher Education.
Griffin, K. (2003). Economic globalization and institutions of global governance. *Development and Change*, 34(5), 789–808.
Harnay, S., & Scialom L. (2015). The influence of the economic approaches to regulation on banking regulations: A short history of banking regulations. *Cambridge Journal of Economics*, 40(2), 401–426.
Helleiner, E. (1995). Explaining the globalization of financial markets: Bringing states back in. *Review of International Political Economy*, 2(2), 315–341.
Hughes, M. P., and C. Palke. (2019). The Bank For International Settlements: An Evolutionary Institution. *Journal of Business Case Studies*, 15(1), 19–28.
Jensen, M. N. (2004). Crisis, conditions, and capital: The effect of International Monetary Fund agreements on foreign direct investment inflows. *Journal of Conflict Resolution*, 48(2), 194–210.
Jones, E., & Knaack, P. (2019). Global financial regulation: Shortcomings and reform options. *Global Policy*, 10(2), 193–206.
Jordana, J., & Levi-Faur, D. (2010). Exploring trends and variations in agency scope. *Competition and Regulation in Network Industries*, 11(4), 342–360.
Jordana, J., & Rosas, G. (2014). When do autonomous banking regulators promote stability? *European Journal of Political Resarch*, 53(4), 672–691.
Jordana J., & Rosas, G. (2018). Central Banks and banking regulation: historical legacies and institutional challenges. In T. Bach and K. Wegrich (eds.), *The Blind Spots of Public Bureaucracy and the Politics of Non-Coordination*. Palgrave-Macmillan.
Kaul, I., Grunberg, I., & Stern, M. A. (Eds.). (1999). Defining global public goods. In *Global public goods: International cooperation in the 21st century* (pp. 2–19). Oxford University Press.
Kenen, P. B. (2008). The G30 at Thirty. Group of Thirty. G30 Publications. https://www.group30.org/images/uploads/publications/G30_G30atThirty.pdf.
Krippner, G. R. (2005). The financialization of the American economy. *Socio-Economic Review*, 3(2), 173–208.
Levi-Faur, D. (2012). From 'big government' to 'big governance'. In D. Levi-Faur (Ed.), *The Oxford handbook of governance* (pp. 3–18). Oxford University Press.
Lipscy, P. Y. (2015). Explaining institutional change: Policy areas, outside options, and the Bretton Woods institutions. *American Journal of Political Science*, 59(2), 341–356.

Maes, I. (2010). Alexandre Lamfalussy and the Origins of the BIS Macro-Prudential Approach to Financial Stability. *PSL Quarterly Review*, 63(254), 263–290.
McKeen-Edwards, H., & Porter, T. (2013). *Transnational financial associations and the governance of global finance: Assembling wealth and power.* Routledge.
Moloney, N., Ferran, E., & Payne, J. (Eds.). (2015). *The Oxford handbook of financial regulation.* Oxford University Press.
Morgan, G. (2008). Market formation and governance in international financial markets: The case of OTC derivatives. *Human Relations*, 61(5), 637–660.
Moschella, M. (2012). IMF surveillance in crisis: The past, present and future of the reform process. *Global Society*, 26(1), 43–60.
Mügge, D., & Perry, J. (2014). The flaws of fragmented financial standard setting: Why substantive economic debates matter for the architecture of global governance. *Politics & Society*, 42(2), 194–222.
Nance, M. T. (2018). The regime that FATF built: An introduction to the Financial Action Task Force. *Crime, Law, and Social Change*, 69(2), 109–129.
Porter, T. (2005). *Globalization and finance.* Polity.
Porter, T. (2009). Financial stability board. In C. Tietje & A. Brouder (Eds.), *Handbook of transnational economic governance regimes* (pp. 345–353). Martinus Nijhoff Publishers.
Posner, E. (2009). Making rules for global finance: Transatlantic regulatory cooperation at the turn of the millennium. *International Organization*, 63(4), 665–699.
Seabrooke, L. (2006). The Bank for International Settlements. *New Political Economy*, 11(1), 141–149.
Singer, D. A. (2007). *Regulating capital: Setting standards for the international financial system.* Cornell University Press.
Stiglitz, J. E. (2006). Global public goods and global finance: Does global governance ensure that the global public interest is served? In J. P. Touffut (Ed.), *Advancing public goods* (pp. 149–164). Edward Elgar Publishing.
Strange, S. (2015 [1986]). *Casino capitalism.* Manchester University Press.
Tsingou, E. (2015). Club governance and the making of global financial rules. *Review of International Political Economy*, 22(2), 225–256.
Underhill, G. R., & Zhang, X. (2008). Setting the rules: Private power, political underpinnings, and legitimacy in global monetary and financial governance. *International Affairs*, 84(3), 535–554.
van der Zwan, N. (2014). Making sense of financialization. *Socio-Economic Review*, 12(1), 99–129.
Vreeland, J. R. (2019). Corrupting International Organizations. *Annual Review of Political Science*, 22, 205–222.
Weisbrot, M & Johnston J. (2016). Voting Share Reform at the IMF: Will it Make a difference? Center for Economic and Policy Research (CEPR).
Westermeier, C. (2018). The Bank of International Settlements as a think tank for financial policy-making. *Policy and Society*, 37(2), 170–187.
Zaring, D. (1998). International law by other means: The twilight existence of international financial regulatory organizations. *Texas International Law Journal*, 33(2), 281–330.
Zysman, J. (1983). *Governments, markets, and growth: Financial systems and the politics of industrial change.* Cornell University Press.

10. The Chinese path to a global financial statecraft strategy: between challenge and adaptation to the global financial governance system

Catalina Espinosa Notrica, Pablo Nemiña and Diana Tussie

1. INTRODUCTION

Twenty-five years ago, the Asian financial crisis exploded. Under the leadership of Japan, a prominent financial power in Asia, the region promoted the creation of the Asian Monetary Fund, a regional financial institution that sought to limit the IMF's upper hand. The US vetoed such a project, which was later reformulated into a reserves swap arrangement known as the Chiang Mai Initiative. At that time, China was growing at an average rate of 10% per year, consolidating itself as a leading global exporter and insinuating a motivation to gain participation in the design of the regional financial architecture.

Today, China, the world's second-largest economy, has developed into a global financial power. Through its development financial institutions, most notably the powerful China Development Bank, it has become the world's largest bilateral creditor (Gelpern et al., 2023). China also holds 35 active bilateral swaps for more than USD 500 billion (McDowell, 2019), and led the creation of two multilateral development banks, the New Development Bank and the Asian Infrastructure Investment Bank (AIIB) (Wang, 2019), the latter a global institution with 109 sovereign members (including 13 prospective members) and a capitalization of USD 100 billion.[1]

China's international financial expansion began in the 2000s and picked up speed after the 2008 crisis (Chin & Gallagher, 2019). The economic crisis gave China a window of opportunity to transform and gain more standing in

[1] Official data as of 17 May 2024.

the decision-making of the financial order that until then had systematically underrepresented the emerging economies. Scholars identified two ways in which the Chinese government acted. A first group of scholars believed that the liberal financial order and the Western institutions would prevail even after the end of the United States hegemony. This is because China acted as a status quo power that benefited economically from the traditional Western order (Ikenberry, 2008; He & Feng, 2020; Larson, 2018). A second group (Tammen et al., 2000; Brooks & Wohlforth, 2008) understood that China would radically change existing institutions because on one hand, reform by accretion did not work, and on the other, because China's interests and values were severely underrepresented. In short, much of the debate around the rise of China was about a dichotomy between status quo or radical change.

Puzzled by this discussion and focusing on the Chinese government strategy from 2000 to 2020, we observed that China behaved neither as a revolutionary power nor as a status quo power; it acted as a revisionist power. Revisionism refers here to a behavior where the hegemon does not destroy the pre-existing order but also takes a proactive role in changing the existing norms, rules, and institutions that are not convenient or strategically favorable (Paradise, 2019). China's economic rise may lead to a power transition (Kim & Gates, 2015), but this process is far from linear, and every field has its own dynamics (Levy, 2008); so, for instance, more financial capabilities do not transfer directly into military power. In this sense, the purpose of this chapter is to present and analyze the Chinese external financial strategy and its implications on global financial governance with a special focus on architecture and institutions. The main questions we address are: What are the main characteristics of such transitioning financial governance? And what is the strategy that China took to reform the existing institutions and to create new institutions in a transitioning global financial governance? To answer these two questions, we use the concept of revisionism and the typology of financial statecraft to analyze Chinese government strategies in the creation of new financial and development institutions. In order to illustrate the power transition, we also analyze the transformation of representation quotas in the traditional Bretton Woods institutions: the International Monetary Fund and the World Bank.

The structure of this chapter is as follows: First, we define what we mean by global financial governance and the main characteristics and changes the order suffered post-2008, after the global financial crisis. Second, we define revisionism and the implications this definition has for our study. Third, we introduce financial statecraft typology in order to later analyze China's strategies and policies toward the new financial order between 2000 and 2020. Fourth, we present Chinese strategies to expand the traditional Bretton Woods institutions. Lastly, we open the door to future questions and scenarios that appear relevant to think about the future of financial governance.

2. TRANSITION PERIODS IN GLOBAL FINANCIAL GOVERNANCE: THE CASE OF POST-2008

In this section, we focus on two points. First, we define what global financial governance means. Second, we characterize and describe the current transition period since 2008, which will be analyzed using financial statecraft theory.

2.1 Defining Global Financial Governance

The literature on global governance is far-reaching, and there are multiple discussions between authors about what type of global governance existed throughout history (see, for example: Bull, 2012; Hurrell, 2007; Huntington, 2003; Krasner, 1983). However, there is a consensus that understands global governance as the different architectural configurations that reflect the values, ideas, and power that the hegemons use to extend and solidify their interests. Global financial governance comprises the rules and arrangements that focus on the financial markets that are part and parcel of the world order. Financial governance refers, in other words, to the norms, rules, procedures, and institutions that govern the transnational regulation and actions of financial markets (Grabel, 2017, 2018).[2] Some examples of elements that conform to any global financial order are the formal rules, such as exchange rate policies, non-banking financial institutions, access to international credits, loans, and conditionality policies, as well as the informal rules, such as the tradition of who can head financial institutions—for example, the tradition of an American presiding over the World Bank (Drezner & McNamara, 2013).

As explained before, the institutions and rules of financial governance have changed over history following the hegemonic power. The gold standard regime in the nineteenth century and early twentieth century was followed by the Bretton Woods regime after the end of the Second World War when the United States emerged as an undisputed creditor to the world. All financial orders experience a life cycle of emergence, dominance, and collapse that ends up in a transition period defined as the coexistence of the traditional institutions with new institutions created by the new hegemon (Acharya, 2018; Stuenkel, 2017). The 2008 financial crisis represented, as we argue later, a period of transition from the United States hegemony post-Washington Consensus order to a post-hegemonic period where regions gained relevance and power attributes (Riggirozzi & Tussie, 2021). In the financial field, governance turned into a complex, fragmented, and pluripolar order reflected in different layers (Grabel, 2017) and the rise of emerging economies, particularly China, as financial

[2] See also the chapter on global finance in this book.

powers, developed alternative arrangements of institutions, currencies, and rules to evade, modify, or resist the existing order (Chin & Helleiner, 2008). In the following paragraphs, we present the main characteristics of the post-2008 transition period that need to be taken into account.

2.2 A Post-2008 World: Global Financial Governance in Transition

The 2008 financial crisis was a tipping point in financial governance since it provided an opportunity to criticize the liberal ideas that the United States had established as the pillars of the global order since the Second World War. During the 1990s, multilateralism was the foundation of financial order, with the construction of binding institutions and regimes to project the power and economic dominance of the United States through binding agreements tied by the IMF and the World Bank (Nemiña & Val, 2021). However, the inability to resolve the crisis and the internal crises of the United States itself led to a transition period. Alternative institutions and rules emerged to challenge the financial order. In other words, the period of uncertainty and doubts about the correct way of stabilizing the global economy after the 2008 financial meltdown marked the beginning of the transition period. The transition of power had particular characteristics: regionalism gained strength compared to the previous unipolar multilateralism based on Washington and Western powers, new rules became more decentralized, new regional financial institutions were created, and existing subregional financial institutions were revamped (such as the Development Bank of Latin America and The Caribbean or Corporación Andina de Fomento - being instituted as the Latin American Development Bank). Additionally, the traditional Bretton Woods institutions gave slightly more voice to developing countries and revisited their conditionality, attempting to take into account domestic contexts (see Broome, 2015; Güven, 2018; Wang, 2017).

To start, the fragmentation between established and new institutions propelled by emerging powers was neither linear nor direct. There were many types of fragmentations between the different areas that conform to the global architecture. New intergovernmental coalitions such as the G20 and the BRICS appeared, along with arrangements characterized by informality, dynamic rapid response, and adaptability to face fluctuating challenges (Wade, 2011). Such coalitions coexisted with new institutional actors like the new regional development banks (for example, the AIIB) and with the old institutional channels (IMF or World Bank). The New Development Bank institutionalized the loosely formed BRICS coalition.

The transition was underpinned by a stronger reliance on regionalism as a governance principle in many other areas, not just finance (Riggirozzi & Tussie, 2021). The 1998 Asian financial crisis had been the first contestation of Bretton Woods, leaving a significant precedent. The decision of the Pacific economies to resort to self-insurance to avoid recurrence to the IMF in a future crisis led to the creation of the Chiang Mai Initiative (CMI), a network of bilateral currency swap arrangements launched by ASEAN plus Japan, China, and South Korea, which allowed swapping local currency for US dollars when a member country was facing a liquidity crisis. CMI represented a clear example of the use of regional institutions as safety nets. From the CMI onwards, the landscape showed the appearance of multiple regional agreements, swap arrangements, and new development banks, such as the AIIB and the New Development Bank, which aimed to strengthen the regional power (Grabel, 2017).

Moving on from the regional perspective, economic governance generally, and financial governance in particular, faced a process of multipolarization that began to offer alternatives to Bretton Woods as a single financial window hegemonized by the United States. A parallel architecture can be identified in the new development banks with differing agendas and practices, such as the AIIB and the New Development Bank (NDB), new liquidity arrangements, such as the BRICS Contingency Reserve Agreement, and the multiplication of Chinese bilateral swap lines (McDowell, 2019) tied to the growth of the RMB as a currency looking to compete with the dollar. All in all, credit creation has been on the rise. Such new practices show a dual role: while they complement the existing order, they also challenge it insofar as they open financial windows where there had been none (Forman & Seegar, 2006).

Regarding the established Bretton Woods institutions, China demanded fairer representation on the board, pushing reforms by accretion—slowly but determinedly—in capital contributions and voting power (Momani, 2015). Major trust funds were established in the Inter-American Development Bank (IADB), the European Investment Bank, the European Bank for Reconstruction and Development, the Caribbean Development Bank, and the Asian Development Bank, giving China legitimacy to move its specific agendas (Humphrey & Chen, 2021). Trust funds are a common practice that enables countries to pinpoint pet issues for lending and as such they do not raise strategic conflicts over the structure of the established banks and voting power in boards. For example, the IADB and the People's Bank of China established the China Co-financing Fund for Latin America and the Caribbean to support sustainable economic growth. This fund aims to alleviate poverty, reduce inequality, boost private investment, and address climate change and gender equality. China's $2 billion contribution will co-finance up to $500 million USD in IADB public sector loans and $1.5 billion in private sector loans, available for three and six years, respectively.[3] That inclusion of countries that were never considered in the decision-making forums showed the changed balance of power and the acceptance of the United States and Europe to adapt to these institutions, if grudgingly and sparingly, so as not to risk their relevance and speed up the alternatives over which they have scant say.

Lastly, but certainly not least, there came a new logic of access to liquidity. As we explain later, the Chinese swap arrangement established a supplementary lending facility regarding the IMF as the lender of last resort. Even if the swaps have not replaced the IMF so far, the access to liquidity without invasive conditionalities turned swaps into an alternative credit-creating mechanism.

In brief, the complexity of the changing global financial governance is marked by overlapping layers of the Bretton Woods Liberal Order created by the United States after the Second World War and an alternative piecemeal order that China and the emerging powers are propelling regionally and multilaterally in a linked step strategy. This alternative order is characterized by an evolution and empowerment of regional arrangements, especially boosted by China particularly and also by Asia more generally, with new competing institutions in monetary and investment issues manifested clearly in a dual fashion: on one hand, in the development banks and on the other, in credit creation without macroeconomic conditionalities. What remains unexplored so far is how the two alternative orders and institutions relate to each other. As we show in our analysis, the type of relationship between the two hegemons has been confrontational but also presents examples of coexistence and even cooperation.

In the next section, we address the definition of revisionism in a broad sense, understanding that the Chinese challenge to the liberal order is likely to be selective and partial rather than outright systemic (Breslin, 2018). Second, we describe the main strategies that the Chinese government has used to build the parallel economic architecture by using the financial statecraft typology as a tool to analyze different financial policy strategies in the building of an alternative order.

3. CHINESE STRATEGY: BEING A REVIONIONIST POWER IN A TRANSITIONING WORLD ORDER[4]

So far, we have described and defined the changes that global financial governance has seen since 2000. In this section, we introduce two key concepts that

[3] See https://www.iadb.org/en/news/china-provide-2-billion-latin-america-and-caribbean-co-financing-fund.

[4] This section draws on Nemiña (2021).

guide our analysis. First, we conceptualize revisionist behavior, and second, we introduce the typology of financial statecraft, which shed light on the evolution of the financial order.

3.1 A Path to Revisionism: How did China's Behavior Evolve since 2000?

As we described before, the traditional literature divided and identified China as either a status quo power or as a radical challenger. However, by analyzing the different Chinese strategies toward the traditional Western financial institutions and the financial institutions and development banks popping up, we realize that China was neither a status quo power nor a radical challenger power; in other words, we see it was a revisionist power. Revisionism in this chapter refers to the proactive role of changing the norms and rules that are not convenient or strategically favorable for the new hegemon, while maintaining those pre-existing rules or institutions that do benefit the hegemon (Paradise, 2019). Reformism lies between the extreme of radical challenger and the untouched maintenance of the status quo. In other words, and according to Stuenkel (2017), after the global financial crisis, China acted as a norm taker but also as a norm shaper. The concept of revisionism explains why the changing global governance is characterized by both continuities and changes compared to the order established since the 1990s under the so-called Washington Consensus, which was hegemonized by the United States.

In the next subsection, we introduce the theory and typology of financial statecraft in order to analyze what types of strategies China used to expand its power in the transitional period of the global financial governance.

3.2 Financial Statecraft Theory and Typology

Financial statecraft is defined by Armijo and Katada (2014, p. 2) as: 'the use, by the governments of sovereign states, of national levers of direct and indirect influence over financial assets, markets, and actors for the purpose of achieving larger foreign policy objectives'. As the authors explain, financial statecraft can be analyzed with three dimensions: offensive or defensive, bilateral or systemic, and monetary or financial (see Table 10.1).

As a tool of foreign policy, financial statecraft can be used either in the bilateral arena in which State A directs its action to State B, or at the systemic level, whereby State A directs its action to global markets or governance institutions. To this binary typology, we add the regional dimension, where State A directs its action to a regional market or institution. In addition, financial statecraft is defensive when a state orients its policy to protect the domestic economy from external financial pressures, while an offensive one implies an objective of

Table 10.1 *Financial statecraft typology revised*

Dimension	Defensive	Offensive
Systemic	Financial	Financial
	• Diversifying sources of international borrowing	• Offer international credit • Reform global international financial institutions or establish new ones
	Monetary	Monetary
	• Reserve accumulation and diversification	• Promote one's currency as a global reserve or transitions currency
Regional	Financial	Financial
	• Regional lending arrangements	• Regional development banks
	Monetary	Monetary
	• Regional clearing in local currencies • Swap arrangements (Chiang Mai, BRICS)	• Propel the use of local currencies or an alternative unit of account toward trade and other transactions
Bilateral	Financial	Financial
	• Default • Develop local credit markets	• Loans or aids to target countries to adopt specific policies
	Monetary	Monetary
	• Diversification of reserves • Swap arrangements	• Trade invoicing in local currency or an alternative unit of account

Source: Author's own elaboration based on Armijo and Katada (2015).

conditioning the way other states behave or their alternatives at hand. Lastly, a policy is labeled as monetary when the policy refers to the cost or quantity of money (i.e., interest rates and monetary creation), monetary regimes, and the strategic use of currencies. We define a strategy as financial when it implies international credit and lending. However, it is important to mention that in terms of financial strategies, there is a difference between development and liquidity finance, the first one being the focus of development banks and the second one of lending institutions like the IMF. As will be shown in the subsequent analytical section, developmental financial strategies have been stronger in disputing the power of the World Bank and the United States than liquidity financial strategies, which have been less successful, explained by the continued dominance of the dollar as the preferred global currency.

Defensive bilateral financial statecraft strategies are frequently used by vulnerable countries to try to defend and shield themselves from the influence or heavy hand of strong advanced industrial countries. In other words, the defensive bilateral strategy consists of a State A that tries to defend itself from the actions of State B, for example, holding gold reserves to avoid sanctions, embargoes, or the like. The diversification of reserves, borrowing from alternative sources, and lastly falling into arrears or defaulting on loans are the most commonly used strategies. Recently, China promoted more than 35 bilateral swap arrangements, which is another form of a bilateral monetary defensive strategy (McDowell, 2019). These arrangements cement diversification of reserves and aid in the process of renminbi internationalization, particularly through the interaction with low- and middle-income countries. Yet internationalization may turn out to be offensive rather than defensive in the long run.

Offensive bilateral financial statecraft is a strategy in which Country A targets Country B. Some authors believe that only major powers can exercise offensive bilateral financial statecraft. In the case of emerging powers, there are some instruments that can be used to achieve a foreign policy goal, for example, promoting a payment system, extending credit or aid to hold the upper hand over neighbors. From a monetary policy perspective, the two most common strategies are: encouraging trade invoicing in local currency and the power to intervene in the exchange rate to oblige the target country to adjust payment imbalances.

Under regional defensive financial statecraft, the main objectives are to secure regional financing and to promote regional clearing in local currencies or a commitment to swap arrangements in case of need, as has been done in the CMI agreement. Defensive financial statecraft aims to protect the region from the vulnerability inherent in the dependence on a single currency. In other words, the aim is to protect the region overall against monetary or financial instabilities.

Offensive regional statecraft consists of promoting regional development banks in addition to propelling the use of local currencies or a unit of account in trade and other economic transactions. When it comes to identifying the reasons behind the new wave of multiple development banks in the past two decades, Palestini (2022, p. 439) identifies two factors that explain the motivation that every region has had to create multiple development banks: the demand for development financing, and the aspiration of developing countries to increase their leverage in the global financial system, that is, expanding financial room vis-à-vis hegemonic interests.

Systemic financial statecraft in general tries to deal with the environment in which global financial and monetary relations occur. In the case of defensive systemic financial statecraft, governments try to defend themselves from the effects of global financial markets. Actions that can count as defensive in financial terms are mainly diversifying sources of foreign lending; in monetary terms, there are a number of actions that central banks can take in order to protect and manage international reserves such as managing domestic interest rates, capital controls, or capital requirements for banks. These policies aim to isolate national economies from negative external shocks or cycles. For example, establishing capital controls or managing interest rates affects the relationship of a given country with its entire counterparts.

Systemic offensive financial statecraft is more encompassing and beyond the reach of smaller players. It is intended to directly influence global financial governance. In terms of offensive financial statecraft, the strategies cover international credit creation, reforming international financial institutions, or establishing alternative ones. At the same time, in monetary terms, reforming global monetary governance norms, as well as establishing the national currency as an international currency, are some policies used as an offensive approach. It must be borne in mind that geopolitics rules here. Bretton Woods was the financial arm of the United States. Ever since, development banks have followed geopolitics. When the Cold War spread to Latin America, the United States agreed to create a regional development bank. When decolonization spread in Asia and Africa, the Asian and African Development banks were created. After the fall of the Berlin Wall, the European Bank for Reconstruction and Development aimed to channel funds to former communist countries. The BRICS created their own bank, and China did likewise with the AIIB.

3.3 Analysis: China's Financial Statecraft

China has used its economic prowess to both promote reforms in existing institutions and transform global financial governance. Regarding the former, as a consequence of a process initiated in 2006, China became the third-largest shareholder in the IMF and the World Bank in terms of voting power. This change, which resulted in a lukewarm redistribution of almost 6% of the total votes from developed to developing countries, stemmed from a general dissatisfaction with the distribution of voting power, especially vocal since the rise of the BRICS that brought with them an overall questioning of the normative authority of the G7 countries (Kingah & Quiliconi, 2016).

The reforms in the voting structure were brought about as an attempt to reflect new realities of the global distribution of power (Tussie, 2018; Breslin, 2018). The negotiations resulted in China having slightly more than 6% of the total votes, while the United States retained its veto power (given that it maintains 16.5% of the votes). At this point, the governance of the IMF was way behind the real distribution of power, and timid change had resulted in a loss of credibility, especially because the mentioned reforms were more rhetorical than practical (Forster et al., 2022).

Regarding developments in global financial governance in the period since 2000, China has shifted from defensive to more offensive financial strategies (see Table 10.2). The typology provided ideal types, yet countries in general, and China in particular, use more than one type and combine defensive and offensive policies in order to achieve their strategic interests (Armijo, 2019). As explained before, we consider that China took a revisionist position during the transition period of global financial governance, meaning that the strategy was more defensive at first and became more offensive since 2010. During the 1990s, China's strategy was defensive due to the need to protect local manufacturing from external competition. In addition, after the Asian financial crisis, the China Central Bank was made aware of the importance of increasing regional power in order to reduce dependence on the IMF lending programs of adjustment (Armijo, 2019). East Asian countries entered into the Chiang Mai swap arrangement and, subsequently, bilateral swap arrangements, as a way of expanding the use of renminbi. Altogether, these moves represent China's strategic path.

Some other important changes showing a more offensive approach in the Chinese strategy were the rise of development banks, such as the New Development Bank and the Asian Infrastructure and Investment Bank, together with the Belt and Road Initiative. These institutions and initiatives are offensive on both a regional and systemic level since they represent a real and active contestation to the World Bank in development financing. Such development finance is naturally a subject of negotiation, but the conditionalities on access to credits seem less intrusive, a reason why emerging economies have been getting closer to China (Gallagher, 2016). In sum, while China diversifies its reserves via initiatives such as the Belt and Road Initiative or the AIIB, these in turn use their capital for funding and trade with China, two core topics

Table 10.2 *Chinese financial statecraft: a synthesis*

Dimension	Defensive	Offensive
Systemic	Reduction in US debt holdings [a]	Asian Infrastructure and Investment Bank
Regional	Chiang Mai Initiative	New Development Bank
Bilateral	Chinese Bilateral Swap Arrangements	China Development Bank

Note: [a] Based on http://www.china.org.cn/business/2023-03/19/content_85177208.htm.
Source: Own elaboration.

at the center of Xi Jinping's economic foreign policy (González Jáuregui & Tussie, 2022).

In the next subsections, we give a detailed description of all the different strategies and initiatives China has used, showing the combination of defensive and offensive financial foreign policy that illustrates the revisionist position and the characteristics of the transitioning global financial order.

3.3.1 China's bilateral swap arrangement

The People's Bank of China has been one of the main drivers of RMB internationalization. With this main objective in mind, the bank began to expand the RMB swap agreements in 2009 and to try to settle trade between local currencies and the RMB without resorting to the use of the dollar. One of the main characteristics of these swap arrangements is that while they add up to a network, they are not part of a multilateral framework like the CMI. In addition, the swap arrangements were not created to make liquidity in dollars available between the banks as the CMI swap agreements do. The first agreement was signed with South Korea, but the strategy was expanded across the world, and in 2017, China maintained a total of 35 swap arrangements equivalent to 500 billion USD dollars (McDowell, 2019). Such an extensive network of swaps can be considered a step in the direction of an offensive strategy of financial statecraft because China uses them as a strategy to internationalize the RMB. Also, it brings some economic benefits, such as the reduction of the exchange rate risk that Chinese firms face, more competition for Chinese banks, and increasing global trade with China. The possibility of China turning into a lender in economic crisis situations makes this strategy very powerful.

The strong position and innovative aspect of the swap arrangements is that the liquidity channel between the banks is created using domestic currencies. Swaps allow foreign central banks to make RMB available to domestic commercial banks that operate with China. The commercial banks can then make RMB available to firms that wish to use the currency to pay for Chinese imports. Of the whole swap network, five countries have activated their swaps: Argentina, Mongolia, Pakistan, Russia, and Ukraine. A clear-cut example of how swaps can become part of an offensive strategy was manifest in the swap arrangement between China and Russia in 2014, aiming to challenge the Western sanctions imposed on Moscow.

3.3.2 Chiang Mai Initiative

The CMI was the first currency swap arrangement launched by the ASEAN+3 countries in May 2000. The aim of this initiative was to address the liquidity difficulties of the region by supplementing existing financial arrangements. The CMI is formed by the ASEAN Swap Arrangement (ASA) and by the network of bilateral swap arrangements among the ASEAN+3 countries. The function or objective of the arrangement was to swap local currency for US dollars when facing a liquidity crisis. In the wake of the 2008 financial crisis, the CMI started the process of multilateralization, transitioning from being a regional defensive strategy to an offensive one. The Chiang Mai Initiative Multilateralization (CMIM) started in 2010 as a single pooled reserve scheme. The multilateralization also brought a cooperation scheme with the IMF that enabled co-financing arrangements with 120 billion USD. In 2012, the CMIM doubled its size to 240 billion USD.

The CMIM does not operate as a centralized fund. On the contrary, the contributions of each country remain in the central banks of the member countries. In the event of a balance of payment or liquidity crisis, a member government can swap its local currency for US dollars from this pool. Each country's borrowing quota is based on its contribution multiplied by its respective borrowing multiplier. The members of the CMIM are China and Hong Kong, Japan, South Korea, Indonesia, Thailand, Malaysia, Singapore, the Philippines, Vietnam, Cambodia, Myanmar, Brunei, and Laos.

The CMI represents an interesting case of a transition from defensive to offensive strategy, but also it shows that the financial governance transitioning period is characterized by cooperation in some cases. The link between CMI and the IMF coordinates the operational and policy aspects of co-financing. In order to smooth the machinery for activation, ASEAN+3 and the IMF have jointly conducted test runs annually (Sussangkarn, 2011).

3.3.3 The New Development Bank

The New Development Bank was created in July of 2015 at the BRICS summit in Brazil. The leaders of the five member countries of BRICS settled on a bank with the aim of mobilizing infrastructure and sustainable development projects in BRICS and other emerging economies and developing countries, as established in the agreement. The founding members are Brazil, Russia, India, China, and South Africa, but the membership is open to members of the United Nations: recently, Bangladesh and the United Arab Emirates joined the bank, and Egypt and Uruguay have been admitted. Showing the ideal of an egalitarian distribution of power between its members, the president of the bank shall be elected from one of the founding members on a rotation basis, and there shall be at least one vice-president from each of the other founding members. The mission of the bank is to support infrastructure and sustainable development efforts in BRICS and other underserved, emerging economies for faster development through innovation and cutting-edge technology. As defined by the bank itself, one of the main values is to become a partner in development that goes beyond the conventional codes of multilateral banks. It represents, operates, and is recognized for its values that fulfill the founding vision. The bank partners with nations through capital and knowledge, achieving development goals with transparency and empathy and creating an equal opportunity for the development of all countries. The initial authorized capital of the bank was 100 billion USD and a subscribed capital of 50 billion USD distributed equally between the member states. The subscribed capital is divided into paid-in shares. The key milestones of the NDB are the cumulative sum of 30.2 billion dollars in approvals for 85 sovereign and non-sovereign projects until 2022. Annual approvals are still far from matching those of traditional development banks; for reference, in 2022, the International Bank for Reconstruction and Development (IBRD) approved loans totaling $33 billion (with the World Bank Group as a whole approving $104 billion), the IADB approved $14.6 billion, and the NDB approved $2.7 billion.[5] However, the NDB is fully operational, and the recent expansion of its membership with the inclusion of Bangladesh, Egypt, and the United Arab Emirates will bolster its client base.

Also, an important aspect of decision-making in the bank is the principle of equality among the BRICS countries. This way of decision-making represents the desire to move away from the practice of traditional multilateral development banks, where members with greater economic weight have more capital shares, affecting the governance system. Instead, votes are distributed equally among all the members regardless of their contribution to the capital of the bank. The maximum number of members on the NDB's Board of Directors shall be 10, with 5 of them representing BRICS countries.

A key feature of the NDB is the commitment to provide local currency financing, which now represents a significant share of the portfolio. Since the beginning, the NDB has been operating with loans in RMB but also in ZAR.

3.3.4 The Asian Infrastructure Investment Bank

The AIIB is a multilateral development bank with a mission to improve social and economic outcomes in Asia. Like the NDB, the AIIB's authorized capital amount was 100 billion USD. The access to finance of this bank is determined by the agreement letter that establishes that the bank will provide or facilitate financing to any member or any agency instrumentally or any agency operating in the territory of the member, but also to international or regional agencies that are concerned with the economic development of the Asian region. The Articles of Agreement allow the Bank to provide financing in different ways, such as making loans, investing in the equity capital of an enterprise, and guaranteeing, as primary or secondary obligor in whole or in part, loans for economic development (Ming Wan, 2015).

---

[5] All data are based on official annual reports.

At the end of 2022, there were 209 approved projects totaling more than USD 40 billion in lending. Regarding the type of projects, 22% were approved to finance energy, 18% were approved for financial institutions, such as local banks, 17% were to finance transport, and 11% were to finance water development. In other words, 68% of the projects are directed toward developing infrastructure in developing countries.

As a part of the Belt and Road Initiative, China's decision to take some form of multilateral leadership in the shape of the AIIB was one of the first signs of a challenge to the existing financial economic order. However, the AIIB is still a system-conforming institution. Breslin (2018) holds that it complements existing funders, rather than being a revolutionary break to replace them. It works in cooperation with the World Bank and the Asian Development Bank. This example shows, as we mentioned before, that the relationship between institutions, even though China has gained a hand in financial governance, can also be cooperative and not only competitive. However, how these dynamics are interpreted often depends on perspective: the emphasis may lie less on the newcomer's intentions and actions, and more on how those who feel challenged perceive and respond to the shift. Since the United States has not applied to enter these banks, the question that arises is whether China is challenging global financial governance per se or if it is challenging United States hegemony. Insofar as the United States has not applied for membership to the AIIB while the bank plays by Western rules, and countries such as Britain, France, Germany, and Canada have applied for membership, one must conclude that the challenge lies in the camp of the United States rather than in overall financial governance.

4. CONCLUSION

Transitions of global governance architectures are complicated. They result from actions taken by rising powers as well as by the reactions of contested powers. The 2008 global financial crisis created a need to diversify holdings and opened a window of opportunity for China to challenge more directly, and in a more offensive way, the existing governance institutions. It was used amply. The financial crisis and the rise of emerging powers taking advantage of their commodity boom allowed fertile ground for the promotion of an alternative and transitioning global governance architecture. China faced its growing relevance in global financial governance in three different ways. In some cases, there were challenges to the pre-existing Bretton Woods institutions, such as propelling the creation of new development banks (AIIB, NDB) or the global boost of Chinese Development Bank lending, which offered attractive development financing alternatives to low- and middle-income countries with no or limited access to global capital markets. In other instances, it unfolds gradually, such as with trust funds which complement existing regional and global multilateral institutions. Finally, there is merely coexistence, such as with bilateral swap arrangements establishing a liquidity financial alternative in the global financial safety net.

Chinese strategies from 2000 have ranged from participating in the status quo to taking on a more offensive approach in a number of ways, whether with institutions or informal networks. The face of development finance has certainly changed and so have the alternatives at hand. This change cannot be underestimated or downplayed. Yet despite the upsurge of such practices, the Bretton Woods institutions, and especially the IMF, still play the role of lender of last resort. In other words, in terms of development finance, there is a multiplication of actors that compete and cooperate with the World Bank, while for liquidity official financing, the IMF is still the dominant institution with China's swap arrangements appearing as a handy alternative for debt-distressed countries with no access to international capital markets. Yet because of the challenges, the rules of conditionality are necessarily less stark and its programs have to take into account the flows provided by China.

China's strategies in terms of expansion changed from being mostly bilateral and defensive to more regional—and later systemic—and offensive. In concrete terms, what started with a pool of USD reserves shared with Japan, South Korea, and ASEAN countries and now has reached 35 bilateral swap arrangements, shows the progressive internationalization of the RMB, and the propelling of two multilateral development banks, the NDB and AIIB. However, the full picture is still in the making and depends very much on how the incumbents react.

At the time of writing, China shows high levels of internal public debt and is facing the progressive retreat of global value chains in the aftermath of the Covid pandemic, reinforced by the economic sanctions on Russia by the G7. Together, these factors have moderated growth records and exposed it to challenges from other competitors (i.e., India). Notwithstanding the progress of the offensive financial and monetary strategy, such as the development of an alternative international payment system and the use of the RMB as an international currency of exchange and credit, may provide further opportunities to sustain its acquired pre-eminent place in the global economy.

Regarding the liberal order, the sanctions following the war in Ukraine or the securitization of global value chains may deepen the transformation initiated by the rise of emerging powers, especially China. Actions lead to reactions. In April 2023, in a speech delivered at the Brookings Institution, Jake Sullivan, US National Security Advisor, took stock of the fracturing economic environment and admitted that ever-greater global interdependence is no longer desirable. Herein lies a challenge to the success and scope of China's financial offensive statecraft strategies in global economic governance, which will be relevant to follow up on in the future.

REFERENCES

Acharya, A. (2018). *The end of American world order.* John Wiley & Sons.

Armijo, L. E. (2018). Chapter 2: Financial Statecraft. In T. M. Shaw, L. C. Mahrenbach, R. Modi, & Y. Xu (Eds.) *The Palgrave Handbook of Contemporary International Political Economy* (pp. 27–41). London: Palgrave Macmillan UK.

Armijo, L., & Katada, S. (Eds.). (2014). *The financial statecraft of emerging powers: Shield and sword in Asia and Latin America.* Springer.

Armijo, L. E., & Katada, S. N. (2015). Theorizing the financial statecraft of emerging powers. *New Political Economy, 20*(1), 42–62.

Breslin, S. (2008). Towards a Sino-centric regional order? Empowering China and constructing regional order(s). *China, Japan and Regional Leadership in East Asia, 131*, 155.

Breslin, S. (2018). Global reordering and China's rise: Adoption, adaptation and reform. *The International Spectator: Special Issue: The liberal order and its contestations, 53*(1), 57–75.

Brooks, S. G., & Wohlforth, W. C. (2008). *World out of balance: International relations and the challenge of American primacy.* Princeton University Press.

Broome, A. (2015). Back to basics: The great recession and the narrowing of IMF policy advice. *Governance, 28*(2), 147–165.

Bull, H. (2012). *The anarchical society: A study of order in world politics.* Bloomsbury Publishing.

Chin, G. T., & Gallagher, K. P. (2019). Coordinated credit spaces: The globalization of Chinese development finance. *Development and Change, 50*(1), 245–274.

Chin, G., & Helleiner, E. (2008). China as a creditor: A rising financial power? *Journal of International Affairs, 62*(1), 87–102.

Drezner, D. W., & McNamara, K. R. (2013). International political economy, global financial orders and the 2008 financial crisis. *Perspectives on Politics, 11*(1), 155–166.

Forman, S., & Segaar, D. (2006). New coalitions for global governance: the changing dynamics of multilateralism. *Global Governance, 12*, 205.

Forster, T., Stubbs, T. H., & Kentikelenis, A. E. (2022). The politics of the International Monetary Fund. In Deciancio, D., Nemiña, P., & Tussie, D. (Eds.), *Handbook on the politics of international development* (pp. 376–391). Edward Elgar Publishing.

Gallagher, K. P. (2016). *The China triangle: Latin America's China boom and the fate of the Washington Consensus.* Oxford University Press.

Gelpern, A., Horn, S., Morris, S., Parks, B., & Trebesch, C. (2023). How China lends: A rare look into 100 debt contracts with foreign governments. *Economic Policy, 38*(114), 345–416.

González Jáuregui, J., & Tussie, D. (2022). China's BRI extension to South America: Challenges and opportunities for the regional order in the post-pandemic. In Deciancio, M., & Quiliconi, C. (Eds.), *Regional and international cooperation in South America after COVID* (pp. 43–62). Routledge.

Grabel, I. (2017). *When things don't fall apart. Global financial governance and developmental finance in an age of productive incoherence.* MIT Press.

Grabel, I. (2018). Toward a pluripolar global financial architecture? The Bretton Woods institutions and the new landscape of developmental finance. *Review of Radical Political Economics*, *50*(4), 653–659.

Güven, A. (2018). Whither the post-Washington Consensus? International financial institutions and development policy before and after the crisis. *Review of International Political Economy*, *25*(3), 392–417.

He, K., & Feng, H. (2020). *Introduction Rethinking China and International Order: A Conceptual Analysis*. University of Michigan Press.

Humphrey, C., & Chen, Y. (2021). *China in the multilateral development banks: Evolving strategies of a new power*. ETH Zurich.

Huntington, S. P. (2003). America in the World. *The Hedgehog Review*, 5(1), 7–19.

Hurrell, A. (2007). *On global order: Power, values, and the constitution of international society*. Oxford University Press.

Ikenberry, G. J. (2008). The rise of China and the future of the West-Can the liberal system survive. *Foreign Aff.*, *87*, 23.

Kim, W., & Gates, S. (2015). Power transition theory and the rise of China. *International Area Studies Review*, *18*(3), 219–226.

Kingah, S., & Quiliconi, C. (2016). Introduction: The BRICS in global and regional governance. In Kingah, S., & Quiliconi, C. (Eds.), *Global and regional leadership of BRICS countries* (pp. 1–11). Springer.

Krasner, S. D. (Ed.). (1983). *International regimes*. Cornell University Press.

Larson, D. W. (2018). New perspectives on rising powers and global governance: Status and clubs. *International studies review*, *20*(2), 247–254.

Levy, J. S. (2008). Power transition theory and the rise of China. In Ross, R., & Zhu, F. (Eds.), *China's ascent: Power, security, and the future of international politics* (pp. 11–33). Cornell University Press.

McDowell, D. (2019). The (ineffective) financial statecraft of China's bilateral swap agreements. *Development and Change*, *50*(1), 122–143.

Ming Wan. (2015). *The Asian Infrastructure Investment Bank: The construction of power and the struggle for the East Asian International Order*. Palgrave Pivot.

Momani, B. (2015). China at the IMF. In Lombardi, D., & Wang, H. (Eds.), *Enter the dragon: China in the international financial system* (pp. 267–291). CIGI.

Nemiña, P. (2021). The rise of the new official creditors in the XXI Century and the challenges to the global financial governance, *Report*, GLOBE – The European Union and the Future of Global Governance, Horizon 2020 – Framework. Available in https://www.globe-project.eu/the-rise-of-the-new-official-creditors-in-the-xxi-century-and-the-challenges-to-the-global-financial-governance_11423.pdf.

Nemiña, P., & Val, M. E. (2021). Debt and international organizations. In *Oxford research encyclopedia of international studies*. Retrieved 25 July 2025, from https://oxfordre.com/internationalstudies/display/10.1093/acrefore/9780190846626.001.0001/acrefore-9780190846626-e-650?rskey=gwrYLh&result=1.

Palestini, S. (2022). The politics of the regional development banks. In Deciancio, D., Nemiña, P., & Tussie, D. (Eds.), *Handbook on the politics of international development* (pp. 435–449). Edward Elgar Publishing.

Paradise, J. F. (2019). China's quest for global economic governance reform. *Journal of Chinese Political Science*, *24*(3), 471–493.

Riggirozzi, P., & Tussie, D. (2021, November 29). Post-Hegemonic Regionalism. Oxford Research Encyclopedia of International Studies. Retrieved 25 July 2025, from https://oxfordre.com/internationalstudies/view/10.1093/acrefore/9780190846626.001.0001/acrefore-9780190846626-e-657.

Stuenkel, O. (2017). *Post-Western world: How emerging powers are remaking global order.* John Wiley & Sons.
Sussangkarn, C. (2011). Chiang Mai Initiative multilateralization: Origin, development, and outlook. *Asian Economic Policy Review, 6*(2), 203–220.
Tammen, R., Kugler, J., Lemke, D., Stam, A., Abdollahian, M., Al-Sharabati, C., … & Organski, A. F. K. (2000). *Power transitions.* Chatham House.
Tussie, D. (2018). Set to shake up global economic governance: Can the BRICS be dismissed? *Global Governance: A Review of Multilateralism and International Organizations, 24*(3), 321–330.
Wade, R. H. (2011). Emerging world order? From multipolarity to multilateralism in the G20, the World Bank, and the IMF. *Politics & Society, 39*(3), 347–378.
Wang, H. (2017). New multilateral development banks: Opportunities and challenges for global governance. *Global Policy, 8*(1), 113–118.
Wang, H. (2019). The new development Bank and the Asian infrastructure investment Bank: China's ambiguous approach to global financial governance. *Development and Change, 50*(1), 221–244.

11. Global climate governance under the Paris Agreement: mobilising collective action at multiple scales

Julia Kreienkamp and David Coen

1. INTRODUCTION AND CHAPTER OVERVIEW

Climate change is often described as a 'super-wicked' problem, not least because it becomes more and more difficult to address the longer action is delayed (Levin et al., 2012). Unfortunately, although the international community has made considerable strides towards addressing climate change since the early 1990s, it has not done so at the pace required. There is now strong scientific consensus that anthropogenic climate change is no longer a distant threat but already a dangerous reality for many vulnerable people and communities across the globe – and that the window for avoiding its worst impacts is closing rapidly (IPCC, 2023).

This chapter provides a snapshot overview of the current state of global climate governance. As a useful point of departure, global climate governance can be defined as 'all purposeful mechanisms and measures aimed at steering social systems towards preventing, mitigating, or adapting to the risks posed by climate change, established and implemented by states or other authorities' (Jagers & Stripple, 2003, p. 385). As this definition implies, scholars of global climate governance are interested in much more than just the intergovernmental negotiations under the United Nations Framework Convention on Climate Change (UNFCCC). Indeed, pluralisation of authority and diversification of policymaking and implementation mechanisms are now key features of this domain.

This new governance reality provides scope for galvanising collective action through political, institutional, and social channels at all scales of governance, from local to global. Rather than a fully integrated regime, the architecture of global climate governance can best be described as a 'regime complex' (Keohane & Victor, 2011) – a loosely coupled set of institutions, comprising the UNFCCC and other state-led regulatory systems as well as a highly diverse non-state actor constituency. Although there is no central authority regulating interactions between these different players, as this chapter documents, the UNFCCC's 2015 Paris Agreement provides an important overarching framework for cooperation and goal alignment.

The Paris Agreement departs significantly from previous attempts to govern climate change through legally binding negotiated commitments. While this shift towards a more bottom-up logic has secured almost universal participation, the success of the Paris Agreement crucially relies on an iterative pledge-and-review process to stimulate ever-increasing ambition among state parties and propel them to put these voluntary commitments into practice. With current ambition levels much too low to keep global temperature rises to 1.5°C – the aspirational temperature goal set by the Paris Agreement – the viability of this mode of governance remains an open question.

This chapter begins by outlining the key objectives of global climate governance – to mitigate global warming and to deal with its impacts through adaptation and loss and damage mechanisms – including brief reflections on why the international community has struggled to make sufficient progress across each of these objectives. It then provides a short overview of the historical development of the global climate change regime, with a focus on the Paris Agreement, its key design features, and prospects for implementation. This is followed by a summary mapping of the various actors involved in global climate change governance, highlighting the opportunities and limitations presented by an increasingly polycentric and multi-scalar global regime complex.

2. CORE OBJECTIVES OF GLOBAL CLIMATE GOVERNANCE

Three interdependent pillars of action inform the core objectives and institutional evolution of the global climate change regime: mitigation, adaptation, and loss and damage. As evidenced below, the exact definition, relative importance, and practical implications of these principal objectives are contested. Notably, the recognition of loss and damage as a distinct policy area has long been resisted by developed state parties. Nevertheless, it is now widely considered the third pillar of climate action under the UNFCCC.

The Paris Agreement also introduced an important additional objective of making global finance flows consistent with a low emission, climate-resilient pathway. Full alignment of all the world's capital with the Paris goals would constitute an extremely powerful lever for tackling climate change and its impacts. However, the Paris Agreement's finance objective has been difficult to operationalise, and there are also concerns that it may distract from other finance-related provisions in the Agreement, notably rich countries' responsibility to provide support to climate-vulnerable countries (Alayza, 2024).

Indeed, finance (in all its forms) remains a major concern and source of contention across all pillars of action in global climate governance and is set to be a priority issue at future negotiations.

2.1 Mitigation

Climate change mitigation refers to the 'stabilization of greenhouse gas concentrations in the atmosphere at a level that would prevent dangerous anthropogenic interference with the climate system' (UN, 1992, Art. 2). The 2015 Paris Agreement provides a measurable interpretation of this goal by committing state parties to keep global warming well below 2°C above pre-industrial levels and pursue efforts towards a 1.5°C limit. In practice, the latter has emerged as the de facto target of global climate governance efforts (Figueres, 2021). However, scientists warn that even global warming of 1.5°C would expose hundreds of millions of people in poorer regions to serious harm (Rockström et al., 2023) and that 'every increment of global warming will intensify multiple and concurrent hazards' (IPCC, 2023, p. 12).

Broadly speaking, mitigation can be pursued via two levers: sources and sinks. The former encompasses any efforts to cut anthropogenic greenhouse gas (GHG) emissions, notably through the drastic reduction or elimination of fossil fuel combustion. Important progress is being made in this regard, with oil, gas, and coal demand projected to reach its peak by 2030 (IEA, 2023a). Still, the current pace of decarbonisation is nowhere fast enough to limit temperature rises to 1.5°C. For this reason, mitigation scenarios and strategies also rely on sinks to 'offset' emissions by removing GHGs from the atmosphere. However, the absorption capacity of natural carbon sinks – such as forests, wetlands, mangroves, or the ocean – is limited and, in some cases, weakening (e.g., Hubau et al., 2020). This has spurred a growing interest in negative emissions technologies, despite concerns over the uncertainties and risks involved in deploying these on a large scale (Dyke, Watson & Knorr, 2021).

So far, 30 plus years of efforts to promote mitigation action under the UNFCCC have not delivered the drastic reductions in GHG emissions needed. The underperformance of global mitigation governance has often been explained through a 'tragedy of the commons' frame (Hardin, 1968): strong incentives to free-ride exist because the costs and benefits of GHG reductions are not directly linked. Simply put, self-interested states are reluctant to take costly climate action unless everyone else does so as well. More recently, however, this framing has been challenged. This is because it does not reflect the complex systemic drivers that perpetuate carbon dependency at multiple levels and scales (Bernstein & Hoffmann, 2019) and does not consider the diversity of reasons why governments and other actors may want to make and implement climate commitments unilaterally, for instance, when faced with pressure from key domestic constituencies (Aklin & Mildenberger, 2020). In addition, portraying climate change as a 'tragedy' may also limit possibilities for positive action by reinforcing defeatism and complacency.

2.2 Adaptation

As mitigation strategies are falling short, adapting to the impacts of a changing climate has become increasingly urgent. An estimated 3.3 to 3.6 billion people are already living in contexts that are highly vulnerable to the adverse effects of climate change (IPCC, 2023). The Paris Agreement established a collective goal to enhance adaptive capability (UNFCCC, 2015, Art. 2.b), reflecting a commitment – at least on paper – to address adaptation with the same urgency as mitigation.

Yet, adaptation remains an under-prioritised domain of global climate governance. In 2023, eight years post-Paris, states finally agreed on a framework aimed at clarifying and operationalising the global goal on adaptation. However, important elements are still missing, notably 'specific, measurable indicators to track on-the-ground action and measure progress' (Hussein et al., 2014). A major challenge is the multifaceted, context-specific, and localised nature of adaptation needs and measures, which can range from building flood defences to establishing early warning systems, cultivating climate-resilient crops, or improving water and land management practices. This makes it difficult to define adaptation, comprehensively account for existing vulnerabilities, allocate responsibilities, and assess progress.

Continued de-prioritisation is also due to political complexities, above all, the question of who should pay for adaptation costs in developing countries. The adaptation finance gap – the difference between what is needed and what is provided through public multilateral and bilateral adaptation finance – is currently estimated at US$194–366 billion per year (UNEP, 2023). A major challenge is that the immediate benefits of adaptation measures are local rather than global. Therefore, unlike mitigation, adaptation has traditionally not been considered a global public good (Persson, 2019).

This view is now slowly shifting. The Paris Agreement defines adaptation as 'a global challenge faced by all with local, sub-national, national, regional, and international dimensions' (UNFCCC, 2015, Art. 7.2). Local adaptation measures have direct and indirect effects whose benefits extend beyond borders, including knowledge creation and sharing, prevention of climate change-related displacement, the enhancement of food security, and co-benefits for mitigation. Importantly, for climate-vulnerable countries, who have contributed least towards climate change, adaptation finance is also a matter of justice. Yet, as Khan et al. (2020) find, wealthy states have been reluctant to employ justice-related frames and criteria to mobilise adaptation finance and support.

2.3 Loss and Damage

The term loss and damage (L&D) refers to climate change impacts that cannot (or are not) avoided through mitigation and adaptation. This includes impacts related to extreme weather events or those caused by slow onset events, such as sea-level rise, ocean acidification, or desertification. L&D has long been a major concern for climate-vulnerable states, but developed countries have historically resisted its institutionalisation within the UNFCCC, due to concerns that this would serve as the basis for compensation claims, given their disproportionate responsibility for climate change.

L&D first entered the official UNFCCC agenda in 2007 through the Bali Action Plan. In 2013, the first dedicated institutional arrangement on L&D, the Warsaw Mechanism on Loss and Damage (WIM), was established. Two years later, the Paris Agreement recognised 'the importance of averting, minimizing and addressing loss and damage' (UNFCCC, 2015, Art. 8.1), albeit with an explicit exclusion of liability and compensation through the accompanying Paris Decision. Most recently, at Conference of the Parties (COP)27 and COP28, state parties agreed for the first time to establish and operationalise a dedicated fund to help vulnerable countries recover from climate-related disasters. While celebrated as a historic breakthrough, initial pledges cover less than 0.2% of the current L&D needs of developing countries (Seega, 2023). Moreover, many critical issues are yet to be resolved, including those related to how, when, in what form, and based on which criteria funds will be distributed.

Although progress has been slow, it is perhaps surprising that agreement on L&D has been reached at all. As Vanhala (2023) argues, this has been facilitated by 'constructive ambiguity': the absence of an agreed-upon definition has allowed different actors to frame L&D in different ways, enabling compromise without resolving fundamental tensions and power imbalances. L&D funding arrangements are explicitly 'based on cooperation and facilitation' (UNFCCC, 2023), rather than principles of distributive and/or corrective justice. It is questionable whether funds motivated by solidarity alone will be sufficient to cover the growing L&D needs of developing countries, meaning that L&D finance is likely to continue to be a fraught issue at future UNFCCC negotiations.

3. THE EVOLUTION OF GLOBAL CLIMATE GOVERNANCE UNDER THE UNFCCC

The last three decades have seen the emergence of a complex institutional architecture to address climate change and its impacts under the UNFCCC. However, more than eight years after parties adopted the widely celebrated Paris Agreement, implementation is 'lacking across all areas and not where it should be' (UNFCCC, n.d.). This section provides a brief overview of the historical evolution of the UNFCCC regime, the key design features of the Paris Agreement, and reflections on its impact and implementation so far.

3.1 Early Efforts to Govern Climate Change: the Kyoto Protocol

The 1992 UNFCCC serves as both the foundational treaty and central convening mechanism for global efforts to tackle climate change. The convention itself is largely procedural in nature, leaving specific targets to be set in subsidiary treaties. It does, however, lay out several principles for cooperation, notably the principle of 'common but differentiated responsibilities and respective capabilities' (CBDR-RC), which recognises that different states have different capabilities and responsibilities to address climate change (UN, 1992, Art. 3.1). Reflecting this principle, the convention divides parties into Annex I (developed) and non-Annex I (developing) countries, with the former expected to take the lead in addressing climate change.

The CBDR-RC principle strongly informed the first international agreement negotiated under the UNFCCC, the 1997 Kyoto Protocol. For the first time, a global-level treaty established binding GHG emissions reduction targets, albeit only for Annex I countries. During a first commitment period of five years (2008–2012), Annex I countries were required to lower their cumulative emissions by 5% compared to 1990 (UNFCCC, 1998, Art. 3.1). Beyond domestic policy measures, they were allowed to use so-called flexible mechanisms to deliver on their individual targets. This included, most prominently, the Clean Development Mechanism, which enabled Annex I countries to offset domestic GHG emissions by funding emissions-reducing projects in developing countries.

There are different views on the legacy of the Kyoto Protocol. While some conclude that its design was fundamentally flawed (Rosen, 2015), others have pointed to high levels of overall compliance, at least partly attributable to genuine policy innovation (Grubb, 2016). The greatest challenge to the protocol's effectiveness was non-participation by major emitters. The US withdrawal in particular posed serious challenges. Other large emitters – notably China – were never included, as they were not listed in Annex I of the convention. This also meant that many Annex I countries were reluctant to participate in the second commitment period of the Kyoto Protocol (2013 to 2020). It became clear that a new legal framework was needed that would facilitate much higher participation.

This new type of framework was widely expected to be agreed upon in 2009, at COP15 in Copenhagen. Yet, parties were unable to bridge their differences. Instead of a new global treaty, the summit produced the Copenhagen Accord, a political agreement hammered out by a small group of states. At the time, COP15 was widely perceived as a disaster, and the division it caused among parties overshadowed subsequent negotiations (Maslin, Lang & Harvey, 2023). In hindsight, Copenhagen presented a turning point, prompting the rise of a more polycentric and flexible global climate change regime, built on a system of nationally determined pledges – thus sowing the seeds for what would later become the Paris Agreement.

3.2 A New Governance Logic: the Paris Agreement

The adoption of the 2015 Paris Agreement represents a shift away from the legalised regulatory logic of the Kyoto regime towards a more inclusive, bottom-up model of global climate governance.

Building on the pledge-and-review approach introduced in the Copenhagen Accord, the Paris Agreement does not contain legally binding individual targets for state parties. Instead, it sets collective targets – most prominently the 1.5–2°C temperature goal – and requires parties to submit their own nationally determined contributions (NDCs) every five years. Importantly, NDCs are prepared by every state party, making the Paris Agreement the first universal climate treaty. Universal participation has been made possible through a more nuanced interpretation of the CBDR-RC principle. The Paris Agreement transcends the static division between Annex I and non-Annex I countries, while acknowledging that responsibilities and capabilities must be evaluated 'in the light of different national circumstances' (UNFCCC, 2015, Preamble). In essence, the Agreement relies on a system of 'bounded self-differentiation' (Pauw, Mbeva & Van Asselt, 2019), whereby countries determine their own responsibilities through the NDCs but are expected to demonstrate maximum ambition and progressively step up their commitments.

In line with this more flexible and facilitative approach, the Paris Agreement relies primarily on peer pressure and reputational costs to ensure compliance. Under the Agreement's enhanced transparency framework, parties are required to report on their emissions and implementation efforts. These reports are subject to technical expert reviews and a multilateral peer review process, however, without the threat of sanctions and in an explicitly 'facilitative, non-intrusive, non-punitive manner' (UNFCCC, 2015, Art. 13.3). Information from the reports will also feed into the Paris Agreement's global stocktake, a five-yearly exercise to assess collective progress made towards the Agreement's long-term goals and with opportunities to ratchet up ambition. The global stocktake is a vital component of the Paris Agreement, serving to demonstrate collective accountability and avoid stagnation of climate ambition.

While these design innovations mark a clear departure from the Kyoto approach, the Paris Agreement still retains some important elements of the 1997 Protocol, notably the inclusion of market-based mechanisms. In Article 6, it sets out the principles for cooperative implementation and the establishment of an international carbon market. However, Article 6 has proven especially difficult to operationalise and slow to implement, with progress also marred by plummeting confidence in voluntary carbon markets (Vaughan & Di Leva, 2023).

Many of the Paris Agreement's design elements reflect a desire to overcome some of the barriers that have traditionally thwarted advancements in global climate governance, above all, the tension between universality, compliance, and ambition (Tørstad, 2020). Getting all states, including all major emitters, on board was only possible because individual commitments are self-determined and unenforceable. The architects of the Paris Agreement accepted that initial NDCs would not be in line with its long-term goals; however, the crux of the Agreement is that it creates a system to ratchet up ambition over time. As such, its success crucially hinges on the consecutive stocktaking exercises and NDC revisions resulting in a virtuous circle of ever-rising ambition. As we will discuss further below, these efforts to ramp up national ambition are also supplemented by the deliberate integration of non- and sub-state action into the UNFCCC regime (Bäckstrand & Kuyper, 2024). However, as the next section shows, there are serious question marks over whether ambition ratcheting is going far and fast enough.

3.3 Implementing the Paris Agreement: Are We on Track?

Reflecting strong political momentum, the Paris Agreement entered into force in record time, on 4 November 2016. Two years later, parties adopted most of the Paris rulebook, detailing rules, procedures, and guidelines for its implementation. On the national level, the Paris Agreement and the influential Intergovernmental Panel on Climate Change (IPCC) Special Report on global warming of 1.5°C inspired a surge of net-zero pledges (Van Coppenolle, Blondeel & Van de Graaf, 2022). The Paris regime also proved resilient, if not unaffected, in the face of the temporary withdrawal of the United States under Donald Trump.

At the same time, progress towards implementing the Paris Agreement has been insufficient. The first global stocktake, completed at COP28 in 2023, shows that parties are significantly off track across all the Agreement's long-term goals (UNFCCC, n.d.). NDCs are still incompatible with a 1.5°C trajectory and often rely on 'false solutions and unrealistic technological fixes' to achieve net-zero targets (Climate Action Tracker, 2023, p. 5). Climate finance flows, whilst increasing, remain wholly inadequate to respond to developing countries' needs, in particular regarding adaptation (OECD, 2023). The failure of rich countries to deliver on their promise, first made in 2009, to mobilise 100 billion USD in climate finance per year by 2020, has already severely undermined trust between negotiators (Lo, 2023). More generally, as

Depledge (2021, p. 1) observes, UNFCCC negotiations have seen increased political squabbling, pointing to 'an evaporation of the constructive "spirit of Paris"'.

At the three most recent COPs, rifts between negotiating parties were on display, for example, in discussions over the inclusion of fossil fuels in formal decisions, with language on 'phasing out' their use replaced by weaker language on 'phasing down' or 'transitioning away' (Lo, 2024). However, this should not distract from the significance of fossil fuels being included in COP agreements in the first place, given that previous conferences had never directly addressed the need to end their use. It is also indicative of global climate governance reaching a crunch point: with the window to reach the Paris climate goals rapidly closing and anti-fossil fuel norms gaining traction (Van Asselt & Green, 2022), COPs can no longer avoid discussion of the main source of emissions. Yet, with powerful vested interests seeking to protect investments, these conversations are bound to be highly contentious. Indeed, since COP26, when fossil fuels featured prominently on the official agenda for the first time, representatives of the oil and gas industry have flocked to COPs in record numbers (McGrath, 2023).

Beyond the official negotiations, global climate action and cooperation have also been affected by major crises and disruptions, above all the Covid-19 pandemic. The long-term impact of the pandemic on global emissions is still uncertain. Although energy-related emissions dropped sharply in 2020, they experienced a strong rebound as pandemic restrictions were easing (IEA, 2023b). Covid-19 stimulus packages have likely contributed to a significant boost in clean energy deployment since 2019 (ibid.). Yet, preliminary assessments show that economic recovery packages are by-and-large not living up to their ambition of delivering a green and just recovery (Tienhaara et al., 2023). More generally, Covid-19 serves as a reminder that encouraging solidarity and collective action does not necessarily get easier in the face of urgent crises.

4. MULTILEVEL CLIMATE GOVERNANCE: A DIVERSE CAST OF ACTORS

Multilateral negotiations alone were never going to halt climate change. As this section seeks to demonstrate, the creation and implementation of global climate policy is not – or no longer – restricted to formal intergovernmental organisations. Indeed, the Paris Agreement has opened new opportunities for mobilisation by a huge diversity of actors (public, private, hybrid) across all levels of governance (international, regional, national, local) and across a growing number of issue areas. Consequently, the architecture of global climate governance has transformed from a relatively mono-centric regime into a polycentric 'regime complex', featuring an array of actors and regulatory elements that are only partially organised hierarchically (Keohane & Victor, 2011; Coen, Kreienkamp & Pegram, 2021). While this fragmentation and hybridisation of global climate governance pose challenges and risks, it also creates new opportunities for bottom-up innovation and experimentation, mutual learning, cooperation, and the exploitation of synergies. The Paris Agreement has the potential to act as a collective compass, steering the actions of diverse actors on multiple scales in the same direction. However, regime complexity can undermine or obscure transparency and accountability, especially in a context of structural power imbalances. It may also divert attention from the (in-)action of states, who remain the principal duty bearers with regard to addressing climate change and its impacts.

4.1 Formal Intergovernmental Organisations

The UNFCCC brings together virtually all countries in the world to negotiate agreements aimed at addressing climate change and its impacts. Its supreme decision-making body, the Conference of the Parties (COP), meets annually to review and assess the implementation of the convention and its subsidiary treaties. The UNFCCC bureaucracy itself serves primarily as an information hub, technical advisor, and negotiation facilitator with limited independence and budgetary resources. However, the secretariat has gradually managed to carve out a more proactive and autonomous role for itself, for instance, by encouraging and coordinating climate action by non-state actors (Hickmann et al., 2019). Although the UNFCCC is no stranger to legitimacy challenges, it is widely seen as the only credible forum for negotiating global climate agreements.

Many of the UNFCCC's activities and decisions are guided by input from another prominent intergovernmental organisation, namely the IPCC. The IPCC is best known for its Assessment Reports, which review and synthesise the latest climate research to provide the international community with scientific guidance on the state of the challenge and the range of possible response strategies. Although reports are prepared by scientists, the IPCC is an explicitly intergovernmental organisation. This poses unique challenges to its work, which needs to be at once 'scientifically sound and politically acceptable' (Agrawala, 1998, p. 621). Despite this and other challenges, the IPCC has played a pivotal role in shaping global climate governance, with some observers arguing that, without it, the Paris Agreement 'seems very unlikely to have emerged' (Hermansen, Boasson & Peters, 2023, p. 30).

Bolstered by the work of the IPCC, the UNFCCC has largely consolidated its role as a central node for global climate action. That said, because the problem of climate change is intrinsically connected to other issues of international cooperation, the UNFCCC is no longer the only formal multilateral forum active in this space. Indeed, almost all major multilateral organisations within and beyond the UN system are seeking to address it in one way or another. This includes, for instance, the United Nations Environment Programme and treaty monitoring bodies associated with other multilateral environmental agreements. Specialised UN agencies, such as the International Civil Aviation Organization and the International Maritime Organization have recently adopted instruments to reduce emissions from international aviation and shipping, although their track record in this regard has been beset by delays and resistance (Deese, 2023). Major international financial institutions, such as the World Bank or the International Monetary Fund (IMF), are exploring ways to use development assistance in a way that contributes towards climate goals (Patrick, 2023). Other intergovernmental organisations are increasingly grappling with the impacts of climate change on issues such as food, health, human rights, or disaster risk reduction.

The cross-cutting nature of climate change provides ample scope for partnerships and collaboration across different intergovernmental organisations. For example, there is growing recognition of the need to expand synergies between the UNFCCC and its 'sister conventions', the Convention on Biological Diversity (CBD) and the UN Convention to Combat Desertification, all of which were established at the 1992 Earth Summit (IISD, 2023). However, there is also a need to address potential conflict. In the case of the CBD, conflict with the goals of the UNFCCC may arise, for instance, where monoculture afforestation is used as a carbon offset solution without consideration of the risks to ecosystems and local communities (Seddon et al., 2021).

4.2 Informal Intergovernmental Organisations

Recent scholarship has revealed the growth of informal intergovernmental organisations (IIGOs) across a range of governance areas (Roger, 2020). In contrast to their formal counterparts, IIGOs are not established through binding legal instruments, such as a charter or a treaty, and they operate without sophisticated bureaucratic structures. However, they meet on a regular basis, have defined goals, consistent practices, and a relatively permanent state-level membership. The most prominent IIGOs active in the climate governance space are the G7 and G20.

Scholars have debated whether small, exclusive clubs may be able to drive forward climate action more effectively than the cumbersome UNFCCC negotiation process; however, the evidence base on this remains thin (Falkner, Nasiritousi & Reischl, 2022). In 2022, the G7 launched a Climate Club to accelerate implementation of the Paris Agreement, with a particular focus on industrial decarbonisation, open in principle to all states that are committed to its goals (Climate Club, n.d.). Details on how exactly the Climate Club aims to accelerate action are still scarce, leading some observers to conclude that it 'amounts to little more than a forum for countries with self-proclaimed "ambitious" climate policies' (Kurmayer, 2023).

IIGOs face potential tensions between representativeness and effectiveness. While smaller gatherings, such as the G7, may be more likely to reach ambitious consensus on climate change, they cannot speak on behalf of the poorest communities – those who will experience the impacts of climate change first and most severely. Therefore, some warn that the G7 and its newly established Climate Club 'could perpetuate global inequalities and exacerbate the climate impacts felt by vulnerable communities in the Global South' (Arhin & Kanugwe Kalaba, 2023). In turn, the G20 is better placed to bridge long-standing differences between the Global North and the Global South; however, member states have found it more difficult to generate consensus on fraught issues, such as cutting fossil fuels (Varadhan & Verma, 2023).

Finally, IIGOs and Climate Clubs also raise a number of questions regarding legitimacy, transparency, and accountability. For this reason, Falkner, Nasiritousi, and Reischl (2022, p. 480) contend that any Climate Club should 'consider how to add to, and not distract from, the multilateral climate regime'.

4.3 Regional Intergovernmental Organisations

Regional intergovernmental organisations, such as the African Union (AU), the Association of Southeast Asian Nations (ASEAN), the European Union (EU), the Inter-American Institute for Global Change Research (IAI), or the Caribbean Community (CARICOM), have the potential to play an important role in driving climate policy innovation, raising collective ambition, and facilitating the implementation of global climate agreements.

The EU in particular has sought to establish itself as an ambitious and proactive actor. It is by far the most advanced example of regional integration, characterised by high levels of institutionalisation and considerable delegation of national sovereignty to the supranational level. The EU is also the only regional organisation to participate in UNFCCC negotiations as a bloc and to submit a joint NDC on behalf of all of its member states. To deliver on its long-term legally binding target of achieving climate neutrality by 2050, the EU has adopted a comprehensive package of policy initiatives and legislation, known as the European Green Deal (Kreienkamp, Pegram & Coen, 2022). However, European climate leadership has not always been consistent, and the EU is not currently on track to achieve its 2030 target of cutting net emissions by at least 55% compared to 1990 levels – a target which is in itself not considered compatible with the EU's commitments under the Paris Agreement (Climate Action Tracker, n.d.).

Other regional organisations are also playing an active role in developing joint climate strategies and policy frameworks; however, their ability to drive transformative policy change is often circumscribed by low institutional autonomy and capacity, as well as a more challenging political context. For example, Bal et al. (2022) find that climate cooperation in the ASEAN region remains underdeveloped, due in part to resistance from powerful domestic politico-business coalitions with preferences for carbon-intensive growth models.

4.4 Sub-National and Non-State Actors

Sub-national and non-state actors are highly heterogeneous. They comprise, for example, cities, regions, and other territorial entities, private businesses, investors, scientific communities, trade unions, non-governmental organisations (NGOs), Indigenous groups, and civil society movements, to name just a few. The global regime complex for climate change provides ample opportunities for sub- and non-state actor participation, which comes in a variety of forms, from advocacy and watchdog activities to policy entrepreneurship, policy creation, and implementation. These activities are often supported through transnational networks or partnerships that facilitate learning, exchange, and the development of shared norms, rules, and standards, among other functions (Tosun & Schoenefeld, 2017).

Under the umbrella of the Paris Agreement, the UNFCCC has strategically embraced and encouraged the diffusion of sub- and non-state climate action through orchestration mechanisms such as the High-Level Champions, who are charged with scaling up ambitious climate action by cities, businesses, and others, or the Global Climate Action Portal, which serves as a repository for non-state climate pledges (Bäckstrand & Kuyper, 2024). The annual COPs have also become gradually more open to non-state observers. While opportunities to access and directly influence the negotiations remain limited, COPs are important platforms for non-state actors to lobby decision-makers, showcase their activities, network, and learn from each other (Lövbrand, Hjerpe & Linnér, 2017). Beyond the COPs, a number of dedicated summits and events have been convened within and outside of the UNFCCC context, aimed at mobilising transnational cooperative initiatives involving sub- and non-state actors (Chan et al., 2022).

These developments have inspired hope that sub- and non-state action could help narrow the gap between insufficiently ambitious NDCs and the aims of the Paris Agreement, in particular in terms of mitigation. Because actors such as cities and private companies are major contributors of GHGs, the mitigation potential of their voluntary pledges is substantial (Hsu et al., 2020). The growing diversity of sub- and non-state climate action also provides, in principle, 'unprecedented opportunities for experimentation and learning', often considered key ingredients for effective responses to highly complex problems such as climate change (Abbott, 2017, p. 738). However, evidence on the effectiveness and broader impact of these actions remains scarce (Hale et al., 2021). A recent assessment of the climate strategies and targets of major companies found that these are 'mired by ambiguous commitments, offsetting plans that lack credibility and emission scope exclusions' (Day et al., 2023, p. 5). Similarly, transnational city networks are not always as ambitious, representative, and transparent as they are made out to be (Bansard, Pattberg & Widerberg, 2017).

To respond to concerns around transparency, a growing number of private standards, certification schemes, and disclosure initiatives have sprung up. However, while corporate actors are increasingly ready to participate in such schemes, this does not appear to consistently translate into significant emissions reductions (Coen, Herman & Pegram, 2022; 2023). Other researchers have warned that the growing emphasis on quantifying non-state contributions may reinforce neoliberal modes of governance (Jernnäs & Lövbrand, 2022) and 'lead to the under-appreciation of variegated social, economic, and environmental impacts' (Chan et al., 2019, p. 2). It is also important to highlight that sub- and non-state actors are not necessarily climate progressive. A significant section of business actors continues to exploit their economic power and privileged access to decision-makers in order to obstruct or delay policies, with the fossil fuel lobby easily outspending climate-supporting industry groups (Downie & Brulle, 2023). Voluntary self-regulation is also not always receiving unequivocal support from political leaders, as exemplified by the recent conservative pushback against environmental, social, and governance (ESG) initiatives in the United States (Dolsak & Prakash, 2024).

Environmental NGOs and civil society groups can provide an important counterweight to actors seeking to delay climate action, and they are also more likely to emphasise concerns related to justice, equity and other social issues (Derman, 2014). NGOs may do so, for example, via traditional advocacy efforts, by partnering with private and/or public actors in carbon disclosure schemes or other initiatives, or by engaging in more adversarial strategies, such as climate litigation. The latter has seen a significant expansion in recent years, with some notable successes (Setzer & Higham, 2023). Beyond such activities by legacy NGOs, more radical and less formal activist movements – such as Extinction Rebellion and the Fridays for Future movement – have also gained significant momentum. However, NGOs and social movements face limitations on their ability to influence global climate policymaking and, in some cases, even active intimidation (OHCHR, 2022). It is also important to highlight that the transnational NGO community itself, while committed to broader representation, is characterised by persistent structural inequalities between the Global North and the Global South (Gereke & Brühl, 2019).

Ultimately, many forms of non-state actor climate action raise questions of legitimacy, representation, and accountability in addition to questions over their effectiveness. Thus, non-state climate engagement does not automatically make global climate governance more democratic and should not distract from the fact that the primary responsibility to act lies with states.

4.5 States and Domestic Mechanisms

The Paris Agreement's success ultimately depends on national ambition and implementation capacity. As Dubash (2021, p. 1) observes, under the bottom-up Paris regime, 'climate politics has become at least as much about understanding dynamics *within* nations as it is understanding the interaction *between* nations'.

Implementing net-zero pledges and other ambitious climate targets requires a far-reaching socio-economic transformation, delivered at high speed. While this is expected to create strong co-benefits, including opportunities for green economic growth (Stern & Valero, 2021), not all sections of society stand to win from net-zero policies in the absence of effective redistributive mechanisms. This includes, for instance, those working in the fossil fuel industry and dependent sectors, but also, more generally, poorer households who cannot easily access low-carbon technologies (Theminimulle et al., 2024). Indeed, as Aklin and Mildenberger (2020) argue, entrenched distributive conflict on the domestic level may be one of the primary obstacles to effective global climate governance. Others have suggested that today's climate politics go beyond distributional concerns, invoking existential fears over 'whose way of life gets to survive' (Colgan, Green & Hale, 2021, p. 592).

The politicisation of climate policymaking highlights the importance of domestic mechanisms and institutions that may be able to address conflict and keep countries on track when implementing their global commitments. This includes, for instance, just transition frameworks and policies aimed at maximising the opportunities of ambitious climate action and mitigating the risks for those most affected (Krawchenko & Gordon, 2021). It also includes climate framework laws that enshrine binding objectives for climate action, thus 'locking in' national ambition (Manguiat & Raine, 2018). Importantly, domestic climate laws and policies must be supported by robust governance machinery and mechanisms to ensure transparency and accountability. A promising development is the emergence of independent national advisory bodies, many of which do not just provide concrete science-based advice but also evaluate progress made on climate action. However, as the example of the UK Climate Change Committee shows, even the most sophisticated and empowered advisory bodies may be sidelined by reluctant governments (Ward, 2024). Ultimately, at least in democratic contexts, domestic constituencies play a key role in influencing policymakers' preferences and holding them to account.

Systematic research into domestic climate governance is still lacking, and existing studies have been strongly biased towards the Global North (Boasson, Burns & Pulver, 2023). As Lincoln (2024, p. 408) warns, the 'net-zero transition will expose a non-negligible number of countries to unprecedented instability'. This includes countries that lack the financial, human, and technological resources to deliver a far-reaching economic transformation, many of which are already faced with a host of complex development challenges exacerbated by the impacts of climate change. Going forward, global climate governance urgently needs to grapple with how socially just transitions can be delivered in different domestic contexts, ensuring that developing countries have the resources they need to deliver on their climate commitments, without taking away from pressing development concerns (Bal et al., 2022).

5. CONCLUSION

Much has changed since climate change first entered the global political agenda towards the end of the twentieth century. Global climate governance is now widely understood as a polycentric process that transcends the UNFCCC, engaging an increasing variety of public and private actors located at different levels of policy implementation, whose actions are loosely coupled to align with the 2015 Paris Agreement. This change in governance structure, away from Kyoto-style regulatory governance, also reflects a change in problem perception. Climate change is no longer considered to be predominantly a problem of multilateral cooperation – whereby the main barrier to action is the lack of effective mechanisms to prevent free-riding – but rather a complex set of problems that will require wide-ranging 'system transitions' across all sectors of our economy and society (IPCC, 2023, p. 28).

To a degree, this reappraisal of the climate change problem allows for an optimistic assessment of the governance structure introduced by the Paris Agreement. When addressing problems as wicked as climate change, regime fragmentation and hybridisation may, in fact, provide important opportunities for bottom-up innovation, experimentation, and learning. As Harrison and Geyer (2019, p. 22) argue, the UNFCCC still has an important role to play in creating the 'ideational environment' to encourage, coordinate, and align bottom-up action and progressively raise collective ambition. Yet, in a context of pronounced power imbalances and pervasive carbon dependency, it remains highly uncertain whether incremental ambition raising will be sufficient to realise the promise of Paris. Major polluting states and other incumbent actors in the global energy system continue to exert disproportionate influence in climate policymaking, within the UNFCCC and beyond (Nasiritousi et al.,

2024). This has produced systemic biases in how climate change is framed and governed and has enabled the exploitation of ambiguities in net-zero commitments in a way that delays decarbonisation efforts (Armstrong & McLaren, 2022). With the 1.5°C target slipping out of reach, climate governance is also set to increasingly confront normative questions of equity and justice – and their distributive implications – both at the national and global level.

The jury is still out on whether the Paris regime constitutes a new 'model for effective global governance' (Slaughter, 2015) or a 'dangerous form of incrementalism' (Allan, 2019 p. 4). As this chapter has sought to convey, wider structural shifts in the architecture of global climate governance present both opportunities and risks. The remarkable diversity of actors and actions demonstrates the huge potential for positive innovation upon existing governance structures, beyond top-down regulation. However, activity does not always equal effectiveness. In addition, many climate governance arrangements have shortcomings in terms of legitimacy, transparency, accountability, and representation. This underscores the need for future scholarship to further assess the promise and limitations of polycentric, multi-scalar governance, balancing a pragmatic concern for problem-solving with a critical appraisal of structural power. Researchers also have much to gain from turning the focus increasingly to capacity challenges and political struggles at the national level – because it is at this level that the Paris Agreement will ultimately succeed or fail.

REFERENCES

Abbott, K. W. (2017). Orchestrating experimentation in non-state environmental commitments. *Environmental Politics*, 26(4), 738–763.

Agrawala, S. (1998). Structural and process history of the Intergovernmental Panel on Climate Change. *Climatic Change*, 39(4), 621–642.

Aklin, M., & Mildenberger, M. (2020). Prisoners of the wrong dilemma: Why distributive conflict, not collective action, characterizes the politics of climate change. *Global Environmental Politics*, 20(4), 4–27.

Alayza, N. (2024, February 15). What is the Paris Agreement's Article 2.1(c) on climate finance, and why does it matter? World Resources Institute. Retrieved February 15, 2024, from https://www.wri.org/insights/article-2-1-c-paris-agreement-explained.

Allan, J. I. (2019). Dangerous incrementalism of the Paris Agreement. *Global Environmental Politics*, 19(1), 4–11.

Arhin, A., & Kanugwe Kalaba, F. (2023). Tackling the climate crisis: Exploring the implications of the proposed G7 climate club on climate and development agendas of African Countries. Africa Policy Research Institute (APRI). Retrieved July 4 2023, from https://afripoli.org/tackling-climate-crisis-exploring-the-implications-of-the-proposed-g7-climate-club-on-climate-and-development-agendas-of-african-countries.

Armstrong, C., & McLaren, D. (2022). Which net zero? Climate justice and net zero emissions. *Ethics and International Affairs*, 36(4), 505–526.

Bäckstrand, K., & Kuyper, J. W. (2024). The Marrakech Partnership for Global Climate Action: Democratic legitimacy, orchestration, and the role of international secretariats. In: H. Jörgens, N. Kolleck, & M. Well (Eds.), *International Public Administrations in Environmental Governance*. Cambridge University Press, 180–200.

Bal, C., Coen, D., Kreienkamp, J., Paramitaningrum, & Pegram, T. (2022). *Explaining Transformative Change in ASEAN and EU Climate Policy: Multilevel Problems, Policies and Politics*. Cambridge University Press.

Bansard, J. S., Pattberg, P. H., & Widerberg, O. (2017). Cities to the rescue? Assessing the performance of transnational municipal networks in global climate governance. *International Environmental Agreements*, 17, 229–246.

Bernstein, S., & Hoffmann, M. (2019). Climate politics, metaphors and the fractal carbon trap. *Nature Climate Change*, 9, 919–925.

Boasson, E. L., Burns, C., & Pulver, S. (2023). The politics of domestic climate governance: Making sense of complex participation patterns. *Journal of European Public Policy*, 30(3), 513–536.

Chan, S., Boran, I., Van Asselt, H. et al. (2019). Promises and risks of nonstate action in climate and sustainability governance. *WIREs Climate Change*, 10(3), e572.

Chan, S., Hale, T., Deneault, A. et al. (2022). Assessing the effectiveness of orchestrated climate action from five years of summits. *Nature Climate Change*, 12, 628–633.

Climate Action Tracker. (n.d.). EU Country Summary. Retrieved from https://climateactiontracker.org/countries/eu/.

Climate Action Tracker. (2023). Warming projections global update. December 2023. Retrieved from https://climateactiontracker.org/documents/1187/CAT_2023-12-05_GlobalUpdate_COP28.pdf.

Climate Club. (n.d.). An inclusive and ambitious high-level forum for industry decarbonisation. Retrieved from https://climate-club.org/.

Coen, D., Herman, K., & Pegram, T. (2022). Are corporate climate efforts genuine? An empirical analysis of the climate 'talk–walk' hypothesis. *Business Strategy and the Environment*, 31(7), 3040–3059.

Coen, D., Herman, K., & Pegram, T. (2023). Market masquerades? Corporate climate initiative effects on firm-level climate performance. *Global Environmental Politics*, 23(4), 141–169.

Coen, D., Kreienkamp, J., & Pegram, T. (2021). *Global Climate Governance*. Cambridge University Press.

Colgan, J. D., Green, J. F., & Hale, T. N. (2021). Asset revaluation and the existential politics of climate change. *International Organization*, 75(2), 586–610.

Day, T., Mooldijk, S., & Hans, F. et al. (2023). *Corporate Climate Responsibility Monitor 2023*. NewClimate Institute. Retrieved from https://newclimate.org/sites/default/files/2023-04/NewClimate_CorporateClimateResponsibilityMonitor2023_Feb23.pdf.

Deese, D. A. (2023). *Controlling International Shipping and Aviation Emissions*. Routledge.

Depledge J. (2021). Introduction: International climate policy after Paris – an update on a changing world. In: J. Depledge, J. E. Viñuales, E. Lees, & D. Reiner (Eds.), *Climate Policy after the 2015 Paris Climate Conference*. Routledge, 1–14.

Derman, B. B. (2014). Climate governance, justice, and transnational civil society. *Climate Policy*, 14(1), 23–41.

Dolsak, N., & Prakash, A. (2024). The rise and fall of ESG. *Forbes*, 23 April. Retrieved from https://www.forbes.com/sites/prakashdolsak/2024/04/23/the-rise-and-fall-of-esg/?sh=3402333474d9.

Downie, C., & Brulle, R. (2023). Big Oil's trade group allies outspent clean energy groups by a whopping 27x, with billions in ads and lobbying to keep fossil fuels flowing. *The Conversation*, 13 February. Retrieved from https://theconversation.com/big-oils-trade-group-allies-outspent-clean-energy-groups-by-a-whopping-27x-with-billions-in-ads-and-lobbying-to-keep-fossil-fuels-flowing-198286.

Dubash, N. K. (2021). Varieties of climate governance: The emergence and functioning of climate institutions. *Environmental Politics*, 30(supl), 1–25.

Dyke, J., Watson, R., & Knorr, W. (2021). Climate scientists: Concept of net zero is a dangerous trap. *The Conversation*, 22 April. Retrieved from https://theconversation.com/climate-scientists-concept-of-net-zero-is-a-dangerous-trap-157368.

Falkner, R., Nasiritousi, N., & Reischl, G. (2022). Climate clubs: Politically feasible and desirable? *Climate Policy*, 22(4), 480–487.

Figueres, C. (2021). COP26 took us one step closer to combating the climate crisis. *The Guardian*, 15 November. Retrieved from https://www.theguardian.com/commentisfree/2021/nov/15/cop-26-agreement-victories-global-economy-climate-crisis.

Gereke, M., & Brühl, T. (2019). Unpacking the unequal representation of Northern and Southern NGOs in international climate change politics. *Third World Quarterly*, 40(5), 870–889.

Grubb, M. (2016). Why it's wrong to label the Kyoto Protocol a disaster. *Climate Home News*, 10 June. Retrieved from https://www.climatechangenews.com/2016/06/10/why-its-wrong-to-label-the-kyoto-protocol-a-disaster/.

Hale, T., Chan, S., Hsu, A. et al. (2021). Sub- and non-state climate action: A framework to assess progress, implementation and impact. *Climate Policy*, 21(3), 406–420.

Hardin, G. (1968). The tragedy of the commons. *Science*, 162(3859), 1243–1248.

Harrison, N. E., & Geyer, R. (2020). The complexity of the governance of climate change. In: A. Orsini et al., Forum: Complex systems and international governance. *International Studies Review*, 22 (4), 1021–1024.

Hermansen, E. A. T., Boasson, E. L., & Peters, G. P. (2023). Climate action post-Paris: How can the IPCC stay relevant? *npj Climate Action*, 2, 30.

Hickmann, T., Widerberg, O., Lederer, M., & Pattberg, P. (2019). The United Nations Framework Convention on Climate Change Secretariat as an orchestrator in global climate policymaking. *International Review of Administrative Sciences*, 1–18.

Hsu, A., Höhne, N., Kuramochi, T., Vilariño, V., & Sovacool, B. K. (2020). Beyond states: Harnessing sub-national actors for the deep decarbonisation of cities, regions, and businesses. *Energy Research & Social Science*, 70, 101738.

Hubau, W., Lewis, S. L., Phillips, O. L. et al. (2020). Asynchronous carbon sink saturation in African and Amazonian tropical forests. *Nature*, 579, 80–87.

Hussein, F., Adow, M., Okereke, C. et al. (2014). Understanding the Paris Agreement's 'Global Goal on Adaptation'. World Resources Institute, 1 February. Retrieved from https://www.wri.org/insights/global-goal-on-adaptation-explained.

IEA. (2023a). *World Energy Outlook 2023*. International Energy Agency. Retrieved from https://www.iea.org/reports/world-energy-outlook-2023/.

IEA. (2023b). *CO2 Emissions in 2023*. Paris: International Energy Agency. Retrieved from https://www.iea.org/reports/co2-emissions-in-2023.

IISD. (2023). Linking the Rio Conventions: Where we saw progress in 2022. IISD Earth Negotiations Bulletin, 14 February. Retrieved from https://enb.iisd.org/articles/linking-rio-conventions-progress-2022.

IPCC. (2023). Summary for policymakers. In: *Climate Change 2023: Synthesis Report. Contribution of Working Groups I, II and III to the Sixth Assessment Report of the Intergovernmental Panel on Climate Change.*

Jagers, S. C., & Stripple, J. (2003). Climate governance beyond the state. *Global Governance*, 9(3), 385–399.

Jernnäs, M., & Lövbrand, E. (2022). Accelerating climate action: The politics of nonstate actor engagement in the Paris regime. *Global Environmental Politics*, 22(3), 38–58.

Keohane, R. O., & Victor, D. G. (2011). The regime complex for climate change. *Perspectives on Politics*, 9(1), 7–23.

Khan, M., Robinson, S.-A., Weikmans, R., Ciplet, D., & Roberts, J. T. (2020). Twenty-five years of adaptation finance through a climate justice lens. *Climatic Change*, 161, 251–269.

Krawchenko, T. A., & Gordon, M. (2021). How do we manage a just transition? A comparative review of national and regional just transition initiatives. *Sustainability*, 13, 6070.

Kreienkamp, J., Pegram, T., & Coen, D. (2022). Explaining transformative changing in EU climate policy: Multilevel problems, policies and politics. *Journal of European Integration*, 44(5), 731–748.

Kurmayer, N. J. (2023). Germany's Scholz to officially inaugurate 'climate club' at COP28. *Euractiv*, 1 January. Retrieved from https://www.euractiv.com/section/energy-environment/news/germanys-scholz-to-officially-inaugurate-climate-club-at-cop28/.

Levin, K., Cashore, B., Bernstein, S., & Auld, G. (2012). Overcoming the tragedy of super wicked problems. *Policy Sciences*, 45(2), 123–152.

Lincoln, J. (2024). Carbon, confusion and conflict: Global governance implications of the net-zero energy transition. In: R. Falk & A. Lopez-Claros (Eds.), *Global Governance and International Cooperation*. Routledge India, 406–427.

Lo, J. (2023). Rich countries 'confident' $100bn climate finance delivered in 2023. *Climate Home News*, 19 September. Retrieved from https://www.climatechangenews.com/2023/09/19/rich-countries-confident-100bn-climate-finance-delivered-in-2023/.

Lo, J. (2024). How fossil fuels went from sidelines to headlines in climate talks. *Climate Home News*. Retrieved January 17, 2024, from https://www.climatechangenews.com/2024/01/17/how-fossil-fuels-went-from-sidelines-to-headlines-in-climate-talks/.

Lövbrand, E., Hjerpe, M., & Linnér, B.-O. (2017). Making climate governance global: How UN climate summitry comes to matter in a complex climate regime. *Environmental Politics*, 26(4), 580–599.

Manguiat, M. S., & Raine, A. (2018). Strengthening national legal frameworks to implement the Paris Agreement. *Carbon & Climate Law Review*, 12(1), 15–22.

Maslin, M. A., Lang, J., & Harvey, F. (2023). A short history of the successes and failures of the international climate change negotiations. *UCL Open Environment*, 5, e059.

McGrath, M. (2023). COP28: Record number of fossil fuel delegates at climate talks. *BBC*. Retrieved December 12 2023, from https://www.bbc.co.uk/news/science-environment-67607289.

Nasiritousi, N., Buylova, A., Fridahl, M., & Reischl, G. (2024). Making the UNFCCC fit for purpose: A research agenda on vested interests and green spiralling. *Global Policy*, 1–8.

OECD. (2023). *Climate Finance Provided and Mobilised by Developed Countries in 2013–2021*. Organisation for Economic Co-operation and Development. Retrieved from https://www.oecd-ilibrary.org/environment/climate-finance-provided-and-mobilised-by-developed-countries-in-2013-2021_e20d2bc7-en.

OHCHR. (2022). Egypt: UN experts alarmed by harassment of civil society actors at COP27 climate summit. Office of the High Commissioner for Human Rights, 18 November. Retrieved from https://www.ohchr.org/en/press-releases/2022/11/egypt-un-experts-alarmed-harassment-civil-society-actors-cop27-climate.

Patrick, S. (2023). The World Bank eyes an overhaul amid the climate crisis. Carnegie Endowment for International Peace. Retrieved October 26, 2023, from https://carnegieendowment.org/2023/10/26/world-bank-eyes-overhaul-amid-climate-crisis-pub-90855.

Pauw, P., Mbeva, K., & Van Asselt, H. (2019). Subtle differentiation of countries' responsibilities under the Paris Agreement. *Palgrave Communications*, 5, 86.

Persson, Å. (2019). Global adaptation governance: An emerging but contested domain. *WIREs Climate Change*, 10(4), 1–18.

Rockström, J., Gupta, J., Qin, D. et al. (2023). Safe and just Earth system boundaries. *Nature*, 619, 102–111.

Roger, C. B. (2020). *The Origins of Informality: Why the Legal Foundations of Global Governance are Shifting, and Why It Matters*. Oxford University Press.

Rosen, A. M. (2015). The wrong solution at the right time: The failure of the Kyoto Protocol on climate change. *Politics & Policy*, 43(1), 30–58.

Seddon, N., Smith, A., Smith, P. et al. (2021). Getting the message right on nature-based solutions to climate change. *Global Change Biology*, 27(8), 1518–1546.

Seega, N. (2023). Rich nations' $700 million COP28 pledges cover 0.2% of climate change loss and damage. Cambridge Institute for Sustainability Leadership, 13 December. Retrieved from https://www.cisl.cam.ac.uk/news/blog/rich-nations-700-million-cop28-pledges-cover-02-climate-change-loss-and-damage.

Setzer, J., & Higham, C. (2023). Global trends in climate change litigation: 2023 snapshot. Grantham Research Institute on Climate Change and the Environment. Retrieved from https://www.lse.ac.uk/granthaminstitute/wp-content/uploads/2023/06/Global_trends_in_climate_change_litigation_2023_snapshot.pdf.

Slaughter, A.-M. (2015). The Paris Approach to global governance. *Project Syndicate*, 28 December. Retrieved from https://www.project-syndicate.org/commentary/paris-agreement-model-for-global-governance-by-anne-marie-slaughter-2015–12.

Stern, N., & Valero, A. (2021). Innovation, growth and the transition to net-zero emissions. *Research Policy*, 50(9), 104293.

Theminimulle, S., Carregha, T., Morrison, E. et al. (2024). Our journey to net zero: Understanding household and community participation in the UK's transition to a greener future. Institute for Community Studies. Retrieved from https://youngfoundation.b-cdn.net/wp-content/uploads/2024/02/Our-journey-to-net-zero-full-report-February-2024.pdf?x59628.

Tienhaara, K., Moerenhout, T., Corkal, V. et al. (2023). *A Green and Just Recovery from COVID-19? Government Investment in the Energy Transition during the Pandemic*. Cambridge University Press.

Tørstad, V. H. (2020). Participation, ambition and compliance: Can the Paris Agreement solve the effectiveness trilemma? *Environmental Politics*, 29(5), 761–780.

Tosun, J., & Schoenefeld, J. J. (2017). Collective climate action and networked climate governance. *WIREs Climate Change*, 8(1), e440.
UN. (1992). United Nations Framework Convention on Climate Change. FCCC/INFORMAL/84. Retrieved from https://unfccc.int/resource/docs/convkp/conveng.pdf.
UNEP. (2023). Underfinanced. Underprepared – Inadequate investment and planning on climate adaptation leaves world exposed. UNEP Emissions Gap Report 2023. Retrieved from https://www.unep.org/resources/adaptation-gap-report-2023.
UNFCCC. (n.d.). Why the global stocktake is important for climate action this decade. Retrieved from https://unfccc.int/topics/global-stocktake/about-the-global-stocktake/why-the-global-stocktake-is-important-for-climate-action-this-decade.
UNFCCC. (1998). Kyoto Protocol to the United Nations Framework Convention on Climate Change. Retrieved from https://unfccc.int/sites/default/files/kpeng.pdf.
UNFCCC. (2015). The Paris Agreement. Retrieved from https://unfccc.int/sites/default/files/english_paris_agreement.pdf.
UNFCCC. (2023). Operationalization of the new funding arrangements for responding to loss and damage and the fund established in paragraph 3 of decisions 2/CP.27 and 2/CMA.4. Report by the Transitional Committee. FCCC/CP/2023/9–FCCC/PA/CMA/2023/9. https://unfccc.int/documents/632319.
Van Asselt, H., & Green, F. (2022). COP26 and the dynamics of anti-fossil fuel norms. *WIREs Climate Change*, 14(3), e816.
Van Coppenolle, H., Blondeel, M., & Van de Graaf, T. (2022). Reframing the climate debate: The origins and diffusion of net zero pledges. *Global Policy*, 14(1), 48–60.
Vanhala, L. (2023). Putting the constructive ambiguity of climate change loss and damage into practice: The early work of the UNFCCC WIM ExCom. *RECIEL*, 32(3), 428–438.
Varadhan, S., & Verma, N. (2023). G20 bloc fails to reach agreement on cutting fossil fuels. *Reuters*, 24 July. Retrieved from https://www.reuters.com/business/energy/g20-draft-tweaked-reflect-dissent-cutting-unabated-fossil-fuels-2023-07-22/.
Vaughan, S., & Di Leva, C. (2023). Will international carbon markets finally deliver? IISD. Retrieved December 14, 2023, from https://www.iisd.org/articles/deep-dive/will-international-carbon-markets-finally-deliver.
Ward, B. (2024). UK Government ignores climate experts at its peril. *Grantham Research Institute on Climate Change and the Environment*. Retrieved January 1, 2024, from https://www.lse.ac.uk/granthaminstitute/news/uk-government-ignores-climate-experts-at-its-peril/.

PART III

Case studies

12. The integration of private actors in the global climate regime: targeting the symptoms rather than the disease?

Kyle S. Herman and David Coen

1. INTRODUCTION

Owing partly to the failure of public climate governance mechanisms to make a dent in greenhouse gas emissions (GHGs), the private sector was enlisted to help manage climate 'governance gaps' (Green, 2013). Since the climate crisis demands rapid action on an unprecedented scale, moreover, many welcomed the increase in private sector participation following the Paris Agreement, wherein the private sector's 'institutionalisation' into the climate change governance system is said to have occurred (Hale, 2016). Following Paris, a 'groundswell' of non-state and private-led climate actors emerged (Chan et al., 2015).

Accordingly, capacity deficits on the part of the public sector have been a major driver of the private sector actors' 'Cambrian explosion' focused squarely on the mitigation of carbon emissions (Keohane & Victor, 2011). The plurality of private actors and their associated interests, nevertheless, also can result in fragmentation in climate governance (Van Asselt & Zelli, 2014; Marx & Wouters, 2015). The infusion of private actors into the global climate governance system, indeed, has led to increased 'regime complexity' (Keohane & Victor, 2011; Hsu et al., 2016; see also Chapter 5 by Vandendriessche, Jordana, & Marx in this book). This regime and its constituent complexities are outlined within the 'Global Climate Governance Regime' (GCGR), developed by Bulkeley (2014), Michaelowa and Michaelowa (2017), Coen, Kreienkamp and Pegram (2020), and Roger, Hale, and Andonova (2019) (see also Chapter 11 by Kreienkamp & Coen in this book).

The growing integration of private actors in global climate governance, and the GCGR, raises crucial questions about the priorities and approaches shaping climate action. Previous research critiques emission mitigation strategies that rely on 'end-of-pipe' technological solutions, arguing that these approaches address the symptoms (emissions) rather than the root cause of the disease (fossil fuel dependency) (Unruh, 2000; Bäckstrand, Meadowcroft, & Oppenheimer, 2011; Corry & Riesch, 2012). Critics have similarly raised concerns about the effectiveness of carbon-centric climate governance (Biermann, Pattberg, & Zelli, 2010) and the risk of greenwashing in carbon-focused policies (Coen, Pegram, & Herman, 2022; 2023; Bernini, Giuliani, & La Rosa, 2024).

While public climate governance has sought to regulate emissions to combat the underlying issue, some argue this logic may have been replicated in private-led climate initiatives (Seto et al., 2016; Meadowcroft & Rosenbloom, 2023). Yet, since global emissions have yet to peak, the question of whether carbon emissions should remain the central focus arises (Biermann, 2010). By framing carbon as the primary target, both public and private actors have become entrenched in a 'carbon frame' that shapes goal-setting and policy outcomes (Köppl, 2012; Paterson, 2014; Coen, Herman, & Pegram, 2020; 2023). This integration has significant implications for the future of climate governance and the need to address the deeper systemic issue of fossil fuel dependence.

Should emissions mitigation remain central to climate governance efforts – and especially if carbon-based governance is to become more privatised as current trends suggest – then there should be a concerted effort, from both public and private governance actors, to expand governance mechanisms beyond one-dimensional, carbon-centric approaches. If climate change governance driven through bottom-up and private initiatives remains attached to the carbon mitigation imperative, then the system of carbon monitoring, disclosing, pledging, and verifying needs dramatic improvement to function effectively.

The shifting composition and roles of private actors in this domain continue to change dramatically with the literature struggling to keep up (Hale, 2016; Meckling & Allan, 2020; Herman, 2024a). This chapter helps to address this gap by providing an analysis of the role of private climate governance actors in the GCGR. The chapter underlines the importance of private actors in global governance and how they relate to the wider regime complex (see Chapter 5 by Vandendriessche, Jordana, & Marx in this book). More specifically, this chapter aims to explore two questions: (1) who are the most consequential private actors in climate governance and how are they networked, and (2) in what frames/phases of the global climate regime do they play a role?

2. BACKGROUND: GLOBAL CLIMATE AND CARBON-BASED GOVERNANCE

Building on the success of global ozone governance – namely the Montreal Protocol and the Vienna Convention – governments created the International

Panel on Climate Change (IPCC) and the United Nations Framework Convention on Climate Change (UNFCCC) to confront climate change. Sensibly, the dominant governance frames to combat climate change have revolved around the mitigation of carbon emissions, considered the most abundant GHGs building up in the atmosphere. However, the political, economic, social, and technological processes to manage GHGs have proved far more difficult than managing ozone-depleting substances; the latter were largely the result of several technologies, but GHGs causing climate change stem from thousands of power plants, billions of cars and trucks – in short, all processes, technologies, and products based on fossil fuels, around the world (Fankhauser, 1994; Hammitt, Bixler, & Noe, 1996).

2.1 Governance under the IPCC and UNFCCC

Throughout the 30-year lifetime of the IPCC and the UNFCC, global GHGs have steadily risen. Below we discuss the evolving policy and scientific frames put forth by the IPCC and the UNFCCC, showing how the governance of carbon emissions has become the central focus for climate governance actors (Herman, 2024a), before moving to our empirical section which discusses the actors within global climate governance (see also Chapter 11 by Kreienkamp and Coen in this book).

In 1988, the IPCC was created to address climate change, based on the SCOPE report (Scientific Committee on Problems of the Environment). The UNFCCC was initiated several years later to guide climate policies and governance. Therefore, while the IPCC is mainly a scientific consensus body, the UNFCCC is an international environmental treaty with the explicit objective to 'stabilize greenhouse gas concentrations in the atmosphere at a level that would prevent dangerous anthropogenic interference with the climate system [to enable] ecosystems to adapt naturally to climate change … and to enable economic development to proceed in a sustainable manner' (Article 2, The United Nations Framework Convention on Climate Change).

Country-level negotiators laid down binding emissions mitigation protocols during the 1990s, culminating in the Kyoto Protocol (KP), with its three main mechanisms: the Clean Development Mechanism (CDM), Joint Implementation (JI), and Emissions Trading (ET). The EU's Emissions Trading System (EU-ETS) became the bedrock for the KP's ET and was the first multi-country climate governance mechanism to attempt to reduce emissions through market-enabling mechanisms (Herman, 2024b). This period witnessed a small but growing involvement of private actors in global climate governance – such as the World Business Council on Sustainable Development (WBCSD) and the World Resources Institute (WRI).

Through their 'symbiotic relationship', in which the line between science and politics is often blurred (Green, 2013), the IPCC and the UNFCCC have evolved through five main frames, each of which takes a different approach to governing GHGs, mainly carbon emissions (see Figure 12.1).

In Frame 1, the stabilisation of GHGs in the atmosphere was the prevailing concept. This carried forward to a slightly revised approach under the KP to stabilise GHGs through market-based mechanisms, such as ET. Therefore, in Frame 2, the KP's CDM, JI, and ET largely sought to deal with carbon reductions through the creation of carbon markets. This marked the first instance of 'carbon-centric' governance because each of the KP's governance mechanisms focused mainly on carbon emissions. The third frame focused not on the percentage of emissions reductions, but the atmospheric concentration of GHGs (e.g., carbon parts per million). We would argue that this frame was the most comprehensive. The fourth frame, somewhat more narrowly, began to focus on *carbon* budgets rather than all GHGs. Finally, following the Paris Agreement, average global temperatures became the scientific focus, with the objective to keep 'global mean temperature rises to well below two degrees Celsius'. This frame rests on the assumption, rather than explicit framing, that driving down carbon emissions should be a main avenue to reach that goal; it also harkens back to the global warming consensus, rather than a focus on climate change, which has surfaced in a non-exact net-zero focus within the latest climate policies (Fankhauser et al., 2022).

These five frames of climate governance under the UNFCCC can be conceptually broken down into three carbon-based governance sequential phases (see Figure 12.2).

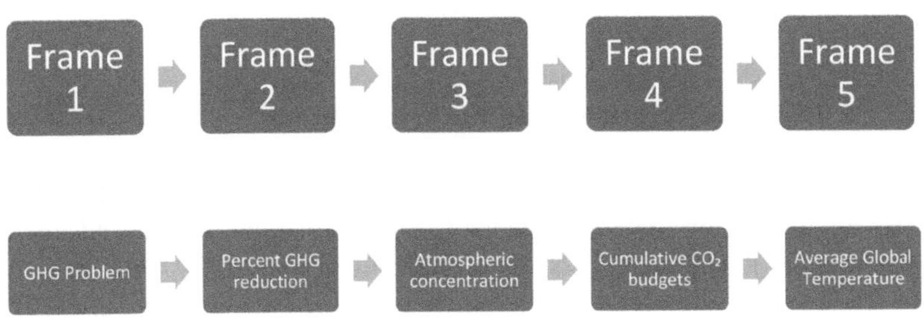

Source: Author's own compilation.

Figure 12.1 *IPCCC/UNFCCC 1990–2021: five science-policy frames for governing GHGs*

Source: Author's own compilation.

Figure 12.2 Phases of carbon-based governance

Phase 1 focused on the stabilisation of GHGs (1990–2000) following the IPCC's second assessment report (IPCC, 1996) which developed guidelines for country-level GHG reporting. These were followed by 'Good Practice Guidance and Uncertainty' (IPCC, 2000), and 'Good Practice Guidance for Land Use, Land-Use Change and Forestry' (IPCC, 2003).

Phase 2 shifted the focus to atmospheric concentration of CO_2 (2001–2011). In this era, bioenergy with carbon capture and storage (CCS), or BCCS, became the technological promise (or technology of prevarication). McLaren and Markusson (2020) argue that BCCS is a technology of prevarication because the technology was not, and still is not, fully developed. Nevertheless, these and other carbon removal technologies became central to assumptions embedded in the majority of integrated assessment models (Carton et al., 2023; Herman & Sovacool, 2024).

Phase 3 saw the rise of technocratic approaches, with solutions like CCS and 'new nuclear' taking centre stage. McLaren and Markusson (2020) describe these as 'technologies of prevarication', driven by political and policy promises (p. 392). This phase also triggered a surge in private actor involvement, both as technical innovators and as stakeholders affected by regulatory shifts (Kok & De Coninck, 2007; Green, 2013; Hale, 2016).

2.2 The Paris Agreement and the Private Sector

The private sector, particularly in developing countries, is often viewed as better equipped than the public sector to mobilise organisational and financial resources for climate action (Kok & De Coninck, 2007). This perspective made the private sector's inclusion in the Paris Agreement a significant milestone (Hale, 2016). A key outcome of this shift was the launch of the UN's NAZCA Portal (Non-State Actor Zone for Climate Action) in 2014 – renamed the Global Climate Action Portal – which now tracks nearly 31,000 climate actors, including over 15,000 private entities (Hsu et al., 2016). The portal, the most comprehensive registry of non-state climate actions, reflects the transnational nature of privately led governance. However, despite the large number of registered private actors, many have minimal impact (Hsueh, 2019). Additionally, the portal does not indicate the relative influence of these actors or highlight which ones hold the most power within global climate governance systems.

While the number of non-state and private sector initiatives has surged since the Paris Agreement, their influence within climate governance remains uneven (Widerberg & Pattberg, 2017). However, some private actors, such as the Carbon Disclosure Project (CDP) and the Task Force on Climate-Related Financial Disclosures (TCFD), wield significant power (Coen, Herman, & Pegram, 2023). For example, in the UK, companies can fulfil emissions disclosure requirements by submitting inventories to the CDP. Additionally, all 'Five Eyes' countries (Australia, Canada, New Zealand, the UK, and the US) either encourage or mandate large publicly traded companies to align climate risk disclosures with TCFD recommendations (Herman, Schiavoni, & Guastella, 2024). Through social network and automated clustering analysis, the following section explores the most influential private actors, their interconnections, and the dominant frames and themes shaping their approach to climate governance.

3. ADDING COMPLEXITY TO THE GLOBAL CLIMATE REGIME

3.1 Empirical Approach to the Study of GCGR and Private Actors

As others have observed in global governance scholarship (Ruggie, 2014), bottom-up and market-based standards are increasingly more relied on for governance (Green, 2013; Hale & Roger, 2014; Marx & Wouters, 2015). The state-led, command-and-control regimes have given way to flexible and voluntary instruments (Hsueh, 2019), which are often orchestrated by private actors (Ciepley, 2013). Centralised private actors gain access to key information and can effectively influence the outcome of informal regulatory mechanisms and standardising processes (Haufler, 2018; Abbott & Snidal, 2001).

As a result, much competition exists among private actors to create, manage, and control carbon standardisation and measurement (Slaughter & Zaring, 2006; Davis, 2012). The climate governance system, as it has become more populated with private actors over the last decade, therefore shares many of the same traits as the prior public climate governance regime. Embedded within these new climate governance mechanisms, indeed, are privately led standard-bearers and initiators that exert much power and influence over the climate change regime (Green & Auld, 2017; Kelley & Simmons, 2019; Herman, 2024b).

Researchers have previously constructed the GCGR to understand the various influences of these actors on climate governance (Van Asselt & Zelli, 2014). It is predominantly seen as a decentralised, partially organised web of actors, initiatives, rules, norms, and standards (Bodansky & Diringer, 2010, p. 23; Abbott et al., 2021). These actors are seen as having a networked rather than hierarchical structure (Widerberg & Pattberg, 2015). It is, furthermore, composed of cooperative initiatives and transnational climate partnerships (Backstrand, 2008; Bulkeley et al., 2014), climate clubs (Weischer, Morgan, & Patel, 2012), and governance experiments (Hoffmann, 2011).

We extend and build upon the GCGR but zoom-in on the private actors that appear to exert the most influence over the network. The result, due to the predominant focus on carbon emissions, is what we label The Carbon-Based Governance Regime (CGR). To construct our revised network, we begin with the central actors already extensively analysed in the literature (Hale & Roger, 2014; Widerberg, Pattberg, & Kristensen, 2016; Widerberg & Pattberg, 2017; Andonova, Hale, & Roger, 2017; Michaelowa & Michaelowa, 2017). Since our focus is on the private sector – we then parse out both private and hybrid actors and initiatives from these databases.

Consequently, we revise and expand the GCGR to incorporate the role of the private sector, paying special attention to the key carbon actors and their relationships throughout the rest of the network. In sum, we reconstruct the GCGR based on the following procedure. Following previous literature, we identify the main standard-bearers, comprising 42 of the original 122 actors derived from the GCGR scholarship. Below is a schematic of the initial sample, with the public anchors at the centre, hybrid 'governors' just outside the core, and the private actors on the periphery (Figure 12.3).

Having constructed a baseline climate governance network, we then considered actors based on their 'steering' and 'publicness' characteristics (Andonova, Hale, & Roger, 2017; Bulkeley et al., 2014; Hoffmann, 2011; Hale & Roger, 2014). Next, we explored the functionalities of these emerging governance actors (Hale, 2016; Bäckstrand, Meadowcroft, & Oppenheimer, 2011). As such, relationships or 'nodes' were added according to shared membership in other climate initiatives (Widerberg & Pattberg, 2017). In our case, the nodes were based on one of six possible relationships: (1) advisor, (2) board member, (3) funder, (4) partner, (5) initiator, or (6) it accepts standards from another actor – (see Coen, Herman, & Pegram, 2020, for more methods details and graphics).

Having set up the CGR, the next step involved the classification of the actors into a total of six actor categories: (1) public climate change 'anchors' (i.e., UNFCCC, EU, IPCC); (2) private 'governors'; (3) other/non-state actors; (4) company/corporate/private investment funds; (5) climate change actors (remaining nodes from GCGR literature); and (6) carbon actors.

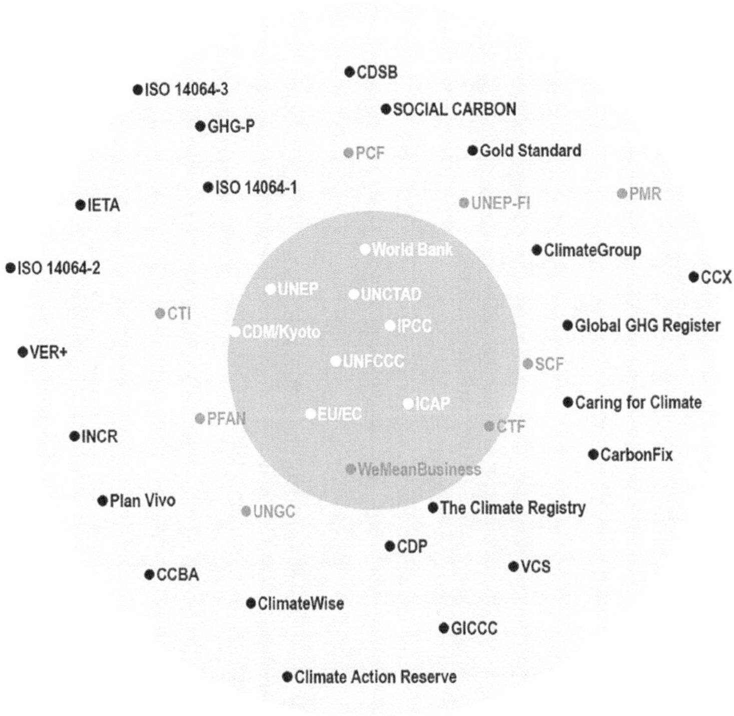

Source: Author's own compilation.

Figure 12.3 *Universe of actors adopted from the GCGR*

3.2 Reassessing the GCGR: the Carbon-Based Governance Regime

In this section, we assess the GCGR by drawing on the results of the CGR Globe study (Coen, Herman, & Pegram, 2020). Table 12.1 briefly outlines the roles and foci of the most central private actors in the CGR. Here we complement our initial mapping of climate actors with an automated network centrality analysis. This clustering analysis had the effect of operationalising the actors (nodes) and their relationships (edges). Further, it enables a deeper exploration of network embeddedness, revealing the concentration of power and activities among a small group of private actors. With automated machine-enhanced transformation, we then ran an algorithm to extract key nodes and topics of the carbon-based governance actors. First, we analysed in-degree centrality. Each

Table 12.1 The roles and foci of the most central private actors in the Carbon-Based Governance Regime

Abbreviation	Full name	Description	Source
CDP	Carbon Disclosure Project	Explicitly aims to collect carbon emissions data from investors, enterprises and governments to accelerate solutions to climate change. By the end of 2021, nearly 10,000 companies disclosed either climate or emissions data to the CDP. Some jurisdictions, including the United Kingdom, consider reporting to the CDP consistent with requirements for publicly traded firms to report GHG emissions.	Cdp.net
CDSB	The Carbon Disclosure Standards Board	Built upon the International Accounting Standards. It aims to make the disclosure of carbon emissions more consistent across sectors and companies. The CDSB explicitly endorses the CDP (for reporting carbon emissions) and the GHGP (for measuring carbon emissions).	Cdsb.net
CERES	Coalition for Environmentally Responsible Economies	Formed to promote corporate sustainability action and to ensure that business had access to decision-makers in high-level intergovernmental forums).	Ceres.org
GHGP	The Greenhouse Gas Protocol	Launched by the World Resources Institute (WRI) and the World Business Council on Sustainable Development (WBCSD) in 2001, it aims to reduce complexities in the measurement and reporting of GHGs. The GHGP specifies that emissions should be measured and reported according to three 'Scopes': Scope 1 are direct emissions, Scope 2 are emissions from energy usage, and Scope 3 are emissions upstream in an organisation's value chain (Phase 2, UNFCCC).	Ghgprotocol.org
GRI	Global Reporting Initiative	A hybrid governance arrangement spearheaded by the United Nations Environment Programme, CERES, and the CDP. It attempts to streamline environmental reporting from the private sector and is now the largest world's largest repository of corporate sustainability reports.	Goldstandard.org

Abbreviation	Full name	Description	Source
GS	Gold Standard	Developed in partnership with the World Wildlife Fund and is a direct outgrowth of the Kyoto Protocol's Clean Development mechanism. It maintains a special position as the orchestrator of public–private verification instruments.	Globalreporting.org
IETA	International Emissions Trading Association	To empower business to engage in carbon markets and climate action.	Ieta.org
ISO-14064-1	International Standards Organization GHG monitoring	Largely consistent with the GHGP, it was launched by the International Standards Organization (ISO). While ISO could be considered a 'hybrid' governance organisation, it can potentially exert more influence over the private sector via its connection to the WTO; it has more regulatory authority. But the ISO GHG inventory standard appears to be going out of favour, as shown in Section 6 of this report (Phase 2, UNFCCC).	Iso.org
ISO-14065	International Standards Organization GHG reporting	Defines requirements for bodies that validate and verify GHG statements. Its requirements cover impartiality, competence, communication, validation and verification processes, appeals, complaints and the management system of validation and verification bodies.	IOIso.org
ISO	International Standards Organization GHG verification	Specifies competence requirements for validation teams and verification teams. It includes principles and specifies competence requirements based on the tasks that validation teams have to perform.	Iso.org

Abbreviation	Full name	Description	Source
SBTi	The Science-Based Targets Initiative	Ensures that companies create emissions reduction plans that align to the IPCC's scientific consensus. Rather than a confusing panoply of carbon reduction pledges, SBTi addresses underlying issues of consistency and accuracy of company emissions inventories, plans and goals. The SBTi defines 'net-zero' emissions as 'zero emissions through a company's value chain (Scope 3), over and above Scope 1 and Scope 2 emissions'. So far, through the SBTi, over 1,000 companies are certified as taking 'science-based' climate action and 411 companies have an approved 'science-based' carbon reduction target. All this science-based target-setting is likely to increase demand for carbon measurement and verification.	Sciencebasedtargets.org
TCFD	The Task Force on Climate-Related Financial Disclosure	A hybrid actor, spearheaded and run by both private and public actors; it was inaugurated by Mark Carney and Michael Bloomberg, with Janet Yellen recently climbing on board. Since many organisations fail to properly account for physical risks that might arise from climate change, the TCFD has attempted to standardise climate risk reporting. It has enlisted over 1,000 companies to disclose climate risks (physical, financial, and material). Several jurisdictions, including the United Kingdom, have recently enshrined the TCFD into public climate change legislations.	Fsb-tcfd.org
VCS	Verified Carbon Standard	The world's most widely used GHG crediting programme. VCS projects have reduced or removed more than one billion tons of carbon and other GHG emissions from the atmosphere.	Verra.org

Source: Author's own compilation.

node group was analysed individually according to its classification. The centrality graphs represent the edge centrality data the software relies on to create the transformed network mapping (Coen, Herman, & Pegram, 2020, p. 63).

Significantly, after applying a machine-learning automated classifier and analysis, a new network emerges with key underlying cluster characteristics. First, the Carbon Lobby group emerges with a strong hold on the carbon framing and could point towards one reason carbon governance has remained the dominant frame. Second, and perhaps unsurprisingly, UNFCCC public anchors (top-down governance actors) continue to form the bedrock of the network. The state-led/World Bank grouping represents another anchoring cluster and is seen to be separate from the IPCC/UNFCCC in line with the much-discussed multilevel governance nature of climate governance (Andonova, Hale, & Roger, 2017; Hale, 2016; Kreienkamp, Pegram, & Coen, 2022; Bal et al., 2023).

Third, a climate risk disclosure cluster has emerged and tends to frame climate change as a risk disclosure imperative, connecting specifically to investors and the insurance industry. Fourth, we see the TCFD carbon disclosure cluster focused mainly on the disclosure of carbon emissions with varying success (see Coen, Herman, & Pegram, 2023). Fifth, the recent renewable energy/verification cluster emerges and suggests that carbon verification and renewables are more locally diffuse. Sixth, the non-state actors, such as philanthropic organisations, are well embedded across the network and seen to operate at many levels of governance (Green & Auld, 2017; Hale, 2016; Bal et al., 2023). Finally, and seventh, it should be noted that carbon governors, such as CERES and WBCSD, are prominent organisations that organise, instantiate, fund and lead many other actors throughout the network (for a detailed graphical analysis of the above networks, see the EU Globe report by Coen, Herman, & Pegram, 2020).

4. WHAT DOES GCR MEAN FOR CLIMATE POLICY-MAKING: A DISCUSSION

Our mapping and relational analyses of global climate actors reveal several salient aspects of how private actors are leveraging and exerting power through public, private, and hybrid governance arrangements. The development of the GCR and analysis shows the emergence and importance of private actors in global climate governance. It also shows, however, that there is substantial competition to carve out carbon governance. This leads to two main findings: (1) private-led climate governance actors are led by a handful of interconnected actors, meaning that power is concentrated in the hands of a few organisations and actors; and (2) the majority of private actors and initiatives focus on the mitigation of carbon emissions, with little focus on other harmful GHGs (e.g., methane and nitrous oxide), and relatively no focus on 'point-of-source' solutions. This is not that surprising considering how the three frames of public climate governance evolved (stabilisation of GHGs, atmospheric concentration CO_2 concentrations, technocratic procedures to address CO_2).

Nevertheless, the GCR and analysis suggest that the emerging bottom-up, carbon-based governance system possesses flaws not dissimilar from those in the public governance paradigm of the past. Evidently, the groundswell of private sector actors engaged in climate change governance is significantly changing the landscape of global climate governance. Consequently, several issues warrant future research attention. First, the unitary focus on carbon emissions. Second, the confusion that might ensue by having multiple private actors responsible for the same activities (e.g., reporting GHGs, Coen, Herman, & Pegram, 2022; 2023). Third, from a more conceptual perspective, the concentration of resources dedicated to the *symptoms* rather than the *disease*.

Some suggest the penultimate problem with private climate governance lies in misguided incentive schemes (Michaelowa & Michaelowa, 2019); in other words, that incentives for the private sector do not align with the public goods benefit of delivering lower emissions (Keohane & Victor, 2011). Others suggest, similarly, that the private sector can only devote limited resources to deal with the collective action problem due to the prisoners' dilemma problem (Geels et al., 2017; Bernstein & Hoffmann, 2018). For example, a company that undertakes costly emissions reductions is not properly rewarded and thus is likely to take only incremental, low carbon action, in lockstep with industry peers (Hickmann, 2017). As such, there is a real worry that carbon-centric governance is just a corporate 'beehive' of activity 'with few tangible outcomes' (Jones & Levy, 2007, p. 436).

There are several limitations to our analysis, however. First, we reiterate that our focus is on the private sector and corporations, which naturally excludes some very important climate or even carbon-based public actors, or those otherwise not dealing with the private sector and corporations. This mapping therefore does not provide an exhaustive listing of all climate change actors and initiatives, but rather the actors that are of salience for the private sector's role in climate change governance. Nor does it provide a full picture of all the carbon-based actors, such as those that are publicly led.

Future research might expand on our CGR to include these other public actors or explore more nuanced versions, such as with a specific regional focus. Furthermore, though there are many similarities with the GCGR, what the CGR shows is how private actors are even more focused on treating the climate change symptoms than were prior public governance mechanisms. In other words, the CGR is overwhelmingly focused on 'carbon governance' (Kolk, Levy, & Pinkse, 2008), demonstrated by the centrality of the private actors that are focused on measurement, reporting, and verification of carbon. Future research might also build on Hsu et al. (2016), Lui et al. (2021), and Kuramochi et al. (2020) while focusing instead on the potential of private carbon governance actors to reduce private rather than public sector emissions.

In sum, the CGR readily maps the previously fragmented climate change regime with respect to the private sector. By conducting this network construction and transformation, we are now able to conduct further empirical investigations into the private and corporate sector's climate governance roles and the respective impacts that these actors have. As an empirical tool, the new CGR has identified the central actors and shown a new taxonomy to classify these actors, and therefore can help to drill down on empirical analyses of these actors and their heterogeneous effects on the corporate sector.

5. CONCLUSION: TARGET THE DISEASE RATHER THAN THE SYMPTOMS

The critiques and analysis presented above have led others to call for a 'post-carbon' governance transition (Farmer et al., 2019). Indeed, as Bernstein and Hoffmann (2018) contend, carbon reduction as the guiding metaphor for climate governance might require substantial revision, especially since trends in emissions worldwide are cause for much consternation. The groundswell of private actors since the Paris Agreement has done little to curtail GHGs, with some highly potent GHGs rising fastest in recent years – such as methane and NOx (Herman, 2024b). This suggests that not only is public climate governance failing, but also the carbon-centric turn of private climate governance is failing, despite the buzz of private sector initiatives since the Copenhagen COP (Jordan et al., 2015).

Drawing on the arguments set forth in the introduction, to reduce the likelihood of emissions lock-in, climate governance mechanisms and related actors might do better to redirect focus towards the *disease* rather than the *symptom*. The ill effect of diagnosing the symptoms rather than the disease can be illustrated by the Global Warming Potential (GWP) conversion system. The GWP conversion method was inherited from the IPCC's First Assessment Report (FAR-1990). In that report, IPCC scientists recommended to standardise carbon as the representative greenhouse gas; it further recommended that all other 'Kyoto gases' should be converted into carbon equivalents to streamline policy. The policy logic was that carbon could serve as a basis for market mechanisms to reduce GHGs. Through a conversion formula called 'Global Warming Potentials' (GWPs), each of the six main Kyoto gases are converted into CO_2-equivalents. However, revisions to this conversion metric are made with each Assessment Report, which is published every 4–7 years, with important implications for carbon-based governance.

Due to these revisions, over time carbon equivalents succumb to fluctuations in measurement, with consequences for carbon markets as well. This effectively undermines the carbon measurement system. For example, nitrous oxide's carbon equivalent – the main culprit of the Volkswagen emissions scandal – has gone up and down according to each IPCC report. This has evidently opened loopholes for industry, while also providing too much leeway for populist politicians. The periodic revisions to GWP metrics with each IPCC Assessment Report (every 4–7 years) therefore introduce inconsistencies with significant implications for carbon-based governance. A deeper rethinking of climate governance frameworks is needed – one that prioritises reducing fossil fuel dependence rather than refining metrics for managing carbon equivalents. Without this shift, governance efforts risk perpetuating the very systemic inertia that they seek to overcome.

The challenges surrounding the standardisation, measurement, and tracking of carbon emissions within private sector governance are not new. Similar concerns have been highlighted in analyses of non-state, private, and hybrid climate governance arrangements (Widerberg & Pattberg, 2017). Despite an expanding regulatory framework that depends heavily on private actors for emissions reporting and management, critical questions remain: Why has carbon-centric governance failed to significantly reduce greenhouse gas emissions? What continues to obstruct the realisation of the ultimate global public good – a clean atmosphere with declining GHG levels? And to what extent can carbon governance be effective without substantial state oversight ?

The continued rise in global emissions raises serious doubts about the efficacy of carbon-based governance frameworks, metrics, and actors. The reliance on long-term targets, such as those set for 2040 or 2050, fails to address the urgent need for immediate reductions. As climate risks escalate, the absence of impactful, near-term solutions underscores the limitations of a governance model that prioritises carbon measurement over the fundamental task of phasing out fossil fuel dependence. A reorientation of climate governance is essential – one that shifts from managing carbon metrics to confronting the systemic drivers of emissions head-on.

REFERENCES

Abbott, K. W., Genschel, P., Snidal, D., & Zangl, B. (2021). Orchestrating global governance: From empirical findings to theoretical implications. In K. W. Abbott & D. Snidal (Eds.), *The spectrum of international institutions* (pp. 171–197). Routledge.

Abbott, K. W., & Snidal, D. (2001). International standards and international governance. *Journal of European Public Policy*, 8(3), 345–370.

Andonova, L. B., Hale, T. N., & Roger, C. B. (2017). National policy and transnational governance of climate change: Substitutes or complements? *International Studies Quarterly*, 61(2), 253–268.

Bäckstrand, K. (2008). Accountability of networked climate governance: The rise of transnational climate partnerships. *Global Environmental Politics*, 8(3), 74–102.

Bäckstrand, K., Meadowcroft, J., & Oppenheimer, M. (2011). The politics and policy of carbon capture and storage: Framing an emergent technology. *Global Environmental Change*, 21(2), 275–281.

Bal, C., Coen, D., Kreienkamp, J., Paramitaninggrum, & Pegram, T. (2023). *Explaining transformative change in ASEAN and EU climate policy*. Cambridge Elements, Cambridge University Press.

Bernini, F., Giuliani, M., & La Rosa, F. (2024). Measuring greenwashing: A systematic methodological literature review. *Business Ethics, the Environment & Responsibility*, 33(4), 649–667.

Bernstein, S., & Hoffmann, M. (2018). The politics of decarbonization and the catalytic impact of subnational climate experiments. *Policy Sciences*, 51, 189–211.

Biermann, F. (2010). Beyond the intergovernmental regime: Recent trends in global carbon governance. *Current Opinion in Environmental Sustainability*, 2(4), 284–288.

Biermann, F., Pattberg, P., & Zelli, F. (Eds.). (2010). *Global climate governance beyond 2012: Architecture, agency and adaptation*. Cambridge University Press.

Bodansky, D., & Diringer, E. (2010). *The evolution of multilateral regimes: Implications for climate change*. Pew Center on Global Climate Change.

Bulkeley, H. (2014). *Transnational climate change governance*. Cambridge University Press.

Bulkeley, H., Andonova, L. B., Betsill, M. M., Compagnon, D., Hale, T., Hoffmann, M. J., … & VanDeveer, S. D. (2014). Introducing transnational climate change governance. *Transnational climate change governance* (pp. 1–16). Cambridge University Press.

Carton, W., Hougaard, I. M., Markusson, N., & Lund, J. F. (2023). Is carbon removal delaying emission reductions? *Wiley Interdisciplinary Reviews: Climate Change*, 14(4), e826.

Chan, S., Van Asselt, H., Hale, T., Abbott, K. W., Beisheim, M., Hoffmann, M., & Widerberg, O. (2015). Reinvigorating international climate policy: A comprehensive framework for effective nonstate action. *Global Policy*, 6(4), 466–473.

Ciepley, D. (2013). Beyond public and private: Toward a political theory of the corporation. *American Political Science Review*, 107(1), 139–158.

Coen, D., Herman, K., & Pegram, T. (2020). *Private sector and climate change: A case study of carbon-based governance*. Globe Report. https://www.globe-project.eu/private-sector-and-climate-change-a-case-study-of-carbon-based-governance_11373.pdf.

Coen, D., Herman, K., & Pegram, T. (2022). Are corporate climate efforts genuine? An empirical analysis of climate 'talk-walk' hypothesis. *Business Strategy and the Environment*, 31(7), 3040–3059.

Coen, D., Herman, K., & Pegram, T. (2023). Market masquerades? Corporate climate initiatives effects on firm-level performance. *Global Environmental Politics*, 23(4), 141–169.

Coen, D., Kreienkamp, J., & Pegram, T. (2020). *Governance of climate change: Policy-making and networked governance*. Cambridge University Press.

Corry, O., & Riesch, H. (2012). Beyond 'for or against': Environmental NGO-evaluations of CCS as a climate change solution. In N. Markusson, S. Shackley, & B. Evar (Eds.), *The social dynamics of carbon capture and storage* (pp. 91–108). Routledge.

Davis, K. (Ed.). (2012). *Governance by indicators: Global power through classification and rankings.* Oxford University Press.

Fankhauser, S. (1994). The social costs of greenhouse gas emissions: An expected value approach. *The Energy Journal*, 15(2), 157–184.

Fankhauser, S., Smith, S. M., Allen, M., Axelsson, K., Hale, T., Hepburn, C., … & Wetzer, T. (2022). The meaning of net zero and how to get it right. *Nature Climate Change*, 12(1), 15–21.

Farmer, J. D., Hepburn, C., Ives, M. C., Hale, T., Wetzer, T., Mealy, P., … & Way, R. (2019). Sensitive intervention points in the post-carbon transition. *Science*, 364(6436), 132–134.

Geels, F. W., Sovacool, B. K., Schwanen, T., & Sorrell, S. (2017). The socio-technical dynamics of low-carbon transitions. *Joule*, 1(3), 463–479.

Green, J. F. (2013). *Rethinking private authority: Agents and entrepreneurs in global environmental governance.* Princeton University Press.

Green, J. F., & Auld, G. (2017). Unbundling the regime complex: The effects of private authority. *Transnational Environmental Law*, 6(2), 259–284.

Hale, T. (2016). 'All hands on deck': The Paris Agreement and nonstate climate action. *Global Environmental Politics*, 16(3), 12–22.

Hale, T., & Roger, C. (2014). Orchestration and transnational climate governance. *The Review of International Organizations*, 9, 59–82.

Hammitt, W. E., Bixler, R. D., & Noe, F. P. (1996). Going beyond importance-performance analysis to analyze the observance-influence of park impacts. *Journal of Park and Recreation Administration*, 14(1), 45–62.

Haufler, V. (2018). Producing global governance in the global factory: Markets, politics, and regulation. *Global Policy*, 9(1), 114–120.

Herman, K. S. (2024a). Doomed to fail? A call to reform global climate governance and greenhouse gas inventories. *International Environmental Agreements: Politics, Law and Economics*, 24(4), 539–564.

Herman, K. S. (2024b). Intermediaries and complexity: Assessing emissions-based governance in the European Union's EU-ETS. *International Environmental Agreements: Politics, Law and Economics*, 24(4), 539–564.

Herman, K. S., Schiavoni, C., & Guastella, G. (2024). Walking, talking, or standing still? Climate commitment and performance in publicly listed firms in five major economies. *Business & Society*, 64(4), 713–756.

Herman, K. S., & Sovacool, B. K. (2024). Applying the multi-level perspective to climate geoengineering: Sociotechnical bottlenecks for negative emissions and cloud seeding technologies. *Energy Research & Social Science*, 115, 103637.

Hickmann, T. (2017). The reconfiguration of authority in global climate governance. *International Studies Review*, 19(3), 430–451.

Hoffmann, M. J. (2011). *Climate governance at the crossroads: Experimenting with a global response after Kyoto.* Oxford University Press.

Hsu, A., Cheng, Y., Weinfurter, A., Xu, K., & Yick, C. (2016). *Understanding NAZCA: Challenges and future of the world's largest voluntary climate action platform.* Yale University Press.

Hsueh, L. (2019). Opening up the firm: What explains participation and effort in voluntary carbon disclosure by global businesses? An analysis of internal firm factors and dynamics. *Business Strategy and the Environment*, 28(7), 1302–1322.
IPCC (1996) 2nd Assessment report of the Intergovernmental Panel on Climate Change. Digital Library of UN.org.
IPCC (2003) Good Practice Guidance and Forestry Use. IPCC.ch/Publications.
IPCC (2020) Good Practice Guidance and Uncertainty Management in National Greenhouse Gas Inventories. PPCC.ch/publication/.
Jones, C. A., & Levy, D. L. (2007). North American business strategies towards climate change. *European Management Journal*, 25(6), 428–440.
Jordan, A. J., Huitema, D., Hildén, M., van Asselt, H., Rayner, T. J., Schoenefeld, J. J., Tosun, J., Forster, J., & Boasson, E. L. (2015). Emergence of polycentric climate governance and its future prospects. *Nature Climate Change*, 5(11), 977–982.
Kelley, J. G., & Simmons, B. A. (2019). Introduction: The power of global performance indicators. *International Organization*, 73(3), 491–510.
Keohane, R. O., & Victor, D. G. (2011). The regime complex for climate change. *Perspectives on Politics*, 9(1), 7–23.
Kok, M. T. J., & De Coninck, H. C. (2007). Widening the scope of policies to address climate change: Directions for mainstreaming. *Environmental Science & Policy*, 10(7–8), 587–599.
Kolk, A., Levy, D., & Pinkse, J. (2008). Corporate responses in an emerging climate regime: The institutionalization and commensuration of carbon disclosure. *European Accounting Review*, 17(4), 719–745.
Köppl, P. (2012). Green lobbying: Is sustainability more than a new frame for old-style lobbying? A consultant's personal point of view. *Journal of Public Affairs*, 12(3), 177–180.
Kreienkamp, J., Pegram, T., & Coen, D. (2022). Explaining transformative change in the EU climate policy: Multilevel problems, policies, and politics. *Journal of European Integration*, 44(5), 731–748.
Kuramochi, T., Roelfsema, M., Hsu, A., Lui, S., Weinfurter, A., Chan, S., … & Höhne, N. (2020). Beyond national climate action: The impact of region, city, and business commitments on global greenhouse gas emissions. *Climate Policy*, 20(3), 275–291.
Lui, S., Kuramochi, T., Smit, S., Roelfsema, M., Hsu, A., Weinfurter, A., … & Höhne, N. (2021). Correcting course: The emission reduction potential of international cooperative initiatives. *Climate Policy*, 21(2), 232–250.
Marx, A., & Wouters, J. (2015). Competition and cooperation in the market of voluntary sustainability standards. In P. Delimatsis (Ed.), *The law, economics and politics of international standardisation* (pp. 215–241). Cambridge University Press.
McLaren, D., & Markusson, N. (2020). The co-evolution of technological promises, modelling, policies and climate change targets. *Nature Climate Change*, 10(5), 392–397.
Meadowcroft, J., & Rosenbloom, D. (2023). Governing the net-zero transition: Strategy, policy, and politics. *Proceedings of the National Academy of Sciences*, 120(47), 1–11.
Meckling, J., & Allan, B. B. (2020). The evolution of ideas in global climate policy. *Nature Climate Change*, *10*, 434–438.
Michaelowa, K., & Michaelowa, A. (2017). The growing influence of the UNFCCC Secretariat on the clean development mechanism. *International Environmental Agreements: Politics, Law and Economics*, 17, 247–269.

Michaelowa, K., & Michaelowa, A. (2019). Transnational climate governance initiatives: Designed for effective climate change mitigation? In L. B. Andonova, T. N. Hale, & C. B. Roger (Eds.), *The comparative politics of transnational climate governance* (pp. 146–178). Routledge.

Paterson, M. (2014). Governing mobilities, mobilising carbon. *Mobilities*, 9(4), 570–584.

Roger, C. B., Hale, T., & Andonova, L. B. (2019). The comparative politics of transnational climate governance. In L. B. Andonova, T. Hale, & C. B. Roger (Eds.), *The comparative politics of transnational climate governance* (pp. 1–25). Routledge.

Ruggie, J. G. (2014). Global governance and 'new governance theory': Lessons from business and human rights. *Global Governance*, 20(1), 5–17.

Seto, K. C., Davis, S. J., Mitchell, R. B., Stokes, E. C., Unruh, G., & Ürge-Vorsatz, D. (2016). Carbon lock-in: Types, causes, and policy implications. *Annual Review of Environment and Resources*, 41, 425–452.

Slaughter, A. M., & Zaring, D. (2006). Networking goes international: An update. *Annual Review of Law and Social Science*, 2, 211–229.

Unruh, G. C. (2000). Understanding carbon lock-in. *Energy Policy*, 28(12), 817–830.

Van Asselt, H., & Zelli, F. (2014). Connect the dots: Managing the fragmentation of global climate governance. *Environmental Economics and Policy Studies*, 16, 137–155.

Weischer, L., Morgan, J., & Patel, M. (2012). Climate clubs: Can small groups of countries make a big difference in addressing climate change? *Review of European Community & International Environmental Law*, 21(3), 177–192.

Widerberg, O., & Pattberg, P. (2015). International cooperative initiatives in global climate governance: Raising the ambition level or delegitimizing the UNFCCC? *Global Policy*, 6(1), 45–56.

Widerberg, O., & Pattberg, P. (2017). Accountability challenges in the transnational regime complex for climate change. *Review of Policy Research*, 34(1), 68–87.

Widerberg, O., Pattberg, P., & Kristensen, K. (2016). *Mapping the institutional architecture of global climate change governance* (Technical Report No. 2). IVM Institute for Environmental Studies.

13. Withdrawal from the Istanbul Convention: a debate between "European" and "native" values

İrem Tuncer Ebetürk and Alexandros Tokhi

1. INTRODUCTION

In recent years, the phenomenon of backlash against international organizations (IOs) has gained increasing attention in scholarly research, particularly when gender rights are at the center of political contestation. Gender has become a highly politicized issue, both domestically and internationally, often serving as a battleground for broader ideological struggles. Antifeminist mobilization is unfolding across multiple arenas: within the European Union (EU) (Datta, 2018; Ebetürk, 2018; Kantola & Lombardo, 2020; Yamin et al., 2018), in domestic contexts (Grabowska, 2014; Kantola & Lombardo, 2020; Kuhar & Paternotte, 2017; Verloo & Paternotte, 2018), and at the international level, particularly in the UN (Cupać & Ebetürk, 2020; 2021; 2022, Verloo & Paternotte (2018); Bob, 2012). One specific aspect of this politicization that has not been extensively explored is the unilateral withdrawal of countries from international treaties, especially those aimed at promoting gender rights. Such withdrawals present a complex interplay between domestic politics, international commitments, and the evolving dynamics of gender equality on a global scale. Understanding the motivations behind these withdrawals, as well as the responses they elicit from IOs and other actors, is essential to comprehending the broader context of contemporary gender politics.

The case of Türkiye's withdrawal from the Istanbul Convention—an international treaty aimed at preventing and combating violence against women—is a prime example of this phenomenon. Türkiye's decision to withdraw, and Poland's similar stance (though less explicitly pursued), reflects a broader contestation of gender rights that is playing out across various national contexts. Both countries' actions must be understood within the broader literature on backlash to IOs and the international politicization of gender rights. Specifically, Türkiye's withdrawal offers a lens through which to examine not only the motivations and implications for the country itself, but also the repercussions for the IO involved—in this case, the EU. This study aims to explore how Türkiye's government leveraged its withdrawal as part of a broader domestic and international strategy and how the EU's response is crucial in shaping the outcome of this political maneuver.

Our central research question focuses on how the case of Türkiye's withdrawal from the Istanbul Convention can be understood through the existing literature on IOs. While previous research has extensively covered motivations for backlash and contestation in domestic politics and in the international arena, fewer studies have examined the withdrawal from international treaties in relation to gender rights. We will analyze Türkiye's actions not just in terms of its domestic motivations but also considering how the EU's response factors into the broader strategy of the Turkish government. The EU's reaction, as we argue, is not merely a side note to the event but is, in fact, central to the success of Türkiye's objectives. This dimension of the study focuses on how international reactions to withdrawals can be as politically significant as the withdrawal itself.

We begin by offering a comprehensive review of the existing literature on unilateral withdrawals from international treaties, with particular attention to the relatively sparse body of work that explores the responses of IOs to such withdrawals. Following this, we delve into the specific case of Türkiye, analyzing the motivations, narratives, and key actors involved in its decision to exit the Istanbul Convention. While the focus remains primarily on Türkiye, we incorporate relevant examples from Poland, though we do not examine this case in detail given that Poland's withdrawal has not yet materialized. Additionally, this section briefly considers the broader contestation of the Istanbul Convention at both domestic and international levels, contextualizing Türkiye's withdrawal within a wider movement of resistance to international norms surrounding gender rights. After reviewing the extant international relations and political science literature that seeks to explain Türkiye's withdrawal, we proceed to an analysis of the EU's response to both Türkiye's withdrawal and Poland's threats to do the same. In the concluding section, we assess the broader implications of the EU's response, arguing that the EU inadvertently perpetuated a narrative of civilizational tension by emphasizing its foundational values, rather than opting for alternative legal or diplomatic mechanisms to address the issue. This, we suggest, echoes and reinforces the dichotomous framing employed by the withdrawing states themselves, particularly Türkiye, in framing the Convention as a battleground of cultural and civilizational identity.

2. LITERATURE ON WITHDRAWALS FROM INTERNATIONAL TREATIES: MOTIVATIONS AND RESPONSES

Unilateral withdrawal from international treaties occurs when a state decides to exit an international agreement without the consent or agreement of the other parties involved. This action raises important questions about state sovereignty, compliance with international norms, and the stability of the international order. Literature on withdrawal from international treaties discusses motivations of withdrawing states, the costs of withdrawal, implications for international order, as well as the reasons behind the existence of withdrawal clauses in the treaties in the first place.

In his seminal work "Exiting Treaties," Laurence Helfer provides a comprehensive analysis of the legal, political, and strategic dimensions of treaty withdrawal. Helfer argues that unilateral withdrawal is legally permissible under the rules of international law, particularly as outlined in the Vienna Convention on the Law of Treaties (1969). He examines how treaties often include exit clauses that allow states to withdraw after providing due notice, thus ensuring flexibility and sovereignty (Helfer, 2005; Krasner, 1999). Similarly, Koremenos et al. (2001) explain the presence of exit clauses as a way to balance commitment with flexibility. The inclusion of exit provisions helps to make treaties more attractive to states by reducing the risks associated with long-term commitments.

Literature on withdrawals from international treaties provides several answers to the question of what motivates states to withdraw from treaties. Helfer (2005) emphasizes that exiting a treaty significantly differs from non-compliance, as it aims to achieve different objectives and has substantially different motivations and implications for the existing states. Helfer highlights several characteristics of unilateral exits that point to their causes and implications. For him, one of the most prominent features of exit behavior is its public nature, which allows the existing state to voice its interests concerning the treaty or to establish a "rival legal norm" to cooperate with like-minded states. Another significant feature is the constellation of actors involved in the exit process. Unlike non-compliance or delays in commitment to treaties—which can be attributed to resource constraints or the behavior of legislators or judges—exit situations often involve a balance of power among government actors. Unlike non-compliance, which can have procedural and technocratic causes, exit from treaties is often the outcome of negotiations, power struggles, and strategic calculations among diverse actors with differing interests, ideologies, and incentives. When states make the decision to exit, it often reflects the preferences of an actor, that is often dominant in the specific political context.

Domestic political actors may push for treaty exit as a way to respond to electoral pressures or to appease specific constituencies. In addition to domestically derived motivations, Helfer identifies three other motivations for treaty exit: cost–benefit calculations in favor of the former, loss of strategic value of a treaty due to a change, for instance, geopolitical calculations or a change in the treaty, and increased sovereignty concerns that are believed to stem from the treaty.

Although her primary focus is treaty compliance rather than withdrawal, Simmons' book, *Mobilizing for Human Rights* (2009), provides valuable insights into why states might choose to exit human rights treaties. Simmons highlights that states often ratify human rights treaties to gain international legitimacy and reputational benefits. If a state no longer values its international reputation in the same way or prioritizes domestic political concerns (e.g., sovereignty, nationalism) over international approval, it may be more likely to withdraw. Simmons also notes that authoritarian regimes are less likely to comply with human rights treaties. For authoritarian or illiberal regimes, withdrawal from human rights treaties can be a pre-emptive move to avoid external accountability or to insulate themselves from international legal frameworks that could embolden domestic opposition. Overall, Simmons' analysis suggests that unilateral withdrawals are frequently linked to internal political dynamics rather than purely international considerations. Finally, Morelli argues that there are two broad sets of motivations for treaty withdrawals: reactions in domestic politics or as an act of state power, often to give a new direction to foreign policy. Domestic political concerns include changes in political leadership, economic considerations, and national sovereignty concerns, while foreign policy motivations might include strategic realignments, broader shifts in international relations, or enhancing bargaining power (Morelli, 2022).

Scholars have also explored the broader consequences of treaty withdrawals, both for the states withdrawing and for IOs and global regimes. While our primary focus is on the motivations behind states' decisions to withdraw and the reactions of IOs, it is crucial to acknowledge that the way IOs perceive these implications may shape their responses to such withdrawals.

The withdrawal from international treaties is seen as a disruptive force that can erode trust, weaken institutions, and undermine global cooperation (Oliver, 2016). Scholars note that treaty withdrawals can have cascading effects, not just on the specific agreement but on the broader international systems, norms, and organizations that rely on global participation and trust. Because withdrawals pose a threat to international cooperation, IOs respond in a variety of ways to safeguard the integrity of global governance. They may resort to diplomatic negotiations aimed at reversing or mitigating the withdrawal, leveraging both political and economic pressures to maintain the status quo. In other instances, they might opt for legal actions that enforce penalties or transitional obligations on the withdrawing state. Some organizations adapt by reforming their internal structures, such as the EU's budgetary and policy adjustments following Brexit (Oliver, 2016). Others emphasize normative reinforcement, doubling down on their core values and mission in the wake of a member state's exit, as the World Health Organization (WHO) did after the US withdrawal in 2020 (Kickbusch & Holzcheiter, 2021). IOs frequently issue statements of concern or public condemnations to maintain the legitimacy of the treaty and to signal to other member states the importance of it. The symbolic power of these reactions serves to discourage other states from following the withdrawing state. IOs may also respond to withdrawals by stigmatizing the exiting state or by threatening reciprocal actions. Helfer argues that reciprocity is a common mechanism used to punish states that unilaterally withdraw. This could include suspension of benefits derived from the treaty or the imposition of countermeasures by other members (Helfer, 2005). These reactions aim to contain the ripple effects of withdrawal, reinforcing the commitment to multilateralism and preventing further erosion of trust and participation in international regimes.

While much has been written about member states' responses to contestation, the reactions of IOs themselves are less explored. A notable exception is Hirschmann's (2021) study, which examines the varied responses of IOs to challenges, using the United Nations Population Fund as a case study between 1987 and 2020. She identifies three key reactions: inertia, adaptation, and resilience-building. Inertia reflects the IO's choice to ignore threats, either strategically or due to blind spots. Adaptation involves accommodating the contesting state through negotiation or policy changes. Resilience-building, however, sees IOs strengthening their capacities to resist contestation, employing tactics like shaming or building alliances with like-minded states and civil society.

A more EU-specific analysis by Oleart and Theuns (2023) explores how the European Commission responded to democratic backsliding in Poland and Hungary. Their findings suggest that a technocratic, depoliticized understanding of democracy shaped the commission's legalistic approach, which they criticize for being insufficiently robust. They argue that this narrow view blocks healthier forms of political contestation, inadvertently fueling deeper conflict, as seen in the rise of populist appeals.

In sum, IO responses to contestation typically oscillate between confrontation and avoidance. In the former, we observe normative pressures such as shaming, whereas in the latter, more technocratic responses or complete avoidance prevail. In the remainder of this chapter, we analyze Türkiye's withdrawal from the Istanbul Convention and Poland's threats to withdraw, along with the EU's responses to these actions, within the framework of the literature previously discussed. Our aim is to explore both the underlying motivations driving the decisions of these states to exit the treaty and the nature of the EU's reactions. Additionally, we will examine alternative responses that could have been possible and assess their potential political efficacy in addressing the challenges posed by such withdrawals.

3. CONTESTATION AND WITHDRAWAL: MOTIVATIONS AND FRAMES

Türkiye's withdrawal marked the first-ever exit from the Istanbul Convention, setting a precedent and sparking widespread debate about the future of international human rights commitments. Poland's repeated threats of withdrawal, while not yet realized, reflect growing internal pressures and ideological shifts within EU member states. By examining these two cases, we can better understand the dynamics of treaty withdrawals and threats thereof within the EU and their implications for the integrity of human rights norms across the region.

We begin by examining the broader contestation surrounding the Istanbul Convention. While Türkiye's formal withdrawal is unique, the Convention has faced significant resistance from various states and actors long before this event. The debate over the Istanbul Convention extends beyond a single case of exit, as numerous countries and groups have challenged the treaty in other ways, often through ideological opposition and political discourse.

The Istanbul Convention, formally titled the Council of Europe Convention on Preventing and Combating Violence against Women and Domestic Violence, stands as a seminal international treaty in the realm of human rights. Adopted in 2011 and entering into force in 2014, the Convention represents a significant milestone in the legal and institutional protection of women from violence. By October 2021, 34 of the 46 eligible member states of the Council of Europe had ratified the Convention. However, despite its broad adoption, the treaty has become a lightning rod for political contention, deeply polarized debates, and controversy.

The process of ratifying the Convention has witnessed substantial mobilization on both sides of the political spectrum, with fierce support as well as strong resistance. In some countries, such as Croatia, the Convention was ratified amid widespread protests, while in others, entrenched opposition successfully blocked its adoption. At the core of the controversy are profound ideological divides. Critics argue that the Convention promotes a concept of "gender ideology," which they perceive as a threat to traditional family structures and values. Furthermore, concerns have been raised about the treaty's potential to infringe upon national sovereignty and its perceived misalignment with local cultural norms and practices.

The array of actors opposing the Istanbul Convention is both diverse and multifaceted, encompassing conservative civil society organizations, religious groups, political parties, think tanks, and state institutions. These actors differ in their organizational structures and national contexts, yet they are united by strong transnational networks that facilitate collaboration. Through these connections, they have crafted cohesive strategies and messaging to challenge the Convention (Corredor, 2019; Krizsán & Roggeband, 2021; Chappell, 2006; Goetz, 2015). This opposition is not confined to isolated national movements; rather, it represents a well-coordinated transnational campaign. Through regular forums and shared platforms, these groups exchange ideas, refine strategies, and reinforce their collective stance against the treaty.

Most studies on the ratification processes and contestation of the Istanbul Convention focus on single cases, with particular emphasis on Central and Eastern European states. Prominent examples include research on Croatia (Bosak & Vajda, 2019; Obajdin & Golušin, 2021; Runjić-Stoilova & Stanković, 2018), Poland (Gwiazda, 2020; Korolczuk & Graff, 2017), Armenia (Ghazaryan, 2021), Bulgaria (Ilcheva, 2020; Stoencheva, 2021; Vassileva, 2018; Popova et al., 2020), Ukraine (Basha, 2018; Ketelaars, 2019; Zorgdrager, 2020), Latvia (Bračina, 2019; Isaacs & Rudzite, 2021; Vizgunova & Graudiņa, 2020), and Türkiye (Elmas et al., 2021; Türközü, 2021). These works provide essential insights into the identities, goals, and narratives of contesting actors, as well as the broader political contexts that shape the ratification or rejection of the Convention. Some scholars also highlight the transnational nature of these contestations and decisions (Kuhar & Paternotte, 2017; Paternotte & Kuhar, 2018), while others compare a limited number of cases to explore the causes and outcomes of these disputes (Krizsán & Roggeband, 2021; Balogh, 2020).

In countries where the Convention remains unratified, resistance typically emerges through collaboration between state and civil society actors. In Türkiye and Poland—the only two nations to actively pursue withdrawal—the governments aligned with contesting groups and initiated the withdrawal. The following sections will examine the withdrawal processes, the frames of contestation in Türkiye, and the ongoing debates in Poland, which has yet to formally exit the Convention.

3.1 Türkiye and Poland: Motivations and Frames

Türkiye officially withdrew from the Istanbul Convention on July 1, 2021, through a presidential decree, while Poland began its withdrawal process in June 2020. Both nations were among the earliest signatories, with Türkiye ratifying in 2012 and Poland in 2015. Over the subsequent decade, both countries experienced significant democratic decline. In each case, gender issues became political tools, instrumentalized by backsliding governments to consolidate support by constructing a unifying narrative against a perceived "common enemy."

In Türkiye, opposition to the Istanbul Convention emerged from a broad coalition of politicians from the ruling AKP party, civil society actors, journalists, and academics. While these groups did not form a formal institutional front against the Convention, their justifications were strikingly aligned, particularly gaining momentum in traditional and social media after President Erdoğan signaled the government's intent to withdraw. The first significant opposition surfaced in 2019, with the government formally announcing its withdrawal plan in 2020. From that point forward, the opposition's rhetoric against the Convention gained heightened visibility, revealing that the contestation was less an organic social movement arising from grassroots mobilization, and more a top-down populist strategy orchestrated by the government (Direk, 2023).

Analyzing the discourse of AKP elites, Turgut (2022) demonstrates how their rhetoric reflects the broader politicization of gender policies during the AKP's second term. A central argument employed by these elites is that the Convention is incompatible with the country's need for "native and national" regulations. This emphasis on "native and national" practices has been a dominant political narrative since the aftermath of the 2013 Gezi protests, positioning "tradition" as the foundation for Türkiye's future, in contrast to what they portray as "external" or "Western" norms. In this context, the withdrawal from the Istanbul Convention is framed as necessary to "protect" women and families through an authentic, localized understanding of gender roles and family structures, rather than relying on international conventions.

Another key justification for opposition to the Istanbul Convention in Türkiye revolves around the alleged promotion of so-called "gender ideology." Like criticisms seen in other countries, the Convention is portrayed as advancing a hidden agenda aimed at undermining traditional family structures and promoting homosexuality and same-sex marriages. A study analyzing the discourse in pro-government newspapers during the period surrounding Türkiye's withdrawal further reinforces this point. It found that the Convention was depicted as an imperialist Western project designed to erode family values, obliterate traditions, and render children "genderless." This framing is often presented through a stark dichotomy between "Islamic, national, native" values and those perceived as "Western, anti-family, and against biological sex" (Kenes & Kocabay-Sener, 2023). This framing taps into broader civilizational tensions, casting the conflict as more than a policy disagreement but part of a cultural struggle between a conservative Türkiye and a liberal, secular West. By portraying the West as an existential threat to traditional values, the Turkish government positions itself as the defender of national sovereignty and cultural identity against Western norms, reinforcing a narrative of civilizational autonomy from the EU.

In Poland, as in Türkiye, the primary justifications for opposition to the Istanbul Convention center on the protection of traditional family values and a rejection of the so-called "gender ideology" allegedly promoted by the treaty. On July 25, 2020, Poland's Justice Minister Zbigniew Ziobro announced that the government would begin the process of withdrawing from the Convention. Poland, which had signed the Convention in 2012 and ratified it in 2015, quickly became a focal point for anti-Convention rhetoric. In a tweet following the announcement, Ziobro denounced the Convention as "an invention, a feminist creation aimed at justifying gay ideology" (Buranyi, 2020). Other government officials echoed this sentiment in the ensuing days, framing the Convention as a foreign imposition on Polish values. Marcin Romanowski, another key political figure, described it as "neo-Marxist propaganda that turns our world of values upside down" (Kafka Desk, 2020).

Beyond merely contesting the Convention, actors in Poland are actively working to create an alternative framework. They advocate for a new international treaty focused on "defending family" by opposing abortion rights and banning same-sex marriage. In 2021, the Polish government circulated a letter to Central and Eastern European countries seeking support for this proposed "family rights convention," which would serve as an ideological counterweight to the Istanbul Convention. The Undersecretary of State at the Ministry of Justice emphasized that defending family values requires more than national policies, asserting that an international effort is essential to counter the influence of norms promoted by the Istanbul Convention.

Like Türkiye, Poland's push for withdrawal is driven by a broad coalition that includes politicians, civil society groups, and religious organizations. However, Poland's contesting actors differ from Türkiye in one significant respect: they are seeking to influence not just the domestic audience but also to galvanize international support for an alternative treaty. This transnational approach aims to reshape not only Polish but also regional standards on family and gender, further broadening the scope of their ideological battle.

3.2 Making Sense of the Withdrawal Decision: What Does the Literature Tell Us About Türkiye?

A brief examination of the discourses surrounding Türkiye's withdrawal reveals that, while the move serves as a symbolic domestic message to the conservative voter base (Aksoy, 2021), it also reflects broader transnational dynamics. The convergence of nationalist rhetoric and newly forming alliances indicates that this withdrawal is not merely a domestic affair but part of a larger ideological movement. Moreover, the decision to withdraw from the Istanbul Convention sends a stronger signal than other forms of contestation, such as non-ratification, delayed ratification, or societal resistance. Scholars studying Türkiye's actions have highlighted various aspects of this phenomenon.

Scholars have analyzed the withdrawal within the frameworks of authoritarian survival and de-Europeanization. On a broader level, the decision reflects the instrumentalization of gender equality as part of populist politics. Ünal (2023) argues that opposing gender equality has been key to creating and sustaining societal antagonisms, mobilizing support, and solidifying political alliances. The government's move to withdraw from the Convention, especially following electoral losses in major cities in 2019, conveyed a strong message of urgency. Gender issues were reframed as a conflict between "traditional values" and "foreign/European" ones, casting gender equality as part of an external threat. The government's securitization of this issue, as scholars of securitization emphasize, moved the debate beyond normal political discourse, justifying emergency actions outside standard political processes (Ünal, 2023, Buzan et al., 1997). This framing helped to explain the abrupt decision to withdraw via presidential decree, bypassing parliamentary debate and portraying Erdoğan as the savior of the nation's core values.

The question then arises: why did this populist strategy hinge on an international convention rather than purely domestic gender issues? The answer lies in the fraught history of Türkiye–EU relations. As Bodur-Ün and Arikan (2022) point out, Türkiye's withdrawal came during a period of stagnation in its relationship with the EU, against a backdrop of a broader contestation of gender equality within and beyond Europe. The withdrawal symbolized the end of the EU's normative influence in Türkiye and was part of a larger de-Europeanization process. By contesting the Istanbul Convention, the Turkish government signaled the rejection of European norms, reframing the EU as an external "norm-imposer" and asserting its commitment to "national and local" values.

Thus, the withdrawal became a tool of populist politics, consolidating support by emphasizing the divide between "us"—those who embrace traditional, national values—and "them"—the Western, European "others" imposing alien values on Turkish society. The Istanbul Convention was particularly suited to this role, as it symbolized "European values" of gender equality. However, this does not imply a wholesale rejection of all EU treaties. As Bayar (2023) notes, the international human rights regime to which the Istanbul Convention belongs made it an easy target for political manipulation. Bayar argues that human rights regimes, which govern the relationship between states and their citizens rather than between states, are more vulnerable to non-compliance and withdrawal, as the costs of withdrawal are lower. This vertical structure made the Istanbul Convention an ideal target for Türkiye's government, where the political calculus for survival made withdrawal both viable and symbolically powerful.

In sum, scholarly analyses of Türkiye's withdrawal suggest that it is deeply embedded in the country's populist and authoritarian survival strategies, wherein gender equality is framed as a security threat within the context of de-Europeanization. From an international relations perspective, the government found withdrawal relatively easy due to the low costs involved, while simultaneously sending a strong message of delegitimizing European norms for domestic political gain. As Helfer (2005) claims, withdrawal provided Türkiye with a strategic tool to recalibrate its legal and political commitments, allowing it to realign international agreements with shifting domestic priorities or governance models.

4. RESPONSES BY THE EU

4.1 Denunciation and Emphasis on "European Values"

Following Türkiye's withdrawal from the Istanbul Convention, 13 civil society organizations within the European Coalition to End Violence Against Women and Girls (EU Coalition VAWG) jointly condemned Türkiye's decision, as well as Poland's intent to withdraw. In an open letter, they warned that these actions endangered the lives of women and girls, directly opposing the EU's fundamental values. The coalition called on European leaders to take a firm stand, urging Türkiye and Poland to reverse their decisions, while also countering false claims that the Convention grants "special rights" to minorities (European Coalition to End Violence Against Women and Girls, 2021).

In the weeks that followed, European leaders echoed these concerns. Council of Europe Secretary General Marija Pejčinović Burić labeled Poland's potential withdrawal as "alarming," emphasizing that the Istanbul Convention's sole aim is to combat violence against women (Council of Europe, 2020). She offered dialogue to clarify any misconceptions and stressed that leaving the Convention would be a regrettable setback for women's protection. In his April 2021 tweet, Charles Michel, the President of the European Council, emphasized that the rule of law and respect for fundamental rights are core EU values, expressing the EU's deep concerns to President Erdoğan over recent developments in Türkiye. He specifically highlighted European worries regarding Türkiye's withdrawal from the Istanbul Convention. Similarly, European leaders such as the EU's High Representative for Foreign Affairs and Security Policy, Josep Borrell Fontelles, described Türkiye's withdrawal as "devastating" and a blow to women's safety across Europe and beyond. These reactions aligned with the coalition's call to reinforce Europe's commitment to gender equality and protection (Diocese in Europe, 2021).

Following Türkiye's withdrawal, EU officials engaged in diplomatic dialogues with Turkish representatives to express their concerns. For example, during visits to Ankara in 2021, Ursula von der Leyen and Charles Michel raised the issue directly with Recep Tayyip Erdoğan, reiterating their disappointment and urging Türkiye to reconsider the decision. Von der Leyen made it clear that protecting women's rights is a core value for the EU and that Türkiye's actions could impact its relations with the EU. Other leaders' remarks further reinforce the narrative around the Istanbul Convention's vital role in combating violence against women. The letter from the Parliamentary Assembly of the Council of Europe (PACE), following discussions on Poland's potential withdrawal, emphasizes that "the prevention of violence, protection of the victims and prosecution of the perpetrators are at the heart of all measures foreseen by the Istanbul Convention, which makes its implementation all the more relevant and important, including in times of crisis" (PACE, 2021).

Overall, the reactions of EU leaders to Türkiye's withdrawal from the Istanbul Convention expressed regret and disappointment. They underscored the EU's commitment to fundamental European values, particularly gender equality and the fight against violence toward women. EU leaders emphasized that the Istanbul Convention is a crucial instrument for protecting women's rights and called on Türkiye to reconsider its decision in light of these shared values.

Other than denunciation, the Parliamentary Assembly of the Council of Europe also took concrete steps to address Türkiye's withdrawal. The assembly adopted Resolution 2376 (2021) on "The functioning of democratic institutions in Türkiye" on April 22, 2021 during its second part session in Strasbourg. In paragraph 8 of the resolution, the assembly acknowledged that while the ratification and denunciation of treaties fall under national sovereignty, "the unprecedented withdrawal from a major Council of Europe convention has raised many questions and concerns about its democratic processes." It further emphasized that, in response to such developments, there should be a reflection on the standards that govern the ratification and withdrawal from international treaties in democratic societies, beyond the minimal legal and constitutional requirements. The assembly therefore called on the Venice Commission to prepare a comparative study and possible guidelines on the modalities that should regulate the ratification and withdrawal from Council of Europe conventions.[1]

[1] This report, published in April 2022, provides a comprehensive analysis of the legal and procedural frameworks governing how countries ratify and withdraw from international treaties. The report calls for robust involvement of national parliaments in both ratification and denunciation decisions, ensuring that such actions are not solely executive decisions. Additionally, the commission stresses that withdrawal from treaties, particularly those related to human rights, should be carefully scrutinized to prevent undermining international commitments.

In response to EU leaders' condemnation, the Turkish government reiterated its commitment to combating violence against women but emphasized doing so through national measures. President Erdoğan's office issued a statement affirming "zero tolerance" for violence against women while justifying the withdrawal by claiming the Convention had been "hijacked" by efforts to normalize homosexuality, which it deemed incompatible with Turkish values. The statement stressed Türkiye's preference for "native and national" solutions over European models it viewed as alien to its social fabric. It also highlighted Türkiye's existing legal framework, its membership in CEDAW, and the forthcoming Human Rights Action Plan aimed at improving protection for women. Vice President Oktay echoed this sentiment, emphasizing the importance of relying on Türkiye's own traditions rather than external models to promote women's rights (Directorate of Communications of the Republic of Türkiye, 2021).

A brief look at the EU response to withdrawal from the Istanbul Convention and the responses of the Turkish government to these reactions demonstrates that the EU's responses often reinforce the same "civilizational tension" narrative that these states invoke, inadvertently reproducing a dichotomy between Western liberalism and other cultural or national identities.

4.2 Path Not Taken?

The previous section illustrates how decisions and threats of withdrawal have been met with expressions of regret by the EU, reinforcing a familiar narrative of civilizational tension. Although the Venice Commission's report offered an alternative to outright denunciation, it remained narrowly confined to an assessment of the existing legal framework and did not extend beyond a technocratic interpretation of what is essentially a political issue.

International law scholars view the EU's reaction to Türkiye's withdrawal as a significant challenge (Çalı, 2021). In a joint paper, Çalı and Helfer (2022) criticize the EU's response for its failure to take more decisive action or to deploy legal interventions. They argue that both the Council of Europe and the EU missed an opportunity to apply stronger legal mechanisms to counter Türkiye's unilateral withdrawal, setting a worrisome precedent for human rights treaties. Specifically, Çalı and Helfer propose that the EU could have called for more thorough scrutiny by invoking a *lex specialis* principle, given the unique nature of human rights treaties, which demand enhanced oversight when a state attempts to withdraw. By doing so, the EU would have prioritized the protection of human rights over sovereign discretion, with a particular focus on the gendered and discriminatory consequences of Türkiye's decision, especially concerning the rights of women and LGBTQ+ communities.

In response to Türkiye, the EU could have approached the situation more effectively by avoiding a reproduction of the civilizational divide that emphasizes European values. Instead, it might have rejected Türkiye's exit through a presidential decree, demanding that the full legal process be followed. Engaging with civil society and democratic forces opposing the Turkish government could have provided symbolic and institutional support. Furthermore, framing the issue not as a clash of norms but as a matter of autocratic populist politics would have been more constructive. However, the EU became entangled in a similar populist logic by focusing on European values against Türkiye, which limited the potential for a more nuanced and supportive engagement.

5. CONCLUSION

Türkiye's unilateral withdrawal from the Istanbul Convention presents a significant case study for analyzing the broader implications of treaty exits, particularly when gender rights are at the forefront of political and ideological contestation. Along with Poland's similar, albeit less formalized, threats to withdraw, Türkiye's decision reflects a larger trend of populist backlash against international norms on human rights. As discussed in the literature, treaty withdrawals are often motivated by a complex interplay of domestic politics, national identity, and international relations (Helfer, 2005; Morelli, 2022). Türkiye's exit from the Istanbul Convention is an example of how governments can manipulate gender politics to bolster support by framing international human rights norms as foreign impositions that undermine national sovereignty and traditional values.

Türkiye's withdrawal is not merely a response to the specific provisions of the Istanbul Convention but part of a broader strategy to construct a civilizational divide between "native and national" values and "Western" or "European" norms. This tactic has been utilized by the Turkish government, under President Erdoğan, to consolidate power by appealing to conservative and nationalist elements within the country. The Istanbul Convention, which seeks to protect women from domestic violence and advance gender equality, became a symbol of Western liberalism and interference in Türkiye's domestic affairs. The government's rhetoric portrayed the Convention as promoting so-called "gender ideology" and undermining family values, effectively turning gender rights into a battleground for broader ideological struggles.

The international response to Türkiye's withdrawal, particularly from the EU, further illuminates the complexities of how IOs react to treaty exits. The EU, alongside the Council of Europe and numerous civil society organizations, strongly condemned Türkiye's withdrawal, framing it as a violation of fundamental European values. The Istanbul Convention was portrayed as an essential instrument for protecting human rights, particularly those of women and marginalized communities. However, the EU's response, while symbolically powerful, inadvertently reinforced the narrative that Türkiye's leadership sought to exploit. By framing the issue as a defense of "European values," the EU allowed the Turkish government to depict the Convention as a foreign imposition, deepening the so-called civilizational dichotomy between Türkiye and the West.

This dynamic aligns with existing scholarship on IOs' responses to treaty withdrawals, which often fall into three categories: resilience-building, avoidance, and confrontation (Hirschmann, 2021). In Türkiye's case, the EU's approach can be categorized as normative confrontation, where the withdrawal was met with strong public condemnation and efforts to stigmatize the Turkish government's decision. However, this strategy may have been counterproductive, as it played into Türkiye's domestic narrative that frames the EU as an external force imposing alien values. The EU's response, while necessary to uphold international norms, failed to engage constructively with the political and cultural dimensions that motivated Türkiye's withdrawal.

In addition, the EU's reaction can be criticized for its failure to go beyond a technocratic response. Scholars such as Çalı and Helfer (2022) argue that the EU and the Council of Europe missed an opportunity to invoke stronger legal mechanisms that could have held Türkiye accountable for its withdrawal. By failing to apply a more robust legal response, such as invoking the *lex specialis* principle, which prioritizes human rights treaties over sovereign discretion, the EU could have emphasized the importance of protecting fundamental rights, particularly given the gendered and discriminatory impact of Türkiye's decision. Such an approach would have shifted the focus from national sovereignty to the protection of universal human rights, a critical angle in cases involving the withdrawal from treaties aimed at promoting gender equality.

Moreover, an important aspect of this case is the role of domestic actors, particularly Türkiye's strong feminist civil society, in resisting the government's withdrawal. Despite the Turkish government's attempt to frame the Convention as a threat to traditional values, feminist groups have mobilized extensively to protest the decision. These groups have organized demonstrations, issued public statements, and formed alliances with international feminist movements, showcasing the resilience of Türkiye's civil society. Their activism illustrates the importance of supporting domestic actors in countries experiencing democratic backsliding, particularly when gender rights are targeted as part of a broader populist agenda.

The EU could benefit from engaging more directly with these civil society movements. Supporting feminist organizations, both financially and through diplomatic channels, could strengthen the domestic opposition to populist policies that undermine human rights. By forging closer relationships with civil society actors, the EU and other international bodies can enhance their ability to counteract populist backlash against international norms. This approach would also provide a more nuanced response to treaty withdrawals, moving beyond stigmatization and confrontation to a more constructive engagement with domestic political realities.

The broader implications of Türkiye's withdrawal from the Istanbul Convention extend beyond the immediate consequences for gender rights. As Ripsman et al. (2016) note, treaty withdrawals can have a cascading effect on global governance, weakening the trust and cooperation necessary for the functioning of international regimes. Türkiye's decision sets a troubling precedent for other countries, particularly those with populist or authoritarian-leaning governments, to follow suit. The risk is that withdrawals from human rights treaties could become a more common tool for governments seeking to insulate themselves from external accountability while promoting nationalist agendas.

Looking forward, future research should explore more effective ways for IOs to respond to treaty withdrawals, especially in cases where gender rights are at stake. One key area of study could focus on the potential of IOs to support domestic civil society actors, such as feminist organizations, who can resist populist backlash and advocate for the protection of human rights. Understanding the long-term effects of withdrawals from treaties like the Istanbul Convention will be essential for developing strategies to prevent the erosion of global human rights regimes.

In conclusion, Türkiye's withdrawal from the Istanbul Convention offers valuable insights into the complexities of treaty exits in the context of gender rights. The case underscores the importance of understanding both the domestic motivations behind such decisions and the international responses they elicit. The EU's reaction, while grounded in a defense of human rights, ultimately reinforced the civilizational tension narrative that Türkiye sought to exploit.

REFERENCES

Aksoy, H. A. (2021). What Lies Behind Türkiye's Withdrawal from the Istanbul Convention? *Stiftung Wissenschaft und Politik*. Retrieved from https://www.swp-berlin.org/publikation/what-lies-behind-türkiyes-withdrawal-from-the-istanbul-convention.

Balogh, L. (2020). The Ratification Status of the Council of Europe's Istanbul Convention Among EU Member States. *MTA Law Working Papers* 7, 1–20.

Bayar, T. (2023). Turkey's Withdrawal from Istanbul Convention: International Human Rights Regime vis-à-vis Authoritarian Survival. *Turkish Studies* 25 (1), 22–42.

Bob, C. (2012). *The Global Right Wing and the Clash of World Politics*. Cambridge University Press.

Bodur Ün, M. & Arikan, H. (2022). Europeanization and De-Europeanization of Turkey's Gender Equality Policy: The Case of the Istanbul Convention. *Journal of Common Market Studies* 60 (4), 945–962.

Bosak, M. & Vajda, M. M. (2019). The Reality Behind the Istanbul Convention: Shattering Conservative Delusions. In *Women's Studies International Forum* (pp. 77–83). Elsevier.

Bračina, E. (2019). Istanbul Convention and the Potential Effect of its Ratification on the Legal System of the Republic of Latvia. https://dspace.lu.lv/dspace/handle/7/48947.

Buranyi, S. (2020). Poland to Withdraw from Treaty on Violence Against Women, Minister says. *The Guardian*, July 26. Retrieved from https://www.theguardian.com/world/2020/jul/26/poland-withdraw-from-treaty-violence-against-women-istanbul-convention.

Buzan, B, Waever, O, & De Wilde, J. (1997). *Security: A New Framework for Analysis*. Lynne Rienner Publishers.

Chappell, L. (2006). Contesting Women's Rights: Charting the Emergence of a Transnational Conservative Counter-network. *Global Society* 20, 491–520.

Corredor, E. S. (2019). Unpacking "Gender Ideology" and the Global Right's Anti-gender Countermovement. *Signs: Journal of Women in Culture and Society* 44, 613–638.

Council of Europe. (2020). Poland Should Not Withdraw from the Istanbul Convention, says Secretary General. July 26. Retrieved from https://www.coe.int/en/web/portal/-/poland-should-not-withdraw-from-the-istanbul-convention-says-secretary-general.

Cupać, J. & Ebetürk, I. (2020). The Personal is Global Political: The Antifeminist Backlash in the United Nations. *British Journal of Politics and International Relations* 22 (4), 702–714.

Cupać, J. & Ebetürk, I. (2021). Backlash Advocacy and NGO Polarization Over Women's Rights in the United Nations. *International Affairs* 97 (4), 1183–1201.

Cupać, J. & Ebetürk, I. (2022). Competitive Mimicry: The Socialization of Antifeminist NGOs into the United Nations. *Global Constitutionalism* 11 (3), 379–400.

Çalı, B. (2021). Withdrawal from the Istanbul Convention by Turkey: A Testing Problem for the Council of Europe. *Blog of European Journal of International Law*. https://www.ejiltalk.org/withdrawal-from-the-istanbul-convention-by-turkey-a-testing-problem-for-the-council-of-europe/.

Çalı, B. & Helfer, L. (2022). The Gender of Treaty Withdrawal: Lessons from Istanbul Convention. *Blog of European Journal of International Law*. https://www.ejiltalk.org/the-gender-of-treaty-withdrawal-lessons-from-the-istanbul-convention/.

Datta, N. (2018). "Restoring the Natural Order": The Religious Extremists' Vision to Mobilize European Societies against Human Rights on Sexuality and Reproduction. European Parliamentary Forum on Population & Development. Retrieved from https://www.epfweb.org/node/690.

Diocese in Europe. (2021). Council of Europe: Istanbul Convention. March 23. Retrieved from https://www.europe.anglican.org/news/latest-news/council-europe-istanbul-convention.

Directorate of Communications of the Republic of Türkiye. (2021). Statement Regarding Türkiye's Withdrawal from the Istanbul Convention. Retrieved from https://www.iletisim.gov.tr/english/haberler/detay/statement-regarding-Türkiyes-withdrawal-from-the-istanbul-convention.

Direk, Z. (2023). On Türkiye's Withdrawal from Istanbul Convention. *Zeitschrift für Vergleichende Politikwissenschaft* 17, 413–432.

Ebetürk, I. (2018). Norms of Gender Equality and the Backlash against Istanbul Convention. *WZB Blog*. Retrieved from https://ordersbeyondborders.blog.wzb.eu/2018/06/06/norms-of-gender-equality-and-the-backlash-against-istanbul-convention/.

Elmas, T., Overdorf, R., & Aberer, K. (2021). Tactical Reframing of Online Disinformation Campaigns Against The Istanbul Convention. https://arxiv.org/abs/2105.13398.

European Coalition to End Violence Against Women and Girls. (2021). Letter from EU Coalition VAWG on Türkiye's Withdrawal from the Istanbul Convention. *End FGM European Network*. Retrieved from https://www.endfgm.eu/editor/0/Letter_from_EU_Coalition_VAWG_on_IC_Türkiye_withdrawal.pdf.

Ghazaryan, M. (2021). Armenia and the Battle to Defeat Ethno-Nationalist Attacks on the Istanbul Convention. *Southwestern Journal of International Law* 27, 167–186.

Goetz, A. M. (2015). The New Competition in Multilateral Norm-setting: Transnational Feminists & the Illiberal Backlash. *Daedalus* 149 (1), 160–179.

Grabowska, M. (2014). Gender Equality in Poland after EU Accession. Expectations and Reality. Heinrich Böll Foundation. Retrieved from https://pl.boell.org/sites/default/files/uploads/2014/07/grabowska_gender_assessment_poland.pdf.

Gwiazda, A. (2020). Right-wing Populism and Feminist Politics: The Case of Law and Justice in Poland. *International Political Science Review* 42 (5), 580–595.

Helfer, L. R. (2005). Exiting Treaties. *Virginia Law Review* 91, 1579–1648.

Hirschmann, G. (2021). International Organizations' Responses to Member State Contestation: From Inertia to Resilience. *International Affairs* 97, 1963–1981.

Ilcheva, M. (2020). Bulgaria and the Istanbul Convention: Law, Politics and Propaganda vs. the Rights of Victims of Gender-Based Violence. *Open Journal for Legal Studies* 3, 49–68.

Isaacs, R. & Rudzite, L. (2021). Conceptualising Culture Wars in the Post-Communist Space: Latvia, the Istanbul Convention and the Struggle for Power. *Europe-Asia Studies* 73 (8), 1418–1440.

Kafka Desk. (2020). Polish Minister Threatens to Withdraw from Istanbul Convention on Gender Equality. *Kafka Desk*. Retrieved from https://kafkadesk.org/2020/05/17/polish-minister-threatens-to-withdraw-from-istanbul-convention-on-gender-equality/.

Kantola, J. & Lombardo, E. (2020). Strategies of Right Populists in Opposing Gender Equality in a Polarized European Parliament. *International Political Science Review* 42 (5), 565–579.

Kenes, H. & Kocabay-Sener, N. (2023). İstanbul Sözleşmesi Tartışmalarında Açık Muhalefetten Zemin Kaydırmaya Farklı Tutumlar: Sabah ve Sözcü Örnekleri. *Federgi* 153–197 (2)

Ketelaars, E. (2019). Geographical Value Spaces and Gender Norms in Post-Maidan Ukraine: The Failed Ratification of the Istanbul Convention. *Review of International Studies* 45, 731–747.

Kickbusch, I. & Holzcheiter, A. (2021). Can Geopolitics Derail the Pandemic Treaty? *British Medical Journal*, 375: e069129. DOI: 10.1136/bmj-2021-069129.

Koremenos, B., Lipson, C., & Snidal, D. (2001). The Rational Design of International Institutions. *International Organization* 55, 761–799.

Korolczuk, E. & Graff, A. (2017). "Worse than Communism and Nazism Put Together": War on Gender in Poland. In A. Graff & E. Korolczuk (Eds.), *Anti-Gender Movements in the Populist Moment* (pp. 67–91). Rowman & Littlefield.

Krasner, S. D. (1999). *Sovereignty: Organized Hypocrisy*. Princeton, NJ: Princeton University Press.

Krizsán, A. & Roggeband, C. (2021). Opposing the Istanbul Convention: Actors, Strategies, and Frames. In A. Krizsán & C. Roggeband (Eds.), *Politicizing Gender and Democracy in the Context of the Istanbul Convention* (pp. 55–119). Springer International Publishing.

Kuhar, R. & Paternotte, D. (2017). *Anti-Gender Campaigns in Europe: Mobilizing Against Equality*. Rowman & Littlefield.

Morelli, A. (2022). *Withdrawal from Multilateral Treaties*. Brill Nijhoff.

Obajdin, D. & Golušin, S. (2021). Narratives of Gender, War Memory, and EU-scepticism in the Movement Against the Ratification of the Istanbul Convention in Croatia. In A. Milošević & T. Trošt (Eds.), *Europeanisation and Memory Politics in the Western Balkans* (pp. 205–230). Springer International Publishing.

Oleart, A. & Theuns, T. (2023). "Democracy without Politics" in the European Commission's Response to Democratic Backsliding: From Technocratic Legalism to Democratic Pluralism. *Journal of Common Market Studies* 61 (5), 882–899.

Oliver, T. (2016). European and International Views of Brexit. *Journal of European Public Policy* 23 (9), 1321–1328.

PACE. (2021, March 15). Poland and the Istanbul Convention: Joint Statement by PACE President, General Rapporteur on Violence Against Women, and Co-rapporteurs on the Monitoring of Poland. *PACE*. Retrieved from https://pace.coe.int/en/news/7966/la-pologne-et-la-convention-d-istanbul-declaration-conjointe-du-president-de-l-apce-de-la-rapporteure-generale-sur-la-violence-a-l-egard-des-femmes-et-des-corapporteurs-pour-le-suivi-de-la-pologne$.

Paternotte, D. & Kuhar, R. (2018). Disentangling and Locating the "Global Right": Anti-gender Campaigns in Europe. *Politics and Governance* 6 (4), 6–19.

Popova, J., Koev, K., & Popova, A. (2020). The Istanbul Convention and its Political, Social, and Cultural Reflections in the Danube Space: The Case with Bulgaria. *Journal of Danubian Studies and Research* 10, 528–540.

Ripsman, N. M., Taliaferro, J. W., & Lobell, S. E. (2016). *Neoclassical Realist Theory of International Politics*. Oxford University Press.

Runjić-Stoilova, A., & Stanković, D. (2018). Populism in Croatia: The Case of Ratification of the Istanbul Convention. *Book of Abstracts*, 4th International Conference on Rhetoric, Postira, 50.

Simmons, B. A. (2009). *Mobilizing for Human Rights: International Law in Domestic Politics*. Cambridge University Press.

Stoencheva, J. (2021). Turkish Yoke, Red Vampires, and Euro-genderists: Strategies of De/legitimization in the Debate Around the Istanbul Convention in Bulgaria. Master's Thesis. https://www.diva-portal.org/smash/get/diva2:1566953/FULLTEXT02.

Turgut, H. (2022). Governing Through Hate. Discourse Strategies used by the AKP Elites on Twitter to Justify the Decision to Withdraw from the Istanbul Convention. *Croatian Journal for Journalism and the Media* 28 (2), 9–40.

Türközü, D. (2021). Türkiye's Withdrawal from the Istanbul Convention: One Step Further, Two Steps Back. *Völkerrechtliche Tagesthemen* 13. Völkerrechtsblog.

Ünal, D. (2023). Securitization of Gender As A Modus Operandi Of Populism: Anti-Gender Discourses on the Istanbul Convention in the Context of AKP's Liberal Transformation. *Southeast European and Black Sea Studies* 1–21.

Vassileva, R. (2018). Bulgaria's Constitutional Troubles with the Istanbul Convention. *Verfassungsblog: On Matters Constitutional*. https://verfassungsblog.de/bulgarias-constitutional-troubles-with-the-istanbul-convention/.

Verloo, M. & Paternotte, D. (2018). The Feminist Project Under Threat in Europe. *Politics and Governance* 6, 1–5.

Vizgunova, E. & Graudiņa, E. (2020). The Trouble with "Gender" in Latvia: Europeanisation through the Prism of the Istanbul Convention. *Baltic Journal of Law & Politics* 13 (1), 108–139.

Yamin, A. E., Datta, N., & Andion, X. (2018). Behind the Drama: The Roles of Transnational Actors in Legal Mobilization over Sexual and Reproductive Rights. *Georgetown Journal of Gender and the Law* 19, 533–564.

Zorgdrager, H. (2020). Churches, Dignity, Gender: The Istanbul Convention as a Matter of Public Theology in Ukraine. *International Journal of Public Theology* 14, 296–318.

14. The challenges of governing sustainable development through goals: prioritization and coordination in Europe and Southeast Asia

Sukmawani Bela Pertiwi, Axel Marx, Charline Depoorter, Kari Irwin Otteburn, Tirta Nugraha Mursitama and Lili Yulyadi Arnakim

1. INTRODUCTION

Fostering sustainable development through international collaboration represents a pressing and vital objective of global governance. It aims to seek harmony between the governance of economic growth, social inclusion, and environmental protection, each of which involves different actors, characteristics, issues, and governance styles. Global governance of sustainable development is a 'governance of governance' (Meuleman, 2019), and it has been transforming and experimenting with different models of governance for the past 50 years to keep up with emerging challenges.

During the early years of sustainable development, norm-setting was the dominant governance model. This model, however, was seen as weak as it was not binding and required a long-term process without clear review and monitoring measures. A more rulemaking-based approach was subsequently introduced with the 1992 Rio Earth Summit by institutionalizing the norm of 'sustainable development' into various international laws and regulations. However, the lack of central authority to enforce rules and the reluctance of member states to bind themselves into international legal frameworks resulted in a minimum amount of participation and level of commitment (Palmer, 1992; Brunnee & Parson, 1993).

Against this backdrop, the adoption of the goal-setting model in the Millennium Development Goals and, subsequently, the Sustainable Development Goals (SDGs) in 2015 was seen as an innovation in the governance of sustainable development. Goal-setting models use common goals instead of rules and norms to steer actors' behavior. It is seen as a middle way between rulemaking and norm-setting as it provides more flexibility than rulemaking but is still equipped with more monitoring mechanisms to track progress than norm-setting. For this reason, the goal-setting model tends to have broad goals and a loose institutional arrangement (Biermann, Kanie, & Kim, 2017).

Based on two case studies carried out previously on the multi-level interactions between regional organizations and their member states (Marx et al., 2021), we find that these features of goal-setting global governance also create two common problems in the implementation of the goal-setting model. First, broad goals mean challenges for countries with limited capacities to meet these goals (Forestier & Kim, 2020) and forces them to prioritize some goals to the detriment of other goals. A loose institutional arrangement characterized by the absence of central authority and binding mechanisms enables further different policy interpretations and goal prioritization among actors. Second, broad goals also require not only partnership but also policy coherence among actors at all levels to implement the agendas. The involvement of many actors in a typically loose institutional arrangement of the goal-setting model, however, makes coordination a common problem. The success of goal-setting, in this sense, lies in the collective ability to deal with these two problems or, in other words, the ability to maintain a balance between accommodating national contexts while ensuring policy coherence.

This chapter aims to further discuss the challenges of goal prioritization and coordination of the SDGs as a goal-setting model of governance of sustainable development by focusing on two regions, namely Europe through the European Union (EU) and Southeast Asia through the Association of Southeast Asian Nations (ASEAN). Some literatures have identified widespread practices of goal prioritization from global (Forestier & Kim, 2020; Heras-Saizarbitoria, Urbieta, & Boiral, 2021) to local levels (Pineda, Cano, & Czerny, 2021; Tremblay et al., 2021; Bandari, Moallemi, Lester, Downie, & Bryan, 2021) as well as policy coherence and coordination problems (van Driel, Biermann, Kim, & Vijge, 2022). However, they address these issues separately and separate them from the goal-setting model as its underlying factor and focus on the international and local approaches to the problems, overlooking the regional level. A region is a group of countries within geographical proximity that have developed unique interactions that differentiate it from other regions. Hence, the regional level is an asset in explaining the dynamics of goal prioritization among member states and the regional coordination to balance these problems.

This chapter is divided into three parts. The first part begins with discussion on the three models of governance as a foundation to understand the goal-setting model and how it is different from the other two models. The second part will describe the evolution of governance models on sustainable development from norm-setting in 1987 to goal-setting in 2015. The final part will then examine the problems of goal prioritization and coordination resulting from the adoption of the goal-setting model in the EU and ASEAN. We end with a conclusion.

2. THE THREE MODELS OF GLOBAL GOVERNANCE

Global governance is a concept aimed at explaining order, coordination, and provision of collective goods in international relations amidst the absence of a global government or an authority (Domínguez & Flores, 2018; Risse, 2012). Models of governance are thus methods developed from the primary instruments used to steer actors' behaviors in establishing or maintaining the order, coordination, and provision of collective goods.

With the dominance of liberal tradition in international relations, rulemaking was the most prominent model of governance, particularly during the Cold War era when states and international organizations were the primary actors in global governance. Liberalists assume that states are rational, hence they behave based on the logic of consequences. Under the uncertainty of an anarchic international system, states are generally reluctant to cooperate with other states. However, states are willing to coordinate their policies in international organizations if they see that policy coordination is more beneficial than individual action or if they seek commitments from other states (Moravcsik, 1993; 1995). Rulemaking, in this sense, reflects how states aim to limit the behaviors of other states by enforcing compliance through – following the logic of consequences – rewards and punishment. Rulemaking operates in hierarchic relations (Meuleman, 2008). In international relations, rulemaking is possible when states, as holders of the highest sovereignty, give consent to international organizations to be the governor, custodian, or authority to enforce these rules (Onuf, 1979; Zürn, 2018). However, as liberalists assume that the identity and interests of states are given, the role of rulemaking is limited to regulating their behaviors. The fact that rulemaking only occurs by the consent of states also means that the power of rulemaking is different across issues based on the preference of member states. Rulemaking on issues with immediate benefits, such as economic cooperation, tends to develop rapidly compared to rulemaking on issues with long-term consequences, such as environmental conservation.

Beginning from the 1990s, international relations scholars witnessed the rise of norm-setting as a new alternative (Finnemore & Sikkink, 1998). The end of the Cold War and the rapid development of globalization have brought new issues and actors to international relations. This fragmentation added a new dimension to actors' relations in global governance. In addition to hierarchical relations between international organizations and the states, there were also network type relations among these emerging non-state actors which are based on equal partnership and informality (Keck & Sikkink, 1998; Monkelbaan, 2019). In this context, rulemaking as a governance model is no longer sufficient since it does not account for the multiplicity of relevant actors. At the same time, there was 'the constructivist turn in International Relations', which brought normative aspects to the field (Checkel, 1998). Constructivists assume that international relations are social relations in which interaction transfers normative values. They also assume that actors behave based on the logic of appropriateness, therefore norm-setting is the most appropriate model to govern their relations. Constructivists also argue that actors' identity and interests are socially constructed instead of given, therefore norm-setting is more powerful as it could be used not only to limit behaviors, but also change actors' identity and interests (Wendt, 1992). In practice, norm-setting has been widely used among international organizations with limited powers to enforce the rule and non-state actors with no authority to influence global governance. Norm-setting relies on socialization and social sanction to preserve the norm. As these are not binding and have no material consequences, states oftentimes underestimate the power of norms.

A recent innovation in global governance is the adoption of a goal-setting model. Goal-setting is designed to tackle long-term policy challenges, which requires broad participation and substantial resource mobilization (Kanie, Bernstein, Biermann, & Haas, 2017; Kanie, et al., 2019). Goal-setting is an old practice, but the systematic study of goal-setting as a global governance model is relatively new. The theory of goal-setting was initially developed in organizational psychology to understand why actors who have equal knowledge and skill have different performance (Latham & Locke, 1991; Locke & Latham, 2019). This theory argues that the answer is motivational, hence goal-setting uses goals to motivate actors' behaviors by focusing attention and efforts on policies relevant to the goal and mobilizing strategies and resources to facilitate the goal (Latham, Ganegoda, & Locke, 2011). This theory also argues that the success of goal-setting depends on actors' capability, commitment, feedback mechanism, situational factors, such as resource availability, and task complexity (Latham, Ganegoda, & Locke, 2011). Its adoption in global governance also follows this line.

The goal-setting model consists of three important aspects: goal substance, goal formation, and goal implementation. Global goals result from the abstraction of local contexts in order to make them applicable universally (Fukuda-Parr, 2013). Many criticize, however, that this process may lead to simplification, reconfiguration, and redefinition of the actual goals (Fukuda-Parr, 2013). The second aspect central in the goal-setting model is goal formulation. Goal formulation can be assigned or negotiated (Latham & Locke, 1979). Research has demonstrated that participative goal formulation is more effective as involving actors builds their sense of belonging and commitment in achieving the goal and in mobilizing resources for the goal. The last aspect is goal implementation. Goal-setting is not binding but involves mechanisms to track progress and give feedback to the ongoing progress (Young, 2017).

This form of goal-setting global governance is considered by some as a promising new governance approach and is further developed in the global experimental governance literature. Theorized by Sabel and Zeitlin in the early 2000s, experimentalist governance is assumed to dissolve a strict distinction between top-down and bottom-up perspectives (Sabel & Zeitlin, 2010; 2012) and enables multi-level governance with the aim of achieving concrete policy-objectives.

2.1 The Evolution of Governance Models on Sustainable Development

Global governance of sustainable development has been experimenting with norm-setting, rulemaking, and goal-setting over the past 50 years. In the beginning, norm-setting was the primary model in governing sustainable development. The introduction of the norm 'sustainable development' in the 1987 Brundtland report (WCED, 1987) was an attempt to mediate the long-standing debate on the relations between economy and ecology that started in the 1960s. The growing concern on the destructive impacts of economic activities on the environment, which according to the 1972 Club of Rome report (Meadows, Meadows, Randers, & Behrens, 1972), may go beyond the Earth's carrying capacity, demonstrated that both were incompatible, and thus, there must be limits to growth. The majority of the world's poor, however, needs economic growth to meet their basic needs. The blame game between developed and developing countries on who should be responsible for environmental destruction while refusing to limit their own growth exacerbated the problem and led the UN to take action.

The 1972 UN Conference on the Human Environment (UNCHE) was the first to include environmental issues in the discussion of economic development, hence marking a shifting paradigm in the relations between economy and ecology. The conference particularly started to recognize the positive correlations between poverty alleviation – a development measure – and environmental conservation. It established the UN Environment Program in 1974 to provide global leadership on environmental agenda and the World Commission on Environment and Development in 1984 to propose long-term environmental strategies for achieving sustainable development (General Assembly Resolution A/Res/38/161). While sustainable development, in this sense, could be understood as a goal, its focus on prescriptive behaviors, its definition of how economy and ecology should interact, and hence, what are acceptable or appropriate in development, make the term mostly normative. As Gro Harlem Brundtland, as the chairman of the commission, also stated, what the commission looked for was 'norms of behavior', 'changes in attitudes' and 'in social values' 'at all levels and in the interests of all' (WCED, 1987, XIV). This norm sets the acceptable development or so-called sustainable development as development that 'meets the needs of the present without compromising the ability of the future generation to meet their own needs' (WCED, 1987, p. 8). This definition acknowledges the need for development, particularly among developing countries, yet still sets the limit for development in terms of 'the ability of the biosphere to absorb the effects of human activities' (WCED, 1987, p. 8). It prescribes developed countries to adopt 'life-styles within the planet's ecological means in their use of energy' and developing countries to maintain population size and growth in line with 'the changing productive potential of the ecosystem' (WCED, 1987, p. 9).

As with other norm-setting models, however, the norm of sustainable development was not binding and thus relied on social mechanisms, such as praising and shaming, to uphold the norm. Hence, with growing environmental threats throughout the 1980s and using the momentum of the twentieth anniversary of the UNCHE, the UN General Assembly called for another conference to be held in 1992 to translate the norm of sustainable development into global agendas and practical guidelines for interstate cooperation, while at the same time reviewing the adoption of the norm at the individual country level (General Assembly Resolution 43/196).

In this sense, the 1992 Rio Earth Summit began the institutionalization of sustainable development into international laws and regulations, hence marking a shift to rulemaking as the primary model governing sustainable development. The Summit produced the Rio Declaration with its 27 principles for the governance of sustainable development and Agenda 21 containing 21 prioritized areas for international cooperation along with the means of implementation. In addition, the Summit agreed legal instruments for specific areas such as the UN Framework Convention on Climate Change (UNFCCC), the Convention on Biological Diversity, and the Declaration on the principles of forest management. The Summit also established the Commission on Sustainable Development to monitor progress on the implementation of these agreements. Separately, in 1995, another world summit was convened to focus on the social pillar of sustainable development. The World Summit on Social Development produced the Copenhagen Declaration as a commitment to put people at the center of sustainable development with ending poverty as the main goal.

The rapid proliferation of agendas, institutions, instruments, and stakeholders in the governance of sustainable development, however, is not without problems. Similar to other rulemaking models, criticisms refer to the lack of central authority to enforce the rule and the reluctance of member states to bind themselves in international legal frameworks, which results in a limited number of parties and level of commitment (Palmer, 1992; Brunnee & Parson, 1993). The broad agendas in yet separate processes for each pillar of sustainable development was another consideration in the UN to streamlining and integrating these structures. For this reason, the UN introduced a new framework for development known as the Millennium Development Goals (MDGs). The MDGs were not only integrated but also focused on achieving development goals rather than rule compliance among actors, thereby shifting the primary model of governance from rulemaking to goal-setting. In defining the goals, the MDGs also departed from the trend of the 1990s that focused more on the environmental pillar. The turn of the millennium was marked with growing concern over the uneven costs and benefits of globalization. Therefore, sustainable development was mostly directed towards achieving inclusiveness and equality among people (General Assembly Resolution A/Res/55/2). The MDGs, however, were superficial in the three core aspects of the goal-setting model. In terms of substance, the MDGs focused mostly on the social pillar and were directed primarily towards developing countries, hence falling short in reflecting the universal nature of sustainable development. The formulation of the MDGs was also conducted top-down without consultation with stakeholders. Lastly, the MDGs also fell short in terms of means of implementation and monitoring mechanisms.

The successors to the MDGs, namely the SDGs, represent a more advanced form of goal-setting. In terms of the goals' substance, the SDGs integrated the three pillars of sustainable development and are universal for both developed and developing countries. The 17 goals of the SDGs are: no poverty, zero hunger, good health and well-being, quality education, gender equality, clean water and sanitation, affordable and clean energy, decent work and economic growth, industry, innovation and infrastructure, reduced inequalities, sustainable cities and communities, responsible consumption and production, climate action, life below water, life on land, peace, justice, and strong institutions, and partnership for the goals. These goals are divided into 169 measurable targets, themselves measured by 231 indicators in total. Hence, the SDG approach is constructed around three levels of governing through goals.

As to goal formulation, the SDGs emerged from two separate processes at the Rio+20 Summit as the continuation of the Rio Earth Summit and the UN process led by the High-Level Panel of Eminent Persons on the Post-2015 Development Agenda. These processes covered intense multi-stakeholders' consultations from the national to international levels, and they both merged to produce the 2030 Agenda for Sustainable Development and the SDGs. In this sense, the SDGs adopted a more participative goal formulation, which gives it a more solid starting point compared to the MDGs.

In terms of goal implementation, the SDGs also have greater means of implementation as well as review and monitoring mechanisms. The SDGs document has put finance, technology, capacity-building and trade as part of its means of implementation and global partnership as one of its goals. In order to track progress, the SDG framework establishes the High-Level Political Forum as a mechanism for countries to share their voluntary national reports (VNR). The VNRs are presented at the yearly High-level Political Forum on Sustainable Development and 'have the central role in overseeing follow-up and review at the global level' (United Nations, 2015, para. 47). Finally, the SDGs do not replace existing international law commitments and conventions but complement and operationalize these commitments. As such, they are mutually reinforcing.

Despite this improvement in the goal-setting model of sustainable development governance through the SDGs, two challenges remain, resulting from the broad goals and the loose institutional character of the SDGs: goal prioritization and coordination between actors.[1] We delve into these two challenges in the following sections through two case studies of SDG implementation at the regional level, namely in the EU and ASEAN.

2.2 Goal Prioritization

In a context of multiple goals, governing by goal might lead to prioritizing one goal over another. Moreover, the 2030 Agenda document stated that goal implementation needs to consider 'different national realities, capacities, level of development and respecting national policies and priorities' (United Nations, 2015). In practice, goal prioritization is highly likely during translation of the SDGs to the national or institutional context. Following the adoption of the 2030 Agenda for Sustainable Development and the SDGs, states would map compatibility between the SDGs and their existing national development plans or incorporate the SDGs into their upcoming plans. In the former case, states tend to prioritize goals that are aligned with the existing national development plan. In the latter case, states are more likely to incorporate all the SDGs but oftentimes still prioritize some goals over others, considering their unique national contexts and limited resources.

Our case studies on EU and ASEAN member states (MS) demonstrate interesting trends of goal prioritization. Both regions consist of highly diverse states

[1] Full details of the case studies can be found in A. Marx et al. (2021), Case Study on the UN Development Policy, GLOBE Project. https://www.globe-project.eu/case-study-on-the-un-development-policy_11414.pdf; and Marx et al. (2021). The case studies were based on an analysis of primary and secondary sources as well as interviews.

in terms of social, cultural, political, and economic aspects. EU MS, however, are more advanced socially and economically and are more integrated politically compared to ASEAN MS. The EU applies membership criteria, thus MS shares similar political and economic values which may guide their collective approach in responding to the SDGs. Meanwhile, ASEAN membership is open to all Southeast Asian countries.

Our findings, however, demonstrate that goal prioritization occurred in both the EU and ASEAN as can be seen in Figures 14.1 and 14.2. Some countries

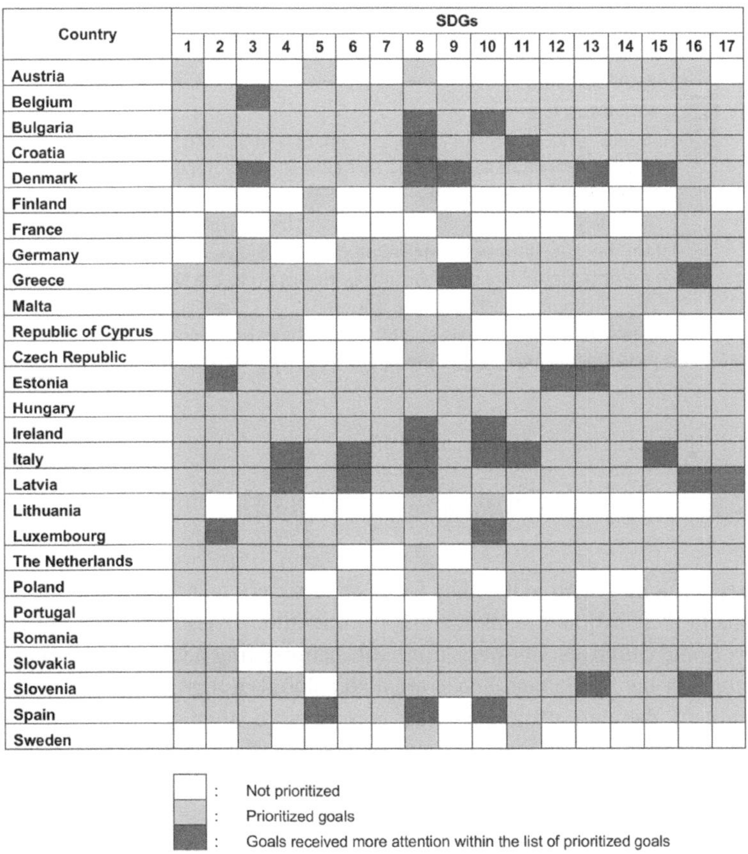

Source: National development plan, VNR, and SDG implementation plan documents of individual countries.

Figure 14.1 Goal prioritization in the EU

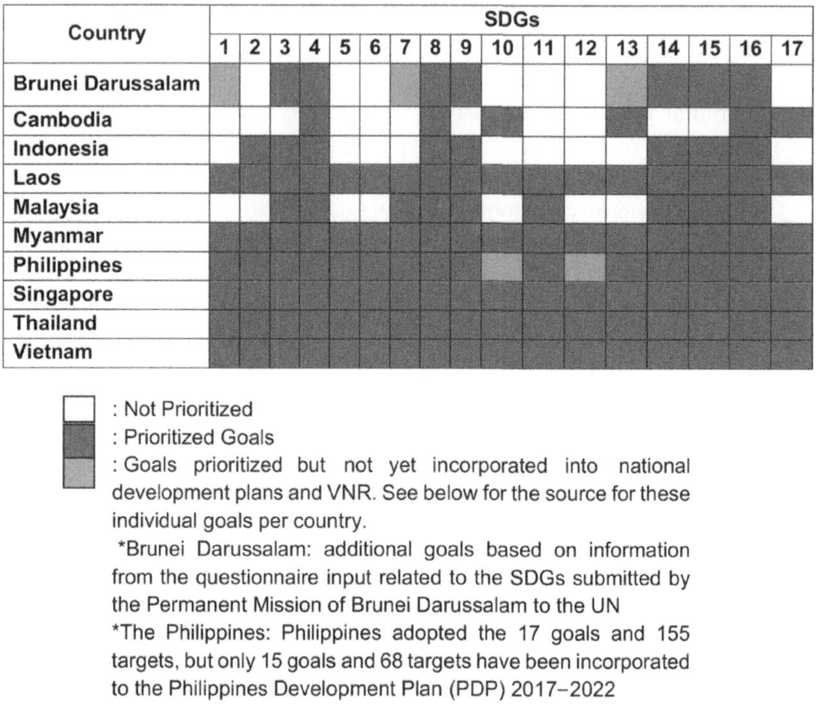

Source: National development plans and VNR.

Figure 14.2 Goal prioritization in Southeast Asia

clearly indicate which SDGs they focus on or simply mention a reference to all SDGs in their national plans without prioritization. These are colored in light gray. Some countries, however, align all their existing national plans with the 17 goals of the SDGs (and hence are also colored in light gray), but from this alignment, there are some goals that receive more attention compared to others, hence they colored in dark gray. For example, the seven thematic priorities in Latvia's Sustainable Development Strategies are aligned with the 17 goals, but goals 4, 6, 8, and 16 are more frequently found across these seven priority areas and are thus colored in dark gray. This finding signals that goal prioritization is a natural tendency resulting from the broad nature of the SDGs. Goal prioritization is still present among EU MS because many SDGs relate to competences on which the EU does not have exclusive power; instead it shares competence with MS or plays only the role of supporting the action of MS.

Meanwhile, the intergovernmental nature of the ASEAN means that MS have full competence in responding to the SDGs with some degree of coordination, as will be discussed later.

Interestingly, despite the differences between the two regions, SDG 8 on Decent Work and Economic Growth ranked number 1 as the most prioritized goal both in the EU and ASEAN. Both regions also share other areas that receive higher prioritization, such as SDG 3 on Good Health and Well-being, SDG 4 on Quality Education, SDG 14 on Life below Water, SDG 15 on Life on Land, and SDG 16 on Peace, Justice, and Strong Institutions. SDG 9 on Industry, Innovation, and Infrastructure is highly prioritized in ASEAN but not in the EU. Similarly, SDG 1 on No Poverty is highly prioritized in the EU but less so in ASEAN. SDG 2 on Zero Hunger and SDG 6 on Clean Water and Sanitation are less prioritized in both regions.

A closer look at the internal dynamics of each region also demonstrates that goal prioritization among MS is not following the line of development divide between old and new MS in both the EU (See Bargaoanu, et al., 2019) and ASEAN. Latvia, Lithuania, and Estonia as neighboring eastern European countries have different goal prioritization on 'People', with Latvia focusing on cultural space, Lithuania focusing on poverty, and Estonia focusing on health. Sweden and Finland as Nordic countries also have different prioritization, on aging society and gender, respectively. In ASEAN, Singapore and Brunei Darussalam, as the most advanced economies and old members of ASEAN, have different goal prioritization, but Singapore shares similar priorities with those of Myanmar and Vietnam. Based on this trend, one might expect new patterns of cooperation among countries with shared goal prioritization. However, goal prioritization may also lead to different progress across the goals particularly when countries prioritize one goal over another not because they are lagging but simply because these areas are important for the development of a country.

2.3 Coordination

The 2030 Agenda document lists policy coherence and coordination as its means of implementation (United Nations, 2015). However, broad goals do not only lead to goal prioritization but also the involvement of many actors to achieve the goals. In the loose institutional arrangement of the goal-setting model, coordination problems are more likely to occur vertically from the global to local level and horizontally among the various actors at the same level. As mentioned in the 2030 Agenda document, these actors include both state and non-state actors at the national, regional, and global level. The success of the SDG goal-setting model, therefore, will rely among other things on its ability to coordinate different actors to maintain policy coherence despite different goal prioritization. Coordination can be facilitated by international organizations, including regional organizations (van Driel, Biermann, Kim, & Vijge, 2022).

In our case studies on the EU and ASEAN, we were able to identify some mechanisms for both horizontal and vertical coordination as well as internal and external coordination in which member states of the EU and ASEAN are active. Vertical coordination refers to actions taken, and mechanisms put in place to align the priorities of different member states of a regional organization with each other and the regional organization itself. Horizontal coordination refers to actions taken on the level of the regional organization to coordinate action on the different priorities that are embedded within the SDGs with the regional organization itself. The degree to which regional organizations can develop horizontal coordination mechanisms will depend on the competences it has in specific policy areas as well as on the level of institutionalization. External coordination refers to actions and mechanisms a regional organization and its members use to coordinate with external factors, such as international organizations or other regional organizations. Internal coordination refers mainly to actions taken within a regional organization to align priorities with the different institutions involved in the regional organizations. The degree to which regional organizations need to develop internal coordination mechanisms will depend on their level of institutionalization. Tables 14.1 and 14.2 detail some of the coordination

Table 14.1 *Types of coordination of the EU on SDGs*

Coordination	Horizontal	Vertical
Internal	Within EU institutions • *Commission's First Vice President lead coordinator on sustainable development* • *Commission's Sustainable Development Project Team* • *Commission's Inter Service Group on the SDGs* • *Council's Working Party on 2030 Agenda*	With EU member states • *European Semester* • *MS VNRs* • *Open Method of Coordination*
External	With external organizations at regional level • *ASEAN* • *African Union*	With external organizations at higher (international): • *UNECE Regional Forum on Sustainable Development*

Source: Author's own compilation.

Table 14.2 Types of coordination of ASEAN on SDGs

Coordination	Horizontal	Vertical
Internal	Within ASEAN institutions • *ASEAN Secretariat Poverty Eradication and Gender Division as SDG coordinator* • *Joint Consultative Meetings of ASEAN Coordination Council*	With ASEAN member states • *AFSNDPA*
External	With external organizations at regional level • *European Union*	With external organizations at higher (international) level • *HLBD* • *ASEAN-UN comprehensive partnership* • *UN ESCAP Asia-Pacific Regional Coordination Mechanism* • *UN ESCAP Asia Pacific Forum on Sustainable Development*

Source: Author's own compilation.

mechanisms that were set in place by EU and ASEAN as well as mechanisms put in place within the UN system, such as the UN Economic Commission for Europe (UNECE) and the UN Economic and Social Commission for Asia and the Pacific (UN ESCAP), respectively (for more details see Marx et al., 2021).

Despite these coordination mechanisms, however, our case studies also found that there are several problems in coordinating various actors, particularly states with different goal prioritization. First, internal horizontal coordination is problematic in ASEAN due to its pillar-based structure, which is no longer present in the EU. So far, ASEAN deals with this problem through the ASEAN Coordinating Council along with its Joint Consultative Meeting.

Second, external horizontal coordination problems are apparent in ASEAN. The EU's closer integration and supranational authority allow the EU to take a central role in the regional governance of SDGs, thereby streamlining communication and cooperation with UN agencies and other external development organizations through a smaller number of authoritative contact points. On the other hand, ASEAN, as an intergovernmental body with fewer competences and resources, cannot function in the same way to speak on behalf of its member states in cooperation with external agencies. While ASEAN has the High-Level Brainstorming Dialogue (HLBD) to coordinate the ASEAN

Community Vision and the UN SDGs as well as the ASEAN Forum on SDGs with National Development Planning Agencies (AFSNDPA) to coordinate the SDGs with MS, the majority of developing Southeast Asian countries have also worked bilaterally with various other UN agencies and investors in various development sectors. The HLBD itself involves a large and diverse group of participants, including ASEAN, UN ESCAP, the United Nations Development Programme (UNDP), the Asian Development Bank, World Bank, the EU, Switzerland and many others. Moreover, the presence of other forums for coordinating SDG governance in the region, such as the ASEAN-China-UNDP Symposium and the UN ESCAP's Southeast Asia Multi-Stakeholder Forum on Implementation of the SDGs, also create possibilities of redundancy and overlap. Therefore, the horizontal coordination of the SDGs implementation in the ASEAN region is complicated by crisscrossing partnerships and many points of contact. Additionally, coordination at the regional level through the HLBD faces challenges due to the broadness of issue areas covered within the forum, including the complementarity between the SDGs and the ASEAN Community Vision; support for the implementation of the SDGs in MS; coordination among dialogue partners, the UN system, and development banks; and monitoring the SDGs' progress. The broad coverage and participation in the HLBD can result in limited time for meaningful dialogue among participants, thereby also limiting the forum's capacity to achieve expected outcomes.

Finally, in relation to vertical coordination, problems emerge in both the EU and ASEAN. Despite the EU playing a more central role, a significant number of SDGs fall under so-called shared or supporting competence, meaning that the degree of vertical coordination relies on the position of EU MS towards the EU to take up a coordinating role. Based on VNRs of the 27 MS, the vast majority of EU MS made explicit reference to EU cooperation and coordination, but there is significant variation on how this is done. First, there are some EU MS which only sporadically refer to the EU while other EU MS emphasize the important role the EU plays or can play. Second, some EU MS only refer to EU cooperation in the field of external relations and most notably development cooperation, while others also focus on the internal dimension and the importance of the SDGs to achieve sustainability internally in the EU through, for example, environmental policy.

In order to analyze this trend further, we assess the quantity of references to cooperation with the EU and ASEAN, and the quality of these references in MS VNRs. The quantity of references depends on the number of times a MS VNR refers to the EU/ASEAN broadly defined. For example, some EU MS, such as Luxembourg, only refer once to the EU, while other countries, such as Cyprus, mention the EU more than 100 times (Government of the Grand Duchy of Luxembourg, 2017; Ministry of Foreign Affairs of the Republic of Cyprus, 2017). Up to five references qualify as *few*, more than five qualify as *many*. To assess the quality of reference to EU cooperation, the focus lies on the relevance of these references. EU MS that mention EU cooperation only as a side note, for instance while providing nationally implemented EU projects as an attest to their SDG efforts or the use of EU statistics to compare their own progress, fall under the *superficial* category. On the other hand, EU MS who see the EU as a pillar of their SDG implementation efforts, for example through explicit statements on cooperation with and within the EU or their efforts to include the 2030 Agenda in EU policy, are coded as having *strong* commitments to the EU. Generally, more weight is given to such statements in the first chapter(s) of the VNRs, where countries elaborate on their general approach towards the SDGs, rather than the later ones, where countries go into more technical detail on each SDG. From this, we distill four trends of vertical coordination between the EU and EU MS: *few-superficial* (strongly EU MS focused), *many-superficial*, *few-strong* and *many-strong* (strongly EU focused) as can be seen in Figure 14.3.

Using the same method, Southeast Asian countries also demonstrate different degrees of quantity and quality of reference to cooperation with ASEAN in their VNRs as can be seen in Figure 14.4. Indonesia, Malaysia, and Cambodia have the fewest references to ASEAN in their VNRs. Meanwhile, Brunei Darussalam has the most references to ASEAN, demonstrating the active participation of Brunei in ASEAN and the importance of ASEAN in Brunei's

		Quantity	
		Few	***Many***
Quality	***Superficial***	Bulgaria, Czechia, France, Hungary, Ireland, Lithuania, Luxembourg, Poland, Slovakia	Belgium, Croatia, Cyprus, Greece, Italy, Netherlands, Slovenia
	Strong	Estonia, Finland, Malta, Spain	Austria, Denmark, Germany, Latvia, Portugal, Romania, Sweden

Source: Author's own compilation.

Figure 14.3 *Overview of different types of EU MS in relation to cooperation with the EU*

		Quantity	
		Few	***Many***
Quality	***Superficial***	Indonesia Malaysia Vietnam Cambodia	Laos
	Strong	The Philippines	Brunei Darussalam Thailand Singapore

Source: Author's own compilation.

Figure 14.4 Different Types of ASEAN MS in relation to cooperation with ASEAN

implementation of the SDGs. Both Thailand and Singapore also have many references to ASEAN, especially when they held ASEAN chairmanship. Meanwhile, no data is available for Myanmar as the country has not presented a VNR up to now.

This differing attitude among MS towards their main regional organizations in the implementation of the SDGs deserves close attention as these organizations are assets to help coordinate the different goal prioritizations among members to ensure policy coherence of the SDGs in this goal-setting model. The different attitudes towards these organizations, however, indicate that MS coordinate their SDG implementation to different degrees at the regional level and that these organizations have not performed sufficiently as coordinators of the SDGs in the regions. This is even more important because the EU and ASEAN are the most advanced regional organizations, thus raising questions about the role of the rest of the regional organizations as coordinators in the goal-setting model of the SDGs.

3. CONCLUSION

Goal-setting global governance offers the potential to address sustainable development challenges that are multi-faceted and broad-ranging. However, this chapter also identifies some challenges with regard to goal-setting global governance.

First, due to the fact that goal-setting tends to include a wide range of global goals, it generates incentives for 'goal-shopping'. This is the root institutional problem that leads to goal prioritization resulting in some goals being more important for some actors compared to others. Goal prioritization can be considered the practice of cherry-picking some goals over others from the agreed global goals. Goal prioritization can be driven by several factors (Forestier & Kim, 2020). First, actors might have a limited budget to implement all goals. Second, some actors might see some goals as being irrelevant in their context. Third, actors might prioritize goals to attract foreign investment and aid.

Second, goal-setting global governance is confronted with a series of different coordination problems. The participation of many actors is a challenge in terms of coordinating diverse actors in the goal-setting model. In the chapter, we identified the different mechanisms developed to facilitate horizontal, vertical, external, and internal coordination. However, our case studies also identify several challenges related to each of these forms of coordination, showing their limited ability to address coherence problems related to achieving the SDGs.

In 2030, we will be able to assess the contribution that goal-setting global governance can make. However, the issues related to goal prioritization as well as coordination highlight the challenges with which global goal-setting governance is confronted and raise some concerns about the effectiveness of this form of global governance.

REFERENCES

Bandari, R., Moallemi, E., Lester, R., Downie, D., & Bryan, B. (2021). Prioritising Sustainable Development Goals, Characterising Interactions, and Identifying Solutions for Local Sustainability. *Environmental Science & Policy, 127*(3), 325–336.

Bargaoanu, A., Buturoiu, R., & Durach, F. (2019). The East-West Divide in the European Union: A Development Divide Reframed as A Political One. In P. Dobrescu, *Development in Turbulent Times* (pp. 26–31). Springer.

Biermann, F., Kanie, N., & Kim, R. (2017). Global Governance by Goal-setting: The Novel Approach of the UN Sustainable Development Goals. *Current Opinion in Environmental Sustainability*, Vol. *26–27*, 26–31.

Brunnee, J., & Parson, E. (1993). Assessing UNCED and the State of Sustainable Development. *Proceedings of the Annual Meeting (American Society of International Law), 87*, 508–513.

Checkel, J. T. (1998, January). The Constructivist Turn in International Relations Theory. *World Politics, 50*, 324–348.

Domínguez, R., & Flores, R. (2018, July 30). *Global Governance.* Retrieved March 2023, from Oxford Research Encyclopedia of International Studies https://oxfordre.com/internationalstudies/view/10.1093/acrefore/9780190846626.001.0001/acrefore-9780190846626-e-508.

European Commission. (n.d.). *About the European Commission.* Retrieved October 27, 2020, from https://ec.europa.eu/info/about-european-commission_en.

European Council. (n.d.). *The European Council.* Retrieved October 27, 2020, from https://www.consilium.europa.eu/en/european-council/.

European Parliament. (n.d.). *European Parliament – Powers and Procedures*. Retrieved October 27, 2020, from https://europarl.europa.eu/about-parliament/en/powers-and-procedures.

European Union. (2007). Treaty of Lisbon Amending the Treaty on European Union and the Treaty Establishing the European Community, Signed at Lisbon, 13 December 2007. *Official Journal of the European Union 2007/C 306/01*. https://eur-lex.europa.eu/legal-content/EN/ALL/?uri=OJ:C:2007:306:TOC.

Eurostat. (2020). *Sustainable Development Goals – Overview*. Retrieved September 26, 2020, from https://ec.europa.eu/eurostat/web/sdi/overview.

Finnemore, M., & Sikkink, K. (1998). International Norm Dynamics and Political Change. *International Organization*, *52*(4), 887–917.

Forestier, O., & Kim, R. (2020). Cherry-picking the Sustainable Development Goals: Goal Prioritization by National Governments and Implications for Global Governance. *Sustainable Development*, *28*, 1269–1278.

Fukuda-Parr, S. (2013). *Global Development Goal Setting as a Tool For Global Governance: Intended and Unintended Consequences*. Retrieved February 2022, from Working Paper No. 108, International Policy Centre for Inclusive Growth (IPC-IG), Brasilia. https://www.econstor.eu/bitstream/10419/71796/1/741212625.pdf.

Government of the Grand Duchy of Luxembourg. (2017, July). *Rapport sur la mise en œuvre de l'Agenda 2030 au et par le Luxembourg*. Retrieved from Sustainable Development Knowledge Platform. https://sustainabledevelopment.un.org/content/documents/15709Luxembourg.pdf.

Heras-Saizarbitoria, I., Urbieta, L., & Boiral, O. (2021). Organizations' Engagement with Sustainable Development Goals: From Cherry-picking to SDG-washing? *Corporate Social Responsibility and Environmental Management*, *29*, 316–318.

Kanie, N., Bernstein, S., Biermann, F., & Haas, P. (2017). Introduction: Global Governance Through Goal Setting. In N. Kanie & F. Biermann, *Governing through Goals: Sustainable Development Goals as Governance Innovation* (pp. 1–28). The MIT Press.

Kanie, N., Griggs, D., Young, O., et al. (2019). Rules to Goals: Emergence of New Governance Strategies for Sustainable Development. *Sustainability Science*, *14*, 1745–1749.

Keck, E. M., & Sikkink, K. (1998). *Activists Beyond Borders: Advocacy Networks in International Politics*. Cornell University Press.

Latham, G., Ganegoda, D., & Locke, E. (2011). Goal Setting: A State Theory, but Related to Traits. In T. Chamorro-Premusiz, S. von Stumm, & A. Furnham, *The Wiley-Blackwell Handbook of Individual Differences* (1st Edition) (pp. 579–587). Blackwell Publishing.

Latham, G. P., & Locke, E. (1979, Autumn). Goal Setting – A Motivational Technique That Works. *Organizational Dynamics*, *8*(2), 68–80.

Latham, G., & Locke, E. (1991). Self-Regulation through Goal Setting. *Organizational Behavior and Human Decision Processes*, *50*, 212–247.

Locke, E., & Latham, G. (2019). The Development of Goal Setting Theory: A Half Century Retrospective. *Motivation Science*, *5*(2), 93–105.

Marx, A., Pertiwi, B., Depoorter, C., Hoornick, M., Mursitama, T., Otteburn, K., & Arnakim, L. (2021). What Role for Regional Organizations in Goal-Setting Global Governance? An Analysis of the Role of the European Union and ASEAN in the Sustainable Development Goals. *Global Public Policy and Governance*, *1*, 421–445.

Meadows, D. H., Meadows, D. L., Randers, J., and Behrens, W. W. (1972). *The Limits to Growth: A Report for the Club of Rome's Project on the Predicament of Mankind*. Universe Books.
Meuleman, L. (2008). *Public Management and the Metagovernance of Hierarchies, Networks, and Markets: The Feasibility of Designing and Managing Governance Style Combination*. Physica-Verlag.
Meuleman, L. (2019). *Metagovernance for Sustainability: A Framework for Implementing the Sustainable Development Goals*. Routledge.
Ministry of Foreign Affairs of the Republic of Cyprus. (2017). *Review on the Implementation of the 2030 Agenda in Cyprus*. Retrieved from Sustainable Development Knowledge Platform. https://sustainabledevelopment.un.org/content/documents/15886Cyprus.pdf.
Monkelbaan, J. (2019). *Governance for the Sustainable Development Goals: Exploring an Integrative Framework of Theories, Tools, and Competencies*. Springer.
Moravcsik, A. (1993). Preferences and Power in the European Community: A Liberal Intergovernmentalist Approach. *Journal of Common Market Studies, 31*(4), 473–524.
Moravscik, A. (1995). Liberal Intergovernmentalism and Integration: A Rejoinder. *Journal of Common Market Studies, 33*(4), 611–628.
Onuf, N. (1979). International Legal Order As An Idea. *American Journal of International Law, 73*(2), 244–266.
Palmer, G. (1992). The Earth Summit: What Went Wrong at Rio? *Washington University Law Review, 70*(4), 1005–1028.
Pineda, A., Cano, J., & Czerny, M. (2021). Governance Approach to the Prioritization of Sustainable Development Goals in the City of Medellin (Colombia). *urbe. Revista Brasileira de Gestão Urbana, 13*, 1–16.
Risse, T. (2012). Governance In Areas of Limited Statehood. In D. Levi-Faur (Ed.), *Oxford Handbook of Governance* (pp. 716–729). Oxford University Press.
Sabel, C. F., & Zeitlin, J. (Eds.). (2010). *Experimentalist Governance in the European Union: Towards a New Architecture*. Oxford University Press.
Sabel, C. F., & Zeitlin J. (2012). Experimentalist Governance. In D. Levi-Faur (Ed.), *Oxford Handbook of Governance* (pp. 169–184). Oxford University Press.
Tremblay, D., Gowsy, S., Riffon, O., Boucher, J. F., Dubé, S., & Villeneuve, C. (2021). A Systemic Approach for Sustainability Implementation Planning at the Local Level by SDG Target Prioritization: The Case of Quebec City. *Sustainability, 13*(5), 2520.
United Nations. (2015). *Transforming Our World: The 2030 Agenda for Sustainable Development*. Retrieved from Sustainable Development – Department of Economic and Social Affairs. https://sdgs.un.org/2030agenda.
van Driel, M., Biermann, F., Kim, R., & Vijge, M. (2022). Cherry-picking the Sustainable Development Goals: Goal Prioritization By National Governments and Implications for Global Governance. *Global Policy, 13*, 669–682.
Wendt, A. (1992). Anarchy is What States Make of It: The Social Construction of Power Politics. *International Organization, 46*(2), 391–425.
World Commission on the Environment and Development (WCED). (1987). *Our Common Future (Brundtland Report)*. United Nations. https://sustainabledevelopment.un.org/content/documents/5987our-common-future.pdf.
Young, O. R. (2017). Conceptualization: Goal Setting as a Strategy for Earth System Governance. In N. Kanie & F. Biermann, *Governing through Goals: Sustainable Development Goals As Governance Innovation* (pp. 31–51). The MIT Press.
Zürn, M. (2018). *A Theory of Global Governance: Authority, Legitimacy, and Contestation*. Oxford University Press.

15. Orchestration in global governance: the Global Compacts on migration and refugees

Andrea C. Bianculli, Miriam Bradley, Robert Kissack and Juan Carlos Triviño-Salazar

1. INTRODUCTION

Recent years have seen some developments in global migration governance, notably the incorporation of the International Organization for Migration (IOM) as a UN-related agency in 2016 and the adoption by UN member states in December 2018 of a Global Compact on Refugees (GCR) and a Global Compact for Safe, Orderly and Regular Migration (GCM). These developments can be understood as efforts to institutionalise the global governance of migration, with the migration regime complex long considered to be 'fragmented' (Kainz & Betts, 2021, p. 66). The refugee regime is well institutionalised, with a central authority—the Office of the United Nations High Commissioner for Refugees (UNHCR), established in 1950 and mandated to negotiate international protection and solutions for refugees—and a hard law framework for refugee protection, the core of which is the 1951 Convention relating to the Status of Refugees and its 1967 Protocol. However, the refugee regime is only one element of the wider migration regime complex, and the global governance of migration more generally has historically lacked a central authority and normative framework.

The IOM, the only intergovernmental organisation dedicated to migration in general, has not fulfilled the role of a central authority in migration governance. In part, this is because, when it was created in 1951, the IOM was deliberately established outside the UN system in order to exclude communist countries from membership (Bradley, 2020, p. 5). Perhaps more importantly, however, the IOM has never had any explicit mandate for the protection of migrant rights, and initially undertook limited and largely logistical operations (Bradley, 2020, pp. 20–21; Pécoud, 2020, pp. 4, 12–13). A number of other UN programmes and specialised agencies are substantially involved in migration issues—for example, the International Labour Organization (ILO) works to promote the rights of migrant workers, and UNHCR has a mandate for refugee protection—but none is dedicated to migration as a whole.

Just as a range of different UN agencies are involved in migration-related issues, a range of different legal and normative frameworks have a bearing on migration, and there exists 'a patchwork of unilateral, bilateral and regional policies' (Newland, 2019a, p. 8). However, there is no comprehensive legal framework concerning migrants' rights. International refugee law is well developed, and the principles of asylum and *non-refoulement* are well institutionalised, but these apply only to those who are expected to face persecution or danger were they to be returned to their countries of origin. With respect to migrants who do not qualify as refugees, there is no body of international migration law as such, but rights and obligations salient to particular groups or categories of migrants can be found across different international legal frameworks. The International Convention on the Protection of the Rights of All Migrant Workers and Members of Their Families, which came into force in 2003, details an extensive range of civil and political as well as economic and social rights that are relevant to migrant workers and their families in countries of transit and employment, but this applies to only a small subset of migrants worldwide and has not been widely ratified (Bradley, 2020, p. 5; Desmond, 2015). While not legally binding, the GCR seeks to extend cooperation on refugee protection and solutions, and the GCM 'is the first comprehensive framework of principles and objectives to guide international cooperation on migration that has been formally negotiated and adopted by states' (Newland, 2019a, p. 1).

This chapter asks two questions. First, how far have the incorporation of the IOM into the UN system, and the adoption by UN member states of the two Global Compacts, served to reshape global migration governance? We argue that the incorporation of the IOM into the UN system has the potential to increase hierarchy in global migration governance, but to date has had limited practical impact. This is in part due to the nature of the IOM's mandate and the conditions under which it was made a UN-related agency, and in part because the majority of its work concerns displaced persons and emergency response, for which UNHCR already had a clear mandate and central role. With respect to the negotiation and adoption of the Global Compacts, we find some elements of orchestration identifiable during drafting and implementation and—to some degree—reduced normative ambiguity in the governance of refugees and other migrants.

Second, we ask how these shifts at the global level have impacted regional migration governance in Latin America. The role and experience of Latin America in the governance of migration are understudied and yet can offer unique insights. Latin American states have for many years taken a 'liberal' stance in managing migration and refugees, and the region has in many ways been a leader in migration and refugee governance (Doña Reveco & Finn, 2021; Hammoud-Gallego & Freier, 2022). Following the Central American crises of the 1970s and early 1980s, for example, states in Latin America agreed to the 1984 Cartagena Declaration on Refugees, with an expanded refugee definition that went beyond that of the 1951 Convention and 1967 Protocol, extending protection not only to those fleeing persecution but also to those fleeing insecurity associated with armed conflict and generalised violence. In 2002, the Agreement on Residence for Citizens of the States Parties of MERCOSUR and Associated States was launched, paving the way for freedom of movement and residence within much of South America.[1] In our two Latin American cases, we found that these developments in global migration governance have had only limited impact for two main reasons. First, the GCR does not go much beyond the pre-existing hard law framework, and several powerful states, including the US, either refused to support the GCM or subsequently backtracked from it, likely weakening its influence globally. Second, the governance of refugees and migration in Latin America anyway often went beyond the commitments set out in the two Global Compacts, such that their influence would likely be limited to reinforcing rather than transforming the work of regional governance mechanisms.

The chapter continues in four parts. The first presents an overview of the IOM outside and later inside the UN system, and of the preparation and substance of the two Global Compacts. The second and third parts examine how these developments in global migration governance have impacted on the regional governance of migration in Mexico and Central America, and in South America. This involved a multi-method data collection strategy, including desk research as well as five semi-structured interviews with academics, experts and policy officers involved in regional processes and organisations in Latin America, and with first-hand knowledge of migration and refugee protection in the region. Finally, the fourth part of the chapter provides a conclusion.

2. DEVELOPMENTS IN GLOBAL MIGATION GOVERNANCE

In just nine months from July 2015 to March 2016, over one million refugees and other migrants arrived in Europe by sea, mainly via the Eastern Mediterranean route to Greece but also via the Central Mediterranean route to

---

[1] See Agreement on Residency for Nationals of Mercosur Member States, Bolivia, and Chile (MERCOSUR/RMI/CT/ACTA No. 04/02).

Italy and—to a much lesser extent—the Western Mediterranean route to Spain (Borton & Collinson, 2017, pp. 1, 3). The number of migrant arrivals would not have been considered exceptionally high in some other regions of the world, either in absolute terms or relative to the size of host populations but was unprecedented in Europe. What quickly came to be referred to as a 'migrant crisis' or 'refugee crisis' caused an enormous amount of friction among the member states of the European Union (EU) regarding who should shoulder responsibility for receiving and hosting these people from their initial entry points in, inter alia, Greece and Italy. The number of asylum claims 'uncovered persistent dysfunctionalities and shortcomings in the Common European Asylum System (CEAS)', and the 'so-called European "refugee" crisis should therefore more accurately be termed a crisis of the CEAS' (Niemann & Zaun, 2018, p. 1).

European states called for action at the international level, and the UN General Assembly convened a high-level meeting on large mixed migration flows in September 2016. As such, this initiative was originally driven by top-down decisions by states rather than bottom-up adaptation (Eilstrup-Sangiovanni, 2022). The main outcomes of the meeting were the formal incorporation of the IOM into the UN system as a 'related organisation', and agreement on the New York Declaration for Refugees and Migrants. The New York Declaration went beyond the issues raised in the Mediterranean, ultimately leading to the GCR and the GCM, which the General Assembly adopted in December 2018. In this section, we trace these developments and argue that they are not as consequential as they may initially appear and have not served to transform the migration regime complex in truly significant ways.

2.1 Incorporating the IOM into the UN System

During the Cold War, 'migration was considered too contentious for general debate in the United Nations' (Newland, 2019a, p. 8). Although a number of UN agencies and programmes—including UNHCR, the ILO, the Office of the High Commissioner for Human Rights, the UN Development Programme, and UNICEF—had significant roles in migration, the UN lacked a migration agency. The IOM, the only intergovernmental organisation dedicated to migration, was not widely seen as a central authority on migration because it was founded outside of the UN system, lacked any normative mandate, and had a chaotic history and only a relatively small number of member states (Bradley, 2020, pp. 20–21; Pécoud, 2020, p. 2). In 1951, the US Congress stipulated that US funding could not go to any international organisation that counted communist-controlled or communist-dominated countries among its membership

(Bradley, 2020, p. 5). This precluded a strong operational role for the UNHCR and meant the IOM[2] was set up outside the UN system.

Almost from its inception, however, the IOM has had significant interactions—at times more competitive and at times more cooperative—with the UN, especially UNHCR (Bradley, 2020, pp. 100–101). The IOM worked closely with the UN on different projects, starting with the establishment of a joint Provisional Intergovernmental Committee for the Movement of Migrants from Europe (PICMME)-UNHCR office in Hong Kong in 1952, which was tasked with resettling refugees of European descent and operated until 1973 (Bradley, 2020, p. 102). The IOM continued to collaborate with the UNHCR, particularly in the area of refugee returns, though there have also been frequent tensions in their relationship (Bradley, 2020, p. 101; 2021, p. 255). Cooperation between the IOM and the UN intensified from the early 1990s, largely through the IOM's increased integration into the UN humanitarian system. In 1992, the IOM was granted observer status at the UN General Assembly, and when the Inter-Agency Standing Committee (IASC)—the main coordination platform for international humanitarian agencies—was established that same year, the IOM was a standing invitee from the outset (Bradley, 2020, p. 102). In 1993, the UN General Assembly extended the scope of the UN Central Emergency Response Fund (CERF)—which collects contributions mostly from governments, and to which operational humanitarian agencies can apply to finance emergency response—to include the IOM (Bradley, 2020, p. 102).

The IOM has generally been viewed as a 'service provider', more akin to a private firm than an international organisation (Betts, 2011, p. 13; Pécoud, 2020, pp. 10–11). This is attributed both to its lack of a mandate to protect migrants and their rights, and to its project-based funding model, according to which donors retain an unusual level of control over what their funds are spent on—and hence what the IOM can do (Bradley, 2020, p. 39; Pécoud, 2020, pp. 12–13). Initially focused on facilitating the out-migration of Europeans displaced by World War II to other regions of the world, the IOM's first task was to provide logistical support for transporting migrants, earning itself a reputation as a 'travel agency' (Bradley, 2020, p. 19; Pécoud, 2020, p. 4). In the early years of the Cold War, the IOM's role progressively expanded to encompass such activities as recruiting migrants, examining their health conditions, and facilitating their integration in receiving countries (Pécoud, 2020, pp. 4–5). Its position outside of the UN system was seen by many, including some member

[2] The IOM was created in 1951 as the Provisional Intergovernmental Committee for the Movement of Migrants from Europe (PICMME). PICMME became the Intergovernmental Committee for European Migration (ICEM) in 1952, was rebranded as the Intergovernmental Committee for Migration in 1980, and became the IOM in 1989 (Bradley, 2020, p. 4).

and donor states, as allowing the IOM to ignore protection concerns, human rights, and humanitarian principles when convenient, increasing its flexibility and usefulness to the states that bought its services (Bradley, 2020, p. 22; 2021).

In the space of 10 months between November 2015 and September 2016, the process of incorporating the IOM into the UN system was completed, and the IOM officially became a UN 'related organisation'.[3] While this fell short of the specialised agency status that the IOM administration had long favoured, the organisation embraced its new status, enthusiastically rebranding itself as the 'UN Migration Agency' (Bradley, 2020, pp. 104–110). Nonetheless, the IOM is not the undisputed lead in all matters of UN migration governance. The IOM sought, but was not granted, the secretariat role for the intergovernmental conference for the GCM (Micinski, 2021, p. 66). In 2018, the UN Secretary-General replaced the Global Migration Group (GMG) with a UN Migration Network, and the IOM pushed hard—and this time successfully—to be appointed as the Network coordinator (Micinski, 2021, p. 73; Newland, 2019a, p. 9). However, it is unclear how far its incorporation into the UN system has served to reshape either the IOM itself or the nature of hierarchy and fragmentation in global migration governance more broadly.

The IOM in 2022 is a very different organisation from that created in 1951, and with a very different role with respect to the UN and the governance of migration. Between 1991 and 2018 alone, the IOM's budget increased from around USD 300 million to USD 1.8 billion, and the number of member states grew from 43 to 172 (Pécoud, 2020, p. 3). Far from being a mere 'travel agency', the IOM is now a major player in refugee and emergency response worldwide, and internally displaced persons (IDPs)—by most definitions, a distinct category from migrants because they have not crossed an international border—are now its largest beneficiary group (Bradley, 2021, p. 254). It is a central actor in the UN-led humanitarian system, among other things as co-leader (with UNHCR) of the global Camp Coordination and Camp Management cluster.

Most of these changes predate the IOM's incorporation into the UN system, and rather than being a consequence of its change in status, they were conditions necessary to bring about that change. By the time of its incorporation into the UN system, member states and IOM staff had already come to see the organisation as bound by humanitarian principles and obligated to protect and promote human rights (Bradley, 2020, p. 22). It is difficult to believe the

[3] IOM Council Resolution 1309 (24/11/2015) began the process, and UNGA resolution A/70/263 (27/4/2015) instructed the United Nations Secretary-General to open negotiations with the IOM. On 30 June 2016, a draft agreement was accepted by the IOM, and the United Nations General Assembly accepted the agreement in Resolution A/70/976 (25/7/2016).

IOM would have been so easily accepted into the UN system if it were not already operating in accordance with UN human rights frameworks. 'IOM staff already worked under UN salary scales, pension schemes, security systems, and the UN Staff Rules and Regulations; IOM had memorandums of understanding and cooperation agreements with dozens of UN bodies, was a de facto member of many UN humanitarian country teams, and accessed various UN funding mechanisms' (Bradley, 2021, p. 255). In many respects, then, the IOM was functioning as part of the UN system even prior to its incorporation in 2016—and the changes it had made to function this way can be seen as part of a process of bottom-up 'cooperative adaptation' (Eilstrup-Sangiovanni, 2022, p. 303).

Furthermore, the stipulations attached to the IOM being made a UN-related organisation limit its scope for change in a number of important ways—notably in identifying the IOM as an explicitly 'non-normative international organisation' and specifying that its funding arrangements would not be altered through its closer relationship with the UN, effectively 'baking in' the projectisation model (Bradley, 2020, p. 39; Micinski, 2021, p. 38). While 'non-normative' is not defined, the senior IOM officials and member state representatives responsible for negotiating the IOM's incorporation into the UN system appear to have meant that the IOM should not become a venue for setting binding standards (Bradley, 2020, p. 23). As such, it is not clear that the IOM has either the mandate or the resources necessary to become an effective actor or central authority in the governance of migration (Newland, 2019a, p. 9).

2.2 The Global Compacts

The final texts of the Compacts were arrived at through two quite different drafting processes. The UNHCR led consultations for the GCR in a cautious effort to prevent backsliding over existing binding refugee protection norms. By contrast, the GCM was drafted through a broader consultation process, including thematic workshops of civil society, experts and states, regional consultation through the UN regional secretariat, and traditional intergovernmental bargaining after the preparation of the zero-draft text. The Global Compacts are soft law frameworks, and they do not impose any new binding obligations on states. Rather, they draw on existing hard law to bring together relevant binding obligations from a range of different sources, and they additionally establish new non-binding commitments. They set out general plans for international cooperation on a range of issues relating to population movements, refugees and other migrants.

Both Compacts exhibit some elements of orchestration, the GCM primarily in the drafting process and the GCR primarily in the terms of the framework and solutions it promotes for refugee response. Orchestration occurs when an international organisation mobilises private actors—including private firms and NGOs—on a voluntary basis in pursuit of shared governance goals (Abbott & Snidal, 2010; Abbott et al., 2016). For both Compacts, hundreds of civil society groups participated in the consultation and stocktaking phases, but the final texts were agreed through intergovernmental negotiations that excluded private actors (Micinski, 2021, p. 73), thus returning to an International Old Governance approach (Abbott & Snidal, 2010, p. 316). The drafting process of the GCM was designed in three phases to provide numerous opportunities for NGOs, experts and practitioners to voice their concerns and suggestions regarding the core issues of international migration, covering thematic, regional and multi-stakeholder dimensions. This resulted in an initial text that was expansive and supported many initiatives favoured by sending and transit states, but over six rounds of negotiations many of these were diluted or removed. 'States are also the ultimate controllers of IOs, and resist orchestration by their own "agents"' (Abbott & Snidal, 2010, p. 326). The implementation of the GCM encourages states to create more accessible pathways for safe and regular migration, with suggestions of how to achieve this, including skills matching initiatives in which employers would sponsor migrants with the required skills, and private sponsorship initiatives (which in many countries involve sponsorship by churches or other faith-based groups) through which vulnerable migrants who do not qualify for asylum could obtain visas (Micinski, 2021, p. 103).

Orchestration also characterised the drafting process for the GCR, with over 400 civil society organisations participating in UNHCR's annual NGO consultation in June 2017 and 2018, although many of their briefs and recommendations did not make it into the final draft (Micinski, 2021, pp. 74–75). Moreover, the GCR envisaged orchestration as a central element of responses to large-scale refugee movements. The Comprehensive Refugee Response Framework (CRRF), which was originally published as an annex to the 2016 New York Declaration, was included without revision as an integral part of the GCR. The CRRF is intended to provide a generic framework or template which can be applied in concrete situations of large-scale movements of refugees. The UNHCR is expected to develop and initiate a CRRF in each such situation, in close coordination with relevant states, with the goal of facilitating international cooperation and burden- and responsibility-sharing. Each application of the CRRF in practice is intended to include multiple stakeholders—including the private sector, faith-based groups, and development and humanitarian actors.

The two Compacts serve to bundle and reaffirm a range of existing rights of refugees and other migrants, and to map a path for future global migration governance (Micinski, 2021, pp. 14–16). In compiling and consolidating rights, norms and values, the GCM in particular has the potential to reduce ambiguity and increase legitimacy within the migration governance regime. The GCM is also innovative in terms of considering the migration process in its entirety and seeking to represent the interests of all three categories of states involved in global migration: sending, transit and receiving (Newland, 2019a, p. 3). Newland identifies the three important roles of the GCM to be 'reducing the negative factors that compel people to leave their homes; amplifying the benefits of migration; and bringing order to the migration process through a better understanding of how migration works, more effective policies, and greater international cooperation' (Newland, 2019b, p. 11). An important contribution of the GCR is to extend the scope of some of the basic norms of refugee protection to individuals who qualify as Convention Refugees but are in a country that is not a party to the 1951 Convention or the 1967 Additional Protocol. In some cases, non-party states have actively engaged in normative interpretation, participated in UNHCR's Executive Committee, and mirrored international norms in domestic law, and it is possible that the GCR will create an additional nodal point to connect major refugee-hosting states to the international refugee protection regime (Gammeltoft-Hansen, 2018, p. 607).

Notwithstanding these contributions, we argue that the Compacts have two major sets of limitations—relating to the substance of the commitments on the one hand, and to the scope and strength of their likely influence on the other. With respect to the substance, the Compacts fail to extend—or even to reaffirm and reinforce—some of the most fundamental existing rights of refugees and other migrants.

The two Compacts fall short of reaffirming the pre-existing binding commitments of states, but they nonetheless compile a number of important commitments. The question remains of how far those important commitments will serve to shape state behaviours. While they are not legally binding, it is hoped that peer pressure and state self-interest will serve to encourage, if not enforce, implementation of the Compacts (Newland, 2019a, p. 6). However, between the negotiations and the adoption of the Compacts, in late 2018 there was a populist backlash against the GCM in particular, with the consequence that several states that had been involved in the negotiations backtracked and withdrew their support (Micinski, 2021, p. 66). The US under Trump refused even to be involved in the negotiation of the GCM, and several other countries, including Austria—then holding the presidency of the EU—eventually refused to endorse the final text (Newland, 2019a, pp. 4–5). The GCM was adopted by the General Assembly in December 2018, with 152 votes in favour, 5 against (Czech Republic, Hungary, Israel, Poland, and the US) and 12 abstentions, including Australia, which cited concerns about the detention-related provisions of the GCM as a reason for rejecting it (Majcher, 2019, p. 93). The GCR aroused less controversy and was adopted by the General Assembly with 181 votes in favour, 2 against (Hungary and the US), and 3 abstentions (Majcher, 2019,

p. 101). While both Compacts were thus endorsed by the General Assembly, and with large majorities, the rejection of the GCM in particular by a number of influential states may serve to reduce the strength of any peer pressure to implement it.

3. MEXICO AND CENTRAL AMERICA

Migration and refugee protection have been key topics in the regional agenda as Mexico and Central American countries (i.e., Belize, Costa Rica, El Salvador, Guatemala, Honduras, Nicaragua, and Panama) have become origin, transit, and destination points of human flows. Three particular characteristics of migration governance in this region prior to 2016 suggest that the incorporation of the IOM into the UN system and the adoption of the two Global Compacts would have only limited effect. First, scholars and policymakers studying the region agree that efforts in the fields of migration and refugee protection seem to be shaped by the interest of the US to regulate migration flows (Ramírez et al., 2019; Vera-Espinoza, 2019). Since the US has such an outsized influence, particularly on Mexico, and under Trump rejected both Compacts, we might expect that the Compacts would have only relatively weak influence in the region.[4] Second, efforts by regional governance mechanisms predate the Global Compacts by decades and indeed fed into the drafting process. Thus, to a significant degree, the commitments in the Compacts encompass actions that were already being implemented in the region. Third, the IOM has long had an important role in several Latin American countries, and it is not clear why its status as a UN-related organisation would either change or strengthen this role. In addition, regional initiatives have counted on input from international organisations—including the IOM and UNHCR—to enhance their technical competence.[5]

The Central American Integration System (SICA), formed by the governments of Belize, Costa Rica, the Dominican Republic, El Salvador, Guatemala, Nicaragua, and Panama, has promoted migratory instruments and agreements among its member states over the last two decades. A noteworthy example

---

[4] The Biden/Harris administration has subsequently stated its support for the GCM. See https://www.state.gov/wp-content/uploads/2021/12/gcm-Accessible_12212021.pdf (accessed 7/12/2022).

[5] Examples of such agreements are the cooperation agreement between SICA and the UNHCR signed on 7 April 2014 (Acuerdo de Colaboración entre la Secretaría General del Sistema de Integración Centroamericano -SG-SICA y el Alto Comisionado de Naciones Unidas para los Refugiados) and the SICA and the IOM agreement; the latter has taken over the OCAM's technical office since 1999 (IOM, 2016).

is the Regional Integral Migration Policy, developed by the SICA General Secretariat since 2010 (SICA et al., 2019). This policy has been formulated under the advice of the IOM and the UNHCR, and it includes provisions on the protection of refugees and other migrants. Another example is the approval and implementation in 2005 of a free mobility agreement for the transit of citizens across El Salvador, Guatemala, Honduras, and Nicaragua. Within the SICA, the Central America Commission of Migration Directors (OCAM) is another central element in its approach to immigration. Although it was created in 1990, before the SICA, as an independent body, it has become part of the regional process. For over three decades, the commission's aims have been to coordinate, consult, and reach consensus in migration management across the region (OCAM, 2020). Focusing on border management and entry requirements, OCAM is tasked with training border and migration officers, standardising common entry requirements, and creating the conditions for the safe and orderly return of regional and extra-regional migrants (OCAM, 2020). Since 1999, the IOM has been responsible for OCAM's technical office as per an agreement signed between both organisations (IOM, 2016).

Outside the Central American integration effort, regional multilateral forums focusing exclusively on migration and refugee protection also exist. The most visible one due to its size, age and reach is the Regional Conference on Migration (RCM) known as the Puebla Process. Created in 1996, the RCM is one of the Regional Consultative Processes (RCP) that the IOM has promoted since 1994 in different regions (Santi Pereyra, 2020).

The RCM includes all the SICA member states plus Canada, Mexico, and the US, and it also includes UNHCR, IOM, and SICA as international and regional observers. The Puebla Process can be framed under IOM- and UN-sponsored efforts in the mid-1990s to promote RCPs as mechanisms of migration governance (Thomas, 2014). In this context, the Puebla Process seeks to become a forum on migration issues that informs political and policy debates that lead to regional coordination and cooperation (Acosta Arcarazo & Feline Freier, 2015). It also seeks to 'strengthen the integrity of each member state's immigration laws, borders, and national security' (RCM, 2022). Although it is a non-binding mechanism, the conference issues recommendations that its members should follow (Acosta Arcarazo & Feline Freier, 2015).

In response to large numbers of people who have fled their homes and are in need of international protection in the region, Belize, Costa Rica, Guatemala, Honduras, Mexico and Panama adopted the San Pedro Sula Declaration in 2017, agreeing to work together to apply the CRRF template in the form of the Regional Comprehensive Protection and Solutions Framework (MIRPS). El Salvador joined the process in July 2019. This is an example of how developments in global migration governance have served to shape the regional governance of migration in Mexico and Central America. Although MIRPS predates the Global Compacts (GCs), it represents the application of a framework which was agreed at the 2016 High-Level Meeting in New York and is a central component of the GCR. MIRPS is a clear example of a mechanism created around the negotiation of the GCR and developed in the region with the technical support of the UNHCR (MIRPS, 2017; 2019).

In certain important respects, the MIRPS goes beyond the CRRF template, to the point that it arguably serves to challenge some tenets of the GCs. For example, the MIRPS operates with a more inclusive approach to those in need of protection than that implied by the categories and dichotomies which characterise the GCs, and 'includes asylum-seekers, refugees, internally displaced persons, deportees with protection needs, as well as the populations affected by violence and insecurity' (UNHCR, 2018, p. 1). The MIRPS also places emphasis on the rights of migrants, partnering with the Central American Council of Ombudspersons in joint border monitoring and advocacy campaigns for forcibly displaced persons, and committing to ensuring that asylum seekers face no penalty for irregular entry and to providing legal guidance to people in transit with protection needs (UNHCR, 2018, p. 1).

Yet in practice, some contradictory policies can be observed, as countries in the region are constrained by pressures from the US to securitise migration and border control (Gómez Castro, 2020). In 2019, Mexico appeared to be reaffirming the MIRPS commitments by assuming and setting out its priorities for the Pro Tempore presidency of the MIRPS, yet at the same time, it agreed to implement the Migrant Protection Protocols (aka the 'Remain in Mexico' policy) with the US. Under the protocols, migrants—including asylum seekers—who enter the US at the Mexican border irregularly or without proper identification are returned to Mexico while their immigration applications are processed (Gómez Castro, 2020, pp. 112–113). Such a policy reinforces rather than challenges the distinction between regular and irregular migration, penalises asylum seekers for irregular entry and—given that migrants often face grave dangers in Mexico—in many cases its application by the US constitutes a violation of the principle of non-refoulement.

Overall, regional responses build upon a rights-based approach that comes from previous regional efforts in migration and refugee protection. Member states in regional forums, as well as the forums themselves, already use a right-centred language when referring to immigrants and refugees. In fact, as multiple meeting minutes of the GCs negotiations show, the common regional position promoted during the drafting carried over previously agreed rights-based and regionally operationalised responses. These dynamics are quite evident for the GCM because, so far, the Compact does not seem to have impacted the language or the practices of regional initiatives, as the innovative aspect was already there. In this case, although the GCM is seen as a useful instrument, regional governance actors do not consider it determinant in their core work, as explained by a high-ranking officer within the RCM:

> The RCM participated a lot in the negotiation of the Global Compact (on Migration). Member states also participated a lot and at the end of 2017, we did a special declaration on the implementation of the Compact … The Compact is an additional mechanism (for the countries), as it is not binding, but the countries have obviously given it a lot of responsibility. And yes, we mention it when there are reports or some special declaration, or some important pronouncement. If possible, we mention it for those countries who are part of it. But actually, there has not been much variation (in our work, compared to the past).

Both the IOM and UNHCR have played a role as norm entrepreneurs in the context of Mexico and Central America, shaping the different regimes at the regional level (Lavenex et al., 2016). The evidence to date does not suggest that the role of either has changed with the incorporation of the IOM into the UN system—it was, and continues to be, important as a provider of technical and financial assistance to regional governance initiatives.

4. SOUTH AMERICA

The norms and organisations of global migration governance have been, and continue to be, important influences on mechanisms of regional migration governance in South America. International organisations, including the IOM and UNHCR, have come to play an increasingly important role in refugee and migration governance in the region. This appears to have been triggered primarily by the large numbers of Venezuelans migrating across the region, but there is also some limited evidence to suggest that the incorporation of the IOM into the UN system has raised its profile in the region, that is, the IOM took over the technical secretariat of the South American Conference on Migration (CSM) in 2016.[6] While global-level norms and institutions are also taken seriously in South American migration governance mechanisms, they are not uncritically accepted, and influence is not unidirectional; South American states and regional institutions have also influenced global-level norms and organisations.

South American countries and regional initiatives in migration and refugees have always referred to international agreements and standards in this policy area. Yet, in the early twenty-first century, South America 'adopted distinctive policies and vocabulary in the area of migration' (Acosta & Brumat, 2020, p.1). Migration governance in the region is among the most progressive in the

---

[6] The CSM was established in 2000 and is the only RCP that does not focus on security issues (Lavenex 2019).

world, and during the 2000s the EU was seen as a negative example against which regional migration governance in South America should be defined and regulated (Brumat & Acosta, 2019; Geddes et al., 2019). This became especially evident in 2008 after the EU Return Directive, which was rejected by regional organisations (OAS, MERCOSUR, UNASUR, CAN), regional parliaments (Parlatino, MERCOSUR Parliament, Central American Parliament, and the Andean Parliament), and the CSM, which added to the criticisms raised by all Latin American governments (Acosta Arcarazo, 2009).

Against this background, South American states and regional governance mechanisms made important inputs into the negotiating processes, particularly for the GCM, in general seeking to incorporate a more expansive range of migrant rights than made it into the final text. In the 2017 CSM Lima Declaration, member states encouraged 'the Global Compact for Migration to consider a Global Framework for the Protection of Human Rights of all migrants and their families based on universal and inter-American instruments on human rights and migrants' rights'. They also 'propose and promote the inclusion of a Framework for Assistance and Care of Migrant Women and their families in the Global Compact for Migration' (CSM, 2017, pp. 2–3). During the XVII Meeting in 2017, the CSM urged for a joint dialogue and action with the CRM to develop 'bi-regional inputs for the Global Compact on Migration' (CSM, 2017a, p. 4). During the negotiations for the GCM, South American countries called for the global recognition of the 'right to migrate', for the universality of migrants' rights and for migration regularisation as a solution to irregular migration, rather than promoting expulsion (Brumat, 2020, p. 153). By the time of the adoption of the GCM by the General Assembly in December 2018, Chile was one of the 12 abstentions. Brazil voted for and signed the GCM but pulled out of the agreement in January 2019 under the Bolsonaro administration.

The signing of the Global Compacts occurred amidst significant changes and new challenges at the regional level in South America. As the economic boom and social distribution strategies of the early 2000s found their limits, some countries saw the emergence of centre-right and right-wing governments. Additionally, since 2014, the deep political, economic, and social crisis in Venezuela has resulted in 'the largest external displacement crisis in Latin America's recent history' (IOM, 2020). According to the UNHCR and IOM, more than 5.4 million Venezuelans fled the country between 2015 and 2020 (Response for Venezuelans (R4V), 2020; United Nations, 2018). Whereas this has certainly challenged the capacity of countries to adequately respond to it, this has been exacerbated by the weakening of regional initiatives and the promotion of new ones leading to institutional overlap (i.e., the Quito Process). Moreover, countries' responses have also shown variation and heterogeneity in terms of how and to what extent they resorted to regional mechanisms.

The response to Venezuelan migrants in the region has included important regional and international elements. In September 2018, the International Technical Meeting on Human Mobility of Venezuelan Citizens in the Region, also known as the Quito Process, was launched under the leadership of Ecuador. Its principal objective was to promote communication and coordination between countries receiving Venezuelan refugees and migrants, while also exchanging information and good practices in migration and refugee matters. The 'Quito Declaration on Human Mobility of Venezuelan Citizens in the Region'—signed by Argentina, Brazil, Chile, Colombia, Costa Rica, Ecuador, México, Panamá, Paraguay, Perú, and Uruguay—reiterated these countries' commitment to fighting discrimination, intolerance, and xenophobia, to protecting vulnerable migrants from human trafficking, to protecting children, and to combating sexual and gender violence. These developments add to the establishment of the Regional Interagency Coordination Platform for Refugees and Migrants from Venezuela by the IOM and UNHCR in September 2018. Under the leadership of the UNHCR and IOM, and as an example of orchestration in practice, the platform coordinates the actions of various UN agencies, NGOs, the Red Cross, financial institutions, religious organisations, and civil society actors, among others. Within this cooperation framework, the UNHCR and IOM launched in December 2018 the Regional Refugee and Migration Response Plan for Refugees and Migrants from Venezuela (RMRP). The RMRP aims to complement and strengthen the response that is taking place at the national and regional levels.

From a regional perspective, the IOM and UNHCR provided technical assistance and support to the Quito Process, and have now taken over the Technical Secretariat of the Quito Process (Joint Declaration of the VI International Technical Meeting on Human Mobility of Venezuelan Citizens in the Region, Santiago, 2020). In all, international actors (i.e., UNHCR and IOM), who had traditionally played a negligible role in the region, are now increasingly important actors in regional migration governance and have been increasingly involved in border controls. "And you go to the borders, and the governments always allow a UNHCR presence, an IOM presence, a UNICEF presence at the border crossing in case there are unaccompanied minors" (Bradley, 2020, p. 28) as expressed by an IDB official. Even if the role of IOM in regional migration governance is relatively new, IOM has already played an important role in individual South American countries, and indeed Colombia and Peru (and, to a lesser degree, Argentina) have been major funders of the IOM. For the period 2007–2016, Peru was the second largest donor (after the United States) to IOM, and Colombia was the fourth largest. However, in both cases, their funding has largely been for projects to be undertaken by the IOM within their own countries.

It is too early to see whether and how the Compacts have affected policy instruments and practices in the region, according to academic and policy experts. On the one hand, they are seen as 'global frameworks that greatly help countries to raise awareness of high standards that are not binding' and they are thus 'a guiding principle' as put by an Inter-American Development Bank official. This is the case even for countries that have not signed the GCM (i.e., Chile). On the other hand, these global agreements seem to have had no impact on the regional level so far as explained by an academic expert. This becomes apparent when analysing the documents issued by the CSM and MERCOSUR after December 2018 and by the new Quito Process. Between its creation in 2018 and December 2020, the Quito Process held six meetings.[7] The Final Declarations make no reference to the GCs, but they emphasise the role of the UN, and specifically the IOM as part of the UN system. In the case of MERCOSUR, the 2020 Declaration of Presidents of MERCOSUR to the GCM does, however, acknowledge 'the relevance and contribution of the "Quito Process", as a regional mechanism that seeks to exchange best practices, articulate coherent and coordinated technical responses to the challenges presented by the human mobility of Venezuelans in the region' (Comunicado Conjunto de Presidentes de los Estados Partes y Estados Asociados del MERCOSUR, 2020, p. 6). In fact, in both that document and the previous year's Declarations of Presidents of MERCOSUR, all references remain strictly regional, including the MERCOSUR Citizenship Statute and the Residence Agreement and its Action Plan. Similarly, MERCOCIUDADES, the network of cities of the bloc, and the Institute of Public Policies on Human Rights of MERCOSUR established different guidelines for 'inclusive migration that respects human rights', where they acknowledge several international agreements dating back to the 1970s, the MERCOSUR Residence Agreement, and both GCs.

5. CONCLUSION

The purpose of this chapter was to determine to what extent the incorporation of the IOM into the UN system and the establishment of the GCM and GCR impacted the global migration regime complex, and furthermore, to consider the impact on the regional governance of human flows in Central and South America. The incorporation of the IOM into the UN system took place relatively quickly, but the process had been under way for a considerable length of time. The alignment with the UN system began a decade before with increased

7 These six meetings include: Quito I, 3–4 September 2018 (Quito); Quito II, 22–23 November 2018 (Quito); Quito III, 8–9 April 2019 (Quito); Quito IV, 4–5 July 2019 (Buenos Aires); Quito V, 14–15 November 2019 (Bogotá); and Quito VI, 23–24 September 2020 (Santiago).

inter-institutional cooperation (in the GMG) and even earlier in the field. The chapter made an empirical contribution to the literature by evaluating the performance of the GCs and IOM in Central and South America in terms of changing state behaviour in the two regions. We noted the degree of influence is shaped by: (1) proximity to the United States; (2) the extent to which regional integration organisations cooperate on migration governance from a rights-based approach; and (3) the length of time the IOM has worked in the region. Factors (1) and (3) are more important in Central America, while (2) and (3) are more important in South America. Moreover, IOM influence is likely to increase through the Quito Process addressing the 5.4 million migrants leaving Venezuela between 2015 and 2020—approximately 4.6 million of whom moved to other countries in the region—including coordinating relief aid.

Regarding the GCs, both Central and South America were proactive in the preparatory stages through the CSM and the RCM of Central America. Both remained committed to protecting migrant rights, although they differ in how frequently and directly they refer to the GCs in migration discourse. The chapter presented evidence of orchestration in the drafting phase and in aspects of their implementation, such as the CRRF. However, the intergovernmental bargaining that finalised the texts points to the IOM remaining important. Two future lines of research are suggested. One, on a theoretical level, focuses on networks and hierarchies within the migration regime (Barnett et al., 2021). The other is to examine over time the extent to which private actors involved in migration voluntarily use the GCs as references for their own regulatory standards. The IOM and other IOs 'could orchestrate more effectively by promoting the use of existing public norms by private schemes; adopting and refining public norms with a conscious view toward their adaptation and use by private schemes' (Abbott & Snidal, 2010, p. 337). Both directions would question the long-term pertinence of the IOM to the global governance of migration.

REFERENCES

Abbott, K., Genschel, P., Snidal, D. & Zangl, B. (2016). Two logics of indirect governance: Delegation and orchestration. *British Journal of Political Science* 46 (4): 719–729.

Abbott, K. & Snidal, D. (2010). International regulation without international government: Improving IO performance through orchestration. *The Review of International Organizations* 5 (3): 315–344.

Acosta, D. & Brumat, L. (2020). Political and legal responses to human mobility in South America in the context of the Covid-19 crisis. More fuel for the fire? *Frontiers in Human Dynamics* 2: 12.

Acosta Arcarazo, D. (2009). Latin American reactions to the adoption of the returns directive. *CEPS*, November. https://www.ceps.eu/ceps-publications/latin-american-reactions-adoption-returns-directive/.

Acosta Arcarazo, D. & Feline Freier L. (2015). Discursos y políticas de inmigración en Sudamérica: ¿Hacía un nuevo paradigma o la confirmación de una retórica sin contenido? *Revista Interdisciplinar da Movilidad Humana* 23 (44): 171–189.
Barnett, M., Pevehouse, J. C. W. & Raustiala, K. (Eds.). (2021). *Global governance in a world of change.* Cambridge University Press.
Betts, A. (2011). *Global migration governance.* Oxford University Press.
Borton, J. & Collinson, S. (2017). Responses to mixed migration in Europe: Implications for the humanitarian sector. *HPN Network Paper 81.*
Bradley, M. (2020). *The international organization for migration: Challenges, commitments, complexities.* Routledge.
Bradley, M. (2021). Joining the UN family? Explaining the evolution of IOM–UN relations. *Global Governance: A Review of Multilateralism and International Organizations* 27 (2): 251–274.
Brumat, L. (2020). Four generations of regional policies for the (free) movement of persons in South America (1977–2016). In G. Rayp, I. Ruyssen & K. Marchand (Eds.), *Regional integration and migration governance in the global South* (pp. 153–176). Springer.
Brumat, L. & Acosta, D. (2019). Three generations of free movement of regional migrants in Mercosur: Any influence from the EU? In A. Geddes, M. Vera-Espinoza, L. Hadj-Abdou & L. Brumat (Eds.), *The Dynamics of Regional Migration Governance* (pp. 54–72). Edward Elgar Publishing.
CSM. (2017). *Lima Declaration on the Global Compact for a Safe, Orderly and Regular Migration.* https://www.iom.int/iscm/lima-declaration-global-compact-safe-orderly-and-regular-migration.
CSM. (2017a). *XVII South American Conference on Migration Final Declaration: 'The inclusion and integration of migrants beyond territorial borders'.* https://csmigraciones.org/es/conferencias-csm/xvii-conferencia-suramericana-sobre-migraciones.
Desmond, A. (2015). The triangle that could square the circle: The UN International Convention on the Protection of the Rights of All Migrant Workers and Members of Their Families, the EU and the universal periodic review. *European Journal of Migration and Law* 17 (1): 39–69.
Doña Reveco, D. & Finn, V. (2021). Conflicting priorities in South American migration governance. *Bulletin of Latin American Research* 41 (5): 802–817.
Eilstrup-Sangiovanni, M. (2022). Ordering global governance complexes: The evolution of the governance complex for international civil aviation. *The Review of International Organizations* 17: 293–322.
Gammeltoft-Hansen, T. (2018). The normative impact of the Global Compact on Refugees. *International Journal of Refugee Law* 30 (4): 605–610.
Geddes, A., Espinoza, M., Abdou, L. & Brumat, L. (2019). Introduction: The dynamics of regional migration governance. In A. Geddes, M. Vera-Espinoza, L. Hadj-Abdou & L. Brumat (Eds.), *The dynamics of regional migration governance* (pp. 1–14). Edward Elgar Publishing.
Gómez Castro, B. (2020). Regionalisation versus securitisation: The pending fate of the refugee protection regime in Central America. *Oxford Monitor of Forced Migration* 8 (2): 103–121.
Hammoud-Gallego, O. & Freier, L. (2022). Symbolic refugee protection: Explaining Latin America's liberal refugee laws. *American Political Science Review* 117 (2): 454–473.

IOM. (2016). OIM y OCAM. Organización Internacional para las Migraciones, Press Note. https://rosanjose.iom.int/site/es/oim-y-ocam.
IOM. (2020). DTM survey of refugees and migrants living in Colombia. https://dtm.iom.int/reports/presentation-dtm-survey-refugees-and-migrants-living-colombia-may-2020.
Kainz, L. & Betts, A. (2021). Power and proliferation: Explaining the fragmentation of global migration governance. *Migration Studies* 9 (1): 65–89.
Lavenex, S. (2019). Regional migration governance – building block of global initiatives? *Journal of Ethnic and Migration Studies* 45 (8): 1275–1293.
Lavenex, S., Jurje, F., Givens, T. E. & Buchanan, R. (2016). Regional migration governance. In T. A. Börzel & T. Risse (Eds.), *The Oxford handbook of regional integration* (pp. 457–485). Oxford University Press.
Majcher, I. (2019). Immigration detention under the Global Compacts in the light of refugee and human rights law standards. *International Migration* 57 (6): 91–114.
MERCOSUR. 2020. Comunicado conjunto de los presidentes de los estados partes del MERCOSUR y estados asociados, LVI Cumbre de Presidentes del MERCOSUR, 2 de julio de 2020.
Micinski, N. (2021). *UN Global Compacts: Governing migrants and refugees.* Routledge.
MIRPS. (2017). *Documento sobre el Marco Integral Regional para la protección y soluciones.* UNCHR library. https://www.acnur.org/es-es/5b50d83b4.pdf.
MIRPS. (2019). Observatorio de Desplazamiento Interno (IDMC) del Consejo Noruego para los Refugiados (NRC). De la Teoría a la Práctica: Un informe de 61 organizaciones de sociedad civil de Belice, Guatemala, Honduras, México y Panamá sobre el Marco Integral Regional de Protección y Soluciones (MIRPS). https://www.refworld.org/es/ref/inforreg/idmc/2019/es/134231.
Newland, K. (2019a). *Global governance of international migration 2.0: What lies ahead?* Migration Policy Institute.
Newland, K. (2019b). *Migration, development, and global governance: From crisis toward consolidation.* Migration Policy Institute.
Niemann, A. & Zaun, N. (2018). EU refugee policies and politics in times of crisis: Theoretical and empirical perspectives. *JCMS: Journal of Common Market Studies* 56 (1): 3–22.
OCAM. (2020). *OCAM en breve.* https://www.sica.int/ocam/inicio
Pécoud, A. (2020). Introduction: The International Organization for Migration as the new 'UN Migration Agency'. In M. Geiger & A. Pécoud (Eds.), *The International Organization for Migration: The new 'UN Migration Agency' in critical perspective* (pp. 1–27). Palgrave Macmillan.
Ramírez, J., Ceja, I. & Alfaro, Y. (2019). La Conferencia Sudamericana de Migraciones y el Proceso Puebla: ¿entre la seguridad y los derechos? PÉRIPLOS | GT CLACSO – Las Políticas Migratorias y el Control de Poblaciones en el Siglo XXI. *Debates, Prácticas y Normativas en América del Sur* 3 (1): 11–37.
RCM. (2022). *Welcome to the Regional Conference on Migration.* https://www.rcmvs.org/en/content/welcome-regional-conference-migration.
Response for Venezuelans (R4V). (2020). Venezuelan refugees & migrants in the region – November 2020. https://www.r4v.info/en/document/r4v-latin-america-and-caribbean-venezuelan-refugees-and-migrants-region-november-2020-en.
Santi Pereyra, S. (2020). La OIM como difusora global de las políticas de migración ordenada: La implantación del control migratorio mediante los mecanismos de cooperación técnica sobre migración y capacity-building. In P. Schuste & K.

Valenzuela-Moreno (Eds.), *Trayectorias y jornadas: Transnacionalismo en acción* (pp. 25–44). Transnational Press London.
SICA, IOM & UNHCR. (2019). *Hallazgos del estudio de línea base sobre migración y desplazamiento en la región del SICA, El Salvador.* https://www.sica.int/documentos/hallazgos-del-estudio-de-linea-base-y-desplazamientoen-la-region-del-sica-como-parte-del-paim-sica-plan-de-accion-para-la-atencionintegral-de-la-migracion-en-la-region_1_120237.html.
Thomas, C. (2014). Transnational migration, globalization, and governance: Reflections on the Central America–United States immigration crisis. *Cornell Legal Studies Research Paper Series*, 14–26.
UNHCR. (2018). *Applying the Comprehensive Refugee Response (CRRF) in North & Central America*, June. https://www.acnur.org/5b58910e4.pdf.
United Nations. (2018). *Global Compact for Safe, Orderly and Regular Migration.* A/RES/73/195.
Vera-Espinoza, M. (2019). Between depoliticisation and path dependence: The role of Mexico in regional migration governance in North America. In A. Geddes, M. Vera-Espinoza, L. Hadj-Abdou & L. Brumat (Eds.), *The dynamics of regional migration governance* (pp. 166–185). Edward Elgar Publishing.

PART IV

Conclusion

16. By way of conclusion: furthering the institutional analysis of global governance

Jacint Jordana, Axel Marx, Marie Vandendriessche and Jan Wouters

1. THE INSTITUTIONAL APPROACH TO GLOBAL GOVERNANCE

In this concluding chapter, we advocate for an institutional perspective on global governance. Although the phenomenon of global governance has been discussed and analysed intensely in recent years, most research (Roger et al., 2022) has combined a conceptual perspective with a comparative approach. We believe there is still a gap in the reflections on the institutional aspects of global governance, including the formal and informal rules that shape international organisations and their relations. While numerous studies have applied the lens of historical institutionalism to international relations (Fioretos, 2011; Rixen & Viola, 2016; Voeten, 2019) and have reflected on how this approach provides explanations of middle-range causal mechanisms, such as sequencing or path dependency for many decision-making processes, its discussion within the context of global governance configurations still seems to be in its infancy. Although international organisations have been examined using a broadly institutional approach (Simmons & Martin, 2013; Rixen et al., 2016), more thorough attention is required for the web of institutions that underpin global governance, especially if we aim to incorporate an approach that is less focused on the role of states and their traditional concept of sovereignty. This book has sought to contribute to this effort by providing new elements for reflection on the role of institutions, norms, and rules that comprise contemporary global governance complexes, including all the different types of actors and institutional practices that they involve.

As global challenges become more complex, interconnected, and transcend national boundaries, the need for collaborative and flexible governance mechanisms has intensified. This has led to the proliferation of institutions designed to address a wide array of pressing global issues, including climate change, international trade, public health, human rights, and migration (Weiss & Thakur, 2010; Acuto, 2013; Lopez-Claros et al., 2020). In this book, we have introduced and analysed several of these global governance complexes, including those that address cybersecurity (Chapter 6), trade (Chapter 7), and finance (Chapter 9).

A central aspect to consider when studying global governance institutions is their fluidity and their ever-changing configurations. Unlike national structures, institutional forms of global governance are often highly variable and react to a wide range of factors. This variability is the result of contextual forces, the nature of the issues addressed, and particularly the absence of a central authority with coercive power that can enforce rules or norms consistently, thus ensuring stability (Raustiala & Victor, 2004; Krisch, 2017; Zürn, 2018). This absence of a clear power centre allows for continuous alterations driven by changing interests, technical innovations, political conflicts, and other dynamic factors. The analysis of global governance has prompted a series of proposals that seek to identify and classify these more fluid forms of governance. Global governance complexes – comprising a variety of entities, such as trans-governmental networks, informal international organisations, and public–private partnerships, among others, which go beyond more traditional entities such as intergovernmental organisations – have become a central topic in the study of global governance. Chapter 5 mapped and discussed current approaches towards studying complexity in global governance.

The spread and adaptation of governance structures worldwide mirror a deepening interdependence between state and non-state actors. This expansion highlights the globalised nature of contemporary policy issues, where no single actor can provide solutions on its own. The institutionalisation of global governance, therefore, embodies the transition towards intricate institutional frameworks that attempt to manage complexity in today's globalised world. In fact, global governance has reached a significant level of institutionalisation, characterised by the development and evolution of institutional arrangements across nearly all policy areas where international cooperation is needed to provide global public goods. This proliferation of institutions and organisational structures, however, does not necessarily guarantee effectiveness in the delivery of the intended goods, despite an increasing delegation of authority in the international system in recent years (Zürn, 2018; Fioretos & Tallberg, 2021).

From the outset of the academic discipline of global governance, many scholars took a perspective on world politics that went 'beyond the state' and beyond the perspectives of classic international relations (Roger et al., 2022, p. 504). Generally speaking, global governance studies commonly reject the assumption that the logic of states and their hierarchical and coherent structures automatically replicate themselves at the international level. According to this assumption, states establish formal intergovernmental organisations (IGOs) based on treaties, and this somehow perpetuates the monopoly of representation at the global level. These formal IGO structures become the centres of power for global public policymaking. All other interactions gravitate towards these centres. This perspective assumes that, over time, IGOs could enjoy a certain degree of autonomy, but always under the supervision of states, which remain the primary actors and determine the IGOs' political and functional autonomy (Barnett & Finnemore, 2004; Lake, 2010). Although many elements of how the international fabric works match this view, it is largely insufficient to make sense of how global governance works in today's world. Currently, studies on the *de facto* autonomy of IGOs show that their secretariats maintain significant room for manoeuvre and that they draw on alternative sources of legitimacy, beyond the legitimacy granted by member states (Lall, 2017; Knill et al., 2019).

In fact, the reality observed in many cases does not align well with this theoretical framework, not even with the relative loss of control that sovereign states experience after delegation to IGOs (Krasner, 2001). Empirical analysis of issue areas in global governance – such as those presented in various chapters of this book – shows that this hierarchical view is more the exception than the rule. Far from a vertical and unified structure, global governance usually manifests as a set of semi-autonomous interacting structures with different configurations of organisations, and without a well-defined centralised logic of control (Henning & Pratt, 2023). Unlike the ministerial logic that dominates national governments, in the global sphere we encounter multiple governance spaces – some highly active and populated by a diverse range of actors, others less dynamic and with fewer participants – that include a variety of entities, including informal institutions, intermediaries, and other non-state and private actors (Büthe & Mattli, 2011; Roger, 2020; Abbott & Snidal, 2021).

2. FROM AN ORGANISATION-CENTRED APPROACH TOWARDS AN INSTITUTIONAL APPROACH

Many studies on global governance have primarily focused on global governance organisations, their behaviour, strategies, and their objectives, as well as the challenges they face in producing global public goods to address a variety of problems in our highly globalised human society. While this book has also analysed some of these actors within the framework of global governance, an important feature was the emphasis placed on institutions that can structure the interactions between organisations and how these institutions can generate patterns and can impose restrictions to potentially facilitate the production of global public goods.

The reason for this focus on institutions is clear: the variety of actor configurations in global governance is extremely high, depending on the policy sector or issue being addressed. This obliges us to closely examine the type of institutions that may, albeit minimally, provide some stability to these dynamic forms of global governance, although this may take place through informal governance processes (Westerwinter et al., 2021; Abbott & Faude, 2022). In a world as globalised as ours – and despite the geopolitical tensions that dominate the present decade – there is no doubt that a better understanding of patterns of stability and change, generated in part by various institutional norms, is essential for analysing global governance and predicting its dynamics. This is a very broad approach, but it provides a different perspective than focusing on agency and structural constraints, and it may allow a different perspective for understanding current developments in global governance.

Studying institutions allows us to identify elements that can offer stability to decision-making (or non-decision-making) processes within the framework of global governance. It may also help us anticipate in which areas and topics we can expect change, based on the strength and acceptance of these rules by the actors involved (cf. the discussion on scenarios in the introductory chapter of this book). As we explore institutional and organisational dynamics, we can better understand where transformations are more likely to occur, or where stability is likely to be maintained, thus anticipating the future trajectories of global governance.

In previous chapters, and from different perspectives, we acknowledged a growing institutionalisation of global governance, which reflects an increasing demand for coordinated action that goes beyond the traditional nation-state system. We also reflected on the crisis of some traditional forms of global governance and the challenges that formal IGOs face in current times. In many cases, the complexity of global problems requires new forms of governance that are more decentralised, more dynamic, and capable of incorporating a wide variety of actors with different expertise, resources, and legitimacy (Abbott & Faude, 2022). However, these structures are not static. They continue to evolve, responding to shifting geopolitical realities, emerging global challenges, unstable inter-institutional dynamics, and the changing balance of power in the international system.

The contributions in this book have addressed issues related to institutionalisation in global governance from diverse angles. In Chapter 2, Charles Roger, Adam Holesch, Jacint Jordana, and Lewin Schmitt offered a wide overview of how research in global governance has evolved since the 1990s – when global governance was rarely discussed – until today, when it is a major focus in academia and policymaking. This chapter traced the evolution of the concept, using a dataset of academic articles to identify three research stages: a formative period, a phase of broad application across literatures, and a recent focus on data-driven, quantitative studies. Chapter 2 highlighted key theoretical developments and gaps while outlining priorities for future research.

Following this broad perspective on global governance studies, in Chapter 3, Alexandros Tokhi, İrem Tuncer Ebetürk, and Michael Zürn examined some key features of global governance and its challenges, focusing on formal policymaking beyond the nation-state. Here, some of the main difficulties of the institutionalisation of global governance by formal IGOs were introduced. The chapter provided a discussion on the role of formal IGOs in shaping global policies and considered the increasingly complex environment in which they operate. Data from the International Authority Database were used to explore the authority of IGOs across various issue areas and to discuss the challenges to formal IGOs' authority as global rule-makers.

Kari Irwin Otteburn and Axel Marx delved further into these obstacles, and in Chapter 4 they examined the significant challenges IGOs face in a changing geopolitical landscape, taking into account their institutional rules and organisational structures. This chapter identified three key limitations: (1) difficulties in balancing stakeholder needs due to rigid governance structures; (2) inadequate policy autonomy to meet their goals; and (3) insufficient resources, including funding and staff, and a lack of procedures to increase self-funding. This contribution also evaluated how informal IGOs address these challenges, and it concluded that informality is unlikely to fully resolve the structural limitations that IGOs face.

Chapter 5, by Marie Vandendriessche, Jacint Jordana, and Axel Marx, explores the variety of collections of international institutions that address specific issue areas in global governance. After World War II, multilateral organisations like the International Monetary Fund, the World Bank, and the United Nations became key actors, while new transnational rule-making bodies emerged after the Cold War. This chapter explains that the growth of formal IGOs slowed, while informal IGOs, private regulatory organisations, and public–private governance initiatives gained prominence in many different policy sectors. Chapter 5 discussed in depth different schools of scholarship on the characteristics of the resulting collections of global governance organisations and focused on one factor that unites them: their propensity for continuous evolution.

The second part of the book adopted a more applied lens. Through a focus on specific sectors, the chapters in this part explored how inter-organisational dynamics and global governance systemic rules can move between fluidity and stability. They discussed how solutions have emerged to manage the provision of global public goods. Cybersecurity, an emerging policy issue, illustrates how complex a new area of global governance can be. This complexity is unravelled by Marie Vandendriessche in Chapter 6. Nearly 70% of the world's population uses the internet – the backbone of the global economy – but it also generates cybersecurity risks like viruses and cyberattacks. Preventing or reducing these risks requires significant coordination at the global level; yet cybersecurity is contentious and involves diverse organisations in a 'hybrid institutional complex'. This complex governance structure reflects how many global issues are managed today, but it also clearly illustrates some of the institutional deficits that we have previously identified.

Chapter 7 covers the governance of global trade – a more traditional area of global governance – and offers a different perspective by focusing on the complexity generated by a diverse array of actors, including states, international organisations (e.g., WTO, UNCTAD, OECD, EU), informal groups (G7, G20, BRICS), and private entities. The two main challenges, as argued by Jan Wouters, the author of the chapter, are: revitalising the WTO – through new agreements and by fixing its dispute settlement system – and fostering cooperation among diverse actors to ensure complementarity. However, achieving these goals is perceived as being complicated by geopolitical tensions, geostrategic competition, and by enduring divisions such as the North–South split. Such divisions exacerbate the weakening of multilateral frameworks and the resurgence of bilateral and unilateral trade strategies.

Another policy field where institutional tensions have emerged is global investment governance, which is dealt with in Chapter 8 by Yoram Z. Haftel and Tomer Broude. The global governance of investment consists of decentralised networks of international investment agreements (IIAs) and investor–state dispute settlement (ISDS) tribunals. Some international organisations – such as UNCTAD and UNCITRAL – play key roles in shaping this complex, primarily through traditional functions such as information-sharing, policy advice, and inter-state negotiations. However, these organisations focus more on coordination and centralisation than on newer governance models like experimentalism or orchestration – governance models that would be more flexible in the turbulent global governance environment of recent times.

Chapter 9 on global finance governance, by David Levi-Faur, Ilana Blumsack, and Dalit Flaiszhaker, illustrates how stable, but very informal, institutional arrangements play a crucial role in our economies and societies. Financialisation is deeply embedded in social, economic, and political life, yet global financial governance is fragmented and lacks a central authority to enforce formal rules for a diverse set of global financial issues. The authors of this chapter argue that better regulatory governance at national, regional, and global levels is essential for stability, sustainable growth, and greater equality, thereby benefiting millions living in poverty.

An example of rising tensions in global finance governance is the new role played by China – the world's second largest economy – which has emerged as a global financial power. China has become the world's largest bilateral creditor and has established multilateral banks like the New Development Bank (within the context of BRICS states) and the Asian Infrastructure Investment Bank. Chapter 10, by Catalina Espinosa Notrica, Pablo Nemiña, and Diana Tussie, illustrates how Beijing has accelerated its financial expansion in recent years to enhance its role in global governance. The authors argue that from 2000 to 2020, China acted as a revisionist power, seeking to reform global financial institutions without fully overturning the existing order and, consequently, tried to alter path dependence without triggering a major institutional crisis.

Climate change is a 'super-wicked' problem, which grows more difficult to address the longer action is delayed. Despite progress in constructing a global governance system since the 1990s to address climate change, efforts remain too slow, and climate change is now a dangerous reality for many vulnerable communities. Chapter 11 by Julia Kreienkamp and David Coen reviews how global climate governance – defined as the mechanisms and measures by states or other authorities to prevent, mitigate, or adapt to climate risks – has evolved in recent years. The global governance arrangements in this field are hybrid and fragmented, and there is no central authority regulating interactions between the different players. Nevertheless, the Paris Agreement under the UNFCCC provides an overarching framework for cooperation and goal alignment. Overall, the polycentric and multi-scalar regime complex for climate change generates both significant opportunities – such as experimentation and learning – and limitations in terms of effectiveness, legitimacy, and accountability.

After this second series of chapters, which focused on different sectors, the third part of this book focused on specific case studies that illustrate particular problems and challenges we discussed in a more comparative form in the first part. In Chapter 12, Kyle S. Herman and David Coen critique the reliance on carbon-centric governance, arguing that it has failed to curb greenhouse gas (GHG) emissions, including potent gases like methane and nitrous oxide. The Global Warming Potential (GWP) system, which converts all GHGs into carbon equivalents, has created inconsistencies and loopholes, thereby undermining carbon markets and enabling industry manipulation. The authors claim that these flaws highlight the need to rethink climate governance, shifting the focus from refining carbon metrics to addressing systemic drivers of emissions, such as fossil fuel dependence. After studying the growing involvement of the private sector, they conclude that long-term targets and insufficient state oversight have hindered significant progress.

İrem Tuncer Ebetürk and Alexandros Tokhi, in Chapter 13, emphasise the backlash against international organisations (IOs) by focusing on the politicisation of gender rights. Türkiye's withdrawal from the Istanbul Convention illustrates the complex interplay between domestic politics, international obligations, and the global struggle for gender rights, making this a relevant case of deinstitutionalisation. Türkiye's case underscores the need for nuanced and coordinated international efforts to prevent the erosion of gender rights and to strengthen global human rights frameworks in the face of growing political resistance. It also outlines the difficulties of sustaining and implementing agreements in a more polarised system of international institutions that face growing difficulties to weave together common values and norms at the global level.

Chapter 14, written jointly by Sukmawani Bela Pertiwi, Axel Marx, Charline Depoorter, Kari Irwin Otteburn, Tirta Nugraha Mursitama, and Lili Yulyadi Arnakim, focused on the global governance of sustainable development. It discussed the relevance of multilevel government institutional arrangements by comparing the cases of the European Union and ASEAN. The authors argued that goal-setting global governance holds promise for addressing the challenges of sustainable development, but that such goal-setting faces significant obstacles. One major issue is 'goal-shopping', where actors prioritise certain goals over others due to limited budgets, contextual irrelevance, or as a way to attract foreign investment. Another challenge is coordination among diverse actors, with institutional mechanisms for horizontal, vertical, internal, and external collaboration often falling short of ensuring coherence. These issues raise concerns about the effectiveness of goal-setting governance for achieving the Sustainable Development Goalss, thus underscoring the need to address the challenges of prioritisation and coordination by 2030.

Chapter 15 focused on new institutions of global governance that are emerging in many policy areas, such as for example in international migration. In December 2018, the United Nations General Assembly adopted the Global Compacts (GCs) on Refugees and Migration, establishing soft-law frameworks that reaffirmed existing binding obligations and introduced new nonbinding commitments. The incorporation of the International Organization for Migration (IOM) as a related organisation into the UN family marked a major shift in migration governance, adding these new institutional designs. In this chapter, Andrea C. Bianculli, Miriam Bradley, Robert Kissack, and Juan Carlos Triviño-Salazar explored – using case studies on Venezuelan migration in South America and Central American migration through Mexico to the US – how the incorporation of GCs and the IOM has reshaped global and regional migration governance.

3. KEY ISSUES IN INSTITUTIONALISING GLOBAL GOVERNANCE

What are the main problems or difficulties in the practice of global governance? We conclude with a summary of some key issues identified by our contributors, ranging from the tensions that traditional IGOs experience when new global governance actors emerge, to differences in path-dependent patterns across policy sectors, and the varying relevance of informal IGOs and other international entities, depending on the global governance complex at hand. We also discuss insights we can gain from the adaptive capacities of major IGOs in steering global governance in certain sectors.

Overall, the chapters in this book have uncovered thought-provoking trends in a landscape of multiple global governance organisations and myriad formal and informal institutions that shape their configurations as well as their interactions. The specific configurations within each area of global governance determine – either formally or informally – the relations between individual actors, and they constrain their choices, even when there is no central authority. Taking this as a starting point may enable us to better understand how governance structures beyond traditional IGOs can contribute to managing global challenges, as well as to identify the strengths and weaknesses of different institutional designs and their corresponding organisational forms.

First, we expect that the future of global governance will not be based on the monopoly of formal IGOs but on a mix of entities with different natures. Some IGOs will become even more powerful and relevant, while others will adopt a low profile and focus on more technical functions. Meanwhile, in key issue areas, private governance – which may comprise a wide range of member types and may take on many different shapes, such as regulatory intermediaries, private companies, knowledge actors, multi-stakeholder initiatives, and many other non-state actors – will become more important in providing global public goods, and will probably become more institutionalised. Private governance can be based on public authorities delegating tasks to private entities – resulting in a transformation from government to governance – but it can also be the product of collective action by private actors that provide important governance functions through their effectiveness, expertise, and reputation. The institutionalisation of these private modes of governance will become stronger and more stable. In some sectors, confrontations between public and private global governance already exist, and these may be accentuated in the near future as tensions for the leadership in global governance increase.

Second, we observed that many well-established IGOs – given increasing interdependence across different policy areas in global governance – tend to expand their mandates in order to engage in new areas of activity. Despite the risk of having only a nominal presence in multiple areas, many IGOs are compelled to expand their operations beyond their core activities and to project their initiatives into different fields, often beyond their original mission. This is partly due either to the connections and dependencies that are more relevant and visible today or to strategic moves and critical events. These transformations will have strong implications for how global governance develops and may impact the role that well-established IGOs will play in the coming years, thus challenging informal collaborative arrangements that exist today between formal IGOs and other types of organisations that operate in the global sphere. We envisage a future in which IGOs will compete fiercely in many cases, but in which they will also eventually cooperate intensively. These dynamics will probably be much more intense than we have observed in previous years. This is because IGOs may establish new structures that involve large non-state actors, with the aim of exploiting synergies and setting policy agendas, while still engaging with the most influential states.

Third, we observed across sectors, that the differences between formal and informal IGOs are blurring. While formal IGOs are expanding their informal dimensions and promoting public–private partnerships, transnational networks, and many other forms of collaboration beyond the formal involvement of nation-states, many successful informal IGOs have strengthened their formal structures, thus ensuring liaisons with the decision-making machinery of major states when necessary. This brings about a new layer of institutionalisation in global governance, with formal and informal rules emerging to articulate such developments. Eventually, some institutional convergence may be expected. This means that certain IGOs – departing from established institutional designs – will display innovative mechanisms to operate in complex environments populated by states of different sizes and power, by autonomous for-profit and non-profit entities, and by civil society actors. The implications for the development of global governance are significant: organisational differences between global governance entities will diminish, and given the nature of each sector and the specificity of the global public goods to be produced, there will be some adjustments.

Fourth, we identified many IGOs that in preceding decades showed a trend of slowly becoming more autonomous from member states, although not completely independent of them. However, differences across sectors were very significant: security remained very state-centric, states remained strong in trade, while in the finance sector, this trend accelerated because formal IGOs were not well established in this field. Regarding future development, it is unlikely that these trends will continue, given current geopolitical transformations that suggest a regression in the autonomy of IGOs. In any case, it appears that nation-states will remain the main suppliers of global institutions and regulations, although privately agreed regulations and the expansion of regulatory intermediaries may undermine their ascendency in some areas of global governance. As global governance is only the top layer of the complex multilevel governance structures that exist in many policy areas today, national-level governments will remain very influential in most cases. Moreover, states will be active in shaping their citizens' views of the roles of IGOs, either in a supportive or in a negative way.

In our understanding, the levels of institutionalisation and policy coverage that global and regional governance will achieve in future years will be largely determined by the strategies and goals of nation-states, and in particular – but not only – by the behaviour of the major powers. However, states are not going to be the only actors setting rules and defining goals in many sectors of global governance. As we have argued, other options may emerge. While successful IGOs will continue over the decade to accumulate resources and reputations globally – allowing them to be more autonomous and operational – they will increasingly share global governance with different organisations and network structures that are less aligned with state strategies and priorities.

Although predicting political developments is beyond our purpose and capacity, we have suggested four world scenarios that roughly cover different directions (Saz-Carranza et al., 2024; see Introduction), accelerating or constraining the trends we have delineated here. In each scenario, state actions combine with a set of dynamics and premises to contribute to the evolution of global governance. Global governance would be very different in a world shaped heavily by a US–China confrontation and continuous geopolitical tensions and conflicts, compared to a world in which countries' desire for regional integration would allow strengthened forms of regional governance that would limit major power confrontations and add stronger voices to world politics and world economies. Such emerging forms of regional governance, however, are contingent on multiple uncertainties – technological, political, economic, environmental – that nation-states can partially influence. However, interactions between non-state actors, IGOs, and nation-states will also contribute to shaping future scenarios.

To conclude, this edited book has contributed to a better understanding of how global governance institutions are evolving and also the related difficulties – in terms of effectiveness, legitimacy, and efficiency, among others – in providing global public goods. Building and consolidating institutions in global governance is not an easy task, and knowledge from state-building experiences cannot be directly transposed to the global level. Traditional treaty-based collective action by states is no longer the only option in global governance. Yet today's panoply of global governance organisations will not automatically generate the global public goods that remain undersupplied. How different forms of global governance continue to interact in a changing international context, and how those interactions will impact the effectiveness of global governance, remain fascinating questions that merit further investigation.

REFERENCES

Abbott, K. W., & Faude, B. (2022). Hybrid institutional complexes in global governance. *The Review of International Organizations*, 17, 263–291.

Abbott, K. W., & Snidal, D. J. (Eds.). (2021). *The spectrum of international institutions: An interdisciplinary collaboration on global governance*. Routledge.

Acuto, M. (2013). City leadership in global governance. *Global Governance*, 19(3), 481–498.

Barnett, M., & Finnemore, M. (2004). *Rules for the world: International organizations in global politics*. Cornell University Press.

Büthe, T., & Mattli, W. (2011). *The new global rulers: The privatization of regulation in the world economy*. Princeton University Press.

Fioretos, O. (2011). Historical institutionalism in international relations. *International Organization*, 65(2), 367–399.

Fioretos, O., & Tallberg, J. (2021). Politics and theory of global governance. *International Theory*, 13(1), 99–111.

Henning, R. C., & Pratt, T. (2023). Hierarchy and differentiation in international regime complexes: A theoretical framework for comparative research. *Review of International Political Economy*, 30(6), 2178–2205.

Knill, C., Bayerlein, L., Enkler, J., & Grohs, S. (2019). Bureaucratic influence and administrative styles in international organizations. *The Review of International Organizations*, 14, 83–106.

Krasner, S. D. (2001). Abiding sovereignty. *International Political Science Review*, 22(3), 229–251.

Krisch, N. (2017). Liquid authority in global governance. *International Theory*, 9(2), 237–260.

Lake, D. A. (2010). Rightful rules: Authority, order, and the foundations of global governance. *International Studies Quarterly*, 54(3), 587–613.

Lall, R. (2017). Beyond institutional design: Explaining the performance of international organizations. *International Organization*, 71(2), 245–280.

Lopez-Claros, A., Dahl, A. L., & Groff, M. (2020). *Global governance and the emergence of global institutions for the 21st century*. Cambridge University Press.

Raustiala, K., & Victor, D. G. (2004). The regime complex for plant genetic resources. *International Organization*, 58(2), 277–309.

Rixen, T., & Viola, L. (2016). Historical institutionalism and international relations: Towards explaining change and stability in international institutions. In T. Rixen, L. Viola, & M. Zürn (Eds.), *Historical institutionalism and international relations* (pp. 3–35). Oxford University Press.

Rixen, T., Viola, L. A., & Zürn, M. (Eds.). (2016). *Historical institutionalism and international relations: Explaining institutional development in world politics*. Oxford University Press.

Roger, C. B. (2020). *The origins of informality: Why the legal foundations of global governance are shifting, and why it matters*. Oxford University Press.

Roger, C., Jordana, J., Holesch, A., & Schmitt, L. (2022). Global governance research: Exploring patterns of growth, diversity, and inclusion. *Global governance: A review of multilateralism and international organizations*, 28(4), 486–508.

Saz-Carranza, A., Rueda-Sabater, E., Vandendriessche, M., Moreno, C., & Jordana, J. (2024). The future(s) of global governance: A scenarios exercise. *Global Policy*, 15(1), 149–165.

Simmons, B. A., & Martin, L. (2013). International organizations and institutions. In W. Carlsnaes, T. Risse, & B. A. Simmons (Eds.), *Handbook of international relations* (pp. 326–351). Sage.

Voeten, E. (2019). Making sense of the design of international institutions. *Annual Review of Political Science*, 22(1), 147–163.

Weiss, T. G., & Thakur, R. (2010). *Global governance and the UN: An unfinished journey*. Indiana University Press.
Westerwinter, O., Abbott, K. W., & Biersteker, T. G. (2021). Informal governance in world politics. *The Review of International Organizations*, 16(2), 177–200.
Zürn, M. (2018). *A theory of global governance: Authority, legitimacy, and contestation*. Oxford University Press.

Index